Dialogues on Human Rights and Legal Pluralism

IUS GENTIUM

COMPARATIVE PERSPECTIVES ON LAW AND JUSTICE

VOLUME 17

For further volumes:
http://www.springer.com/series/7888

René Provost • Colleen Sheppard
Editors

Dialogues on Human Rights and Legal Pluralism

Springer

Editors
René Provost
Faculty of Law
Centre for Human Rights and Legal Pluralism
McGill University
Montreal, QC, Canada

Colleen Sheppard
Faculty of Law
Centre for Human Rights and Legal Pluralism
McGill University
Montreal, QC, Canada

ISBN 978-94-007-4709-8 ISBN 978-94-007-4710-4 (eBook)
DOI 10.1007/978-94-007-4710-4
Springer Dordrecht Heidelberg New York London

Library of Congress Control Number: 2012945667

Printed on acid-free paper

Springer is part of Springer Science+Business Media (www.springer.com)

Acknowledgments

McGill University established the Centre for Human Rights and Legal Pluralism in 2005, reflecting a longstanding engagement with international human rights dating back to the important role played by Professor John Humphrey in the drafting of the 1948 Universal Declaration of Human Rights. The Centre's founding aimed to address the perceived gap between the myriad formal human rights at the local, national, regional, and international level, on the one hand, and the continued reality of inadequate enforcement and ongoing violations of fundamental human rights around the world, on the other. Situated within a Faculty of Law committed to engaging with multiple and interacting legal regimes, the Centre was established to build knowledge and understanding regarding the universality of human rights in a legally plural world.

As the founding Director and Research Director of the Centre, we began to engage with numerous scholars across disciplines about their understanding of the connection between human rights and legal pluralism. All of the contributors to this book have presented their insights on the complexities of human rights in a legally plural world in various fora at our Faculty and Centre – at conferences, special workshops, seminars, lectures – and in so doing, have contributed to a dynamic dialogue about the multiple, contested and complex intersections of human rights and legal pluralism. This book attests to the rich diversity of thought and scholarship in this domain. We thank the contributors for sharing their insights and for helping us to begin a dialogue on how universal human rights must be given meaning in legally plural contexts. We view this book as a starting point for a continuing conversation about human rights and legal pluralism in our global community.

In preparing this book, we owe a tremendous debt of gratitude to Dia Dabby, a doctoral student at the McGill Faculty of Law, and former Aisenstadt Fellow at the Centre for Human Rights and Legal Pluralism, for her excellent research, editorial, and translation work. She played an invaluable role in bringing this project to fruition. We also wish to thank our current Dean Daniel Jutras, for his stalwart support of the Centre for Human Rights and Legal Pluralism, as well as our former Dean, the Honourable Justice Nicholas Kasirer, under whose leadership the Centre was established. Finally, we thank Springer Press for their editorial assistance.

We acknowledge the permission to reproduce Sally Engle Merry's "Transnational Human Rights and Local Activism: Mapping the Middle", which was first published in 2006 in American Anthropologist, Volume 108, Issue 1, 38–51, and Angela Campbell's article "Wives Tales: Reflecting on Research in Bountiful", first published in (2008) 23 Canadian Journal of Law and Society 121–141. Two of the chapters are revised versions of papers previously posted online: Val Napoleon's chapter is based on a paper which was written for the National Centre for First Nations Governance and posted online in 2007 at http://fngovernance.org; Colleen Sheppard's chapter expands on a paper presented at the Centre for Research (CRISE) Oxford University workshop, *How Can the Law Help Reduce Group-Based Inequalities?* (May 2009), posted online in February 2010 at: http://www.crise.ox.ac.uk/pubs/workingpaper75.pdf.

As noted above, this book project had its genesis in the creation of the Centre for Human Rights and Legal Pluralism. However, our continued engagement on this project has only reinforced our belief in the critical need to continue to explore diverse perspectives and contexts within which human rights intersect with legal plurality. We see this book, therefore, as the first steps in what will no doubt be a much longer journey.

McGill University
Montréal

Colleen Sheppard and René Provost

About the Contributors

Jean-Guy Belley is a Professor Emeritus at the Faculty of Law at McGill University and Visiting Professor at the Faculty of Law at the Université de Montréal. His teaching and research interests are in contract and general theory of law from the perspective offered by the social sciences, mainly sociology and economic analysis of law. A former fellow of the Canadian Institute for Advanced Research (Law in Society program), he has co-ordinated the collective book *Le droit soluble* (LGDJ, 1996) and a special issue of the *Canadian Journal of Law and Society* on legal pluralism (1997). He has also contributed to another special issue devoted to the same topic by the *Canadian Journal of Law and Society* in 2011 (volume 26, number 2).

Angela Campbell is an Associate Professor at the Faculty of Law at McGill University and Director of the McGill Institute of Comparative Law. She is also a member of McGill's Centre for Human Rights and Legal Pluralism and an associate member of the McGill Centre for Research on Children and Families. She conducts research in the area of family law, with a specific focus on how formal laws envisage family relationships and how well these laws capture different social perceptions of what "family" means. Recent publications include "Bountiful's Plural Marriages" (2010) 6 *International Journal of Law in Context* 343–361; "Exploring Judicial Appreciations of Parental Addiction in Child Custody and Access Decisions: Quebec as a Case Study" (2010) 28 *Windsor Review of Legal and Social Issues* 1–24; and "Bountiful Voices" (2009) 47 *Osgoode Hall Law Journal* 183–234.

Julie Desrosiers is a full Professor at the Faculty of Law at Université Laval. Her research interests include criminal law, human rights, and child and youths' rights and protection. She is the author of *L'agression sexuelle en droit canadien* (Éditions Yvon Blais, 2009) and *Isolement et mesures disciplinaires dans les centres de réadaptation pour jeunes* (Éditions Wilson et Lafleur, 2005).

Carlos Iván Fuentes is a doctoral candidate at the Faculty of Law at McGill University and former O'Brien Fellow at the Centre for Human Rights and Legal Pluralism. Under the supervision of Prof. Evan Fox-Decent, he is exploring the normative plurality within the international legal order, particularly international human rights law. His interests include inter-American human rights law, international humanitarian law, sustainable development, and public governance. He currently works as an Associate Legal Officer at the Treaty Section of the Office of Legal Affairs, United Nations. The views expressed herein are those of the author and do not necessarily reflect the views of the United Nations.

Jane Matthews Glenn is a Professor Emeritus in the Faculty of Law and School of Urban Planning, and Associate Member of the McGill School of Environment at McGill University. Her research interests are in the general area of property law and include urban planning, housing, environmental, and agricultural law. Recent publications include "Informal Formality: Tenantries, *Ejidos* and Family Land", (2008) 4:2 *International Journal of Law in Context* 135–148; "GM Agriculture in Canada: A Courtroom Drama" in Luc Bodiguel & Michael Caldwell (eds.), *The Regulation of Genetically Modified Organisms: Comparative Approaches* (Oxford, Oxford University Press, 2010); and "Crown Ownership in Water *in Situ* in Common Law Canada: Public trusts, classical trusts and fiduciary duties" (2010) 51 *Cahier de droit* 493–519.

Roderick A. Macdonald is the F.R. Scott Professor of Constitutional Law at the Faculty of Law at McGill University. He teaches and publishes in the areas of civil law, commercial law, administrative law, constitutional law, jurisprudence, and access to justice. Professor Macdonald has been President of the Law Commission of Canada (1997–2000), Trudeau Fellow (2004–2007), winner of the Killam Prize for the Social Sciences (2007), President of the Royal Society of Canada (2009–2011), and is currently a Commissioner on the Inquiry into Corruption in the Construction Industry in Quebec. Recent publications include "Three Metaphors of Norm Migration in International Context" (2009) 34 *Brooklyn Journal of International Law* 603–653; "The Political Economy of the Federal Spending Power" in (2008) 34 *Queen's L.J.* 249–304; "Access to Civil Justice" in P. Cane & H. Kritzer (eds.) *Oxford Handbook of Empirical Legal Research* (Oxford: Oxford University Press, 2010) at 492–521; and "Custom Made: For a Non-chirographic Critical Legal Pluralism" (2011) 26 *Canadian Journal of Law and Society* 301–327.

Frédéric Mégret is an Associate Professor of Law at the Faculty of Law at McGill University. He holds the Canada Research Chair on the Law of Human Rights and Legal Pluralism and is the Director of the McGill Clinic for the Sierra Leone Special Court. Professor Mégret is the author of *Le Tribunal pénal international pour le Rwanda* (Pedone, 2002). He is currently co-editing the second edition of *The United Nations and Human Rights: A Critical Appraisal* (Oxford University Press, 2012) with Philip Alston.

Sally Engle Merry is Professor of Anthropology, Law and Society at New York University. She is the author of several books, including *Gender Violence: A Cultural Perspective* (Blackwells 2009); *Human Rights and Gender Violence: Translating International Law into Local Justice* (University of Chicago Press, 2006), which was awarded the J.I. Staley Prize of the School of Advanced Research in 2010; and *Getting Justice and Getting Even* (University of Chicago Press, 1990).

Val Napoleon was appointed Law Foundation Professor of Aboriginal Justice and Governance at the Faculty of Law, University of Victoria on January 1, 2012. She is from north east British Columbia (Treaty 8) and a member of Saulteau First Nation. She is also an adopted member of the Gitanyow (Gitksan) House of Luuxhon, Ganada (Frog) Clan. Prior to joining the Faculty of Law at UVIC, she was a cross appointed associate professor with the Faculty of Native Studies and Faculty of Law, University of Alberta. Her dissertation on Gitksan law and legal theory was awarded the UVIC Governor General's Gold Medal for best dissertation in 2009. Several of her major initiatives include the JID (joint JD and indigenous law degree) program and establishing an indigenous law clinic. Her other current projects include Dechinta (land-based pedagogy and bush university in the NWT), and a collaborative national reconciliation and justice with the Indigenous Bar Association, Truth and Reconciliation, and the Ontario Law Foundation. Professor Napoleon's current research focuses on indigenous legal traditions, indigenous legal theory, indigenous feminism, citizenship, self-determination, and governance.

René Provost is an Associate Professor at the Faculty of Law at McGill University and was the Founding Director of the Centre for Human Rights and Legal Pluralism (2005–2010). He is the author of *International Human Rights and Humanitarian Law* (Cambridge University Press, 2002), the editor of *State Responsibility in International Law* (Ashgate/Dartmouth, 2002), and a co-editor of *Confronting Genocide* (Springer, 2011) with Payam Akhavan and of *International Law Chiefly As Applied and Interpreted in Canada* (Emond Mongtgomery, 2006).

Colleen Sheppard is a full Professor at the Faculty of Law at McGill University and Director of the Centre for Human Rights and Legal Pluralism since September 2010. She was Research Director for the Centre for Human Rights and Legal Pluralism from 2005 to 2009. Her research and teaching focus on comparative constitutional law, equality, and feminist theory. Recent publications include: *Inclusive Equality: The Relational Dimensions of Systemic Discrimination in Canada* (McGill-Queen's University Press, 2010); *Multiple discrimination in the World of Work*, Working Paper No. 66, International Labour Organization, Geneva: Prepared for the *Global Report on Equality at Work* (December 2011); and "*Systemic Discrimination and Gender Inequality: A Life-cycle Approach to Girls' and Women's Rights*" in Errol P. Mendes & Sakunthala Srighanthan (eds.), *Confronting Discrimination and Inequality in China* (Ottawa: University of Ottawa Press, 2009), pages 232–243.

Guylaine Vallée is a full Professor in labor and employment law at the School of Industrial Relations at the Université de Montréal. She is also co-coordinator of the Interuniversity Research Centre on Globalization and Work (CRIMT) and Associate Researcher at the Centre de recherche en droit public (CRDP). Her recent publications concern the incidence of the non-standard work and enterprise on the effectiveness of the labor and employment law, the effect of human rights on labor law, the question of the control over working time for standard and non-standard workers, and the articulation of the plurality of sources of labor and employment law. She is also co-author of books concerning labor and employment law published in 1997, 2003, and 2006. Besides these academic publications, she is co-author of an Experts' Committee Report on the social protection of non-standard workers submitted to the Minister of Labour of Québec in 2003. Since 2009, she is the co-editor with Katherine Lippel of the collection "Droit du travail" (in two volumes) of the JurisClasseur Québec, a major encyclopedia of Québec and federal law in French.

Samuel G. Walker was a Gates Scholar at the University of Cambridge, where he received a master's in international law (LL.M.). He holds a B.A. in History from Yale University (2005), as well as an LL.B. and B.C.L. from the McGill University Faculty of Law (2010).

Contents

1 **Introduction: Human Rights Through Legal Pluralism** 1
René Provost and Colleen Sheppard

Part I Universality and Plurality: Foundational Claims

2 **Pluralistic Human Rights? Universal Human Wrongs?** 15
Roderick A. Macdonald

3 **E Pluribus Unum – Bhinneka Tunggal Ika? Universal Human Rights and the Fragmentation of International Law** 37
Carlos Iván Fuentes, René Provost, and Samuel G. Walker

4 **International Human Rights and Global Legal Pluralism: A Research Agenda** 69
Frédéric Mégret

Part II Human Rights Values and Multiple Legal Orders: Connections and Contradictions

5 **The Protection of Human Dignity in Contemporary Legal Pluralism** 99
Jean-Guy Belley

6 **Equality Through the Prism of Legal Pluralism** 129
Colleen Sheppard

7 **Labour Law in Canada as a Site of Legal Pluralism** 145
Guylaine Vallée

8 **The Rigidity and Density of Discipline in Youth Rehabilitation Centres … Or Rules That Counter Rights** 165
Julie Desrosiers

9 Reconceptualising Social and Economic Rights: The Right to Housing and Intersecting Legal Regimes 187
Jane Matthews Glenn

Part III Communities, Human Rights and Local Practices

10 Transnational Human Rights and Local Activism: Mapping the Middle 207
Sally Engle Merry

11 Thinking About Indigenous Legal Orders 229
Val Napoleon

12 Wives' Tales on Research in Bountiful 247
Angela Campbell

Selected Bibliography on Human Rights and Legal Pluralism 269

Index 275

Contributors

Jean-Guy Belley Faculty of Law, McGill University, Montreal, QC, Canada

Angela Campbell Faculty of Law, Institute for Comparative Law, McGill University, Montreal, QC, Canada

Julie Desrosiers Faculty of Law, Université Laval, Québec, QC, Canada

Carlos Iván Fuentes Treaty Section, Office of Legal Affairs, United Nations, New York, NY, USA

Jane Matthews Glenn Faculty of Law, McGill University, Montreal, QC, Canada

Roderick A. Macdonald Faculty of Law, McGill University, Montreal, QC, Canada

Frédéric Mégret Faculty of Law, Centre for Human Rights and Legal Pluralism, McGill University, Montreal, QC, Canada

Sally Engle Merry Department of Anthropology, New York University, New York, NY, USA

Val Napoleon Faculty of Law, University of Victoria, Victoria, BC, Canada

René Provost Faculty of Law, Centre for Human Rights and Legal Pluralism, McGill University, Montreal, QC, Canada

Colleen Sheppard Faculty of Law, Centre for Human Rights and Legal Pluralism, McGill University, Montreal, QC, Canada

Guylaine Vallée École des relations industrielles, Université de Montréal, Montréal, QC, Canada

Samuel G. Walker Faculty of Law, McGill University, Montreal, QC, Canada

Chapter 1
Introduction: Human Rights Through Legal Pluralism

René Provost and Colleen Sheppard

At first glance, human rights and legal pluralism make strange bedfellows. To begin with, they are not conceptual analogues: the first is normative in its essence, capturing a bundle of rights reflecting the interests most fundamental to any human being; the second is conceptual, offering a model of how to construct legal normativity in a society. There are, beyond this distinct nature, further layers of difference which separate rather than unite notions of human rights and legal pluralism, explaining the fact that studies on human rights rarely have embraced a legal pluralism approach and, conversely, that legal pluralistic analysis by and large focuses on norms other than human rights. This book interrogates the chasm that seems to exist between these two notions, to highlight the potential for legal pluralism to bring innovative perspectives to our understanding of human rights, which have become a critical component of modern legal systems. Human rights have experienced momentous growth during the post-World War II era. At the international, state, and local levels, human rights laws, declarations, charters, and covenants have multiplied and endorsed a recurring core of rights and obligations linked to the protection of fundamental human dignity, equality and justice. Nevertheless, there has been a growing concern that simply ratifying or legislating human rights conventions and laws does not lead to the effective enjoyment of human rights in the daily lives of millions of individuals. Legal pluralism offers an approach that translates abstract and broad human rights standards into the vernacular of everyday life, transplanting these norms into ordinary human relations where they can truly achieve their transformative potential.[1]

Human rights, in the way that they have been classically captured in legal standards, protect the individual against oppression by the state. Built on the painful experiences of abuses at the hand of governments, human rights thus correspond to a series of

---

[1] See Sally Engle Merry's contribution (Chap.10) to this volume.

R. Provost (✉) • C. Sheppard
Faculty of Law, Centre for Human Rights and Legal Pluralism,
McGill University, Montreal, QC H3A 1W9, Canada
e-mail: rene.provost@mcgill.ca; colleen.sheppard@mcgill.ca

R. Provost and C. Sheppard (eds.), *Dialogues on Human Rights and Legal Pluralism*, Ius Gentium: Comparative Perspectives on Law and Justice 17,
DOI 10.1007/978-94-007-4710-4_1, © Springer Science+Business Media Dordrecht 2013

obligations imposed upon the state, including either duties to abstain from interfering within a protected zone shielding every individual, or duties to provide everyone with the opportunity to develop and realise their full potential. Human rights have transformed the way in which we conceive of the place of the individual within the community and in relation to the state in a vast array of disciplines, including law, philosophy, politics, sociology, and geography. The published output on human rights over the last five decades has been enormous, but on the whole bound tightly to a notion of human rights that links individuals and groups directly to the state. The community, as an object of study and a locus of normativity, has been largely left out of human rights studies. Legal pluralism, on the other hand, grew out of anthropological analysis of the ways in which traditional communities structured their collective lives prior to and following colonization, and highlighted the existence of norms and customary laws which played a role parallel to that of formal law in colonizing nations. Anthropological studies also revealed the ways in which colonial legal orders attempted to co-opt indigenous customary law by formally deeming it applicable in certain circumstances, leading to a transformation of both legal orders in ways which were often unintended, unanticipated, and often misunderstood. The interest was to capture a notion of normativity which did not correspond to an idealised understanding of law in western thought, necessarily centred upon the state. Within such a perspective on law, there is little space for a focus on human rights standards.

Over the last two decades, there has been a gradual enlargement of the scope of human rights, moving them beyond claims against the state to contest human rights violations by non-state actors. Initially spurred by feminist critiques of the exclusion of domestic violence as a human rights concern, a move to reinterpret human rights has meant that more and more rights can be claimed to protect victims from abusers which have no relation to the state.[2] Examples include the Inter-American Convention on the Prevention, Punishment, and Eradication of Violence against Women, the rise of individual criminal responsibility for war crimes committed by rebel fighters, and the Montreux Document on Private Military and Security Companies. This so-called *Drittwirkung*[3] application of human rights nevertheless has by and large remained anchored in a positivist understanding of law, calling for the state to remain centrally involved as arbiter or enforcer, despite an acknowledgment that there are considerable obstacles to generating compliance by actors not institutionally connected to the state. Legal pluralism offers an approach that captures the process whereby communities beyond the state take ownership of human rights norms and transform them to

[2] See Andrew Clapham, *Human Rights Obligations of Non-State Actors* (Oxford: Oxford University Press, 2006); Andrew Clapham, "Human Rights Obligations of Non-State Actors in Conflict Situations" (2006) 88 *International Review of the Red Cross* 491.

[3] See, for instance Hans-Joachim Cremer, *Human Rights and the Protection of Privacy in Tort Law: A Comparison between English and German Law* (London: Routledge, 2011); András Sajó and Renáta Uitz, eds., *The Constitution in Private Relations: Expanding Constitutionalism* (Utretch: Eleven International Publishing, 2005).

reflect their specific identities and aspirations. Human rights are thus pluralised and given meaning outside of the formal apparatus of state law, woven into the fabric of community relationships, duties and obligations.

One important new way of thinking about human rights is to examine how they arise in multiple and diverse ways in a legally plural world.[4] Such an approach diverges from the general tendency to presume that human rights law is exclusively about *universal* norms and principles and instead situates human rights norms within multiple or plural legal orders, including both formal and informal legal regimes. These multiple legal regimes, moreover, do not operate in isolation from one another but constantly interact and intersect. The challenge in the domain of human rights law, therefore, is to examine how formal human rights laws intersect and interact with diverse, co-existing legal regimes and systems, both formal and informal. For example, how might human rights norms take into account indigenous legal regimes, and the multiplicity of informal institutional legal orders in economic, political and social contexts, including workplaces, educational institutions, families, and religious, ethnic and cultural communities? How does private law intersect with the public law of human rights, domestic with international, regional with local? In examining human rights in a diverse and legally plural world, this project will draw on important interdisciplinary perspectives on legal pluralism and respect for human rights, and expand in new directions a burgeoning literature on the application of legal pluralism in international law.[5]

Developing a legal pluralist perspective on human rights law has two key dimensions. First, it provides important new insights into the obstacles to effective enforcement of formal human rights protections – obstacles institutionalized and embedded in both official and unofficial law. Second, it illuminates how official human rights law can be reinforced and strengthened by recourse to multiple sources of formal law (e.g. international, regional, domestic), and by integrating human rights norms into informal and customary law as well as institutional norms and practices (e.g. workplace, community codes of conduct). In so doing, the universal ideals embodied in international human rights documents are linked to local law, understandings, social practices and institutional processes.

This collection of essays brings together authors with diverse perspectives on the intersection between legal pluralism and human rights to explore the ways in which these concepts can be mutually reinforcing or in tension with each other. The essays reveal that there is no unitary conclusion but that the question of how human rights and legal pluralism interact opens up a rich domain of inquiry for those interested in how human rights can either affect the behaviour of individuals, collectivities, and institutions or be secondary to other institutional norms, formal and informal laws.

[4] Most recently, see the special 2010 issue on human rights and legal pluralism in the *Journal of Legal Pluralism and Unofficial Law* (volume 60); International Council on Human Rights Policy, *When Legal Worlds Overlap: Human Rights, State and Non-State Law* (Switzerland: International Council on Human Rights Policy, 2009).

[5] Paul Schiff Berman, "Global Legal Pluralism" (2007) 80 *Southern California Review* 1155.

1.1 Universality and Plurality: Foundational Claims

Part I of the volume addresses a number of foundational claims about the conceptual relationship between human rights and legal pluralism, focusing on the discourse of universal human rights in Post-World War II international law. One important theme addressed in Part I concerns the tendency for human rights discourse to veer towards essentialism regarding the human condition. Reflecting the natural law justification for the universality of human rights, it is assumed that the rights listed in documents like the Universal Declaration of Human Rights and the conventions that followed are reflective of the very nature of human beings and, as such, not subject to variation from place to place. This view is very much challenged by all three of the essays in Part I.

Instead, they construct an alternative understanding of human rights, based on one of the fundamental dimensions of legal pluralism, to the effect that law is not handed down to individuals or groups from a superior authority, but rather produced by legal actors whose behaviour we seek to regulate through legal norms. As such, the agency of a wide range of legal actors is recognised, from states to individuals, nongovernmental organisations to corporations. In these discrete and interacting normative sites, legal standards are not only interpreted and applied but also produced. This approach speaks to a sense of ownership or appropriation of rules and by the same token to the responsibility borne by each of us for human rights standards that we feel should govern our lives: these can no longer be viewed as imposed either by some higher authority or by a more valid approximation to the essence of what it means to be a human being. Instead, they evoke a notion of law as an imagined alternative to which we are invited to subscribe and contribute. As explained by Roderick Macdonald in his essay, "[l]egal pluralism is not a truth claim. It is a way of characterizing an interpretive choice for citizens about how they wish to conceive law, themselves and the relationship they have to law."

In addition to the pluralisation of law as a reflection of the multiplicity of legal sites in which norms are produced, legal pluralism articulates the idea that there is necessary and constant interaction among these various normative sites. This is explored by Carlos Fuentes, René Provost and Samuel G. Walker in the context of the emergence of universal and regional human rights regimes, underscoring the fragmented nature of human rights law. As Frédéric Mégret also points out, regional regimes illustrate how formal human rights instruments can define different paths towards the achievement of humanitarian ideals. As legal agents, we can no more step out of the normative universe in which we are situated than we can step out of the physical universe. As a corollary, the suggestion of agency cannot be taken as a claim of absolute liberty in which legal actors are free to make unconstrained choices about the norms to which they will adhere. That normative universe encases the range of options which we feel are legitimate and open to rational interpretive option. Seen in this light, the constant and variable exchanges, tensions, clashes, and confluences, among approaches to human rights norms do not challenge the viability, binding character or usefulness of human rights law; rather they highlight its nature as a privileged site for engagement with diversity.

A second foundational theme explored in the three essays in Part I centres on the cultural dimension of the process whereby international human rights standards are given meaning. With the idea of the delocalisation of international legal standards away from a community constituted only of states necessarily comes a cultural pluralisation of human rights norms. This pluralisation entails a process that reflects the identity of legal agents engaged in giving meaning to abstract legal standards. That identity is, needless to say, multidimensional. In a more traditional reading of human rights law, states are the norm entrepreneurs and the normative process and output partake in their shared identity as states, grounded in the idea of sovereignty. What is more, human rights issued from an exclusive focus on the state, conceptualise the state as the source of the threat against which human rights were erected as a barrier. Even at that level, cultural specificity still does emerge to a limited extent, filtered through the state, in regional regimes that will contain somewhat distinct approaches to human rights, lists of fundamental rights that change, and specific rights defined in variable and at times contradictory ways. Cultural exceptionalism has also been reflected in some of the reservations issued by states at the time of ratifying international human rights treaties, most famously the reservations of some states seeking to be bound only to the extent that the treaty imposes obligations compatible with Islamic law. It bears reminding that there are still some parts of the world in which there is no applicable regional regime, leaving each state to relate to the international human rights regime in a manner unmediated by instruments or institutions reflecting a presumably thicker consensus among a smaller group of states. Some governments, moreover, have abstained from ratifying human rights treaties altogether, operating in a purely customary environment in which there is still greater space for interpretive choices. Leaving aside a more traditional outlook on law to embrace legal pluralism as a conceptual framework, the agency of every class of legal actors in the process of giving meaning to human rights norms suggests that the cultural plurality of agents will generate a cultural plurality of legal norms. These non-state legal agents do not share a corporate identity grounded in the idea of sovereignty, and the cultural fragmentation resulting from what Robert Cover described as *jurisgenesis* will invariably be greater than that observable when considering only state intervention.[6] For non-state agents, human rights norms become part of a constellation of markers of identity. They are a projected statement of an idealised world and a claim to *a priori* legitimacy, an intimation of difference and a delineation of communal boundaries.

Human rights law thus stands as a fragmented, polycentric regime, and has been so since its emergence into positive international law. The phenomenon of normative fragmentation does not necessarily lead to the conclusion that there is in fact no human rights regime to speak of. Formal institutions created pursuant to different human rights instruments have their own particular source of authority and apply a

[6] Robert Cover, "The Supreme Court 1982 Term – Foreword: Nomos and Narrative" (1983) 97 *Harvard Law Review* 4.

designated instrument or set of instruments, but they nevertheless do not apply human rights standards in an isolated manner; on the contrary, they speak to each other either directly through what has sometimes been called transjudicialism or indirectly by referring to the law of other jurisdictions. Even informally, legal actors will often invoke the provisions of instruments which are in no way directly applicable to the situation at hand to strengthen their arguments. In this fashion, the universal is localised and the vernacular is globalised, with these internormative trajectories shaping a cosmopolitan human rights regime. For the authors of the three chapters in Part I of this volume, the nomadic character of human rights, the spaces in-between, and the moments of encounter among the fragmented segments of the regime, all present privileged sites in which to investigate the nature of human rights.

1.2 Human Rights Values and Multiple Legal Orders: Connections and Contradictions

Questions about the interplay between human rights and legal pluralism arise in complex ways in the institutional contexts of everyday life. Part II confronts the intersection between multiple sources of formal and informal law and the fundamental values at the heart of formal human rights law – values that include human dignity, equality, non-discrimination, protection of vulnerable individuals and groups, physical and psychological integrity, security of the person and children's rights. It is evident that the relationship between formal human rights law and the informal codes, practices and norms of institutional governance is complex and contested. In corporations, labour unions, schools, state institutions for child protection and detention, to name but a few – human rights issues arise in the lived experiences of individuals and groups, are accentuated by structural and systemic power inequities and vulnerability, and contested in acts of everyday dissent and protest. Yet they are not often discussed or recognized within the legal discourse of human rights. It is critical, nonetheless, to take institutional realities into account in thinking about the effective enjoyment and enforcement of human rights – both in terms of understanding significant obstacles to respect for human rights and in order to assess the potential to incorporate human rights norms into the everyday institutional decision-making processes of public and private institutions. In this domain, we see the competing claims of state-based human rights norms confronting, for example, the informal rules, policies and practices of public and private institutions, "soft" law institutional codes of conduct, and negotiated collective agreements. Two contradictory arguments emerge when we examine the intersection between the informal law of institutional orders and human rights.

One important argument underscores how institutional norms, codes of conduct, policies and practices can significantly undermine fundamental human rights. In his essay on legal pluralism and human dignity, Jean-Guy Belley concludes that the relationship between these two concepts is "conflictual rather than mutually reinforcing."

Belley traces the broad historical shifts from pre-modernity to modernity to the contemporary global context and laments the growing hegemony of technocratic and bureaucratic corporate power. The legal pluralism embedded in the informal laws of the private, transnational corporation, in Belley's view, erodes respect for human dignity – a concept central to human rights. While Belley's chapter focuses on the private, transnational corporation, Julie Desrosiers' essay reaches a similar conclusion about the antinomy between legal pluralism and human rights in the domain of public institutions – specifically institutions set up to protect youth in need of protection. Within these state-run institutions, Desrosiers poignantly demonstrates how institutional rules and regulations contribute to the recurrent and systemic violation of basic human rights to liberty, freedom of expression and security of the person of some of the most vulnerable members of society – children and youth in state custody because they are considered in need of protection. State-based institutions, designed for child and youth protection, have themselves become sources of rights violations. Colleen Sheppard's chapter exploring equality rights through the prism of legal pluralism also highlights the importance of understanding how transformative formal human rights laws are often undermined by institutional resistance, obstacles and backlash. Indeed, the legal concepts of indirect discrimination, also referred to as disparate impact or adverse effects discrimination and systemic or structural discrimination, are based upon recognition of the ways in which institutional norms and practices can undermine inclusion and equality.

Thus, understanding legal pluralism provides important insights into why it is so difficult to secure the effective enforcement of formal human rights guarantees in many institutional contexts. Such guarantees confront the power of institutional norms, rules and practices anathema to respect for human rights. Despite the generally negative conclusions reached by Belley and Desrosiers, both point to internal resistance and critique to challenge institutional denials of human dignity and rights. For Desrosiers, one promising transformative pathway would be to give greater voice and decision-making power to the youths themselves – an idea that resonates with a more positive vision of the intersection between informal and formal law. Belley underscores the need to develop and maintain a critical perspective on alternative forms of "soft law" regulation, rather than assuming that they are necessarily or always progressive. While recognizing systemic and institutional obstacles to equality, Sheppard insists that the effective enforcement of human rights demands a bottom up strategy embedded in everyday institutional practices and policies.

Recognition of the possibility of institutional transformation from within is the basis upon which a powerful alternative argument is constructed – one that maintains that legal plurality can be a potential mechanism for enhancing rather than undermining rights. It is suggested that the objectives of formal human rights norms may be reinforced by informal norms and practices at the institutional level. Processes such as collective bargaining, internal participatory and consultative decision-making, institutional dispute-resolution mechanisms and the internalization of human rights norms as guideposts in institutional governance constitute effective ways to prevent and redress human rights violations outside of the formal complaints processes of human rights law.[7] Guylaine Vallée examines the potential for legal pluralism to enhance rights by examining the historical specificity of labour law and collective bargaining. Labour law has historically affirmed legal pluralism, according special legitimacy to rules created by workers and employers through the processes of collective negotiation. From a human rights perspective, labour law can be understood as part of a global movement towards the affirmation of economic and social rights of workers. Vallée examines the interplay between formal state laws and the collectively negotiated law of the workplace in areas touching upon the rights of vulnerable workers. Sheppard also emphasizes the importance of legal pluralism in light of the historic inadequacy of formal retroactive state-based complaints about discrimination. She suggests that an important pathway to the more effective enjoyment of equality rights requires the construction of internal participatory and democratic processes for preventing, contesting and remedying systemic and structural inequalities.

Affirming the importance of non-state actors, Vallée also suggests that unions act as "co-legislators" (a term she coins), acting as a bridge between collective agreements and state law. Extending the role of unions and arbitrators beyond the collective agreement and obliging them to engage with state law endorsing equality and protections for vulnerable workers heightens the level of accountability for all concerned. The rise of co-legislators, therefore, lends weight to the need to recognize the multiplicity of formal and informal legal orders and their fluid cohabitation. As instigators of change, moreover, the presence of "co-legislators" suggests that a multiplicity of voices and a plurality of legal orders can bridge the local and the global. This idea is also advanced by Sheppard, who highlights the ways in which international legal standards and global solidarity networks can be drawn upon to reinforce local claims. For Sheppard, "it is critical to examine how law is being used in multiple, creative and diverse ways, globally and locally by social actors seeking to foster a more equitable and inclusive world." The human right to equality, from this perspective, engages both law and politics.

In the final essay of Part II, Jane Matthews Glenn examines social and economic rights, and in particular the right to housing through an innovative legal pluralism lens. She considers whether social and economic rights can be reconceptualised in a way that places more emphasis on concrete implementation issues, thereby attenuating more abstract and perceived problems of justiciability. Glenn's disaggregation of rights emphasizes the non-linear approach to what is termed 'discrete rights' and provides an alternative framework to how socio-economic rights are addressed and perhaps enforced. For Glenn, the cases chosen to call attention to the right to housing (and access to justice more broadly) also highlight the multiplicity of actors and intersecting and overlapping forms of normativity: "[m]ore generally, it also shows a willingness on the part of the courts to hear, at least, cases that affect government policy decisions and the use of public resources."

---

[7] See Susan Sturm, "Second Generation Employment Discrimination: A Structural Approach" (2001) 101 *Columbia Law Review* 458.

Thus, the contributions in Part II of this volume explore how the intersection between formal and informal legal orders is complex and multifaceted, revealing simultaneously the potential of legal plurality either to reinforce or to undermine the advancement of fundamental human rights values.

1.3 Communities, Human Rights and Local Practices

The chapters in Part III of the volume turn to consider some implications of giving greater significance to the use and impact of human rights norms by communities operating in a manner that is not formalized in codes or fixed institutional arrangements. The three chapters by Sally Engle Merry, Val Napoleon and Angela Campbell touch on the problems at the interface between internal formulation of norms and human rights law, the role played by human rights in the governance of discrete communities, and the concern for sub-groups marginalized within such communities.

A focus on small groups like a polygamous Church of the Latter Day Saints community (Campbell), indigenous communities (Napoleon), or individuals trying to provide protection for women victim of domestic violence (Merry), brings to the fore the need to transpose international human rights standards into a vernacular that will be reflective of local practices and values. Without this proactive translation, international or national standards on the protection of fundamental rights will often appear as too remote or too aligned with the interests of the state to be useful in a small-scale context. Merry underscores the critical role played by translators, occupying a middle position between the community and international or national standards or institutions. This is a position of power but also of vulnerability: the power reflects the authority flowing to the translator as knowledge broker, able to bring into a conversation arguments which can be seen as transcending the positions of parties to a dispute; the vulnerability echoes the reality that a translator's status depends on her ability to bridge the international/state/formal approaches to particular issues and those embedded in local lore. This bridge may often be accomplished only at the expense of concessions by both sides. Campbell adds to this analysis by situating herself as partly an outsider and partly a translator to whom the women of a polygamous community would turn to find reassurance or support in formal legal norms. Whereas Merry opposes local to global in an effort to illustrate the existence of 'cultural translators', Campbell uses locality to demonstrate that the line between outsiders and insiders is fluid rather than static. Both authors point in distinct manner to the permeability of boundaries between the formal human rights regimes and vernacular local norms. While Merry points to the process of replication or hybridization to illustrate the presence of cultural translators, Campbell points to the researcher recognizing and coming to terms with their outside (and perhaps conflicting) perspectives on what has been called "culturally challenging practices". Napoleon uses locality in a different manner, namely in order to indicate the decentralization of peoples in western Canada. Locality, in this sense, is said to refer to a *reconciliation* of legal orders rather than a *translation* between legal orders. As a result,

Napoleon's starting point is the damage caused to Indigenous legal orders by the community's exposure to state-driven norms. The challenge is therefore of a different nature, namely to "effectively reconcile the modern and historic forms of governance and law making authorities at the local level". As an example of the direction that a legal order may take with a localized setting, Napoleon evokes the Gitksan community where law "takes place horizontally among the members on a decentralized basis, and not vertically as when government is centralized."

As the last point regarding the law of certain indigenous communities makes clear, there is a variety of structures which can reflect law in general and human rights principles in particular. This is so, Napoleon underscores, even among different First Nations in Canada so that what the Gitskan consider to be law will not necessarily be thought of as such for the Cree or the Wet'suwet'en. There are as many models of governance inspired by human rights principles as there are communities. If we take the notions of law and communities as mutually constitutive, then there is no model that necessarily flows from human rights standards, even beyond the contested nature of many of these standards. That said, human rights do travel from one sphere to another through the intercession of translators, as we have seen, and offer a common language in which to express values and articulate practices. As such, Merry writes, "[u]nderstanding how human rights circulate and are transplanted raises larger questions about how cultural life is changing in response to globalisation and its deepening inequalities in wealth and power". It is in this fashion that the vernacular of how equality standards are rendered by a woman in a polygamous marriage in a secluded religious community in British Columbia, for instance, can meaningfully contribute to the construction of a global ethnography of human rights discourse. It is thus in the merger of the methodological concerns of anthropology and the law's attention to human rights discourse that legal pluralism offers the possibility of a far more complex understanding of the contribution of international and domestic human rights norms.

The acknowledgment of the culturally-bounded nature of norms, including human rights, raises the question of the processes whereby communities determine their governance structures. In other words, do human rights standards provide us with a valid reference point to understand and assess the practices of a given community? A focus on the self-perceptions of wives in a polygamous community, on efforts by non-governmental organisations in Asia working to tackle violence against women, and on the contribution of female elders in Aboriginal communities, offers not only a gendered understanding of the impact of human rights standards but also paints a picture of marginalisation and the extent to which human rights offer a tool to defend against it. As studied by Campbell, the informality of group structures often provides an opportunity for elites to impose their viewpoint and marginalise groups like women. This dominant narrative can be further reinforced by formal human rights discourse affording a degree of deference towards communities in the articulation of human rights. The internal, parallel narrative which allows marginalised sub-groups to validate their role may well not be recognised as valid from an external standpoint, condemned as false-consciousness. One reaction noted by Merry is that the language of human rights may be abandoned altogether in favour of a more purely vernacular narrative, mentioning the example of women's groups in Nigeria fighting to advance the rights of women on the basis of Shari'a rather than the Universal Declaration of Human Rights. The three chapters concur in affirming the need to acknowledge the validity of multiple, competing and overlapping narratives about human dignity, and to refrain from a reading of human rights standards that amounts to an assertion of an essentialising monopoly in the legitimation of community structure, practices and values. In looking at discrete, marginalised and insular communities, the authors of this final part of this book provide important insights on the multiple points of interaction between norms and human rights law, illustrating the importance of the roles of conciliator and translator in these overlapping, concomitant, and coexisting worlds.

1.4 Conclusion

A central paradox of the international human rights regime further to its entrenchment in documents like the Universal Declaration of Human Rights was that it sought to impose a unique benchmark for measuring the behaviour of powerful institutions across the infinitely variable landscape of cultural, social and political realities. As a result, it was often assumed and argued that human rights stood for a single model of rights protection.[8] The chapters of this volume, taken together, underscore the fallacy of such a proposition while at the same time upholding the usefulness of human rights as a rhetorical tool to sustain dialogue across boundaries of one sort or another. The chapters taken from the domestic as well as the international fields demonstrate that there is flexibility within the concept of human rights, an idea which was already observed at the international level in the elaboration of the 'margin of appreciation' recognised to states in the internal application of international standards; the chapters push this much further to suggest that even beyond the open-textured nature of human rights norms, there is a phenomenon of fragmentation at the international and domestic levels resulting in multiple, overlapping human rights regimes attaching to a broad range of institutions and communities. Legal pluralism explains this phenomenon as inherent to any manifestation of legal normativity. The picture of the global human rights regime which emerges from these converging perspectives is one of a multivalent legal tradition in which the occasional contradictions of the parts do not deny the unity of the whole.

[8] See Mary Ann Glendon, *A World Made New: Eleanor Roosevelt and the Universal Declaration of Human Rights* (New York: Random House, 2001).

Part I
Universality and Plurality: Foundational Claims

Chapter 2
Pluralistic Human Rights? Universal Human Wrongs?

Roderick A. Macdonald*

2.1 Introduction

The burden of moral philosophy is to reason towards universal truths. To do so requires philosophers to abstract from the complex, diverse, messy world in which real people lead real lives, and in which tyranny, slavery, inequality and injustice are everyday experiences. The burden of descriptive sociology, by contrast, is to explore how human societies function and to draw appropriate distinctions between what may initially look like identical situations. For better or for worse, most contemporary reflection about human rights by law professors, lawyers and judges approximates the philosophical rather than the sociological viewpoint.

Let me straightaway register a counterpoint to the preoccupations of my juristic colleagues. In my empirical research into access to justice over the past 35 years, I have found nothing but social diversity and legal plurality. I would expect a like

This essay was initially delivered in the fall of 2006 to a workshop sponsored by the McGill Centre for Human Rights and Legal Pluralism. In December 2008, parts of the essay were incorporated into an address at the conference – *The Universal Declaration of Human Rights: 60 years later* – sponsored by the Association of Canadian Studies. That speech was later revised as an essay now published in a special edition of the Association's magazine *Canadian Diversity.* I have retained some of the material from that published speech that was originally part of this essay.

*I should like to thank my colleagues, Kim Brooks, François Crépeau, Robert Leckey, Hoi Kong, Vrinda Narain and Shauna Van Praagh, and my doctoral students Tom McMorrow and Suzanne Bouclin, for their insightful comments on an earlier draft of this essay. I am grateful to Colleen Sheppard and René Provost of the MCHRLP for their invitation to deliver the initial address, and for their subsequent comments on the revised version of the essay. Lucan Gregory (B.C.L./LL.B. 2010) closely read the final version and saved me from numerous inconsistencies, illogical derivations and incompletely elaborated assertions. None, of course, bears responsibility for any claims made here.

R.A. Macdonald (✉)
Faculty of Law, McGill University, Montreal, QC H3A 1W9, Canada
e-mail: roderick.macdonald@mcgill.ca

R. Provost and C. Sheppard (eds.), *Dialogues on Human Rights and Legal Pluralism*, Ius Gentium: Comparative Perspectives on Law and Justice 17,
DOI 10.1007/978-94-007-4710-4_2, © Springer Science+Business Media Dordrecht 2013

finding to result were I to undertake empirical research into human rights.[1] For this reason, in my title I have inversed the standard presentation of human rights themes, emphasizing particularity over universals. In doing so, I do not disparage the jurist's quest for high-level explanatory theory. Rather, my goal is to reorient that quest. The pressing challenge is to elaborate a theoretical approach adequate to the variety of contemporary practices of human rights.

Might I introduce the point by calling forth what has sometimes been described as the "best first sentence in western literature"? That sentence is:

All happy families are happy alike; all unhappy families are unhappy in their own way.

So begins Leo Tolstoy's *Anna Karenina.*[2] To me, the opening of *Anna Karenina* reveals a key fact about human beings, about human society and about human institutions – except that, by focusing on an abstraction, I believe Tolstoy got the analysis exactly backwards. In my experience *unhappy* families tend to be unhappy alike, and *happy* families tend to be happy each in their own way. I don't mean to make a large claim here about the "essential nature" of happiness or unhappiness. After all, I suppose that there are as many different ways of being unhappy as there are ways of being happy. Rather, I suggest that members of happy families who reflect on their happiness realize that there is no single formula for happiness. Happiness results from attending to the specific features of a family relationship, the specific character and personality of each member of the family and the specific circumstances within which the family finds itself.

On the contrary, members of unhappy families who reflect on their unhappiness (and I suspect that many do not) often seek some recipe, some distilled wisdom of the ages, that can be expressed in a universal set of principles meant to ensure their happiness. For members of such unhappy, but reflective, families, happiness is not typically something that demands an investment of emotional energy, a humility about one's own circumstances, and an ongoing quest for grace that fails as often as it succeeds. No, for them, happiness is the necessary outcome of adhering to an apparently proven and, if possible, memorizable mantra. Unfortunately, however, in most cases the mantra requires of them saint-like conduct which human beings are simply incapable of achieving – and the failure of achievement only compounds their unhappiness.

As a meditation on the human condition, the inversed form of Tolstoy's epigram may be deployed to guide reflection not just about happiness, but about "all things human". Transposed particularly to human rights, the epigram would come out something like this:

All unhappy experiences of human rights are unhappy alike, and all happy experiences of human rights are happy in their own way.

My goal in this short essay is to tease out, in the particular, the implications of this revised epigram for the theory and practice of human rights, not just in some far off locale "in need of guidance" but also right here in Canada.

---

[1] I am comforted in this conclusion by the essays collected in E. Jensen and T. Heller, eds., *Beyond Common Knowledge: Empirical Approaches to the Rule of Law* (Palo Alto: Stanford University Press, 2002).

[2] English translation by Louise and Aylmer Maude, republished by Oxford University Press, 1995.

One might begin by noting that there is a substantial literature contesting the very *idea* of human rights.[3] In addition, some scholars take the view that, while the *idea* of universal human rights is not incoherent, it is nonetheless incoherent to attempt to instantiate these rights in a document that purports to inventorize justiciable "universal human rights". The claim is that if enforcement of this set of abstract propositions is left to the institutions of particular states that define themselves precisely by exclusionary boundaries that make some human beings alien, then the notion of universality is a chimera.[4] I do not propose to revisit either of these types of critique here. Both have their place. Indeed, they are useful in pointing to the need to attend to on-the-ground beliefs and practices of States whenever international norm entrepreneurs in any domain seek to homogenize social diversity under a single legislative instrument.[5]

Still, abstract declarations of rights, even if non-justiciable in a global forum, do have their value. Contemporary critiques of the universalizing urge often miss this point because they fail to account for the symbolic power of human rights as a way of talking about the dignity of human beings, the dignity of diverse human identities and the dignity of human cultural expression. Of course, in rendering our most meaningful symbols and practices of social solidarity (rites, chants, rituals, icons, sacred music, dance, and feasts, to mention only some) into textual representations like the *Universal Declaration of Human Rights*, we ought not, in the manner of unhappy families, to express our expectations in too great detail or set our aspirations too high: to be normative, aspirations must be framed as general canons of virtue, not a litany of minimum duties; and they must be realistic – that is, within the realm of approximate achievability by mere mortals. Ought ought to imply can.

Moreover, it is not enough simply to aspire; the reason we frame our aspirations as we do is because we conceive them as actually informing our practices. Translating aspiration into action requires us to take account of the diverse sites of these practices and of the processual modes inherent in these sites. We cannot, I argue, recuse ourselves from the hard work of deriving a menu of possible procedural and institutional forms by and through which the paths pointing in the direction of these aspirations may be traced.[6]

---

[3] For a compendium of recent literature on critiques of human rights, and responses by human rights advocates, see W. Twining, *General Jurisprudence: Understanding Law from a Global Perspective* (Cambridge: Cambridge University Press, 2009), chapters 6 and 7.

[4] I derive this formulation from W. Conklin, "A Phenomenological Theory of the Human Rights of the Alien" (2006) 13 *Ethical Perspectives: Journal of the European Ethics Network* 245.

[5] For an application of the critique of universalism to private law instruments, see, notably, P. Legrand, "The Impossibility of Legal Transplants" (1997) 4 *Maastricht Journal of European and Comparative Law* 111, and J.M. Miller, "A Typology of Legal Transplants" (2003) 51 *American Journal of Comparative Law* 839. A review of the metaphors of harmonization, transplants and viruses as explanations of international norm entrepreneurship is presented in R.A. Macdonald "Three Metaphors of Norm Migration in International Context" (2009) 34 *Brooklyn Journal of International Law* 603.

[6] My thinking on this point has been deeply influenced by Lon Fuller's "eunomics project". See K. Winston, (ed.), *The Principles of Social Order: Selected Essays of Lon L. Fuller* (2d) (Oxford: Hart Publishing, 2002). See further W. Witteveen and V. van der Burg, (eds.), *Rediscovering Fuller: Essays on Implicit Law and Institutional Design* (Amsterdam: University of Amsterdam Press, 2000).

Conceiving the *idea* of human rights as aspiration rather than rights claims and perceiving the diversity of practices for instantiating that idea ground my skepticism about much contemporary human rights discourse. Little is to be gained by further contributions to Manichean debate. My ecumenism about human rights theory and practice also rests on what I see as facts on the ground that were not present at the time the commitment to textualize human rights in the form of a *Universal Declaration of Human Rights* crystallized. The world we now inhabit is shrinking in ways scarcely imaginable half a century ago. Advances in communications and transportation technologies are handmaidens to the increasing scope and scale of interpersonal and intergroup interaction across social, religious, cultural and geographic boundaries. The consequent transfers of ideas, institutions and conceptions of the good and the just are creating a new, dare I say multi-centred, dialogue about the human condition; far from a monochromatic singularity, the global commons we are now forging is a richly textured, richly coloured and multivariate commons. In addition, we are witnessing a greatly increased capacity of manifold organized interests (be these in the form of the State, private militias, the mafia, multi-national corporations, international trade unions and NGOs) to impose their will on others. In combination with the incredible effectiveness of weapons of violence and oppression purveyed through the international arms trade, the resources now wielded by organized interests threaten the always fragile processes and institutions through which law may discipline power.

Once we acknowledge the scope of transnational interaction and recognize the challenge that cross-border violence and oppression by non-governmental forces poses for State-based legal institutions and for international instruments developed by States, entirely new dimensions of the *idea* of human rights are revealed. First, we begin to see how these multiple centres of power also threaten human rights – often in ways that States do not. Second, we begin to see that reliance on domestic human rights law as developed in constitutions, bills of rights, human rights codes and like artefacts to control such abuses within enacting States is wishful thinking, even in those States that hold themselves out as exemplars of the Rule of Law. Third, we begin to see that international human rights instruments to which States subscribe or which are imposed on them by the "world community" also have insufficient scope and lack the normative purchase to rein in non-State human rights abusers. However powerful the *idea* of human rights in both domestic and international settings, in a world of unbridled militias, organized human trafficking, and rapacious multinational organizations, the traditional conception of human rights law as being exclusively linked to the political State reveals its limitations. Whether the State is acting domestically as legitimated normative authority or internationally as a consenting party to negotiated extra-systemic norms, it is still acting as if it were the exclusive norm subject.[7]

[7] The point is not new. See, for example, P. Alston, ed., *Non-State Actors and Human Rights* (Oxford: Oxford University Press, 2005); T. Campbell and S. Miller, eds., *Human Rights and the Moral Responsibilities of Corporate and Public Sector Organizations* (Dordrecht: Kluwer, 2004).

To ground a more potent practice of international human rights I suggest, as an alternative to the Statist vision of law, a legal pluralistic conception of the legal endeavour. In the understanding I intend here, legal pluralism foregrounds four key ideas: (1) in any given physical or socio-intellectual environment, several legal orders are in direct competition for authority; (2) these legal orders are typically independently-legitimated – that is, they do not derive their legitimacy from another, hierarchically superior legal order; (3) the State legal order is not always the most powerful, or even the most legitimate, of these competing legal orders; and (4) the trajectory of legal rules among these various legal orders (the phenomenon of internormativity) is multi-directional: sometimes, the rules of the State legal order, including any rules that may derive from adherence to international instruments, penetrate into the legal systems of non-State actors; sometimes the rules of non-State legal orders, especially those that might, at first blush, appear to offend officially-accepted notions of the Rule of Law, substantive equality and procedural due process, are imported into State legal systems.[8]

Legal pluralism theory has much to contribute to our understanding of human rights in general, and international human rights in particular. Our contemporary focus on human rights instruments enacted by States leads some to assume, wrongly in my view, that these instruments are the exclusive site of human rights aspiration and action. By contrast, thinking in the logic of legal pluralism about law as a complex set of interacting legal systems even within a single State recalls my inversion of Tolstoy's epigram. States that respect the *idea* of human rights and that seek to instantiate it in their practices realize that there is no one formula enshrined in a canonical legal artefact and certainly not the specific formula that they purport themselves to follow for achieving this state of grace.

Only by every State attending to the specific features of the official legal system actually in place, only by attending to the specific features of the diverse legal systems that are in competition with it, and only by attending to the specific contextual circumstances that the State legal system is called upon to regulate can the contingency of success be managed. Not only are the universal mantras so familiar to human rights law too abstract to provide workable guidance about procedures and institutions for States in this governance project, they often require conduct that many States under economic and political stress are simply incapable of achieving. More to the present point, these mantras provide a convenient cover for States that adopt them to displace human rights abuses to other sites (such as Guantanamo), or other agents (foreign rendition), or to legalize abuses like judicial murder (capital punishment) under the guise of the Rule of Law.[9]

---

[8] I have addressed these themes in M.-M. Kleinhans and R.A. Macdonald, "What Is a *Critical* Legal Pluralism?" (1997) 12 *Canadian Journal of Law and Society* 25; and R.A. Macdonald, "The Legal Mediation of Social Diversity" in A. Gagnon et al., (eds.), *The Conditions of Diversity in Multinational Democracies* (Montreal, QC: IRPP, 2003), 85.

[9] I have chosen illustrations from the current practices in the United States of America since they are widely known. For a brief consideration of like duplicity in Canada, see R.A. Macdonald, "Human Rights and Identity – Human Identities and Rights", [2009] *Canadian Diversity* 6–64 (Spring 2009 edition).

2.2 Three (Un)Certain Critiques of Universal Human Rights

A perusal of recent writing about international human rights reveals a vast array of ideas, justifications, critiques and reformulations: Baxi, Sen, Tasioulis, and Griffin are only some who have recently contributed novel insights to reflection about the possibility, scope and content of universal human rights.[10] While some of the critical literature is focused on the *Universal Declaration of Human Rights*, the main defenders of human rights speak to the *idea* of universal human rights, and not just to the document. The different foci of *critique* and *replique* put into relief a number of issues familiar to those who toil in the field of public administration. Notably, these sometimes incommensurable foci require us to address questions of agency, and self-representation. This inquiry, in turn, induces deeper reflection about rational justification of western legal artefacts, not just for proponents of universal human rights, but also for those who argue the contrary. In brief, if respect for the *idea* of human rights leading to on-the-ground respect for human rights in practice is the public policy goal to be achieved, the key questions are "what tools of government?" and "what policy instruments?" are most suited to realizing that goal.[11]

Regrettably, many who make the claim for universal human rights do so for reasons that might charitably be described as ethnocentric. Their claim is less about human dignity than it is about the superiority of certain agency-enhancing practices with which they are familiar. This is particularly true of scholars from western States. But why should an economic system that trumpets freedom while reinforcing an invidious social class structure necessarily be preferable to a social system that deploys a caste structure to create the conditions of freedom within a caste? Systems of regulation that aim to increase the scope of human agency through libertarian constitutional constraints on State action can run the risk of limiting agency through economic or social exclusion. Consider, from the perspective of a capacity to profit from the human rights with which they are vested, the relative status of the poorest and richest 5% of the population in the United States of America. Now consider, from the same perspective, the relative status of the lowest and the highest castes in post-independence India. What, in addition to mere rhetoric about freedom, equality, and the *idea* of human rights, would we have to know in order to make a calculation of actual respect for human rights across the entire population of these two States?

Likewise, but in contrast, many of the anti-universalist critiques of universal human rights have a darker side. For example, the critique of symbolic over-reaching

[10] See U. Baxi, *Human Rights in a Posthuman World* (New Delhi: Oxford University Press, 2007); A. Sen, "Elements of a Theory of Human Rights" (2004) 32 *Philosophy and Public Affairs* 315; J. Tasioulis, "The Moral Reality of Human Rights" in T. Pogge, ed., *Freedom from Poverty as a Human Right* (Oxford: Oxford University Press, 2007); J. Griffin, *On Human Rights* (Oxford: Oxford University Press, 2008).

[11] On these "tool" choices see L. Salamon, *The Tools of Government* (Oxford: Oxford University Press, 2002); and R.A. Macdonald, "The Swiss Army Knife of Governance" in P. Eliadis, et al., eds., *Designing Government* (Montreal: McGill-Queen's University Press, 2004).

by those who promote universal human rights often reflects a self-interested refusal to hold up existing practices to critical scrutiny, and a preference for practices that fail to reach even a minimum standard of procedural and institutional decency. This is particularly true in connection with gender issues. The failure by many (perhaps most or even all) western States to achieve absolute gender equality in all matters public and private cannot be equated to the tolerance by some other States of gender-based physical mutilation or psychological coercion. From a secular human rights perspective, to exclude women from the priesthood is indefensible, if not ludicrous. But, the practices of suttee, clitorectomy and honour killings are both appalling and atrocious. To defend honour killings in some States on the basis of the continuing practice of excluding women from the priesthood is indecent.

2.2.1 Instrumental and Symbolic Effects of Legal Regulation

In general, both the claims for and the critiques of the *idea* and practice of universal human rights are unhelpful to the extent that they fail to account for the non-instrumental importance of human rights discourse. Regardless of whether the formulation of any particular dignity claim as a human right – say, freedom of speech, gender equality, or the right to a childhood – is or is not a western, neo-colonial imposition, it remains the case that the discussion of these claims, along with similar claims emanating from all parts of the world, makes an important contribution to reflection about social and political organization. Regardless of whether any particular claim is framed exclusively as a rights-claim against the State or whether it can also be framed as a rights-claim against non-State power exercised by militias, corporations, unions, cultural and linguistic groups, ethnic aggregations, or religious organizations, the framing exercise permits discussion about larger issues of global concern.[12] Creating the conditions in which the *idea* of human rights becomes a key feature of inter-State discourse and global communication and exchange among people has been no mean accomplishment of the past half century.

The signal distinction between instrumental and symbolic effects of legal regulation – a distinction sometimes cast as that between law seen as the endeavour of imposing rules of duty and entitlement and law seen as the aspiration to facilitate peaceful coordination of human interaction – is central to understanding all types of legal constraints on collective action.[13] A quarter-century ago, upon the coming into force of the *Canadian Charter of Rights and Freedoms*, I observed only partly in jest: you can't live with a *Charter*, but you can't live without one either.[14] My primary

---

[12] R. McCorquodale, "Overlegalizing Silences: Human Rights and Nonstate Actors" (2002) 96 *American Society of International Legal Procedure* 381.

[13] L. Fuller, "Law as an Instrument of Social Control and Law as a Facilitation of Human Interaction" (1975) 1 *Brigham Young University Law Review* 85.

[14] "Postscript and Prelude: The Jurisprudence of the Charter – Eight Theses," (1982) 4 *Supreme Court Law Review* 321.

concern at that point was to note the evolution in the way in which jurists came to frame legal responses to human rights claims. Neo-Hegelian determinism seemed to lie behind their belief in the progressive perfection of legal instruments to protect human rights: an evolution from customary practice, to judicially recognized limitations on freedom of contract, private property and state action, to legislative framing of discrete rights, to quasi-constitutional codifications, to entrenched constitutional enactments. Why, I asked, was it thought necessary to adopt a constitutional *Charter* at that juncture? What about the world of law and politics in Canada in 1982 induced Canadian jurists to believe that a constitutional *Charter* was necessary? and What exactly did they expect to gain from it? In brief, what, apart from pure ideology, would justify the choice of a constitutional *Charter* as a governing instrument for human rights claims as most appropriate for Canada in 1982 and beyond?

Further reflection on the question led me to suggest, a decade later, that it was the symbolic effect of the *Charter* – what has come to be known as *Charter*-patriotism – that mattered most.[15] That is, the *Charter* was primarily important for what the specific configuration and labeling of constitutional rights, and the specific judicial and legislative escape-hatches it enacted, reveal about the *idea* of human rights in Canada. Despite the litany of orthodox Bill of Rights prescriptions, the Canadian document was very much a context specific – both temporally and geographically – statement of aspiration about what a society should look like, and how its governing structures should respond to that particularity. In 1982, a number of sections – notably sections 1, 15(2), 23, 25, 27, 28, 29 and 33 – would have been inconceivable in just about every other State that was contemplating the enactment of a constitutional *Charter*.[16] Some, such as sections 23, 25, 27, and 29, speak to rights relating to language of education, aboriginal peoples, multiculturalism, and religious schools particular to the Canadian context; others, such as sections 1 and 33, speak to Canadian formulations of the relationship between democratic legislatures and courts – both methodologically and procedurally; still others, notably sections 15(2) and 28, provide a distinctly Canadian take on equal protection and gender equality.

At the time I first wrote about the *Charter*, my observations were only marginally rooted in a coherent theory of law or rights. They were more the product of my life experiences in the 1960s and 1970s. In those decades, one often saw greater good being accomplished by agencies of the State in contesting the abuses of private power than by courts hiding behind a rhetoric of the Rule of Law and rights to limit administrative

[15] "Procedural Due Process in Canadian Constitutional Law: Natural Justice and Fundamental Justice" (1987) 39 *University of Florida Law Review* 218; "The New Zealand Bill of Rights Act: How Far Does It or Should It Stretch?" in *Proceedings of the 1993 New Zealand Law Conference* (Wellington: New Zealand Law Society, 1993), 94. For an initial consideration of this idea see P. Russell, "The Political Purposes of the Charter of Rights and Freedoms" (1983) 61 *Canadian Bar Review* 30.

[16] For a comprehensive elaboration, see P.W. Hogg, *Constitutional Law of Canada*, 5th ed. (Toronto: Thomson Carswell, 2007).

action aimed at policing the moneyed, the smart and the powerful.[17] Today I hope I have a richer theoretical understanding of why I wrote as I did back then.

In 1982, I did not appreciate that my sense of law as grounded in human interaction carried implications beyond the recognition of the dialogic character of law's authority. At the time I sought only to understand law as a purposive human endeavour. My queries were these: when, why and how do human societies develop normative practices and forms of interaction within which self-policing coordination is possible? what is the relationship between explicit and canonical forms of normativity (modes of law) and institutional settings (sites of law)? what is the relationship between implicit and inferential forms of normativity and implicit and inferential institutional settings? and what conception of human agency and freedom underlies the pursuit of law as a way of symbolizing human interaction? Today, I have come to realize that once one enters this terrain of interaction and dialogue, one inevitably winds up in the precincts of legal pluralism.

2.2.2 Critical Legal Pluralism

In Part Three I trace out how the particular theory of legal pluralism that I have adopted might contribute to our understanding of human rights. For the moment, I am simply concerned to re-situate the key contemporary critiques of universal human rights as reflections of orthodox legal theory. Let me begin with a brief statement of the theoretical tenets of classical State legal positivism. There are five, each of which can be captured by a convenient "ism".

1. Monism: the belief that law is formal and institutionalized such that a single normative order has a legal monopoly over a given geographic territory.
2. Centralism: the belief that law is exclusively the product of the institutions of the political State.
3. Positivism: the belief that law is an artefact that can be distinguished from that which is not law (the contemporary "sources" thesis) by an *ex ante* hard criterion (for example, a rule of recognition).[18]

---

[17] See, for later and more detailed elaborations of this theme, H.W. Arthurs, "Constitutional Courage" (2003–2004) 49 *McGill Law Journal* 1; and A. Petter, *The Politics of the Charter* (Toronto: University of Toronto Press, 2010).

[18] I acknowledge that I am reformulating this classical position in two ways. First, the "separation thesis" as it has been traditionally applied to positivism denies a necessary connection between law and morality (H.L.A. Hart, "Positivism and the Separation of Law and Morals"), while the "sources thesis" is primarily about the conditions of legal validity (J. Raz, *The Authority of Law*) – legal validity as a question of social fact not moral merit. Second, while for present purposes this account of positivism focuses on human endeavours, it applies equally to some versions of scholastic natural law theories that would identify the hard criterion as being the word of God. Indeed, in this perspective, such natural law can be seen to share all the listed tenets of traditional analytical positivism.

4. Prescriptivism: the belief that law is about externally-imposed formulaic rules and analogous normative statements meant to impose duties or confer powers.
5. Chirographism: the belief that law is primarily, if not exclusively, about norms that can be, and usually are, fully expressible in words.

Each of these tenets has an exclusionary ambition and reflects a different preoccupation with delineating the legal from the non-legal – whether numerically (monism), spatially (centralism), analytically (positivism), ontologically (prescriptivism) or semiotically (chirographism). Together they comprise the core of analytical jurisprudence as propounded by H.L.A. Hart and his followers.[19] I acknowledge that there is nothing necessary in analytical jurisprudence that requires acceptance of principles one and two, although adherents do seem to adopt them.[20] I also acknowledge that recent analytical jurists have seriously attenuated Hart's separation thesis that purportedly serves as the positivist litmus test.[21] In like fashion, it is not necessary for analytical jurists to hold to the chirographic commitment and to claim language as the exclusive (or even necessary) vehicle of legal normativity. Nonetheless prescriptivism seems to be an essential feature of classical State legal positivism. In this hypothesis there are authorized rules of the legal system enacted and administered by officials, and then there is the "rest of the world" on which they operate. One might summarize classical State legal positivism as resting on the idea of a nomopoly (a *nomos* monopoly).[22] While each of the specific commitments noted differs as to what sphere constitutes the nomopoly, one thing is consistent: the human being (as legal subject) is outside that sphere.

What would it mean to imagine human beings, and not State-authorized law-making and law-applying agents, as the foundational feature of law? One consequence is this: that which authorized agents claim is law would be conceived only as hypothesis. In such an aretaic conception, every human being in interaction with others is law-maker and law-applier – a legal agent.[23] That is, before we can be legal

[19] H.L.A. Hart, *The Concept of Law* (Oxford: The Clarendon Press, 1961), (2d ed, 1994).

[20] For example, Hart never claimed that the normative regime of the Roman Catholic Church could not be a legal system, and he never adopted Kelsen's normative monism. See e.g. H. Kelsen, *The Pure Theory of Law* (Berkeley: Stanford University Press, 1967).

[21] Notably, J. Raz, *The Authority of Law: Essays on Law and Morality* (2d) (Oxford: Oxford University Press, 2009).

[22] R.A. Macdonald and D. Sandomierski, "Against Nomopolies" (2006) 57 *Northern Ireland Legal Quarterly* 610.

[23] L.B. Solum, "Virtue Jurisprudence: An Aretaic Theory of Law" (unpublished, October 2004); L.B. Solum, "Virtue Jurisprudence: A Virtue-Centered Theory of Judging" (2003) 34 *Metaphilosophy* 178. In a legal pluralistic conception, everyone is a law-maker and a law-applier, but some actually are conceded to have general authority by virtue of their wisdom. The manifestly foolish human being, interacting with others, is a law-maker and a law-applier, but no one accepts her or his actions as authoritative; by contrast the wise human being, engaged in the same activities, can be conceded to be an authority and other human beings, even as agents, will typically defer to her or his understandings.

subjects – thrown under law – we must be legal agents. Although we use words expressing duties and entitlements in order to distance ourselves from our acts of law-making and law application, as others have noted,[24] these words also serve to conceal a simple truth. We recur to formal legal texts that aim to be authoritative and definitive when we are uncertain about the "other", which is to say, of course, when we are uncertain about ourselves.[25]

2.2.3 Human Rights Critique in the Lens of Critical Legal Pluralism

With this brief background about a *critical* legal pluralism in view, let me turn to contemporary critiques of universal human rights. Three of the most often repeated critiques are: (1) that human rights discourse is meaningless since enforceable rights are uniquely the creation of positive law; (2) that there is no justifiable foundation for universal human rights claims because truth has no objective existence and is simply a matter of consensus; and (3) that human rights discourse is redundant and adds nothing of value to our moral vocabulary. [26] All three aim at the relationship between law and morals and recall the classical legal positivist conception of legal normativity. However important the inquiry into the justification of moral judgement may be as a philosophical endeavour, for a legal pluralist concerned with social facts in diverse contexts, the above three critiques are less interesting critiques of universal human rights.

Rather, a legal pluralist perspective would focus on other themes that are evoked in contemporary debate about the *idea* of human rights, especially when framed in broad documentary enunciations like the *Universal Declaration of Human Rights*. I have in mind the following claims:

1. The *idea* of human rights is flawed because of its universalizing (read Western colonial) ideology.
2. The *idea* of human rights is flawed because it is overly individualistic and does not adequately attend to social and economic rights.
3. The *idea* of human rights is flawed because its invocation leads, by ricochet, to the invocation of the cultural defence to defend egregious practices visited especially against women and children.

[24] Trudy Govier, *Dilemmas of Trust* (Montreal: McGill-Queen's University Press, 1998).

[25] Of course, the aversion to uncertainty manifests itself in numerous other mechanisms by which human beings seek security in relationships: a financial bond, the offering of a hostage, the surrender of arms, self-denial in the mob and, in the Hobbesian universe, deference to a sovereign.

[26] Other frequently encountered critiques are: (4) human rights theories are individualistic and atomistic; (5) human rights theories inadequately accommodate feminist concerns; (6) human rights theories reflect western colonial ideology; (7) modern human rights simply expand real rights into immeasurable territory. For a discussion of all seven, see W. Twining, *supra*, note 3, chapters 6, 7, 13.

A legal pluralist would disagree with each of these assertions. The *idea* of human rights is not flawed because of any of its inherent characteristics, but because of what its proselytizers have made it into. Imagining human rights in action as the application of propositional knowledge to particular cases misperceives the character of law. Again, the *idea* of human rights is not flawed primarily because of what it leaves out, but because of what its proselytizers have failed to read in. Imagining human rights as involving only those matters that have currently been enacted in human rights instruments misperceives the true sources of legal authority. And still again, the *idea* of human rights is not flawed primarily because it leads by ricochet to the invocation of the cultural defence, but because its proselytizers have failed to call upon those who would invoke that defence to justify their positions in the language of human rights and not just in the language of culture. Imagining the cultural defence as anti-law misperceives the character of law as mediator of the irreducible diversity of human society, and fails – as I explain below – to account for internormative trajectories between competing normative orders.

2.3 Legal Pluralism Theory and Universal Human Rights

In order to explore these three (un)certain critiques in a way that reveals the contribution of legal pluralism theory to analysis of universal human rights claims, I shall reframe them in everyday legal language. I consider, in turn, conceptual issues, methodological issues, and operational issues, basing my analysis on a particular version of legal pluralism – critical legal pluralism.

2.3.1 Conceptual Issues: Universal Human Rights and Western Neo-colonialism

A central virtue of legal pluralism theory in general is that it directly contests not only *where* jurists draw boundaries, but the necessity of *ex ante* boundary-drawing itself. Consider these boundary-contesting aspects of legal plurality.

First, the plurality of sites of law.[27] Systemically, legal pluralism invites us to imagine that there are multiple legal orders operating in the same social and geographical space. Hence, there can be multiple regimes of human rights law interacting in the same social and geographical space: (1) various international regimes of human rights norms embedded within international legal regimes generally; (2) national regimes of human rights norms (however thin they may be in certain places); (3) multiple local, regional, national and transnational regimes of economic relations; (4)

[27] R.A. Macdonald, "Metaphors of Multiplicity: Civil Society, Regimes and Legal Pluralism" (1998) 15 *Arizona Journal of International and Comparative Law* 69.

multiple local, regional, national and transnational regimes of religious norms; and (5) multiple local, regional, national and transnational regimes of social norms.

Second, the plurality of modes of law.[28] Legal pluralism invites us to imagine that there are multiple forms of legal normativity operating within the same legal regime, wherever we choose to locate it. Even within the official state legal order, we perceive a plurality of normative types: explicit canonical norms; implicit canonical norms; explicit inferential norms; and implicit inferential norms.

Third, the plurality of internormative trajectories.[29] Contrary to many theories of internormativity, migration of norms occurs in all four frames, and is not unidirectional. So, for example, implicit canonical (customary) norms may migrate from one customary field to another; explicit canonical (enacted) norms may migrate from one institutional site to another; explicit inferential (*stare decisis*) norms may migrate from one decision-making frame to another. Likewise just as customary norms may migrate into decisional and enacted norms, so too decisional norms may migrate into both cognate and agnate customary regimes.

Fourth, the plurality of legal agents.[30] Legal pluralism invites us to imagine that there are multiple official institutions within each of these normative orders. These may be understood in the same typology as norms themselves. In addition, within each of the official institutions there are multiple agents – that is, the people that in traditional lexicon are the subjects of law. All these agents generate law, both formally and informally, both chirographically and performatively.

In brief, legal pluralism invites scholars both to recognize that to understand these several legal orders they may need also to imagine several different ways of conceiving law, and to recognize that there are also several different ways of imagining legal pluralism itself.[31] This means that we have to stand back from our "can't-helps" and our "it goes without sayings". Legal pluralism invites us to reject questions like "what is law?" to the extent they attempt to settle definitional questions on a purely conceptual basis, and foreclose inquiry into struggles for justice. Legal pluralism invites the more destabilizing inquiry framed by questions like "to what types of beliefs and behaviours does adopting a pluralistic approach commit us?" Rethinking the way we should pose the traditional question "what is law?" implies two conceptual points.

---

[28] R.A. Macdonald, "Pour la reconnaissance d'une normativité implicite et inférentielle" (1986) XVIII *Sociologie et sociétés* 47.

[29] R.A. Macdonald, "Custom Made: For a Non-chirographic Critical Legal Pluralism" (2011) 26 *Canadian Journal of Law and Society* 301.

[30] R.A. Macdonald, "Les Vieilles Gardes. Hypothèses sur l'émergence des normes, l'internormativité et le désordre à travers une typologie des institutions normatives" in J.-G. Belley, ed., *Le droit soluble [:] Contributions québécoises à l'étude l'internormativité* (Paris: Librairie générale de droit et de jurisprudence, 1996), 233.

[31] R.A. Macdonald, "Here, There … and Everywhere: Theorizing Legal Pluralism; Theorizing Jacques Vanderlinden" in N. Kasirer, ed., *Étudier et enseigner le droit: hier, aujourd'hui et demain – Études offertes à Jacques Vanderlinden* (Montreal: Éditions Yvon Blais, 2006), 381.

One is this. Much reflection on law today presupposes that the idea of law is relatively uncontroversial. Law as a phenomenon is just out there. Then, there are theoretical approaches to it. Unsurprisingly, most people who study law adopt the view that classical State legal positivism is descriptive; by characterizing critical approaches as external, they are able to preserve their conception of the core of law as non-ideological. Typically those who take a critical perspective feel the need to present and assert this same core in order to justify the validity of their critique. But there is no core that simply is. Law is a label human beings attach to a set of human phenomena; before they apply the word law, these phenomena are just data in the world.[32] Through our labeling we construct these phenomena as law rather than as something else. So, ontological contestations aside, the real question is: who bears the burden of the "uncomfortable adjective"?[33] In other words, through our labeling we are deciding both who bears the burden of creating the uncomfortable adjective (i.e., a question of authority that points directly at us), and who is burdened by the uncomfortable adjective (i.e., who is subjected to the requirement to specify meaning). If law is the product of the political State, then legal pluralists must always add the adjective "informal" in order to embrace their concerns; conversely, if law means normative regimes grounded in justice claims, then State positivists must always add the adjective "official" in order to target their concerns. It follows that contemporary critiques of western legal neo-colonialism operate not only at the specific level of chirographic international human rights norms, but also at the more general level of what it is that adherents to classical State legal positivism are prepared to acknowledge as law. Once one accepts the premises of classical state legal positivism, then the only way to generate human rights norms is through a type of enacted instrument like the *Universal Declaration of Human Rights*.

A second point flows from the first. It speaks to the definitional exercise itself. Why do we have definitions? What are they for? And what is special about definitions of social phenomena? The legal pluralist recognizes that all definitions of law are political acts that imply political purposes. The questions then are, "What assumptions about knowledge, communication, social organization and human behaviour underlie this particular hypothesis?" and "What normative commitments do adherents of the standard account adopt so as to address the problems of law and legal ordering?" The standard five commitments – monism, centralism, positivism, prescriptivism, and chirographism – imply not only the framing of the inquiry in relationship to universal human rights, but also in respect of any claim to cultural specificity. The pluralist hypothesis casts a burden of justification on those who would claim the primacy of their own normative system. These conceptual beliefs are coherent with a particular notion of the meaning of universal in human rights documents such

---

[32] Of course, by referring to human phenomena I mean to exclude the normativity of other phenomenal communities (animal species including higher primates) and noumenal communities (including angels).

[33] R.A. Macdonald, "Triangulating Social Law Reform" in Y. Gendreau, ed., *Dessiner la société par le droit* (Montreal: Les Éditions Thémis, 2004), 119.

as the *Universal Declaration of Human Rights*. They do not inhere in the *idea* of human rights itself, or in any particular document by which that *idea* is instantiated. To see what it would mean to challenge these assumptions, consider now a second theme: methodology.

2.3.2 Methodological Issues: Universal Human Rights as Individualistic Negative Rights

Every particular conception of law – that is, every set of *ex ante* stipulations about a terrain of action and a set of problems, and every set of unargued assumptions about human behaviour and motivation – is a simplification of a complex web of human engagement meant to give plausibility to the methodological protocols through which we address the problems we have decided are properly those of law. Of course, the legal pluralist hypothesis should, as much as the standard account, also be seen as a simplifying conceptual frame – but, with these differences: the frame is heterogeneous and unstable.[34] The legal pluralist query may be phrased in this way: "what are the internormative trajectories between *local law* – which is said to be located in the actual practices of local culture – and *universal* or *cosmopolitan law* – which is said to be grounded in the aspiration to give rational content to the notion of human dignity?"[35]

Because human rights instruments are typically seen as propounding constraints upon State action, they rest on a prescriptive conception of law as a means of social control. A quartet of beliefs inheres in this account of the province of law. In their extreme form they are: (1) law is a specialized field for experts – people can't be trusted; (2) human communication must be explicit and formalized in precise language – if you can't say it, you can't know it, and you can't communicate it[36]; (3) people have little capacity to organize themselves and to co-ordinate their behaviour without a coercive structure of authority – law is needed to exit a state of war of all against all; (4) human beings are essentially Pavlovian dogs – they are not agents, they have no autonomy and they must be closely regulated.[37] But law can also be understood

[34] R.A. Macdonald, "Legal Republicanism and Legal Pluralism: Two Takes on Identity and Diversity" in M. Bussani and M. Graziadei, eds., *Human Diversity and the Law* (Brussels: Bruylant, 2005), 43.

[35] I do not mean to argue that all laws characterized as universal are necessarily of this character. Some descriptive universal laws relating to human beings such as "all humans must die" do not directly give rational content to the notion of human dignity.

[36] The dimensions of this belief as concerns law are explored in R.A. Macdonald and C. Kehler Siebert, "Orchestrating Legal Multilingualism: *12 Études*" in J.-C. Gémar and N. Kasirer, eds., *Jurilinguistique: entre langues et droits* (Montreal: Thémis, 2005), 377.

[37] See notably, E. Melissaris, "Perspective, Critique and Pluralism in Legal Theory" (2006) 57 *Northern Ireland Legal Quarterly* 597; *Ubiquitous Law* (Surrey, Eng.: Ashgate, 2009). Compare M.-M. Kleinhans and R.A. Macdonald, *supra,* note 8.

as a facilitation of human interaction. For a legal pluralist, law may be hypothesized as "*the endeavour of symbolizing human interaction as governed by rules*".[38]

The pluralist hypothesis is an argument that law is not a *datum* of experience but an intention. Law is an idea that can be understood only if it requires more of us than simple cognition – it demands that we commit ourselves towards its achievement. The pluralist also argues that law results from the mental activity of perception, reflection and symbolization – even in those cases where we want to claim that the urge to law and obedience is simply conditioned or reflexive. The pluralist hypothesis is an argument that law is bi- and multi-lateral, lying in relationships with other human symbolizers more than the field within which the relationship is built. In recognizing agency, the pluralist hypothesis implies orienting oneself and one's intentions and behaviours by reference to a point of reference external to the act or the intention – even in those cases where the reference point is largely of one's own making.

Understanding law as a symbolic endeavour invites us to reflect on the different resources at our disposal for promoting a culture of human rights, and how we might use them. When we think of our most effective compasses for orienting reflection about the human condition, formal legal artefacts rarely rank at the top of the list. What, we might ask, is the relative contribution of the Parable of the Good Samaritan, Gabrielle Roy's *Bonheur d'occasion*, Mark Twain's *Huckleberry Finn*, Victor Hugo's *Les misérables*, James Agee's *Now Let us Praise Famous Men*, the movies *Goin' Down the Road* and *Lives of Others*, Buffy Ste-Marie's *Universal Soldier*, the Range's 1986 pop-music classic *The way it is,* Picasso's *Guernica*, the Canadian *Memorial at Vimy Ridge* and the remains of the Extermination Camp at Auschwitz to our understanding of identity and human dignity?

Much more so than the texts of treaties, conventions and statutes, the judgments of courts, and the speculations of legal philosophers and lawyers, these grounded, contextual evocations of the human aspiration to interpersonal justice confront us with our social pathologies. No doubt, each can be read as implying some universal insight. But they speak powerfully mainly because they speak locally, in local idiom, to local concerns.[39] When I talk of cultural resources in different media, I do not mean subway advertising posters celebrating ethnic or religious diversity, toleration, or our obligation to promote social solidarity by contributing to charitable endeavours. While propaganda, like prescriptive law, has its place in creating awareness of the other, like prescriptive law, propaganda habitually forecloses self-examination: the other as external object disjoined from us. Literature, theatre, music, art, and dance, by contrast, compel self-examination precisely because they directly invite

[38] This hypothesis is derived from L. Fuller, *The Morality of Law* (2d), (New Haven: Yale University Press, 1969), 106.

[39] For this reason I have selected artefacts known to me. In doing so I do not mean to suggest that other such artefacts found in other cultures – I. Andric, *The Bridge over the Drina* (New York: New American Library, 1967), or A. Paton, *Cry the Beloved Country* (New York: Scribner's, 1948) to take two examples – do not have similar import.

engagement and performance by the reader, listener, watcher and audience. Our challenge is to use these cultural resources to best effect locally, while inviting others to use their own analogous resources to promote a culture of human rights.[40]

A legal pluralist analysis rejects the statist assumption that official documents are the primary drivers of a cultural practice of human rights. Using our cultural artefacts to imagine, evoke and respond to the destroyed or compromised lives that have been the price of our "civilization" is by far the most powerful contribution we can make to promoting human rights. For it does so by inviting every country, every State, every culture, and every citizen to do likewise. This invitation opens up a third dimension of the legal pluralism perspective: how do we operationalize legal pluralism as an approach to human rights?

2.3.3 Operational Issues – Universal Human Rights and the Cultural Defence

For most legal scholars, theoretical concern with law leads to investigation of practices. Such is the case with reflection about human rights norms: universal prescriptions breed relativistic factual counter-prescriptions, and these counter-prescriptions inevitably become the primary site of condemnation of instruments like the *Universal Declaration of Human Rights*. So, for example, defenders of universal human rights point out that claims about the need to respect local practice quickly mutate into what has become castigated as the cultural defence: that is, a defence of local practices that are inimical to the rights of women and children.[41]

From these concerns about local practices emerges an increasingly vocal condemnation of legal pluralism as providing a theoretical justification for such practices. But this assault on legal pluralism misperceives both the theory and its application in the realm of human rights. To begin, it ascribes to law a role as the exclusive mediator of the irreducible diversity of human society; in addition, it fails to account for internormative trajectories between the multiple normative orders that compete for authority and loyalty in particular social spaces. Of course, this internormative challenge confronts both the local and the cosmopolitan: many proponents of local law consider this indigenous law as a subordinated legal order that is a site of resistance to the tyranny of global normativity; and many proponents of cosmopolitan law see universal claims as a necessary antidote to tyranny masquerading as indigenous difference. The challenge has a crucial operational dimension that merits elaboration.

[40] Other examples of locality and local adaptation can be found wherever universal rules exist – whether in law, cuisine or sports. Compare, for example C.L.R. James, *Beyond a Boundary* (London, 1969) with the anthropological documentary *Trobriand Island Cricket*.

[41] For a recent reflection in Canada, in the context of religious tribunals, see J.-F. Gaudreault-Desbiens, (ed.) *Le droit, la religion et le "raisonnable"* (Montreal: Thémis, 2009).

How ought we to understand the pluralities of legal pluralism? I make two points. First, even within the rationalist cosmopolitan universal human rights tradition there is normative plurality. It makes no sense to consider that international criminal law, international humanitarian law, international children's rights law, and so on, are indistinguishably part of the same normative system. Each mediates rationality and practice (logic and experience) differently and cosmopolitan jurists do their cause a disservice by insisting that the only site for universal norms is at a level so abstract that conceptual and field differentiations vanish. Here I mean to highlight not only the plurality of indigenous law, but also the plurality of cosmopolitan law. Of course, I also acknowledge the deep pluralism of vernacular law. Every time that someone makes a claim about the normative weight of indigenous law, it is important to note that this is the same claim that cosmopolitan law makes about itself. A local norm entrepreneur asserts local law as an incontrovertible normative proposition – not as a raw datum of human experience; but other local norm entrepreneurs within that indigenous tradition may have other, often quite divergent, views.[42] This is the second point.

To illustrate these pluralisms, I'd like to explore a significant contemporary manifestation of the cultural defence logic – the desire to have matters of family and filiation decided by religious tribunals.[43] Because religious tribunals operate within a comprehensive socio-cultural normative framework, many are concerned that officially recognizing faith-based tribunals would run the risk of legitimating an entire religious private law regime and that this regime would come to displace secular civil law in the hearts and minds of the faithful. Consequently, the argument goes, the State should not act in any way that would permit religious courts to gain a toe-hold in people's consciousnesses; and, the argument continues, this is especially important in immigrant communities where traditional cultural and religious values are believed to be in competition with Canadian values, where linguistic and cultural barriers may further isolate women in particular from the broader society, and where theocratic as opposed to secular views of the relationship of church and state may still be dominant.[44]

If we are genuinely committed to the idea of a secular, pluralistic, multicultural and religiously diverse society, however, there will always be a place for faith-based tribunals – not just in matters of family and successions, but also in contract and commercial law as well. The true challenge is to frame an appropriate relationship between religious law and secular law, and the jurisdiction of faith-based tribunals

[42] Sally Merry discusses instantiations of the vernacularization of human rights in multiple dimensions in "Transnational Human Rights and Local Activism: Mapping the Middle"(2006) 108 *American Anthropologist* 1.

[43] See R.A. Macdonald and A. Popovici, "Le catéchisme de l'islamophobie" in M. Jezequel, dir, *La justice à l'épreuve de la diversité culturelle* (Montreal: Éditions Yvon Blais, 2007), 19.

[44] A. Shachar, "Privatizing Diversity: A Cautionary Tale from Religious Arbitration in Canada" (2008) 9 *Theoretical Inquiries in Law* 573.

in relation to that of the official, secular courts so that the goals one seeks to accomplish by law are realized in fact. The best way to ensure a tolerant secular liberal-democratic State in a culturally and religiously diverse society is to maintain a rigorous *distinction* between different legal regimes and in particular between religious law and secular law. But this does not mean totally *separating* these various legal regimes from State law. As with the debate about whether students should be permitted to wear religious symbols in public schools, the issue with faith-based tribunals is how to achieve the best mutual accommodation of religious observance and secular Canadian values.[45]

An example may illustrate the point. Are there circumstances where a legal pluralist would contemplate the wearing of a burqa as acceptable practice, notwithstanding the apparent subordination of women that it appears to reflect? Those who begin with universal human rights condemn the practice because it is said to infringe basic conceptions of gender equality. A legal pluralist would ask, in particular contexts and in respect of particular women who seek to wear a burqa, whether the agency of *those* women in *that* society is augmented or diminished by wearing the garment. In the lens of legal pluralism, one no longer imagines legal inquiry only in relation to formal artefacts like the *Universal Declaration of Human Rights*, but also in respect of informal artefacts like the claim to cultural specificity. One no longer opposes "universal western *law*" to "indigenous local *practice*". The query is rather about competing legal orders and their legitimating conditions. We need to ask: What is the meaning for citizens of universal western law, both as concerns its rationalistic aspirations and as concerns its actual outcomes in practices and decisions by official institutions in the West? In like manner we also need to ask: What is the meaning of indigenous, local law, both as concerns its actual outcomes in practices and decisions by official institutions and as concerns the rationalistic aspirations which it implies?

In other words legal pluralists recognize both the possibility of aspiration to universal human rights and the undeniable presence of culturally diverse instantiations of that aspiration. They also acknowledge the power of internormative trajectories between the ideal and the actual, the cosmopolitan and the local. Simply because a claim grounded in cultural specificity is advanced to justify egregious practices does not mean either that the claim is a justifiable interpretation of cultural practice, or that even if it were, the claim must always trump aspirational norms. The imprecation "render unto Caesar that which is Caesar's and render unto God that which is God's" reminds us that our lives are lived in multiple normative universes. Whether Caesar is a Roman emperor in 0012 or a political State in 2012, and whether God is a Supreme Being or an aspiration to human justice expressed in an international

[45] For a discussion of how this issue has recently played out in Quebec, see R.A. Macdonald and T. McMorrow, "Myths of Miscegenation" in B. Iancu, ed., *The Law/Politics Distinction in Contemporary Public Law Adjudication* (Utrecht: Eleven international publishing, 2009), 89.

human rights instrument matters little. As in all conflicts between legal regimes the questions to be decided are what is Caesar's? and what is God's?[46]

The interplay of universal norms and particular identities is becoming increasingly complex as we come to a better understanding of human psychology. Today we recognize that people use the notion of identities not just to isolate themselves from others, but also to claim relationships. Consequently, the meaning of identity is now quite removed from the list of 14 markers of invidious discrimination identified by *Human Rights Codes* and a far cry from the historic analytical triptych of gender, race and class. To be a vegetarian, a vegan or a tee-totaler is to claim a particular space more important for many than gender; to adopt a libertarian political stance, or to be a Marxist, or in Quebec to be a separatist, is to make a powerful identity claim. For Canada's self-positioning in discussions of human rights, it is paradoxical that we continue to expand our list of protected identity claims while simultaneously denying that identity involves a complicated interplay between self-ascription and other-ascription. Human rights cannot be reduced to a bourgeois flavour-of-the-month that bears little connection to foundational generic exclusions or to individualized perceptions of particular mis- or non-recognition. A legal pluralist analysis reveals the dangers of our assumption that legislative categories can exhaustively capture the diversity of human identities, and that we can fully specify the meaning of identity claims for those who assert them.

2.4 Conclusion

My central argument has been that the political project of legal pluralism constitutes an important contribution to human rights discourse. The project is emancipatory in that it requires each of us to take responsibility for what we consider law to be, and the manner in which we reconcile different conceptions of human justice. Let me re-iterate and re-formulate the theoretical point. We are required to inquire about every claim to law – whether appearing in the form of a canonical *Universal Declaration of Human Rights*, or in the form of an inchoate appeal to local justice:

1. What is the source of legitimacy of authority?
2. Are norms of due process, however variegated and in whatever form articulated, being respected?
3. Is there a rational justification for the substantive norms that are being invoked?

[46] Recall that the Preamble of the *Canadian Charter of Rights and Freedoms* states – "Whereas Canada is founded upon principles that recognize the Supremacy of God and the Rule of Law…" – an assertion that compels us to recognize that neither God nor the Rule of Law are reducible to the other. See B. Polka, "The Supremacy of God and the Rule of Law in the Canadian Charter of Rights and Freedoms: A Theologico – Political Analysis" (1987) 32 *McGill Law Journal* 854.

In the present context, the pluralist hypothesis is subject to a strong objection: aren't legal pluralists preaching an extreme form of cultural relativism?[47] In one perspective, this objection amounts to asking if the legal pluralist hypothesis really matters. Does it add anything to our understanding of human rights as a legal phenomenon, or does it simply dress up an old debate in new language?

I claim that the pluralist hypothesis does matter precisely because of the way that it acknowledges old debates, but transforms the manner by which they are engaged. Legal pluralism is not a truth claim. It is a way of characterizing an interpretive choice for citizens about how they wish to conceive law, themselves and the relationship they have to law. The legal pluralist hypothesis invites legal subjects to imagine themselves as legal agents – to discover the constitutive potential of their own actions. The pluralist perspective offers a hypothesis about how human rights entrepreneurs should conceive their endeavour and how they should spend their energies. The hypothesis means, irredeemably, that we can no longer excuse our lack of engagement with all dimensions of human rights by deferring (1) to questions as formulated by others, and (2) to agendas that are framed exclusively in a universalizing language that stands apart from human experience; nor can we maintain the conceit that we need not trouble ourselves with creating the institutions by which human rights claims are actually given effect.

For a legal pluralist, the idea of law is itself a site of political struggle. Every conception of law is a simplification of a complex web of human engagement. We deploy assumptions, protocols and stipulations to identify, to organize and to frame issues that we have decided are properly those of law. It follows that any discussion of human rights implies a like simplification and framing of inquiry.

If we are to truly celebrate the *idea* of universal human rights we can no longer smugly characterize as *human rights unhappiness* the failure of States to adopt the consecrated formulae of human rights such as the text of the *Universal Declaration of Human Rights,* while ignoring their local on-the-ground practices and indigenous critiques of other practices that actually reflect the *Declaration's* aspirations. And, if we are to truly celebrate the *idea* of universal human rights we can no longer excuse our own humanitarian failures by pointing to universal formulas for *human rights happiness* that we adopt, while ignoring the specific practices in the particular contexts of our everyday human experience that testify to these failures. Indeed, the

[47] Another objection has also been advanced against legal pluralism theory: if everything is law – nothing is law. On this point, see B.Z. Tamanaha, *A General Jurisprudence of Law and Society* (Oxford: Oxford University Press, 2001). In my view this objection has been comprehensively refuted in recent publications defending the pluralist hypothesis. See, notably, E. Melissaris, "The More the Merrier? A new take on legal pluralism" (2004) 13 *Social and Legal Studies* 57, and R.A. Macdonald, "Critical Legal Pluralism as a Construction of Normativity and the Emergence of Law" in A. Lajoie, et al., eds., *Théories et émergence du droit: pluralisme, surdétermination, effectivité* (Montreal: Éditions Thémis, 1998), 12.

aspiration to the *idea* of universal human rights presupposes that its on-the-ground instantiations are pluralistic.[48]

In turning our attention to understandings of how human beings interact with diverse representations of legal norms, we may discover that the commitments we hold – or tell ourselves that we hold – are imperfect translations of a self we do not know, or want to know. We may learn something unpleasant about how we perceive the human agency of others, and surprise ourselves by our own implicit psychology of subservience to an external normative order. But such are the risks of declining the invitation of classical state legal positivism to conceive ourselves only as legal subjects. In the end, the assertion of legal agency implied by declining the invitation is the challenge of human rights.

[48] A slightly different presentation of this point is elaborated by Sally Merry in *Human Rights and Gender Violence: Translating International Law into Local Justice* (Chicago: University of Chicago Press, 2006).

Chapter 3
E Pluribus Unum – Bhinneka Tunggal Ika? Universal Human Rights and the Fragmentation of International Law

Carlos Iván Fuentes[*], **René Provost**[†], **and Samuel G. Walker**[‡]

3.1 Introduction

The adoption of the Universal Declaration of Human Rights (UDHR) by the United Nations General Assembly in 1948 has been presented as a global embrace of human rights, reflecting an international community united in a coherent statement of its aspiration to protect the fundamental rights and freedoms of every individual and, to some extent, groups. The UDHR is now commonly seen as having achieved

"In pieces, yet one", the national motto of Indonesia, taken from a fourteenth century Javanese poem. See Gary Bell, "Indonesia – The Challenge of Legal Diversity and Law Reform", in Ann Black and Gary Bell, eds., *Law and Legal Institutions of Asia: Traditions, Adaptations and Innovations* (Cambridge: Cambridge University Press, 2011) at 262.

[*] Doctoral candidate and former O'Brien Fellow, McGill Centre for Human Rights and Legal Pluralism; Associate Legal Officer, Treaty Section, Office of Legal Affairs, United Nations (carlos.fuentes@mail.mcgill.ca). The views expressed herein are those of the author and do not necessarily reflect the views of the United Nations.

[†] Founding Director, McGill Centre for Human Rights and Legal Pluralism, and Associate Professor, Faculty of Law, McGill University (rene.provost@mcgill.ca).

[‡] BCL LLB 2010, Faculty of Law, McGill University.

C.I. Fuentes
Treaty Section, Office of Legal Affairs, United Nations, New York, NY 10017, USA
e-mail: carlos.ivan.fuentes@mail.mcgill.ca

R. Provost (✉)
Faculty of Law, Centre for Human Rights and Legal Pluralism,
McGill University, Montreal, QC H3A 1W9, Canada
e-mail: rene.provost@mcgill.ca

S.G. Walker
Faculty of Law, McGill University, 4043 Hingston Ave, Montreal, QC H4A 2J6, Canada
e-mail: samgwalker@gmail.com

R. Provost and C. Sheppard (eds.), *Dialogues on Human Rights and Legal Pluralism*, Ius Gentium: Comparative Perspectives on Law and Justice 17,
DOI 10.1007/978-94-007-4710-4_3,

customary status, and thus applicable to every state. To what extent does this signal the existence of a unified human rights regime under international law? Does a finding that the human rights regime is fragmented necessarily lead to the conclusion that it cannot be considered universal? We will argue that universality and unity represent distinct conceptual propositions, the first relating to a normative claim, the second to a structural relation. A pluralistic understanding of universality, far from an oxymoron, offers a model in which regime fragmentation actually sustains universal values in a manner more effective than a unified regime grounded in nowhere in particular, if not nowhere at all.

The essay first recalls the story of the emergence of human rights into positive international law, underscoring the extent to which it became an ideological battlefield between East and West, all the while excluding a significant portion of the world's population still subsumed by vast colonial empires. Beyond the UDHR, human rights regimes began to materialize at different speeds in various regions, without any assured uniformity in the guarantees thus entrenched, a phenomenon which was actually supported by the UN. In a second section, the debate regarding the fragmentation of international law is presented, including the reasons which triggered the International Law Commission (ILC) to appoint a working group on the subject and the main conclusions reached by the ILC. The doctrinal discussion regarding fragmentation is then related directly to the field of human rights, to assess the extent to which factors such as the emergence of discrete regimes and the multiplication of institutions have had an impact on the unity of international human rights law. Finally, in a third section, the essay questions the conceptual relationship which can be said to exist between universality (rather than unity) of human rights and the fragmentation of that regime. Relying on a legal pluralist critique of international law, the essay challenges the normative assumptions underlying the concept of universality, to ultimately question whether it is possible and indeed desirable that the universal human rights regime be unfragmented.

3.2 The Contested and Fractured Emergence of Human Rights

A kind of idealistic nostalgia pervades the popular narrative regarding the adoption of the UDHR in 1948, in which it is imagined that the global community became united at last in a coherent expression of our shared fundamental values. Such characterizations tend to gloss over the contentious ideological battlefield between East and West from whence the UDHR emerged, a debate which all the while excluded a significant portion of the world's population living in the shadow of colonialism. Even if the UDHR can optimistically be characterized as having reached some normative unity today, at the time of its adoption it was, historically speaking, a discordant compromise. That compromise is reflected in the fact that shortly after the UDHR's adoption, regional human rights regimes began to develop independently and arose in part from a desire to impute the specific demands of local culture on otherwise 'universal' norms. This section reviews the inception of both the

UDHR and regional mechanisms in order to demonstrate that the view of human rights as beginning in unity but subsequently splintering is misguided. In fact, from its very inception, human rights law strived to accommodate contested meanings.

3.2.1 The Universal Declaration of Human Rights

John Humphrey, the Canadian author of the original draft of the UDHR, recounts the remarkable debate that took place in the General Assembly in 1948 as "something of a miracle" given that the "political atmosphere in which the committee had to work was charged to the point of explosion by the Cold War with irrelevant recriminations coming from both sides."[1] With the Eastern bloc suspecting that the UDHR was a Trojan Horse for Western individualism and market capitalism, delegates argued over everything from the philosophical underpinnings of human rights to minute wording in the draft document. At one point, the discussion descended into venomous exchanges, with the US accusing the Soviets of persecuting religion, censoring the press, and denying political dissidents a fair trial, among other abuses, and the Soviets responding that the US was a "hypocrite servant of capitalism" by talking self-righteously about human rights while denying fundamental freedoms to its own black citizens in the South.[2]

Beyond political accusations, concerns about the fragmentation of international human rights surfaced from the very beginning. At the first session of the Commission on Human Rights in January 1947 there was a considerable amount of handwringing over whether human rights could be "universally claimed by all people without distinctions as members of the larger human family, or in a fragmented world with many different forms of government [and] value systems... restricted to membership within a given state, culture, or stages of development."[3] The Indian representative, fearing that the entire project would be sidetracked, suggested that the Commission "not enter into this maze of ideology", but the discussion raged on.[4]

Another debate was ignited over the very source of human rights itself. "[T]he most controversial issue," according to Humphrey, "was whether it should contain

[1] John P. Humphrey, *Human Rights & the United Nations: A Great Adventure* (Dobbs Ferry, NY: Transnational Publishers, 1984) at 64.

[2] Paul Gordon Lauren, *The Evolution of International Human Rights: Visions Seen* (Philadelphia: University of Pennsylvania Press, 1998) at 228. For a contextualization, see Samuel Moyn, *The Last Utopia – Human Rights in History* (Cambridge, MA: Harvard University Press, 2010), 44–83.

[3] Lavren, *Ibid.* at 221.

[4] Cited in Habib C. Malik, ed., *The Challenge of Human Rights: Charles Malik and the Universal Declaration* (Oxford: Charles Malik Foundation, 2000) at 31. The Indian statement drew a piquant rebuttal from Malik himself: "Well, unfortunately, whatever you say, Madam, one must have ideological presuppositions and, no matter how much you fight shy of them, they are there and you either hide them or you are brave enough to bring them out into the open and see them and criticize them." *Ibid.*, at 37.

some reference to the deity."[5] With some countries vociferously arguing variously that the preamble should contain some reference to 'the Creator,' 'nature,' or nothing at all, the eventual compromise of 'human dignity' was arrived at, which offended no one.[6] As one author has put it, "Characterizing human rights in terms of human dignity, while providing a conceptual foundation for this area, simply postponed the definitional dilemma to a later stage of inquiry. The question then becomes – what is 'human dignity'?"[7]

Some of the wording was agreed upon with the tacit assumption that it would *not* hold universal meaning: "[A]greement on a text sometimes concealed an unexpressed disagreement over the meaning of particular words. Thus the word 'democratic' in Article 29 would probably be interpreted differently in London and Moscow."[8] Indeed, the intentional vagueness of norms is a common strategy to manage substantive disagreement and pave the way to an agreement on an international instrument.[9]

Similarly, René Cassin recalls how during the drafting negotiations an effort was mounted to reorganize the Declaration's provisions in a hierarchical fashion by grouping articles under headings that would identify some rights as more 'fundamental' than others. This initiative immediately encountered controversy, however, and was hastily abandoned. Cassin reflects that this concession was in some sense a compromise designed to conceal disagreement: "une Déclaration des Droits de l'Homme n'est pas un traité scientifique: ses auteurs avaient le droit, imitant en cela les architectes qui enlèvent les échafaudages d'une construction achevée, de retirer les divisions et têtes de chapitre pouvant masquer l'ordonnance de leur oeuvre."[10]

Thus significant parts of the UDHR, as well as its structure, were borne out of political compromise and left deliberately ambiguous.[11] This foreshadowed future claims of relativism and helped to justify evolving or localized interpretations. A way of stating things had to be found which was not vague, but still, according to René Cassin, "sufficiently flexible to cover all systems."[12] The representative of

[5] Humphrey, *supra* note 1 at 67. See also René Cassin, "La declaration universelle et la mise en oeuvre des droits de l'homme" (1951) 79 *Recueil des droits* 237–367, at 284.

[6] *Ibid.*; Karin Mickelson, "How Universal Is the Universal Declaration", 47 University of New Brunswick Law Journal 19 (1998) at 22.

[7] Mickelson, *supra* note 6 at 23.

[8] Humphrey, *supra* note 1 at 66.

[9] See Richard Bilder, *Managing the Risks of International Agreements* (Madison: University of Wisconsin Press, 1981).

[10] Cassin, *supra* note 5 at 277.

[11] *Cf.* Gudmundur Alfredsson and Asbjorn Eide, *The Universal Declaration of Human Rights: A Common Standard of Achievement* (The Hague: Martinus Nijhoff Publishers, 1999) at 14 (The "five facilitating factors" which allowed the UDHR to achieve compromise, according to Ashild Samnoy, were (1) rejecting controversial issues; (2) general and vague formulations; (3) limitation clauses; (4) not including a philosophical foundation; and (5) crosscutting argumentative cleavages).

[12] See Johannes Morsink, *The Universal Declaration of Human Rights: Origins, Drafting & Intent* (Philadelphia: University of Pennsylvania Press, 1999) at 21, citing UN Doc. E/CN.4/SR.6 at 5.

the Philippines held the view that the UDHR had to "be accepted by all Members of the UN and... should take the different cultural systems of the world into account."[13] Similarly, the Chilean delegate observed that "different ideologies need[ed to] find common ground."[14] In other words, as Cassin again put it: "On ne saurait donc considérer que le progrès vers l'universalité dont témoigne la Déclaration, conduise à l'*uniformité*".[15]

It is possible that these ambiguities were in part tolerated because it was widely assumed that the UDHR would never really become a binding instrument of international law.[16] In fact, before work on the drafting of the UDHR ever took place, the Commission on Human Rights endured several days of heated debate about which project deserved priority: a non-binding declaration or a covenant.[17] At the start of the Second Session of the Commission, Eleanor Roosevelt bluntly announced the U.S. position: "[P]riority should be given to the draft Declaration, and [the] latter should not be drawn up in such a way as to give the impression that Governments would have a contractual obligation to guarantee human rights."[18] On this point the USSR was in agreement, and its representative, Alexandre Bogomolov, moved to close debate so that work on the declaration alone could begin. The UK representative, Charles Dukeston, was livid: "History showed that Declarations imposing no juridical obligation had remained inoperative for centuries... His delegation would never agree to the Commission elaborating a Declaration without a Convention."[19] The Belgians maligned that it would be no more than an "academic vote" and that it "might even endanger the Commission's existence and would cause immense disappointment to a world that was awaiting positive solutions capable of influencing human destiny... [The Belgian representative] pointed out that behind the divergences of view on procedure lay disagreement on matters of substance."[20] Only when the UK delegation softened did the Commission decide to set aside the covenant for the time being. According to René Cassin, who took credit for the British turnaround, the UK began to realize that the political climate was becoming simply too hostile to warrant an ambitious project: "Already, the Cold War had begun and threatened to compromise the adoption of a declaration, as well as of a convention."[21]

[13] UN Doc. E/CN.4/SR.9 at 2.

[14] Morsink, *supra* note 12 at 21.

[15] Cassin, *supra* note 5 at 283 (referring specifically to the fact that the UDHR, unlike previous historic rights documents, did not confine its protections to citizens or otherwise discriminate on the basis of nationality, but nevertheless did not require that countries treat nationals and non-nationals alike in all matters).

[16] Humphrey, *supra* note 1 at 65.

[17] Morsink, *supra* note 12 at 17.

[18] UN Doc. E/CN.4/SR.25 (1947) at 10.

[19] UN Doc. E/CN.4/SR.28 (1947) at 7 (amongst those explicitly opposed to a Declaration without a Covenant, in addition to the UK and Belgium, were India, Australia, and the Philippines).

[20] *Ibid.* at 2–5.

[21] René Cassin, *La Pensée et l'action* (Paris: Editions F. Lalon, 1968) at 112.

Even though there is no doubt that today the UDHR has taken on binding significance in customary law, the historical reality that many of the delegations foresaw precisely the opposite fate in store is important when considering that much has been made of the fact that on December 10, 1948, the UDHR was passed without any State voting against. While true, eight States did abstain (Byelorussia, Czechoslovakia, Poland, USSR, Ukraine, Yugoslavia, South Africa, and Saudia Arabia). The Eastern bloc states complained of the UDHR's foundation in Western ideology and its inadequate recognition of economic, social, and cultural rights, as well as collective rights and duties. At the General Assembly, the Soviet delegate did not mince words in a direct attack on the universalist nature of human rights: "Human rights could not be conceived outside the State; the very concept of right and law was connected with that of the State."[22] While the Soviet ideological opposition to the universalist spirit of the UDHR was unwavering, they apparently decided to abstain because the very reason they had agreed to be involved in the first place was so as to have a platform from which to condemn Nazism and fascism. That political goal, only a mere few years after World War II, remained paramount.[23]

Saudi Arabia objected to the right of persons to change their religion or belief, which contradicted the Koran, and claimed that the UDHR reflected Western culture and was "at variance with patterns of culture of Eastern States".[24] South Africa, for its part, feared that the UDHR would be elevated to a binding norm, threatening the apartheid State.[25] Moreover, it is little known that Canada had threatened to abstain, having declined to support the UDHR in an earlier vote in the Third Committee. This was explained at the time as arising from protests from the Canadian business community over endorsing too "revolutionary" a document, and, unconvincingly, due to concerns that in signing it the federal government would be encroaching on provincial constitutional powers.[26] In a secret telegram sent to Lester B. Pearson (then the Foreign Affairs Minister), declassified only several decades later, it was also advanced that some of the language was so "lacking in precision so as to make some articles incapable of application," such that "Article No. 19, conferring the right to public employment irrespective of political creed, must be read as requiring the employment of Communists in the government service, while Article 16 would

---

[22] United Nations *Official Records*, General Assembly, 3rd session, Part I, 1948, Plenary Meetings, p. 924.

[23] Morsink, *supra* note 12 at 23.

[24] Cited in Ann Elizabeth Mayer, *Islam and Human Rights: Tradition and Politics*, 3rd ed. (Boulder, CO: Westview Press, 1999) at 10–11. Mayer notes that the Saudi representative's remarks "provoked sharp dissent from the representative of Pakistan, who took the position that Islam unequivocally endorsed freedom of conscience" (at 11). She further notes that "[t]his debate on whether Muslim countries could approve the UDHR thus presaged decades of subsequent disputes in the Muslim world about whether in endorsing international human rights Muslims were betraying Islamic law and submitting to Western cultural domination. In the end, when it came time to vote on the UDHR, Saudia Arabia was alone among Muslim countries in abstaining…" (*ibid*).

[25] Kindred et al., *International Law Chiefly as Interpreted and Applied in Canada*, 7th ed. (Toronto: Emond Montgomery, 2006) at 838.

[26] *Ibid*. at 837.

permit the unrestricted activities of sects such as Jehovah's Witnesses."[27]. Ultimately, as Humphrey tells it, the Canadians decided to vote in favor on December 10 because "the government did not relish the company in which it found itself" (referring mainly to the fact that abstaining States were part of the communist bloc). [28]

More importantly, perhaps, is the fact that in 1948 the UN consisted of only 56 member states, excluding much of the developing world. In 1997, Prime Minister Mahathir Mohamad of Malaysia would come under withering criticism from human rights activists for suggesting that for its 50th anniversary, a 'review' of the UDHR should be undertaken since the membership of the UN had more than tripled since 1948, with the diversity of views undergoing a similar expansion.[29] But Mahatir was not alone in this view, especially amongst former colonized states, whose exclusion was taken as a given by the Western powers that principally drafted the UDHR.[30] As Kéba M'baye, the original drafter of the African Charter on Human and Peoples' Rights, and no enemy of universalism, tells us, "on ne peut pas nier le fait que, en 1948, trois Etats seulement du continent africain étaient à l'O.N.U. et que leur participation à l'élaboration des différentes règles a été nulle."[31] For example, it has been suggested that the lack of a right to self-determination in the UDHR is patently a consequence of its principal drafters being colonialist powers.[32] Similarly, other minority rights did not make it into the final draft of the UDHR because member states in the 'new world' were concerned that the recent waves of WW2-related immigrants would resist cultural assimilation.[33]

Given the level of discord heretofore obscured by the UDHR's 'unanimous' adoption, it is no surprise that regional human rights regimes, with their own substantive law as well as procedural mechanisms, quickly began to develop even after 'universal' principles had ostensibly already been agreed upon. A review of the drafting history of the regional human rights regimes in Europe, the Americas and Africa reveals that each acknowledged transcendent principles enshrined in the UDHR and other fundamental treaties, but nevertheless sought to infuse their systems with local and specific understandings of human rights. The independent development of regional regimes is therefore reflective of the fractured emergence of human rights.

---

[27] *Ibid.* at 837, fn. 4 (citing H. Mackenzie, ed., *Documents on Canadian External Relations*, Vol. 14 (1994), at 359). See also A.J. Hobbins, "Eleanor Roosevelt, John Humphrey and Canadian Opposition to the Universal Declaration of Human Rights: Looking Back on the 50th Anniversary of the UNDHR" (1998) 52 *International Journal* 325–342; and W. Schabas, "Canada and the Adoption of the Universal Declaration of Human Rights" (1998) 43 *McGill Law Journal* 403–41.

[28] Humphrey, *supra* note 1 at 72 and 79.

[29] Mickelson, *supra* note 6 at 21.

[30] Albert Verdoodt, *Naissance et signification de la déclaration universelle des droits de l'homme* (Louvain: Editions Nauwelaerts, 1964) at 61.

[31] Kéba M'baye, *Les droits de l'homme en Afrique* (Paris: Pedone, 1992) at 41. These three countries were: Ethiopia, Egypt and South Africa.

[32] *Ibid.* at 42. See Moyn, *supra* note 2.

[33] William Schabas, *Preventing Genocide and Mass Killing: The Challenge for the United Nations* (Minority Rights Group International, 2006). See generally Morsink, *supra* note 12, at 274 ff.

3.2.2 Europe: A Binding and Continental Treaty

In Europe, discussions on forming a regional political unit began to take shape soon after WW2,[34] leading to the creation of an International Committee of Movements for European Unity [hereinafter, the European Movement] under the leadership of Sir Winston Churchill.[35] The Committee convened a congress in The Hague in May 1948 in which the representatives promoted the idea of a union or federation of European States respectful of democratic principles and human rights.[36] The resolutions of this 'Congress of Europe' expressed the desire for a Charter on Human Rights and a Court of Justice that would enforce it.[37] The Statute of the Council of Europe, which made several references to human rights and even made respecting them a condition of membership, was signed soon after the UN General Assembly approved the UDHR.[38]

The European Movement prepared a preliminary draft convention which was submitted to the Committee of Ministers of the Council of Europe.[39] At the Committee of Ministers, a schism emerged, with some fearing that a European human rights project would interfere with the analogous process at the UN Commission on Human Rights. Pierre-Henri Teitgen, one of the drafters of the European Movement draft, recalled that "when the Committee met up to draw up the agenda for the session, there emerged four opposition groups, who argued [...] that the Council of Europe ought moreover to wait until the [UN] had completely finished its work relating to the agreements for implementation of its Universal Charter."[40] Carlos Sforza, the Italian minister of foreign affairs at the time, stressed that "la circonstanza che le stesse avessero realizzato la Dichiarazione del 1948, esspresamente definita comme 'universale', non doeva costituire un impedimento alla creazione di una Carta 'continentale', modellata sulla cultura, i valorie e le tradizioni peculiari all'Europa."[41] The representative of Denmark had a similar reaction:

---

[34] See e.g. Francis Geoffrey Jacobs, *The European Convention on Human Rights* (Oxford: Clarendon Press, 1975) at 1.

[35] John Truscott Wright, *The European Convention on Human Rights: An Analysis and Appraisal*, (Thesis (Doctoral), New School for Social Research (New York, N.Y.), 1978) at 4 [unpublished].

[36] Ralph Beddard, *Human Rights and Europe: A Study of the Machinery of Human Rights Protection of the Council of Europe*, 2nd ed. (London: Sweet & Maxwell, 1980) at 17.

[37] A. H. Robertson, *Human Rights in Europe; Being an Account of the European Convention for the Protection of Human Rights and Fundamental Freedoms Signed in Rome on 4 November 1950, of the Protocol Thereto and of the Machinery Created Thereby: the European Commission of Human Rights and the European Court of Human Rights* (Manchester: Manchester University Press, 1963) at 6.

[38] Beddard, *supra* note 36 at 19.

[39] The draft can be found in Council of Europe, *Collected edition of the "travaux préparatoires" of the European Convention on Human Rights*, vol. 1 (The Hague: Martinus Nijhoff, 1975).

[40] Pierre-Henri Teitgen, "Introduction to the European Convention on Human Rights" in Ronald St J. Macdonald, Franz Matscher and Herbert Petzold, eds., *The European System for the Protection of Human Rights* (Dordrecht: Martinus Nijhoff, 1993) at 16.

[41] Carlo Russo and Paolo M. Quaini, *La Convenzione europea dei diritti dell'uomo e la giurisprudenza della Corte di Strasburgo*, 2nd ed. (Milano: Giuffrè, 2006) at 4.

> The Universal Declaration lacked precision. It could not be otherwise in view of the differences in civilization and forms of Government existing in different Member States of the United Nations. It would be a very different matter if the question was reconsidered on a purely Western European basis, in which case a text might be elaborated which would be binding in the legal sense.[42]

Eventually, in August 1948, the Committee of Ministers agreed to discuss at the first session of the Consultative Assembly the "measures for the fulfillment of the declared aim of the Council of Europe [...] in regard to the maintenance and further realization of human rights and fundamental freedoms."[43] In less than a year and a half the Convention was signed in Rome, leaving the controversial issues for a Protocol that would eventually be adopted in March 1952.[44]

Lord McNair put it best when he said: "This Convention of 1950 is an illustration of the fact that in international affairs it is often easier to advance on a regional than on an universal basis."[45] Most authors affirm that the UDHR served as the basis of the European Convention,[46] but it must be noted that "les droits garantis [in the European Convention] sont moins nombreux et moins largement définis que dans la Déclaration universelle."[47]

Recalling the history of this process reveals an interest on the part of the promoters of the European Union to make democracy and human rights inherent qualities of the new and united Europe, a desire evidently arising out of horror at the atrocities of the Second World War. As explained above, it was in response to the reaction of some governments to slow the European process in favour of the UDHR that culture became the rhetorical flag of regionalism. In a rather interesting anecdote, Teitgen relates that René Cassin, one of the 'founding fathers' of the UDHR, "was reluctant to accept the idea of a regional system of protection of human rights being set up outside his universal charter (which was not compulsory and did not provided for sanctions), even if such a system was perfectly compatible with the Charter of the United Nations (but compulsory and much more effective)."[48]

---

[42] Council of Europe, *supra* note 39 at 24.

[43] *Ibid.* at 28.

[44] See European Commission of Human Rights, *Documents and/et Decisions of the European Commission on Human Rights 1955–1957* (The Hague: Nijhoff, 1971) at 92.

[45] Lord McNair, "Foreword", in British Institute of International and Comparative Law, ed., *The European Convention on Human Rights* (London: British Institute of International and Comparative Law, 1965) vii, at viii.

[46] Iain Cameron, *An Introduction to the European Convention on Human Rights*, 4th ed. (Uppsala: Iustus Förlag, 2002) at 33.

[47] M. R. Pelloux, "Précédents. Caractères généraux de la Convention Européenne", in Université de Strasbourg. Faculté de droit et des sciences politiques et économiques, ed., *La protection internationale des droits de l'homme dans le cadre européen. Travaux du colloque organisé par la Faculté de droit et des sciences politiques et économiques de Strasbourg en liaison avec la Direction des droits de l'homme du Conseil de l'Europe, 14–15 novembre 1960* (Paris: Dalloz, 1961) at 64.

[48] Teitgen, *supra* note 40 at 11.

3.2.3 *The Americas: Universal and Particular*[49]

On the other side of the Atlantic, the process unfolded differently, and proved less hesitant at moving beyond the UDHR. From the nineteenth century, the idea had persisted that international law as applied in the American continent had special traits which could not be found in other regions, and that some principles merely enunciated in Europe had been brought to life in Latin America.[50] Alejandro Alvarez, a former judge of the ICJ, was among the strongest voices defending the particularities of American International Law:[51]

> Not only has the contribution of Latin America to the development of International Law been of vast proportions, but the manner in which the contribution has been made has also been of the most important consequence to that same law. It has shown, in fact, most clearly that although the general community of nations possesses solidarity and recognizes the same international precepts, those precepts are not always universal, that is to say, they are not applied in all cases and in like manner on both continents.[52]

Undoubtedly linked to the fact that its members did not suffer the devastation and division of the Second World War, the American process began earlier and moved more decisively, at least at first, than the Universal and European processes towards the adoption of a binding document. The Inter-American Conference on Problems of War and Peace of 1945 commissioned the Governing Board of the Pan-American Union and the Inter-American Juridical Committee with the drafting of two declarations, one on the rights and duties of States and the other on the rights and duties of man, which would be annexed to a binding charter for the strengthening of the Inter-American System of International Law.[53] The Committee did its part and elaborated a draft Declaration of the International Rights and Duties of Man. Although the 1945 Conference contemplated adopting this Declaration as a binding convention,[54] a conference for that purpose was never called.[55]

The Declaration was eventually adopted at the Ninth International Conference of American States as the "American Declaration of the Rights and Duties of Man" in April 1948. But over the course of the next decade, the efforts to adopt a binding

---

[49] See *infra* note 63 and accompanying text.

[50] See especially Alejandro Alvarez, "Latin America and International Law" (1909) 3 *American Journal of International Law* 1.

[51] See also Jorge L. Esquirol, "Alejandro Alvarez's Latin American Law: A Question of Identity" (2006) 19 *Leiden Journal of International Law* 931; Katharina Zobel, "Judge Alejandro Alvarez at the International Court of Justice (1946–1955): His Theory of a 'New International Law' and Judicial Lawmaking" (2006) 19 *Leiden Journal of International Law* 1017.

[52] Alvarez, *supra* note 50 at 346.

[53] General Secretariat of the Organization of American States, *Inter-American Yearbook on Human Rights 1968* (Washington, DC: OAS, 1973) at 65.

[54] Rafael Nieto-Navia, *La Corte y el sistema interamericano de derechos humanos* (San José: Corte IIDH, 1994) at 8.

[55] *Inter-American Yearbook on Human Rights*, *supra* note 53 at 65.

Convention, with an accompanying Inter-American Court, would be repeatedly stifled. It was not until the Fifth Meeting of Consultation of Ministers of Foreign Affairs in 1959 that priority was given to the elaboration of an American Convention and the establishment of a system of institutions for human rights protection and promotion. It took two Special Inter-American Conferences (one in 1965 and the other in 1967) to agree on the details.

The issue of the intersection of the Inter-American regional human rights system with international law came to the fore at the 1967 gathering. The Commission of Juridical and Political Affairs of the Permanent Council met in May 1967 to discuss the current draft of the declaration, and initially put special emphasis on the fact that the UN Covenants had already been open for signature in the General Assembly. The Commission saw fit to ask the governments present if these Covenants should be taken as the universal and unique substantive elaboration of human rights. If so, it advanced that the American Process should be limited to establishing an institutional and procedural framework for the application of the Covenant(s).[56]

The replies from governments were diverse. On one side, Argentina expressly requested a halt to consideration of an American Convention, echoed by Brazil which stated that "international agreements already adopted on the matter do represent a universally applicable and sole set of standards on human rights."[57] On the other side, Bolivia, Chile, Ecuador, and the United States, among others, stressed that coexistence and coordination between the universal system and the regional system presented in the draft Convention was possible.[58] Costa Rica went further and affirmed that "the coexistence of regional and universal conventions for the protection of human rights is not only possible, but advisable."[59] Colombia also stated that "[a]long with the creation and operation of the Inter-American Commission and Court on Human Rights, there should be prepared a system of substantive law that would either pick-up the declarations and principles of the universal conventions or would be adapted to the practices of America in this field."[60] Similar calls for regional particularities were made by Ecuador ("it should not be ignored that there exist on the American Continent juridical institutions and features which could and ought to be given emphasis through substantive law"[61]) and Costa Rica ("[s]uch [substantive] provisions should not be made separate from those established by the United Nations and should merely be complemented by those that are required by the politico-social reality of the Inter-American System"[62]). After studying these opinions,

[56] Nieto-Navia, *supra* note 54 at 12–13.

[57] OAS, Inter-American Commission on Human Rights, Comparative Study of the United Nations Conventions on Civil and Political Rights and in Economic, Social and Cultural Rights and the Draft Inter-American Convention on Human Rights, OR OEA/Ser.L/V/II.19/doc.18 (1967) at para. 13, in *Inter-American Yearbook on Human Rights*, *supra* note 53 at 174.

[58] *Ibid*. at para. 11, in p. 173, 175.

[59] *Ibid*.

[60] *Ibid*. at para. 15, in p. 177.

[61] *Ibid*. at para. 14, in p. 175, 177.

[62] *Ibid*.

and undertaking a comparative study of the draft and the UN Covenants, the Inter-American Commission on Human Rights concluded that:

> III. The need for, and the desirability of, a regional convention for the Americas are based on the existence of a body of American international law built up in accordance with the specific requirements of the close relationship that exists between human rights and regional economics [sic] development and integration [...]
> IV. Consequently the Inter-American Convention on the Protection of Human Rights should be autonomous rather than complementary to the United Nations covenants, although it should indeed be coordinated with those covenants.
> V. To this end, the substantive [text] [... should ...] include other rights that are not contemplated in that covenant, but the international protection of which is demanded because of conditions peculiar to the Americas.[63]

The American Convention was eventually adopted in 1969. The Convention contains all the rights covered by the International Covenant on Civil and Political Rights, but also includes additional rights such as the right to property, right of reply, and the prohibition on arbitrarily depriving a person of their nationality or the right to change it.[64] In particular, the Convention is unique in guaranteeing the right to life "in general, from the moment of conception",[65] a formulation seen to restrict abortion and reflective of the Roman Catholic identity of much of the region.[66] It also provides for a more extensive set of non-derogable guarantees applicable during states of emergency.

The essential conclusion from this history is that even though the Inter-American System has always tried to mark its difference vis-à-vis international law, the OAS briefly contemplated the possibility of establishing a purely institutional and procedural scheme that would apply the 'universal' law of the UN Covenants. The result, however, is a regional system that builds on the rights established in international law, but also promotes their particular cultural adaptation.

3.2.4 Africa: "Assimilating Without Being Assimilated"[67]

When the Organization of African Unity (OAU) was founded in 1963, the only mention of human rights was made in the Preamble to its Charter, where it stated that "the Charter of the United Nations and the Universal Declaration of Human Rights, to the Principles of which we reaffirm our adherence, provide a solid foundation for peaceful and positive cooperation among States."[68] This formulation,

[63] *Ibid.* at para. 96, in p. 211.

[64] *Ibid.* at para. 44–79, in p. 191 ss.

[65] Art. 4(1).

[66] See B.G. Ramcharan, *The Right to Life in International Law* (Dordrecht/Boston: Martinus Nijhoff Publishers, 1985) at 277, note 6.

[67] Leopold Senghor, quoted in Fatsah Ouguergouz, *The African Charter on Human and Peoples' Rights* (The Hague: Nijhoff, 2003) at 41.

[68] Charter of the Organization of African Unity, 479 U.N.T.S. 39, entered into force Sept. 13, 1963, Preamble.

which emphasized that human rights were primarily about "positive cooperation among States", indirectly reflected the cool reception that Africa initially gave to universal human rights. It had not gone unnoticed that only three African states were even members of the United Nations at the time the UDHR was adopted, and even they had had very little role in its drafting.[69] The OAU was roundly suspicious that human rights were merely an agent for further domestic interference in a continent ravaged by decades of colonialism, an era of dominance that had too often been justified under the banner of various forms of humanitarianism. [70] Thus, as commentators have frequently noted, OAU founders "laid great stress on safeguarding recently won independence against infringements of any sort".[71] The Charter enshrines the principle of "non-interference in the internal affairs of [member] states" (Article 3(2)).

Nevertheless, in the years following 1948, 50 African states expressed support for the UDHR, which reflected their support for "asserting and protecting human dignity... It is this goal which is universal in character and hence in this sense human rights apply to all people wherever they live."[72] But beyond this shared fundamental premise, African states would demonstrate that they felt no obligation to slavishly abide by others' interpretation of particular rights.

Movement towards a truly African treaty began in earnest in 1978 with a UN Human Rights Commission resolution calling for the Secretary General to support the Organization of African Unity in its efforts to instate an African human rights commission.[73] In 1979, the OAU adopted a resolution calling for a draft African Charter[74] and at a Ministerial Conference in Dakar, Senegal in November 1979, a group of 20 legal experts under the Chairmanship of Judge Kéba Mbaye met to prepare the first draft articles.[75] In a telling anecdote, Bello recalls that at this meeting:

> To the surprise of the assembled group of experts, they discovered that the OAU Secretariat had prepared a preliminary draft Charter which was not dissimilar to the provisions in both European and Latin American Conventions on Human Rights... [T]he group of experts, having reviewed the situation, agreed that the Organization of African Unity needed a different and special Charter to deal with the problems of human rights in Africa. A replica of the European Convention would therefore be inconsistent.[76]

---

[69] M'baye, *supra* note 31.

[70] Gino J. Naldi, "Future Trends in Human Rights in Africa: the Increased Role of the OAU?" in *The African Charter on Human and Peoples' Rights: The System in Practice, 1986–2000*, Malcolm D. Evans and Rachel Murray, eds. (New York: Cambridge University Press, 2002) at 2.

[71] Claude E. Welch, "The O.A.U. and Human Rights: Towards a New Definition" (1981) 19 *Journal of Modern African Studies* 401, at 402.

[72] R.M. D'Sa, "The African Charter on Human and Peoples' Rights: Problems and Prospects for Regional Action" (1981–1983) 10 *Australian Year Book of International Law* 101, at 103.

[73] M'baye, *supra* note 31 at 148. This followed a series of conferences and discussions amongst African jurists beginning in the 1960s: E.G. Bello, "The African Charter on Human and Peoples' Rights: A Legal Analysis" (1985-V) 194 *Recueil des cours* 9–268, at 21–29.

[74] Decision 115(XVI) Rev I, OAU Doc AHG/115(XVI) 1979.

[75] D'Sa, *supra* note 72 at 106.

[76] Bello, *supra* note 73 at 28.

Thus, the "stated objective of the drafters was to prepare an African Charter on human rights which could be truly 'African' in its legal philosophy and in its response to the needs of the African peoples."[77] As M'baye put it, "Ses rédacteurs ont entendu, tout, en s'imprégnant des idées directrices de la Déclaration universelle et des autres déclarations, faire une oeuvre adaptée aux besoins de l'homme africain."[78] After a series of discussions and conferences, at the 18th OAU Assembly in Nairobi in June 1981, the African Charter on Human and Peoples' Rights was at last adopted.[79]

While the Charter reiterates the pledge to "promote international cooperation having due regard to… the Universal Declaration of Human Rights" in its Preamble, the OAU member states also take into consideration "the virtues of their historical tradition and the values of African civilization which should inspire and characterize their reflection on the concept of human and peoples' rights".[80] Thus at Article 60, the Charter only mandates the Commission to "*draw inspiration* from international law on human and peoples' rights" and at Article 61 to "*take into consideration, as subsidiary measures* to determine the principles of law, other general or special international conventions".[81] The Charter is notable for other marked departures from the UDHR, in particular its emphasis on the rights of "peoples," its inclusion of not only rights but responsibilities, its enshrining of 'new' rights such as the right to development and a clean environment and, according to Kéba M'baye, one of the Charter's original drafters, an entirely different conceptual foundation from the UDHR in that "En Afrique, le droit n'est pas conçu comme une sorte d'épée mise entre les mains de l'individu pour lui permettre de se défendre contre le groupe. Il est plutôt considéré comme un ensemble de règles protectrices de la communauté dont l'individu fait partie."[82] A reflection of this distinct foundation is the absence from the African Charter of a right to privacy, which was considered but discarded as being overly individualistic.

M'baye, however, is not cynical about the UDHR and suggests that there is a "marche inévitable des droits de l'homme vers l'universalisme."[83] But he identifies a discordance inherent in the UDHR, and universalism itself, that has only been resolved by recognizing the necessity for the specificity of human rights: "La virulence de l'antagonisme entre les conceptions occidentales et tiers-mondistes des droits de l'homme s'est considérablement atténuée. À sa place s'est érigée la notion de spécificité."[84]

---

[77] *Ibid.*

[78] M'baye, *supra* note 31 at 162.

[79] *Ibid.*

[80] African Charter on Human and Peoples' Rights, Preamble.

[81] Emphasis added.

[82] M'baye, *supra* note 31. See also Bello, *supra* note 73, at 32–34.

[83] *Ibid.* at 43.

[84] *Ibid.* at 41.

Considering that the UDHR was proclaimed to be a universal standard for all peoples, it is interesting to recall that after 1977 the UN General Assembly explicitly encouraged the creation of regional human rights regimes,[85] a direct contribution to the formal fragmentation of international human rights. The possibility of fragmenting the international human rights regime was, in fact, the very reason consensus was, and continues to be, possible. As John Clayton has put it, "The 1948 Universal Declaration was a *historic* document. It is rightly regarded as a key moment in shaping the post-war world. In the meantime, however, it has become also a *historical* document. It can now be seen to mirror the concerns of that time and to embody its asymmetry of political power."[86]

All of the above shows that the concept of universality in international human rights law, today considered one of the most controversial issues, was always a source of contention from the very first meeting of the UN Commission on Human Rights. A similar study could be carried out in reference to the regime fragmentation of human rights along thematic rather than geographic lines. The creation of dedicated regimes on children, women, migrants, disabled people, torture, racial discrimination, etc. is not systematically posited as merely giving greater specificity to these norms. The possibility of dislocation between the Convention on the Rights of the Child and the Convention on the Elimination of All Forms of Discrimination Against Women, for example, cannot be easily discounted, and it would thus be fair to say that international human rights law was never unquestionably unified to begin with. The existence of the regional systems do show that, although it seemed to generate relatively few misgivings, the question of cultural adaptation was always on the mind of those in charge of elevating human rights into positive international law. Even during a recent debate about cultural relativism in human rights at the 1993 UN World Conference on Human Rights in Vienna, the fear of fragmentation did not appear to influence the discussion; interpretive flexibility seemed necessary for the global promotion of universal human rights standards.[87] That the Inter-American process quickly dismissed the idea of a purely procedural system applying international law demonstrates that fragmentation was hardly seen as a problem – on the contrary, a plurality of institutions and norms seemed like the most plausible way to protect human rights the world over. The process of fragmentation is still ongoing,

---

[85] In 1977 the General Assembly passed a resolution entitled "Regional arrangements for the promotion and protection of human rights" in which it invited "States in areas where regional arrangements in the field of human rights do not yet exist to consider concluding agreements with a view to the establishment within their respective regions of suitable regional machinery for the promotion and protection of human rights." (UN Doc. A/RES/32/127) The same sentiment was expressed in 21 General Assembly resolutions from session 32 (1977) to 61 (2006); see especially, *Alternative approaches and ways and means within the United Nations system for improving the effective enjoyment of human rights and fundamental freedoms: report of the Secretary-General*, UN GAOR, 32th Sess., UN Doc. A/32/178 (1977) at paras. 107–111.

[86] Quoted in Mickelson, *supra* note 6 at 47.

[87] World Conference on Human Rights, *Vienna Declaration and Programme of Action*, UN GAOR, 1993, UN Doc. A/CONF.157/23 at paras. 5, 13 and 37.

with new instruments emerging to articulate human rights norms reflective of specific communities defined on a regional basis, such as the ASEAN Human Rights Declaration or the Arab Charter on Human Rights adopted by the League of Arab States. Thus while the possibility of multiple and diverging interpretations seems to be a source of great worry amongst some theorists of international law, in fact the very 'universality' of human rights norms was seen from the very beginning to depend on their specificity. As M'baye elegantly put it, "l'universalisme n'empêche pas la diversité."[88]

3.3 Fragmentation and International Human Rights Law

The theoretical study of international law has, for some time, suggested that it has a certain level of cohesion that makes it independent from national legal systems. Consequently, international law is seen as *complete* in the self-referential sense of the word[89] – that is, it is supposed that there is no need to look outside the system for its rules and principles.[90] Nowadays, that view has changed. International law is now seen as a system in constant evolution. As its normative base grows in size, the propagation of institutions and sub-regimes also grows and reshapes the whole system.

In this section we turn to the phenomenon of the fragmentation of international law and its relevance to international human rights law. Fragmentation is understood as the:

> proliferation of international legal rules and institutions, the autonomous character of some international legal regimes and expansion of international law in those areas of relations that were not considered fit for international legal regulation before.[91]

The debate about the fragmentation of international law is not a new one. For many years scholars have been concerned about the proliferation of international institutions and its effects on the unity of international law.[92] Recent accounts of

---

[88] M'baye, *supra* note 31 at 44.

[89] Allain Pellet, "Article 38" in Andreas Zimmermann, Christian Tomuschat and Karin Oellers-Frahm, eds., *The Statute of the International Court of Justice: A Commentary* (Oxford: Oxford University Press, 2006) at 704; for a defense of the completeness of international law, in regards to the problem of non-liquet, see Hersch Lauterpacht, "Some Observations on the Prohibition of 'Non Liquet' and the Completeness of the Law", *Symbolae Verzijl, présentées au professeur J. H. W. Verzijl à l'occasion de son LXX-ième anniversaire* (The Hague: Martinus Nijhoff, 1958) at 196.

[90] The sole exception may be the reference to 'general principles of law recognized by civilized nations' in article 38.1.c of the Statute of the International Court of Justice.

[91] Roman A. Kolodkin, *Fragmentation of International Law? A View from Russia* in Ronald St. John Macdonald and Douglas M. Johnston, eds., *Towards World Constitutionalism: Issues in the Legal ordering of the World Community* (Leiden: Martinus Nijhoff, 2005) at 224.

[92] See e.g. C. W. Jenks, *The Prospects of International Adjudication* (New York: Oceana Publications, 1964) at 178–81; Ian Brownlie, "Problems Concerning the Unity of International Law", in *Le droit international à l'heure de sa codification: études en l'honneur de Roberto Ago*, vol. I (Milano: Giuffrè, 1987).

the issue of fragmentation project a grim outlook on the possible consequences of the expansion of international law. Commentators have stated that "the problem of fragmentation is more serious than is commonly assumed because it operates to sabotage the evolution of a more democratic and egalitarian international regulatory system and to undermine the reputation of international law for integrity."[93] Particularly in human rights law, there has always been uncertainty as to the coexistence and coordination of the universal and regional systems for the protection of human rights.[94]

It was not until the beginning of the twenty-first century that the International Law Commission (ILC) decided to study the phenomenon of fragmentation and include it as a topic in its works.[95] The ILC first took note of certain cases where the Vienna Convention on the Law of Treaties could not provide a clear solution in the event of conflicting obligations. The cases of *Richard Waite and Terry Kennedy*[96] and of *Beer and Regan*,[97] both against Germany before the now-extinct European Commission of Human Rights, provide interesting examples. Although not finding a violation of the European Convention, the European Commission stated *obiter dictum* that there is an incompatibility between the immunity from civil liability accorded to large groups or categories of persons and article 6.1 of the European Convention (which provides for the right to a fair hearing).[98] Interestingly enough, the European Court on Human Rights would arrive to the same conclusion, with a slightly stronger wording.[99] According to Gerhard Hafner, author of the ILC

[93] Eyal Benvenisti and George W. Downs, "The Empire's New Clothes: Political Economy and the Fragmentation of International Law" (2007) 60 Stan. L. Rev. 595 at 595.

[94] Marc-André Eissen, "The European Convention on Human Rights and the United Nations Covenant on Civil and Political Rights: Problems of Coexistence" (1972) 22 Buffalo Law Review 181; Rodolfo E. Piza Escalante, "Coordination of the Mechanism for the Protection of Human Rights in the American Convention with those Established by the United Nations" (1980) 30 American University Law Review 167.

[95] *Report of the International Law Commission on the Work of Its Fifty-Fourth Session*, UN GAOR, 57th Sess., Supp. No. 10, UN Doc. A/57/10 (2002) [*ILC Report-54th Sess.*].

[96] Eur. Comm. H. R., Richard Waite and Terry Kennedy v. Germany, App. No. 26083/94 Report of the Commission adopted on 2 December 1997, paras. 53–54.

[97] Eur. Comm. H. R., App. No. 28934/95 Beer and Regan v. Germany, Report of the Commission adopted on 2 December 1997.

[98] Waite and Kennedy, *supra* note 96 at para. 54.

[99] "The Court is of the opinion that where States establish international organisations in order to pursue or strengthen their cooperation in certain fields of activities, and where they attribute to these organisations certain competences and accord them immunities, there may be implications as to the protection of fundamental rights. It would be incompatible with the purpose and object of the Convention, however, if the Contracting States were thereby absolved from their responsibility under the Convention in relation to the field of activity covered by such attribution. It should be recalled that the Convention is intended to guarantee not theoretical or illusory rights, but rights that are practical and effective. This is particularly true for the right of access to the courts in view of the prominent place held in a democratic society by the right to a fair trial." *Waite and Kennedy v. Germany* [GC], no. 26083/94, ECHR 1999-I, 42 Y.B. Eur. Conv. H.R. 83; see also August Reinisch, "Waite and Kennedy v. Germany, Application No. 26083/94; Beer and Regan v. Germany, Application No. 28934/95. European Court Of Human Rights, February 18, 1999" 93 A.J.I.L. 933.

preliminary report on fragmentation,[100] the European Commission "took the view that the immunity from jurisdiction accorded to international organizations or members of diplomatic or consular missions of foreign States cannot be regarded as delimiting the very substance of substantive rights under domestic law."[101] That is, the law of diplomatic immunity – quintessentially an issue of public international law – could jeopardize the right to access to justice as enshrined in the European system for the protection human rights.

Hafner was of the view that three elements, resulting from the lack of a centralized organ, transformed international law into a heterogeneous, unorganized system: the enlargement of international law, the specialization and variation in the structure of its norms, and the emergence of parallel and competing regulations.[102] Although the topic was first included in the long-term program of work of the Commission as "Risks ensuing from fragmentation of international law",[103] the study group soon realized that the "proliferation of rules, regimes and institutions might strengthen international law."[104] In order to recognize that fragmentation both evidences the vitality of the international system as well as produces potentially negative consequences,[105] the title of the topic was changed to: "Fragmentation of international law: difficulties arising from the diversification and expansion of international law." The result of the study is a document with 42 conclusions which deal with the possible clashes of norms in international law,[106] and a lengthy report prepared by Martti Koskenniemi which accompanies and contextualizes these conclusions.[107]

In relation to international human rights law, the difficulties of fragmentation are focused on four aspects: (1) the proliferation of institutions, (2) the issues deriving from regionalism, (3) the nature of the so called 'self-contained regimes', and (4) the hierarchization of norms within the international system. Each of these will be discussed in turn, both with respect to the relationship between international human rights law and international law, and among the human rights sub-regimes (both thematic and regional).

---

[100] Report which was further elaborated here: Gerhard Hafner, "Pros and Cons Ensuing from Fragmentation of International Law" (2003–2004) 25 Michigan Journal of International Law 849.

[101] *Report of the International Law Commission on the Work of Its Fifty-Second Session*, UN GAOR, 55th Sess., Supp. No. 10, UN Doc. A/55/10 (2000) at 143.

[102] *Ibid.*

[103] *Ibid.* at 147 (In the Annex to the report, Prof. Gerhard Hafner notes "The disintegration of the legal order is conducive to jeopardizing the authority of international law. Doubts could be raised as to whether international law will be able to achieve one of its primary objectives, dispute avoidance and the stabilization of international relations and, thus, achieve its genuine function of law. The credibility, reliability and, consequently, authority of international law would be impaired").

[104] *ILC Report-54th Sess., supra* note 95 at 239.

[105] *Ibid.*

[106] *Report of the International Law Commission on the Work of Its Fifty-Eighth Session*, UN GAOR, 61th Sess., Supp. No. 10, UN Doc. A/61/10 (2006) at para. 251 [*Conclusions*].

[107] International Law Commission, *Report of the Study Group – Fragmentation of International Law: Difficulties arising from the Diversification and Expansion of International Law*, UN Doc. A/CN.4/L.682 (2006) (finalized by Martti Koskenniemi) [Report].

3.3.1 Proliferation of Institutions

The institutional dimension of fragmentation is self-evident: "Decisions reaching different conclusions on the same international law subject by a variety of tribunals may undermine the appearance, if not the fact, of a unitary international legal system."[108] The last (and outdated) version of the synoptic chart prepared by the Project on International Courts and Tribunals showed over 100 international judicial and quasi-judicial entities, of which 86 are currently functioning.[109] As the trend in the last quarter of a century shows an increasing number of both *ad hoc*[110] and permanent[111] judicial and quasi-judicial institutions, it is not unreasonable to believe that the specialization of tribunals and commissions might produce diverging opinions regarding the same set of facts.

However, it is evident that "à chaque niveau de densité normative correspond un certain niveau de densité institutionnelle permettant aux normes d'être mises en œuvre de manière satisfaisante."[112] In practice, international courts constantly cite and refer to decisions of other international courts, which shows that – at least in the human rights field – the proliferation of institutions promotes the production of common principles. At the very least, the fact that human rights issues are discussed in diverse institutional settings reveals their ubiquity in international politics, and their relevance for the promotion of the international rule of law. For instance, after the ICTY decided that the prohibition on torture had reached the level of a peremptory norm of international law,[113] decisions of the European Court of Human Rights[114] and the Inter-American Court[115] followed in the same direction by making direct reference to the criminal tribunal. Moreover, in cases related to freedom of expression, it is quite normal for the Inter-American Court to take note of the decisions of the European Court due to its experience in the subject.[116] The same happens among

[108] Jonathan I. Charney, "Is International Law Threatened by Multiple International Tribunals?" (1998) 271 Rec. des Cours Hague Acad. D. Int'l Haye 1001.

[109] Philippe Sands, Ruth Mackenzie and Yuval Shany, *Manual on International Courts and Tribunals* (Butterworths, London 1999) at 167–251; Project on International Courts and Tribunals, "Synoptic Chart v.3.0" online: PiCT <http://www.pict-pcti.org/publications/synoptic_chart/Synop_c4.pdf>.

[110] For example, the ICTY and the ICTR.

[111] Such as the ICC.

[112] Georges Abi-Saab, "Cours général de droit international public" (1987) 207 Rec. des Cours Hague Acad. D. Int'l Haye 8; Georges Abi-Saab, "Fragmentation or unification: some concluding remarks" (1999) 31 N.Y.U.J. Int'l L. & Pol. 919.

[113] *Prosecutor v. Furundžija*, IT-95-17/1, Judgment, (10 December 2003) at para. 153–157 (International Criminal Tribunal for the Former Yugoslavia).

[114] See *Al-Adsani v. United Kingdom* [GC], no. 35763/97, [2001] XI E.C.H.R. 79 at para. 61.

[115] See especially *Case of Maritza Urrutia (Guatemala)* (2003), Inter-Am. Ct. H.R. (Ser. C) No. 103, at para. 92.

[116] *Case of "The Last Temptation of Christ" (Olmedo-Bustos et al.) (Chile)* (2001), Inter-Am. Ct. H.R. (Ser C.) No. 73, at para. 69; *Case of Ivcher-Bronstein (Peru)* (2001), Inter-Am. Ct. H.R. (Ser C.) No. 74, at paras. 152, 153 and 155; *Case of Herrera-Ulloa (Costa Rica)* (2004), Inter-Am. Ct. H.R. (Ser C.) No. 107, at paras. 113, 122, 125, 134 and 170; *Case of Palamara-Iribarne (Chile)* (2005), Inter-Am. Ct. H.R. (Ser C.) No. 135, at paras. 178, and 219.

the international[117] and hybrid[118] *ad hoc* criminal tribunals, which constantly cite each other, especially the remarkably important precedents of the ICTY. More recently, the International Court of Justice (ICJ) noted that its interpretation of a particular provision of the African Charter of Human and Peoples' Rights was consistent with the interpretation by the European Court and Inter-American Court of analogous provisions in their respective substantive instruments.[119]

3.3.2 Regionalisation of Human Rights

Regionalism, as understood by the Report of the ILC, refers to methods for examining the law, techniques for law-making, or the geographical exception to the application of a universal rule. Probably the least controversial of these is that of law-making. As seen in the previous section, regional institutions have been among the main forces behind the evolution and promotion of international human rights law. Beyond the formal human rights structures of the Inter-American and European system, other regional organizations, such as the OECD, the EU and ASEAN, have worked towards the development of regional human rights standards. On the other hand, when speaking of regionalism as a particular theoretical perspective or an exception to 'universally accepted norms', the clash between the general and the particular does emerge. Interestingly enough, the ILC study group decided that: "the question of the universalism vs. regionalism opposition in human rights law (…) goes deep into the philosophical question of cultural relativism –and as such falls outside the ILC project on fragmentation".[120]

The problem is that, according to the ILC, coherence seems to imply unity: "the emergence of new and special types of law, 'self-contained regimes' and geographically or functionally limited treaty-systems creates problems of coherence in international law".[121] The fact that international human rights law is developed by a multi-pronged universal system and three regional arrangements does not make its study easy,

---

[117] *Prosecutor v. Ayyash et al.*, STL-11-01/I/TC, Decision to Hold Trial in Absentia, (1 February 2012) at para. 38 (where the Special Tribunal for Lebanon relayed on the ICTY's interpretation of "reasonable steps", in order to find that all reasonable steps required before proceeding to conduct a trial *in absentia* had been taken).

[118] *Co-Prosecutors v. Kaing Guek Eav*, 001/18-07-2007-ECCC/SC, Appeal Judgment, (3 February 2012) (The Supreme Court Chamber of the Extraordinary Chambers in the Courts of Cambodia for the Prosecution of Crimes Committed during the Period of Democratic Kampuchea found that, in considering the question of cumulative convictions, the Trial Chamber correctly resorted to the *C elebicìi* test elaborated in ICTY and ICTR jurisprudence).

[119] *Ahmadou Sadio Diallo (Republic of Guinea V. Democratic Republic of the Congo)*, Judgment (30 November 2010), at para. 68 (International Court of Justice), online: ICJ <http://www.icj-cij.org/docket/files/103/16244.pdf>.

[120] *Report*, *supra* note 107 at para. 216.

[121] *Ibid.* at para. 15.

but even in the independence of the systems and the cultural adaptation of claims, one can easily find a common architecture. In our opinion, regional production of norms is not only desirable but necessary for the evolution of international human rights law. For instance, it was not until 2006 that the United Nations created a binding universal instrument for the protection of people against forced disappearances, while in the Inter-American System a regional instrument has been in force since 1996. In fact, in other areas of international law the creation of a common universal framework has required the promotion of regional institutional arrangements that develop, contextualize, apply and enforce the universal rules.[122] As for the issue of cultural relativism, it is hard to understand why the ILC would consider this issue outside the scope of the project. As we have shown in the first section, the creation of regional institutions was highly influenced by the discourse of regional particularities, a positive cultural relativism which seeks to adapt and promote – rather than limit – the protection of human rights.

This analysis can be taken to a further level of fragmentation to consider the direct influence of state practice on the gradual development of international human rights. It is acknowledged that customary law emerges in large part as a result of the heterogenous positions taken by various states. The variety of domestic legal norms also shapes general principles of international law, the main vehicle used by the ICTY and ICTR to develop international criminal law in the last 15 years. All this is to show that international law, and particularly human rights law, is inherently dependent on the activities of local and regional arrangements to facilitate the negotiation and production of norms.

3.3.3 Human Rights as Self-Contained Regimes

A self-contained regime is a special set of rules including rights, obligations and sometimes institutions which precludes the systematic application of general international law. At this point, international human rights law is generally regarded a self-contained regime within international law.[123] For the purposes of the Report,

[122] The clearest example is that of the regime for the conservation and management of fish stocks created by the United Nations Fish Stocks Agreement, which rests on the premise that States will cooperate either through direct agreements or through subregional or regional fisheries management organizations or arrangements; *Agreement for the Implementation of the Provisions of the United Nations Convention on the Law of the Sea of 10 December 1982 Relating to the Conservation and Management of Straddling Fish Stocks and Highly Migratory Fish Stocks*, 4 August 1995, 2167 U.N.T.S. 3, 34 I.L.M. 1542 at art. 8.

[123] For instance, in the *Case of the Mapiripán Massacre*, the Inter-American Court rejected Colombia's argument about the applicability of the International Law Commission's *Draft Articles on Responsibility of States for Internationally Wrongful Acts*, stating that the American Convention "is inspired by higher shared values (focusing on protection of the human being), they have specific oversight mechanisms, they are applied according to the concept of collective guarantees, they embody obligations that are essentially objective, and their nature is special vis-à-vis other treaties that regulate reciprocal interests among the States Parties"; *Case of the Mapiripán Massacre (Colombia)* (2005), Inter-Am. Ct. H.R. (Ser. C) No. 134, at para. 104.

the existence of the regime in itself does not produce difficulties. A self-contained regime relates to general international law as any special norm would relate to a general one (*lex specialis derogate legi generali*). Difficulties only arise in the event of lacunae or the failure of the regime, whereupon general international law must be applied.

For the purposes of this essay, the question is not whether the emergence of international human rights law as a special regime has had an impact on the rules of general international law,[124] but whether the dislocation of human rights into sub-regimes undermines its universality. Focusing on international human rights law as the normative context in which we will work (that is, leaving behind international law as the conceptual framework and only looking within that field) it is possible to find fragmentation both in a thematic[125] and regional sense. The relationship between the three regional regimes and the universal system is one of cooperation. That is, while performing their duties autonomously, the diversity in the methods and results generally complement each other. For instance, the general rule is that the Inter-American system would not accept cases which are pending in other international fora.[126] However when the results which would be obtained in other institutions would differ from the possible reparations awarded in the system, both the Court and the Commission have heard and decided cases.[127] In this sense, regional institutions take seriously the nature and character of their judicial decisions, while respecting the political measures of, and the solutions thereby provided by, the special procedures of the United Nations' Charter and treaty bodies. Within the Universal System, and to a certain extent in the regional systems, there are different sets of rules and institutions which relate to special issues such as children's rights, equality and eradication of discrimination, the rights of migrant workers, domestic violence, etc. In both senses, the institutional arrangements are quite distinct, have different procedures, with different levels of participation of the victims and produce diverse formal outcomes.

The question is whether there is a clash of self-contained regimes in international human rights law. In the substantive aspect, human rights norms do not compete with each other. As seen before, regional instruments were created not to compete but to complement the universal normative base. In practice, both the Inter-American

[124] Lucius Caflisch and Antônio A. Cançado Trindade, "Les Conventions américaine et européenne des droit de l'homme et le droit international general" (2003) 108 Revue Général de Droit International Public 5.

[125] Or, as Mégret puts it: "one of the defining phenomena of the human rights project today is its increasing fragmentation along group lines", Frédéric Mégret, "The Human Rights of Older Persons: A Growing Challenge" (2011) 11:1 *Human Rights Law Review* 37 at 39.

[126] *American Convention*, *supra* note 65 at art. 46.1.c.

[127] In *Baena Ricardo*, the Court rejected Panama's argument that the case had already been dealt with by the International Labour Organization and the United Nations, by stating that the remedy provided by the Committee on Freedom of Association was of a collective nature, while the Court was hearing a case about individual rights, *Case of Baena Ricardo et al.(Panama)* (1999), Inter-Am. Ct. H.R. (Ser. C) No. 61; nowadays the Inter-American Court routinely hears cases which had already been discussed by the Special Rapporteurs of the United Nations, or by charter or treaty based bodies of the Universal System.

and European Courts share similar views and often quote each other.[128] Even the ICJ has noted the interpretation given by other tribunals to their respective instruments[129] and has "ascribe[d] great weight to the interpretation adopted by" the Human Rights Committee.[130] At the institutional level, human rights entities work under the principles of complementarity and coordination – that is, they will only receive a case if internal remedies have been exhausted and if it has not been sent to another international institution which might potentially decide on a similar issue. So the possibility of twice judging the same State for the violation of the same victim under the same set of facts in different human rights regimes is remote.

3.3.4 Hierarchies of Norms

The ILC noted that "[a]s a legal system, international law is not a random collection of such norms. There are meaningful relationships between them. Norms may thus exist at higher and lower hierarchical levels"[131] *Jus cogens* is defined by the ILC as "A rule of international law [...] superior to other rules on account of the importance of its content as well as the universal acceptance of its superiority."[132] This means that whenever there is a relationship of conflict between two norms in which one is *jus cogens*, the latter will prevail. This is relevant for the purposes of human rights in the sense that even self-contained regimes have to comply with the general peremptory norms established outside the regime. Interestingly enough, the report enumerates the norms most frequently cited as *jus cogens*: "prohibition of aggression, slavery and the slave trade, genocide, racial discrimination apartheid and torture, as well as basic rules of international humanitarian law applicable in armed conflict, and the right to self-determination."[133] Most of the above are either human rights norms, or norms which are necessary or corollary to the respect of human rights. Even if established in universal instruments, it is hardly an issue that a human rights entity would derogate from one of these norms in the benefit of another right. However, the ICJ has suggested that the conflict between norms, one being a *jus cogens* norm, would have to be direct for the latter to prevail over the other. In the words of the Court: "[t]o the extent that it is argued that no rule which is not of the status of *jus cogens* may be applied if to do so would hinder the enforcement of a *jus cogens* rule, even in the absence of a direct conflict, the Court sees no basis for such a proposition."[134]

---

[128] See Caflisch and Cançado Trindade, *supra* note 124.

[129] *Ahmadou Sadio Diallo*, *supra* note 119 at para. 68.

[130] *Ibid.* at para. 66.

[131] *Conclusions*, *supra* note 106 at para. 251 (1).

[132] *Ibid.* at para. 251 (32).

[133] *Ibid.* at para. 251 (33).

[134] *Jurisdictional Immunities of the State (Germany v. Italy: Greece Intervening)*, Judgment (3 February 2012), at para. 95 (International Court of Justice), online: ICJ <http://www.icj-cij.org/docket/files/143/16883.pdf>.

All of the above shows that the debate over fragmentation seems to overlook the benefits of institutional multiplication and regionalism, and tends to overstate the possibility of normative clashes. At the heart of the issue is the desirability of a plural international law for a plural world.

3.4 A Fragmented But Universal Human Rights Regime?

The idea of fragmentation is one which resonates with respect to not only international law but the idea of law in general. We now offer a critique grounded in the insights offered by legal pluralism, situating the fragmentation debate within a broader discussion of the degree to which law can be said to be unified. On that basis, this section explores some of the implications of a more nuanced idea of unity for the claim to universality embedded at the heart of the human rights regime.

The world is a pluralistic place, while legal normativity aspires to coherence, predictability and (at least relative) equality. There lies a tension at the heart of the idea of law which is most commonly resolved in practice by attributing to an entity, nowadays usually the state, a monopoly for enacting and enforcing law. The legitimacy and efficiency of such monopolies have long been questioned but, under a positivistic reading, the relative efficiency of formal law provides a layer of satisfaction which has relegated this debate to the more rarefied theoretical spheres. Public international law stands as an oddity in this respect, because of the near absence of any institution like a super-state to which might be granted the kind of monopolies given to the state in the domestic context. A standard reaction has been to simply deny that public international law is law at all, under a rather narrow positivistic reading of the concept of law.[135] Approaches eschewing this narrow vision of law in favour of a broader notion of legal normativity are confronted in perhaps a more immediate and necessary manner with the tension between diversity and law. This explains the comparatively greater salience of a debate regarding the universality of international law than its equivalent under domestic law, however equally warranted that latter debate might be in some respects.

How likely is it that the universalist narrative conveyed by international human rights law could be verified by the normative fabric of its legal standards? Even if a process could be imagined whereby truly cross-cultural or trans-cultural values could be identified and given a legal expression, it would seem unlikely to correspond to the ways in which treaty standards have been agreed upon, customary norms produced, and general principles sublimated. As shown earlier in this paper in the section retelling the troubled path needed to ensure the emergence of the Universal Declaration and other human rights instruments, all norms represent value

[135] Cf. H.L.A. Hart, *The Concept of Law* (Oxford: Clarendon Press, 1961); Eric Posner, *The Perils of Global Legalism* (Chicago: University of Chicago Press, 2009). On unity, see Mario Prost, *The Concept of Unity in Public International Law* (Oxford: Hart Publishing, 2012).

choices which will not necessarily be embraced by all. The idea of violence at the core of this creative process was forcefully articulated by Robert Cover, describing how courts in reaching decisions smother alternate narratives in favour of a chosen one.[136] To this idea, first developed in the context of domestic constitutional adjudication, must be added that of the intercultural nature of the selection process when considering international human rights standards. In municipal law, the suppression of other legal narratives in favour of a state-sanctioned one might not be necessarily as intercultural because of the tighter bonds linking different members of the polity within a given state. The democratic nature of public institutions is a second factor which might endow official norms with a measure of legitimacy despite the reluctance of some to embrace the substance of a given norm. Turning to international human rights law, while it would surely be an exaggeration to suggest that cultural debates will systematically arise with respect to the emergence of every norm, and that cultural difference will be more prominent than ideological, economic, political and other types of differences, it seems reasonable to conclude that the acknowledged cultural plurality of the world 'community' will play out in the process whereby international norms are created. Likewise, despite the presence of safeguards to ensure the formal equality of states and the broad fairness of the creation of international law, that process is far from meeting any definition of democracy. As a result, it appears that international human rights law cannot realistically be assumed to escape cultural profiling.

In cultural terms, international law navigates between hegemonic unity and anarchical diversity.[137] In a hegemonic model, norms are adopted because they are presented as universalised goods which ought to be pursued and embraced by all. Differences which might arise are presented as relating to particular articulations or applications of a universal set of values. This need not necessarily rest on an objective, natural or transcultural notion of truth, although such justifications are commonly presented. It can also reflect a pragmatic claim that the values embodied in international law represent a greater aspiration, subject to its eventual displacement by something said to be even better.[138] In an anarchical model, cultures are presented as immanently transient, contingent, fragmented, with only passing and limited areas of convergence linking some of them at some point. Within that model, the identification and adoption of transcultural or intercultural norms are well-neigh impossible, save perhaps for the most general principles which will offer little guidance and impose only the lightest constraints on international agents. A perfect embodiment of either the hegemonic or anarchical model is unlikely to be found in positive international law, but they help understand the dynamics of the norm-creation process.

[136] Robert M. Cover, "The Supreme Court 1982 Term—Foreword: Nomos and Narrative" (1983) 97 Harvard Law Review 629.

[137] See Mireille Delmas-Marty, *Le relatif et l'universel: Les forces imaginantes du droit* (Paris: Seuil, 2004) at 414.

[138] See Richard Rorty, "Solidarity or Objectivity" in Lawrence Cahoone, ed., *From Modernism to Postmodernism: An Anthology* (Cambridge: Blackwell, 1996) at 573; Richard Rorty, "Human Rights, Rationality and Sentimentality" in Stephen Shute and Susan L. Hurley, eds., *On Human Rights* (New York: Basic Books, 1993) at 111.

In the hegemonic model, the pluralisation of the processes whereby international human rights law is created has meant that it is now much more difficult for a relatively homogenous grouping of states to directly impose its approach on the rest of the world community, as could perhaps be done in an earlier epoch of international law. This is not to underestimate the influence of power asymmetries, along various vectors, but rather to suggest that the image so vividly conveyed by Cover of one actor being able to "kill" alternate legal narratives seems realistic only under a positivistic outlook on law. When law is reduced to the normative by-product of the state, then a monopoly perhaps can effectively be created. On the other hand, under a more pluralistic vision of law which considers multiple, overlapping and interacting normative regimes, it seems unlikely that any single actor – even the state – could effectively eliminate competing legal narratives. Even when considering domestic constitutional adjudication, it seems plausible that not everyone will embrace the approach chosen by the courts. To repeat, positivism leads us to conclude that the rejected narrative is simply not "the law". For pluralists, however, rejection by the state's organ will affect the rejected narrative but probably not succeed *ipso facto* in eradicating it. Indeed, resistance to the formal legal narrative will contribute to identifying the boundaries of official law and shaping its content and identity.[139] Returning to international law, we find basically no monopolies of the kind embodied by courts in the domestic adjudication process. Even the International Court of Justice is granted only a peripheral and optional competence, relating solely to states party to a case pursuant to their express consent. Likewise, the International Criminal Court suffers from significant limitations to its competence. This leaves out many states, many issues, and many other international legal actors. In that context, the possibility of creating a fully hegemonic international legal order appears remote. For the reasons just outlined, there cannot be any purely institutional solution, and even a world human rights court could not bring about true unity when law is considered from a legal pluralist perspective.

At the other end of the spectrum, the anarchical model revolves around the notion that diversity, cultural and otherwise, results in an international 'community' (for lack of a better word) which is fragmented in so many different ways that normative consensus is impossible. While it is plausible that such diversity is always present, the model appears unlikely to be materialised in international law because it fails to acknowledge to a sufficient degree the convergence of interests among particular classes of actors, around identified issues, in a given conjuncture. In this respect, the legal pluralism literature and, in particular, the critical legal pluralists, seem to give insufficient attention to the state in their attempt to underscore the significance of non-state normative regimes. Even in the context of domestic law, writers with a degree of sympathy for a pluralist understanding of law have questioned the extent to which the state could be marginalised in an analysis of legal normativity.[140] The critique plays out equally forcefully in the international legal sphere, in which

[139] See Nathaniel Berman, "In the Wake of Empire" (1999) 14 *American University International Law Review* 1515 at 1547.

[140] Jeremy Webber, "Legal Pluralism and Human Agency" (2006) 44 Osgoode Hall L.J. 167.

the state remains the privileged actor around which the entire normative structure is organised.[141] Still today, the architecture of the international human rights regime owes much to its initial conception as a bulwark protecting the individual against abuses from the state. Thus statehood is one factor of commonality among those centrally empowered to create international law. The need of all states to legitimise their own existence and power can be taken as one point of convergence around which norms can be created.[142] Pockets of convergence will thus emerge within the fabric of international relations, not necessarily incorporating all states but at times a group sufficiently influential to pave the way for agreement on some international norms. In the human rights field, this resulted in the emergence over time of regional and specialised regimes rather than, or in addition to, universal comprehensive human rights codes.

International law is a regime which encompasses a series of normative pockets in which it proved possible to identify converging interests. Absent any institution entrusted with the responsibility to oversee the development of international law as a whole, it has always grown in fits and starts, responding to passing crises or visionary aspirations. In the emerging period of positive international law, for example, there seemed to have been no particular concern for coherence between, say, state responsibility for injury to aliens and the laws of war. What lately has come to constitute the terms of the debate over the fragmentation of international law corresponds to the acceleration of the creation of more and more pockets of law.[143] Where James Brierly could note 70 years ago that international law imposed no restriction on the imposition of tariffs on transnational trade or the manner in which a Government treated its own citizens on the national territory, the notion of a reserved domain shielding state activities from international regulation has been steadily shrinking since then.[144] There is little state or human activity today which lies beyond the application of some international legal standard; few issues, if any, are not amenable to being cast as a human rights claim. The widening breadth of international law did not correspond to a structured and controlled widening of a coherent regime. Much as there was a degree of relative autonomy between rules on state responsibility for the treatment of aliens and the laws of war in the nineteenth century, there remains a lack of integration among the constellation of normative pockets forming international law today. Thus, trade law, human rights law, environmental law, space law, the law of the sea, and many others, each coexist as a specialised

[141] See Volker Röben, "What About Hobbes? Legitimacy as a Matter of Inclusion in the Functional and Rational Exercise of International Public Power" in Rüdiger Wolfrum and Volker Röben, eds., *Legitimacy in International Law* (Berlin: Springer, 2008) at 356 (Whether states can be expected to obey international law depends in essence on their being included in the exercise of this [public] power).

[142] See Jörn Rüsen, "Human Rights from the Perspective of a Universal History" in Wolfgang Schmale, ed., *Human Rights and Cultural Diversity* (Goldblach: Keip Publishing, 1993) at 40.

[143] See *Conclusions*, *supra* note 106.

[144] J. L. Brierly, *The Law of Nations: An Introduction to the International Law of Peace*, 1st ed. (Oxford: Clarendon Press, 1930).

field operating in many ways in relative ignorance of the others.[145] Within the field of human rights, regional systems in Europe, the Americas and Africa have evolved with a degree of relative autonomy from one another as well as with regard to corresponding global human rights regimes.

The idea of pluralism is useful here again, in that it enriches the notion of plurality. Whereas plurality speaks to the existence of multiple entities, in this case normative regimes, pluralism underscores the necessary interaction among these regimes.[146] To this corresponds the critique of the notion of "self-contained regimes" which would ultimately operate in full isolation from the rest of international law. Regimes which at one point were presented as self-contained, for example international trade law or the law of the European Union, have been shown conclusively to be rooted in notions belonging to other parts of international law (eg. the law of treaties, state responsibility) and to interact constantly with other regimes (eg. environmental law, human rights law).[147] This corresponds in the field of human rights to a well-documented practice whereby institutions of one regime will give due consideration to approaches developed in another one.[148] A striking example is the propagation of a state's duty to prevent, investigate and punish violations of human rights even if they cannot be attributed to the state itself, first developed by the Inter-American Court of Human Rights in the *Velasques-Rodriguez* case but later adopted in a variety of other human rights regimes.

That said, the accelerating institutionalisation of international law, often taking the form of specialised adjudication bodies, does not necessarily forecast greater coherence among the various component regimes. As noted by Pierre-Marie Dupuy:

> [C]ertains des régimes conventionnels existants étant dotés d'un système spécifique de contrôle de leur légalité, la multiplication de ces organes risque d'aboutir, plus encore qu'à une fragmentation du droit, à l'émergence de féodalités normatives. Chacune, jalouse de ses prérogatives ou de son originalité, sera tentée de privilégier ses règles sur toute autre et de donner à des principes pourtant communs une interprétation singulière.[149]

Not only does the creation of more institutions not in itself signal a convergence among the various regimes forming international law, but it would be dangerous to assume that incoherence is limited to the interaction among these regimes. Even within a unified conventional regime equipped with sophisticated institutions, including courts competent to issue binding decisions, coherence cannot be taken

---

[145] *Conclusions*, *supra* note 106 at para. 251 (11).

[146] Mireille Delmas-Marty, *Le pluralisme ordonné: les forces imaginantes du droit (II)* (Paris: Seuil, 2006) at 18.

[147] See *Report*, *supra* note 107 at 248; Pierre-Marie Dupuy, "L'unité de l'ordre juridique international: cours général de droit international public" (2002) 297 Rec. des Cours Hague Acad. D. Int'l Haye 9 at 432.

[148] Carlos Iván Fuentes, " Normative Plurality in International Law: The Role of Soft Law in the Jurisprudence of the Inter-American Court of Human Rights" (Paper presented at the conference 'Theorizing the Global Legal Order', Swansea University, 21–22 May 2008) at 10, online: SSRN <http://ssrn.com/abstract=1134101>.

[149] Dupuy, *supra* note 146 at 429.

for granted. This is well illustrated by the doctrine of the margin of appreciation under the European Convention on Human Rights, allowing for limited fragmentation in a regime bringing together a relatively homogenous group of states and endowed with one of the best enforcement mechanisms in international law.[150] The margin of appreciation amounts to the formal recognition within a regime of diversity which, more often than not, will remain unacknowledged as such.

The fragmented evolution of international law described up to now has focussed on the episodic convergence of state interests. While the international legal system remains structured around the state, it has grown over the last century to give greater recognition to actors other than states. International organisations, peoples, individuals, corporations, and NGOs all have benefited, to significantly variable degrees, of an increasing willingness to ascribe legal personality to non-state actors. One might mention the ICJ *Advisory Opinion on Reparations for Injury Suffered in the Service of the United Nations*, on the ability of the UN to present a claim under the law of international responsibility, the ICTY decision in *The Prosecutor v. Simic*, regarding the International Committee of the Red Cross' customary immunity against compelled testimony before international tribunals, and *Presbyterian Chruch of Sudan v. Talisman Energy*, a US Federal Court decision which found that a corporation could directly violate the prohibition of genocide under international law.[151] The emergence of new legal persons has had an impact on the processes whereby international norms are created. Resolutions of international organisations have been taken to influence, under certain circumstances, the emergence of customary international law[152]; the practice of the International Committee of the Red Cross has been considered as relevant by the ICTY in its assessment of the existence of a customary rule[153]; non-governmental organisations have been shown to have exerted real influence in every phase of the negotiations of international instruments.[154]

---

[150] Delmas-Marty, *supra* note 146 at 15.

[151] *Reparation for Injuries Suffered in the Service of the United Nations*, Advisory Opinion, [1949] I.C.J. Rep. 174; *Prosecutor v. Blagoje Simi et al.* IT-95-9-A, Decision on the Prosecution Motion Under Rule 73 for a Ruling Concerning the Testimony of a Witness, 27 July 1999 (International Criminal Tribunal for the Former Yugoslavia, Appeals Chamber); *Presbyterian Church of Sudan v. Talisman Energy, Inc.*, 374 F.Supp.2d 331, at 335–336 (S.D. N.Y. 2005), aff'd 582 F.3d 244 (2d Cir. 2009); see also *Sosa v. Alvarez-Machain*, 542 U.S. 692 at fn. 20 (2004). In the United States, the Supreme Court likely will pronounce on this issue, probably sometime in 2013, in the case of *Kiobel v. Royal Dutch Petroleum Co.*, 621 F.3d 111 (2d Cir. 2010).

[152] *Texaco Overseas Petroleum Company & California Asiatic Oil Company v. the Government of the Libyan Arab Republic* (1977), 17 I.L.M. 1 at paras. 80–90, 53 I.L.R. 389, 104 J.D.I. 350 (Sole Arbitrator: René-Jean Dupuy); *Legality of the Threat or Use of Nuclear Weapons Case*, Advisory Opinion, [1996] I.C.J. Rep. 206 at para. 70–73. See Jose Alvarez, "Are Corporations 'Subjects' of International Law?" (November 5, 2010) Santa Clara Journal of International Law, Forthcoming; NYU School of Law, Public Law Research Paper No. 10–77. Available at SSRN: http://ssrn.com/abstract=1703465

[153] Prosecutor v. Duško Tadić (Prijedor Case), IT-94-1, Decision on the Defence Motion for Interlocutory Appeal on Jurisdiction, 2 October 1995, at paras. 108–108 (International Criminal Tribunal for the Former Yugoslavia, Appeals Chamber).

[154] Gaëlle Breton-Le Goff, *L'influence des organisations non gouvernementales (ONG) sur la négociation de quelques instruments internationaux* (Bruxelles: Bruylant, 2001).

Over the last 50 years, the aspirations embodied in the human rights regime have evolved. Rooted in the horrors of the Second World War, the Universal Declaration of Human Rights primarily aimed at preventing abuses of individuals and groups at the hand of states. While the necessity and centrality of a focus on the state have never really seriously been challenged, a widening range of other issues have been analysed using the human rights toolkit. Some of the very same entities identified as having emerged under international law with a degree of legal personality – international organisations, multinational corporations, nongovernmental organisations, armed insurgents, individuals – have also been singled out as the authors of violations of human rights. This widening aspiration has some times taken the form of a focus on duties, as exemplified by the 1998 Valencia Declaration on Human Duties and Responsibilities, and other times been cast simply as the application of existing standards to non-state actors.[155] This can be taken to correspond to another form of fragmentation of the human rights regime, given that there are normative and institutional features of mainstream human rights law which are unsuited or formally inapplicable to actors other than states. One can mention the ideas of derogations in times of emergency and the doctrine of the margin of appreciation as examples of the former, and the explicit state focus of the competence of most human rights bodies as an instance of the latter. Here again, legal pluralism can offer some interesting insights, articulating a notion of (human rights) law capable of accommodating a certain incoherence among various legal fragments, insisting on the richness of both the interaction among the parts and the normative *métissage* which is its ineluctable result.[156] In considering every actor as a site of both production and application of human rights, the idea that states bear the responsibility for the governance of the human rights regime is jettisoned, making every actor bear some of the burden of building and supporting the regime.[157]

What are the implications for the universality of human rights law of a perspective which abandons the positivist idea of fragmentation in favour of a pluralist notion of multiple, overlapping and interacting human rights regimes? Is every government, corporation, organisation, individual, a normative island, inhospitable to any overarching claim by a universal human rights regime? Does it amount to the cultural relativist

[155] Andrew Clapham, *Human Rights Obligations of Non-state Actors* (Oxford: Oxford University Press, 2006).

[156] Nicholas Kasirer, "Legal Education as Metissage" (2003) 78 Tulane Law Review 481; Emmanuelle Jouannet, "Universalism and Imperialism: The True-False Paradox of International Law?" (2007) 18 European Journal of International Law 379.

[157] See Martti Koskenniemi, "International Law: Between Fragmentation and Constitutionalism", (Paper presented in Camberra, 27 November 2006) online: Australian National University <http://cigj.anu.edu.au/cigj/link_documents/KoskenniemiPaper.pdf>; David Kennedy, "One, Two, Three, Many Legal Orders: Legal Pluralism and the Cosmopolitan Dream", (Paper presented to the International Law Association-British Branch, 4 March 2006) online: HLS <http://www.law.harvard.edu/faculty/dkennedy/speeches/LegalOrders.pdf>; Iulia Motoc, "Conception of Pluralism and International Law" in Helene Ruiz Fabri, Emmanuelle Jouannet and Vincent Tomkiewitz, eds., Select Proceedings of the European Society of International Law (Oxford: Hart Publishing, 2008).

defeat of any universalistic claim by human rights? One does not follow from the other. In the debate surrounding cultural relativism in human rights, the latter were challenged as being specific to Western constructs, alien to 'other' cultures. Indeed, in this debate, the clash was presented as involving law on the one hand and something else on the other.[158] The radical asymmetry perceived to exist between legal norms and cultural standards resulted in a sense that law had either to overcome the cultural particularity of a given context or be limited by way of concessions to this context.[159] According to a legal pluralist perspective, human rights law cannot be taken as a monolithic edifice clashing with an equally monolithic cultural context. Human rights, as we have argued, are composed of fragmented, multiple, overlapping sets of norms. Likewise, cultural referents can be taken as normative, subject to constant intersections and exchanges with other traditions.[160] Conversely, it can also be said that human rights law has become a form of cultural practice, itself the proper subject of anthropological enquiry, liable to interact as such with distinct cultures.[161] Under both characterisations, the human rights regime, of which the Universal Declaration can be taken to be the centrepiece, becomes a privileged space for deliberation on values and rules among a great diversity of actors, rather than simply a set of targets or minimum thresholds to be imposed on everyone.[162]

3.5 Conclusion

The recent debate about the fragmentation of international law helps to illuminate the ways in which the Universal Declaration of Human Rights ought to be seen as truly living up to its name. In the field of human rights, invoked every day by victims in their hour of need in the most immediate fashion, the urge to instrumentalise these norms in the most positivistic fashion can prove irresistible. But the human rights regime can hardly live up to such exacting expectations, for reasons which owe more to the nature of legal discourse than to any institutional weakness in the human rights 'system'. Rights are a powerful rhetorical tool which can achieve a degree of social engineering, but it seems unrealistic to conceive of them as standing

[158] Karen Engle, "From Skepticism to Embrace: Human Rights and the American Anthropological Association from 1947–1999" (2001) 23 Human Rights Quarterly 536; Sally Engle Merry, "Human Rights Law and the Demonization of Culture (And Anthropology Along the Way)" (2003) 26 PoLAR: Political & Legal Anthropology Review 55 at 60; Annelise Riles, "Anthropology, Human Rights, and Legal Knowledge: Culture in the Iron Cage" (2006) 108 American Anthropologist 52.

[159] Mickelson, *supra* note 6.

[160] See generally H. Patrick Glenn, *Legal Traditions of the World: Sustainable Diversity in Law*, 3rd ed. (Oxford: Oxford University Press, 2007).

[161] Riles, *supra* note 158.

[162] Jouannet, *supra* note 156 at 397.

above or outside of the space occupied by social values. The human rights regime, itself fragmented horizontally among various sub-regimes and vertically among diverse categories of actors, is properly taken as a universally significant element in a permanent process of deliberation about fundamental human values. It is by providing common terms in a dialogue about visions of a just society that human rights can make a claim to universality. Legal instruments like the Universal Declaration are thus distillations of collective struggles and learning.[163] In this fashion, as exemplified by the idea of unity in diversity, the concepts of universality and unity appear not only distinct but even in tension. In other words, it is through fragmentation that human rights can aspire to universality.

[163] Seyla Benhabib, "The Legitimacy of Human Rights," (2008) 137:3 *Daedalus* 94–104; Seyla Benhabib, "Another Universalism: On the Unity and Diversity of Human Rights," (2007) 81:2 *Proceedings and Addresses of the American Philosophical Association* 7–32.

Chapter 4
International Human Rights and Global Legal Pluralism: A Research Agenda

Frédéric Mégret

International human rights and legal pluralism may seem like strange bedfellows. On the one hand, human rights is a normative project that is largely seen as unifying and cosmopolitan in inspiration vying, perhaps, to become a sort of supra-national, global law; legal pluralism, on the other hand, typically describes the coexistence of irreducible legal orders within a similar space, and their emergence from a variety of fragmented sources. Nonetheless, the two arguably more in common than immediately catches the eye, in that international human rights is more legally pluralistic than is sometimes assumed, and legal pluralism is an interesting way of understanding the process of production of international human rights norms.

This chapter will be interested specifically in the idea of *international* human rights law, as the projection of the idea of rights protection, originally primarily conceived as a reality domestically, onto the international sphere. Because of lack of space but also because it is analytically a different issue, this chapter will not be concerned with the question of international human rights law's impact on issues of *domestic* legal pluralism and rights.[1] I am interested in how international human rights as a normative system comes into being and persists as a form that is both

[1] I note that this is obviously a big omission and that one of the ways in which the international human rights/legal pluralist paradigm could be very useful is in dissecting how international human rights might encourage/discourage forms of legal pluralism. Examples that come to mind are the emergence of religious courts in otherwise secular states to cater to the demands of religious minorities (N. Bakht, *Family Arbitration Using Sharia Law: Examining Ontario's Arbitration Act and Its Impact on Women*, 1 MUSLIM WORLD JOURNAL OF HUMAN RIGHTS (2004).), the use of legal pluralism in (re)constructing domestic legal orders in fractured societies (e.g.: B. R. Rubin, *Transitional Justice and Human Rights in Afghanistan*, 79 INTERNATIONAL AFFAIRS (ROYAL INSTITUTE OF INTERNATIONAL AFFAIRS 1944) 567–581 (2003). L. Grenfell, *Legal Pluralism and the Rule of Law in Timor Leste*, 19 LEIDEN JOURNAL OF INTERNATIONAL LAW 305–337 (2006)).

F. Mégret (✉)
Faculty of Law, Centre for Human Rights and Legal Pluralism, McGill University,
Montreal, QC H3A 1W9, Canada
e-mail: frederic.megret@mcgill.ca

R. Provost and C. Sheppard (eds.), *Dialogues on Human Rights and Legal Pluralism*, Ius Gentium: Comparative Perspectives on Law and Justice 17,
DOI 10.1007/978-94-007-4710-4_4,

deeply unitary and fragmented. International human rights arguably radicalize some of the anxieties of human rights about this form which, if anything, make a legal pluralist analysis even more useful. I lay no claim to a canonical understanding of legal pluralism, although I fully acknowledge the term has particular associations and connotations in socio-legal discourse. For the sake of clarity, the legal pluralism paradigm this study will be closest to is that sometimes associated with the expression "global legal pluralism," one focused on "multiple, overlapping normative communities" and their "inevitable intermingling".[2] However, I will also draw on the legacy of other forms of legal pluralism that have been identified either in the colonial or post-industrial context and which have a bearing on the issue if only because they have enlightened our understanding of the theoretical bases of multiple coexisting normativities.

This chapter seeks only to outline the contours of what might be a research agenda focusing on the intersection between the two, its potential and its limits. In doing so, I will draw on existing work, but also suggest new directions. There has been relatively little research, at least until recently, at the intersection of international human rights and legal pluralism. Several factors explain this relative lack of interest that are linked to (human rights) biases about both human rights and the nature of things international. As far as the former are concerned, one obstacle is the Enlightenment view of human rights as very much about transcending a particular form of legal pluralism, namely that of the *Ancien régime*, which saw different rules apply to different "*corps intermédiaires*". Indeed, there is a strong sense that human rights, in their universality and already being something of a minimum, should apply equally to all. This means that conceiving of rights as being mediated by particular legal spheres, a fortiori not positively legal spheres, is likely to raise some resistance. There may be a subtle perception that diversity in rights, a fortiori of the legal orders in which they become located somehow negates the idea of rights, that what makes rights (as opposed to say mere rules) is that they must the same everywhere. Another obstacle is a construct of human rights as being opposed to the untrammeled demands of the sovereign and as therefore in a sense already preempting some of the critique of legal pluralism.

None of these arguments are particularly convincing to the legal pluralist. The universality of rights does not in and itself lead to a claim about the necessary

---

[2] P. S. Berman, *The New Legal Pluralism: Defining the Field*, ANNUAL REVIEW OF LAW AND SOCIAL SCIENCE, 226 (2009); R. Michaels, *Global Legal Pluralism*, ANNUAL REVIEW OF LAW AND SOCIAL SCIENCE (2009); R. Michaels, *Re-State-ment of Non-State Law: The State, Choice of Law, and the Challenge from Global Legal Pluralism, The*, 51 WAYNE LAW REVIEW 1209 (2005); O. Perez, *Normative Creativity and Global Legal Pluralism: Reflections on the Democratic Critique of Transnational Law*, 10 INDIANA JOURNAL OF GLOBAL LEGAL STUDIES 25 (2003); S. E. Merry, *International Law and Sociolegal Scholarship: Toward a Spatial Global Legal Pluralism*, 41 STUDIES IN LAW, POLITICS AND SOCIETY 149–168 (2008); S. E. Merry, Human rights and global legal pluralism: Reciprocity and disjuncture, in F. von Benda-Beckmann, K. von Benda-Beckmann & A. Griffiths (eds) *Mobile people, mobile law. Expanding legal relations in a contracting world*. Aldershot: Ashgate 215–232 (2005). P. S. Berman, *Global Legal Pluralism*, 80 SOUTHERN CALIFORNIA LAW REVIEW 1155 (2006).

uniformity of their application. Simply because international human rights law shares with legal pluralism a concern with state centralism, moreover, hardly means that the two are identical. In fact, one could argue that international human rights law challenges state centralism "from above" and with a view to reducing states' distinctiveness, where legal pluralism challenges state centrism from below, and with a view to opening up domestic legal orders to a much greater diversity of legal regimes. These are two distinct projects, and international human rights law does not have a monopoly on challenging the state's stronghold. In fact, the claim that human rights is "against" the state can be overdone and human rights discourse, in being classically and almost obsessively addressed to the state, has often ended up being very dependent on its central position in law making, and even arguably become part of the fabric of the legitimization of (the right sort of) sovereignty. Conversely, legal pluralism is in some ways more genuinely skeptical and dismissive of the state as the central locus of norm generation.

The argument can also been made that international human rights is obsessed with issues concerning the *international* deployment of human rights, emphasizing a top-down and unitary approach at the expense of the diversity of logics involved. In this respect, international human rights is always at risk, like much of international law, of incorporating wholesale in its conceptual apparatus notions of law derived from the ideology of "legal centralism". The emphasis is typically on an "international human rights system",[3] with its overtone of a well-organized, coherent and hierarchical body of rules and institutions. In some ways, international human rights law can be seen as a normative system that aspires to be sovereign itself. In some ways, international human rights it the ultimate manifestation of an aspiration to see the international system operate under the guidance of a unique framework,[4] and therefore a negation of legal pluralism.

It should be noted, in all fairness, that legal pluralists had until recently shown little interest for analyzing the international realm, or indeed for thinking about the relationship of the paradigm to human rights. After the study of colonial and post-colonial societies, and subsequently the rediscovery of the multiplicity of legal centres that populate industrialized societies, global legal pluralism has only recently emerged as a sort of "third generation" of legal pluralism. Notwithstanding, there are many reasons to think that international human rights law is a natural candidate for analysis in terms of legal pluralism. My main contention will be that international human rights law is seen too much as a cosmopolitan law in the making, and not enough as a decentralized, disorderly, internally diverse process.

[3] J. W. Nickel, *Is Today's International Human Rights System a Global Governance Regime?*, 6 The Journal of Ethics, 4 (2002). Henry J. Steiner, Philip Alston & Ryan Goodman, *International human rights in context: law, politics, morals: Text and materials/Henry J. Steiner, Philip Alston, Ryan Goodman*, 3rd ed. (Oxford [UK]; New York: Oxford University Press, 2008).

[4] The current project to set up an international human rights court might be seen to be part of this drive. M. Nowak, *The Need for a World Court of Human Rights*, 7 Human Rights Law Review 251–259 (2007); S. Trechsel, *World Court for Human Rights, A*, 1 Northwestern University Journal of International Human Rights i (2003).

I suggest a more complex view of international human rights law as a branch of law deeply dependent on legally plural forms that sit in uneasy tension with international human rights unifying thrust. The international human rights project is marked by a fundamental "centralization/decentralization dynamic" that is made even more complex by the emergence of supranational norms.[5] International human rights law develops through its interaction with both constituted legal orders and a variety of informal ones. I will suggest that acknowledging its debt to a plurality of legal forms is one of the ways in which international human rights law can better understand how it comes into being as a system of norms. Indeed, I will argue that it is only a misplaced view of how international human rights is *supposed* to work (through an analogy with state law that overestimates the extent to which state law itself functions the way it is sometimes presented as functioning) that leads to perennial disappointment about its perceived "failures". A better understanding of the contribution of legal pluralism to international human rights law is also needed to counter over-broad, excessively functionalizing and potentially hegemonic claims made on behalf of international human rights.

I suggest two, quite distinct, ways in which international human rights and legal pluralism might be articulated, which roughly correspond to John Griffith's understanding of "weak" and "strong" legal pluralism.[6] First, international human rights might be seen as itself *a form of legal pluralism* (i.e. as an internally pluralistic order), tolerant of a wide range of different legal and normative orders. This is a sort of "top down" legal pluralism, one that sees pluralism as the product of a particular international legal form. It is also what might be described as an "internal" look on international human rights law, one that understands pluralism as a constitutive category. Second, international human rights might be seen as coming into being *through* the operation of a diversity of legal orders. This is the "bottom up" version of legal pluralism, one that emphasizes how legal pluralism both challenges and (thus) produces international human rights law. It is a more distinctly "external" take on international human rights, although not a fully external take on the law (in that the law is understood to include these islands of normativity, even if they do not acknowledge each other). These two meanings are in some ways radically distinct and even in some ways incompatible, but can also be seen as part of a complex loop: international human rights tolerates a certain diversity, and that diversity then energizes the international human rights project.

[5] J. G. Belley, "*L'État et la régulation juri dique des sociétés globales. Pour une problématique du pluralisme juridique*", 18 Sociologie et Sociétés 11–32 (1986).

[6] J. Griffiths, *What Is Legal Pluralism*, 24 Journal of Legal Pluralism & Unofficial L. 1 (1986).

4.1 International Human Rights as Legal Pluralism

A first way in which one might think about international human rights and legal pluralism is by considering that international human rights as a legal system in itself tolerant and even encouraging of forms of pluralism. This closely parallels a tension in international human rights between "universalism" and "relativism", one which legal pluralism may be particularly apt at transcending. Pluralism here might be the opposite of "monism" not as it is traditionally understood in international law doctrine (i.e.: the approach that says that international law norms are directly applicable domestically), but as a monism of regime. In this section I suggest some of the ways in which international human rights law may have evolved naturally plural forms.

4.1.1 The Foundations of International Human Rights' Pluralism

4.1.1.1 International Human Rights, Value Pluralism and Normative Diversity

A legal pluralistic agenda might begin by emphasizing the extent to which international human rights law is perhaps all the more prone to encouraging a certain diversity that it is conceptually a product of diversity. The human rights project itself might be seen as an the heir to a profound realization that values are irreducible. From a classical liberal perspective, the ambition of human rights is to permit competing views of the good society to take hold whilst protecting certain basic social goods. Of course that supposedly "thin" theory of justice is always vulnerable to the accusation that it is in fact quite "thick" and, in particular, embedded in certain presuppositions intimately linked to Western social and political developments, in particular about the individual and the nature of political association. In practice human rights seek to present themselves as a minimal ideology, one that is not only tolerant but highly protective of a number of world views; of course, however, that pluralism has its limits and diversity is, ultimately, constrained by human rights' core tenets.

Moreover, international human rights law can be seen as the product of numerous normative strands which have led it to develop as a "normative system of normative systems", one that is arguably naturally prone to a certain broad inclusiveness. First, international human rights law is already a fusion of different concepts of law: human rights were conceived as natural rights, yet became embedded in positive public international law, and their development is marked by a constant tension between the two. Second, international human rights is the product of the tension between many thriving, domestic cultures of human rights. Needless to say the adoption of the UDHR or the Pacts has not put an end to, for example, a constant process of experimentation with constitutional rights and civil liberties entrenchment. Third, international human rights is the product of many different national and regional traditions of ethics, political theory and concepts of justice. Of course that argument, especially in the early years, was always at risk of being overdone: it was precisely the absence of many of the states of the third world at the negotiations of the 1948 Universal Declaration of Human Rights that spurned subsequent criticism that the Declaration merely reflected Western standards. Nonetheless, even though there can be something a little simplifying and self-serving about talk of "inter-civilizational dialogue" aimed at "discovering" indigenous sources of human rights, research on the multiplicity of human origins and, most importantly, of influences that continue to bear on them paves the way to a better understanding of human rights' pluralism.

4.1.1.2 International Human Rights and Its Embededness in Public International Law

The human rights project has come to be embedded, for better or for worse, in the matrix of public international law (even as it significantly contributes to reshape that law). International human rights law undeniably emerges in an international legal arena that it itself very pluralistic. In fact, one could say that legal pluralism is the very founding principle of the Westphalian compromise. "Cujus regio, ejus religio", although it may occasionally have meant internally the very negation of legal pluralism, is certainly in its external application a principle that renounced the imperial domination of one religious form for Europe (and more generally of a single faith or ideology for the whole world).[7] International law by itself thus provides for an obvious legal pluralism, at least in the weak sense.[8]

International human rights law's relation to international law, of course, is famously fraught with complexity.[9] On one hand, international human rights is precisely about transcending at least the more extreme consequences of plural sovereignties; on the other hand, international human rights absorbs some of the key features of public international law, if only through its reliance on the state as its prime subject, and its recognition of a right such as self-determination. This reliance on the state then contributes to disaggregate the seemingly unitary system of international human rights into multiple normative fragments. For example, even when it comes to human rights, fundamental principles of voluntarism still very much hold sway, meaning that if nothing else different states will join different treaties. This leads to a veritable mosaic of human rights commitments, a sort of human rights "by the menu".

This sense of internal pluralism, of various "communities of commitment", is reinforced by an extensive practice of reservations which even among state parties

[7] The point has been restated recently by Peter Danchin. P. G. Danchin, *The Emergence and Structure of Religious Freedom in International Law Reconsidered*," 23 Journal of Law and Religion 455 (2008). (describing state sovereignty as the "'group rights' solution of the early liberal tradition to the problem of religious and cultural pluralism").

[8] S. L. Bunn-Livingstone & R. Jennings, *Juricultural pluralism vis-à-vis treaty law: state practice and attitudes* (Martinus Nijhoff, 2002) at 51.

[9] For a recent doctrinal exposition see Frédéric Mégret, *The Nature of Human Rights Obligations*, International Human Rights Law (2010).

to a treaty means that different states may in fact commit to different understandings of such a treaty.[10] Even customary international law is an ambiguous means to transcend the partial geographic applicability of international human rights for all but a few rights. True enough, custom has sometimes been used to confirm the status of certain rights in international law but this was often on the basis of the existence of significant treaties. Moreover, the acquisition of customary character by rights only really relates to the existence of rights, rather than to the specific ways in which they should be applied.

4.1.1.3 International Human Rights and Colonialism's Legacy

One of the great contributions of early or "classical" legal pluralism is to the understanding of colonial and post-colonial legal systems. As early as the East India company (or even after the reconquista), "pockets" of local law were recognized, particularly in private matters. In other words, colonialism is legal pluralism's "locus classicus." This legacy raises interesting dilemmas for international human rights law. There are certainly ways in which international human rights law operates in ways that are not entirely at odds with the colonial law of yesterday.[11] Colonial law was, after all, not primarily conceived of as an imposition of external violence, but as bringing the gift of universal standards of civilization. Conversely, the spread of international human rights law has not gone without violence and imposition (think, for example, of the practice of "humanitarian intervention"). There is a sense that the very existence of international human rights law, as a law that is supposed to apply domestically either in parallel to or over and above domestic law, raises problems familiar from an earlier era.

A legal pluralist research agenda for international human rights might seek to analyze the experience of colonial legal pluralism in search of ways in which a "higher" legal order might nonetheless tolerate certain local practices. Although this would be particularly interesting in analyzing the evolution of domestic human rights and legal pluralism (an issue beyond this chapter), it also provides clues as to the organization of the international human rights system itself. Human rights have increasingly displaced earlier references to "conscience" or "principles of civilization" as an international standard of what societies/states should achieve. In colonial times, tolerance for local law was tempered by the need to enforce minimum standards of civilization through such mechanisms as, for example, the "repugnancy clause".[12]

---

[10] Of course, doctrinally, international human rights law does its very best to limit the scope and ambit of these reservations. However, in practice, it is still these reservations that are the most telling indicator of the reality of states' commitment to international human rights norms, rather than the timid pronouncements of international bodies understandably wary of their multiplication.

[11] Jack Donnelly, *Human Rights: A New Standard of Civilization?*, 74 International Affairs (Royal Institute of International Affairs 1944–) 1–23 (1998); D. P. Fidler, *Return of the Standard of Civilization, The*, 2 Chicago Journal of International Law 137 (2001).

[12] L. Sheleff, *Human Rights, Western Values and Tribal Traditions: Between Recognition and Repugnancy, Between Monogamy and Polygamy*, 12 Tel Aviv University Studies in Law 237 (1994); C. O. Akpamgbo, *Woman to Woman Marriage and the Repugnancy Clause: A Case of Putting New Wine into Old Bottles, A*, 14 Journal of Legal Pluralism and Unofficial Law 87 (1977).

A certain reemergence of the "repugnancy clause" has been apparent in cases where international law has been directly applicable as the law of the land over and above domestic law, in situations of "international territorial administration". For example, although the Secretary General has sometimes taken a stance in favor of legal pluralism in post-conflict settings administered by the UN, and Kosovo's UNMIK was to a degree supposed to apply Yugoslav law, he has also insisted that this must be done "in conformity with … international standards".[13]

The debate, as with colonial law, can be framed as whether legal pluralism is a deficient state of affairs to be remedied through the advent of centralization and the bringing of all communities under the same legal roof,[14] or whether it is in fact something willed by the system itself and desirable per se. From the perspective of colonial law, the answer was generally that legal pluralism was a pragmatic device to manage an uncomfortable coexistence between indigenous populations and people of European descent. Since customary laws were not endowed with any intrinsic worth (they were typically seen as backward), colonization would sooner or later replace legal pluralism with the straightforward application of colonial law. The neo-colonial project followed this lesson in some cases, and rejected it in others. Whilst customary norms might serve as models for the law of newly independent states, in many cases, their fate was to become absorbed by the law of the state, whilst in a few cases the continuation and even deepening of legal pluralism was seen as the way of emancipation.

However, despite the appeal of some of these similarities, notable differences emerge between colonial law's and international human rights' relation to legal pluralism. Colonial law was very much in favor of its own form of legal pluralism, but this bias was inextricably linked to the technology of colonization. It emerged from the improbable encounter between a European and a non-European people, and the particular legal quandaries this created. Its tolerance for local customs was essentially pragmatic and political rather than principled (except insofar as its racism could be perversely described as "principled"). Tolerance for local law had little to do with recognition for the intrinsic worth of local cultures – often (although not always), quite the contrary. It also inevitably meant that Westerners escaped the reach of local law and were submitted to an entirely different set of rules than those over whom they ruled. This was true even outside colonization stricto sensu in countries, such as China, Siam, or Persia, where Western visitors, through the capitulations regime, imposed a form of exorbitant legal pluralism on dominated nations.

International human rights law, by contrast, presumptively deals with states, including post-colonial states, which on the one hand are not confronted with the exceptional circumstance of colonization and, on the other hand, are sovereign and therefore much more in a position to decide on their own affairs. This means that the degree of legal pluralism existing in any given country will be much less a direct

[13] Security Council, Report of the Secretary-General on the Rule of Law and Transitional Justice in Conflict and Post-Conflict Societies, S/2004/616 (2004), at para. 5.

[14] See Quermonn, at 50–55.

product of international human rights law than it was of colonial law. At the same time, and even though it is less causally significant, international human rights law is more prone to think of legal pluralism (as it does of everything) in strong normative terms, and not simply as a technique of control. International human rights law is more clearly about transforming legal systems than colonial law was.

4.1.2 Manifestations of Legal Pluralism

4.1.2.1 International Human Rights and Regionalization

Although this is curiously under-analyzed as a phenomenon, international human rights law has witnessed a very significant trend of regionalization. The main regional human rights instruments typically refer in their preambles to at least the Universal Declaration[15] and are typically presented as part of the overall drive towards international human rights,[16] the relationship between "universal" and "regional" human rights is little understood. There has been very little serious academic study of this phenomenon, or what its normative foundations might be.[17] Commentators seem generally content that regional human rights instruments are a way of bringing rights closer to the people they are meant to apply[18] and, pragmatically, that they often come with more efficient enforcement mechanisms (typically, adjudication) than would be achievable at the universal level.

But it is clear that regional human rights instruments are more than simply functional translations of universal human rights into more manageable regional settings. They are grounded explicitly or implicitly in an understanding that certain regions, for historical, cultural, social, or political reasons, have subtly and not so subtly different understandings of rights. Indeed, membership is presumably restricted to members of the corresponding regional organizations (Council of Europe, OAS, or AU),

[15] Second preambular line of the ECHR.

[16] Conversely, they are treated as such by universal human rights instruments and mechanisms. For example, a typical rule of non-receivability before regional or international human rights bodies is that the relevant case is already being considered by another similar regional or international human rights body. In other words, despite enforcing a significantly different law, these bodies consider themselves as sufficiently close to be "functional equivalents".

[17] B. H. Weston, R. A. Lukes & K. M. Hnatt, *Regional Human Rights Regimes: A Comparison and Appraisal,* 20 Vanderbilt Journal of Transnational Law (1987); L. T. Buergenthal, *International and Regional Human Rights Law and Institutions: Some Examples of Their Interaction*, 12 Texas International Law Journal 321 (1977). The phenomenon of regionalization is typically ascribed to the fact that the regional environment is generally more conducive to enterprising human rights initiatives, but the normative implications of regionalization not discussed.

[18] Regionalization remains-problematized largely from the point of view of its constituent entities, rather than from the point of view of the "international". See, e.g.: C. M. Shaw, *The Evolution of Regional Human Rights Mechanisms: A Focus on Africa,* 6 Journal of Human Rights (2007) 2. H Hashimoto, *The prospects for a regional human rights mechanism in East Asia* (Routledge, 2004).

and human rights often presented as one of the foundations of corresponding regional cooperation or integration projects, to which they remain deeply indebted.[19] The ECHR, for example, refers to "governments of European countries which are like-minded and have a common heritage of political traditions, ideals, freedom and the rule of law" and are thereby resolved "to take the first steps for the collective enforcement of certain of the rights stated in the Universal Declaration".[20] There is a sense that regional human rights instruments are as much the manifestation of a regional constitutive process, than they are the localization of a universal project.

Indeed, human rights instruments have been seized by the "regions" that adopt them as a way to define quite substantially different substantive "paths" to human rights. For example, the European Convention entirely neglects social and economic rights; the Inter-American Convention considers that the right to life protects the unborn child, thus prohibiting abortion; and the African Charter clearly puts emphasis on a number of human duties as well as rights. Needless to say, these initial differences have been amplified by the jurisprudence of the various courts tasked with these instruments' implementation. Without going into detail, there are in fact quite ample differences even in the conception of what rights entail and how they should be understood. For example, the ECHR has developed a theory of the "margin of appreciation" whilst neither universal bodies nor other regional bodies have. Although this may evolve in the future, it is striking that one regional system considers that rights can be substantially interpreted at the margin to take into account local specificities, whilst other seemingly do not.[21] It is almost as if these regional groups subscribed to the basic ideology of rights (e.g.: that individuals have basic entitlements that trump other legal demands), but then invested that "vehicle" with quite strikingly different meanings.

There are therefore, many different regional human rights legal orders coexisting under international human rights law which reinforces the basic claim of international human rights' fundamental pluralism. The emergence of these regimes in many cases (Europe and the Americas) is simultaneous to the emergence of an international human rights regime, as if the two were co-terminous. A legal pluralist research agenda would identify the factors that have led to this regionalization, as well as its ongoing dynamic. The coexistence, under the label "international human rights" of several regional and national legal subsystems of human rights may not strike as an obvious form of legal pluralism. Certainly, it is not a perfect legal pluralism in that regional or domestic orders are better understood as porous rather than self-contained. But because of the way in which it clearly delineates several integrated normative spaces, it does come close to at least a "soft" version of

[19] E. K. Quashigah, Les droits de l'homme et l'intégration in Réal P. Lavergne, (ed), *Intégration et coopération régionales en Afrique de l'Ouest* (IDRC-CRDI, 1996) 301.

[20] 6th preambular paragraph. See also American Declaration of the Rights and Duties of Man, first preambular paragraph ("The American peoples have acknowledged the dignity of the individual, and their national constitutions recognize that…"); American Convention on Human Rights, first preambular paragraph ("Reaffirming their intention to consolidate in this hemisphere (…)").

[21] It is of course possible that other bodies have simply not theorized fully their theory of the margin of appreciation but this seems improbable.

pluralism. International human rights is system of legal systems and would probably collapse under the strain if it were to portray itself as unitary.

This tension between the universalism of rights and the particularlism of their application creates many interesting jurisprudential dilemmas. In a sense, it significantly downgrades the classical expectation that human rights inhere unproblematically in human nature. Or rather: they may, but that matters little to our understanding of them, and certainly does not provide a key to their interpretation because human rights still need to be "translated" into regional vernaculars. It also portrays the exercise of promoting internationally protected human rights not as an exercise of simply "applying" or "implementing" law but really of "deciding in terms of human rights in particular, localized settings". International human rights bodies are the upholders of states' commitment to the framework of human rights as a way of thinking about their own tradition of justice and the good life, rather than of a rigid, inflexible and homogeneous international norm. So much so, in fact, that fears were expressed from the start by human rights lawyers that regionalization might affect the very claimed universalism of rights.[22] A legal pluralist study of international human rights would downplay these fears and on the contrary see regional diversification as an inevitable property of any global system of human rights norms.

4.1.2.2 International Human Rights and the Margin of Appreciation

A further very significant way in which international human rights encourages forms of legal pluralism is through a device such as the "margin of appreciation".[23] Although this doctrinal construct is perhaps most explicitly the brain child of the ECHR, it is not impossible to view it as more generally a device to manage human rights within complex regional groupings that combine a shared commitment to supranational human rights with a strong degree of actual divergence in terms of legal systems and traditions.[24] Of course, at a certain level the margin of appreciation can be seen as a simple concession to sovereignty with a view to encouraging states to ratify human rights instruments. The margin of appreciation doctrine has been criticized for creating inconsistencies in the application of the ECHR,[25] and for occasionally allowing too much leeway.[26]

---

[22] K. Vasak, *Human Rights: A Thirty-Year Struggle: The Sustained Efforts to Give Force of Law to the Universal Declaration of Human Rights*, 30 UNESCO Courier 316–325 (1977).

[23] H. C. Yourow, *The Margin of Appreciation Doctrine in the Dynamics of European Human Rights Jurisprudence* (1996).

[24] Indeed, the case has been made that it could serve a very useful purpose if an international human rights court were to be created. B. Wilkins, *International Human Rights and National Discretion*, 6 The Journal of Ethics 373–382 (2002).

[25] Sia Spiliopoulou Akermark, *Limits of Pluralism – Recent Jurisprudence of the European Court of Human Rights with Regard to Minorities: Does the Prohibition of Discrimination Add Anything, The*, 2002 Journal on Ethnopolitics and Minority Issues in Europe [i] (2002).

[26] J. A. Sweeney, *Margins of Appreciation: Cultural Relativity and the European Court of Human Rights in the Post-Cold War Era*, 54 International and Comparative Law Quarterly 459–474 (2008).

However, there is also clearly a more positively pluralistic dimension to it,[27] which the European Court itself has stressed. The margin of appreciation acknowledges the fact that human rights will have to be implemented differently within each society, and in ways that are to a degree impenetrable from outside. It highlights certain rights as being less susceptible to interpretation, whilst others will be quite "elastic" to certain traditions, be they legal, cultural or religious. Moreover, it gives a sort of majoritarian spin to human rights interpretation. As long as European states are quite evenly split on an issue (typically an issue involving mores), the ECHR will not "impose" a human rights solution to complex social debates. By the time the great majority of European states have begun recognizing something as entailing rights (e.g.: homosexuality), then those who lag behind will find it increasingly hard to have their "margin of appreciation" acknowledged. This also anchors the implementation of human rights in something like a notion of the "standards of the community", where the community is a group of states that have resolved together to promote certain principles – but not to become one, or truly federate, or adhere to the same political project. Human rights in the European context tend to evolve with the society(ies) in which they are meant to apply.

4.1.2.3 International Human Rights and Personal and Functional Diversification

Finally, international human rights has increasingly in the last several decades gone through a process of personal diversification, based on a recognition of the importance of the differences that constitute human beings beyond their common humanity.[28] Human rights were once conceived as applying primarily to a prototypical universal human subject, and made little allowance for differences between fundamental categories of humanity. Increasingly, however, the project has tended to become plural not only in a conventional geographic dimension (regional, national), but also in that it applies differently to different populations. The populations in question may be "universal" (children, women), but they may also be localized and even constituted groups. Indigenous peoples are a particularly clear instance of this pluralization. One could argue that the global indigenous rights regime that is slowly emerging as part of the development of international human rights is creating a distinct rights regime for indigenous peoples the world over. The same thing is probably true, although to a lesser extent, of the Convention on the rights of migrant workers, or the Convention on the rights of persons with disabilities.[29] Coupled with

---

[27] Mireille Delmas-Marty & Marie-Laure Izorche, *Marge Nationale D'Appreciation et Internationalisation du Droit: Reflexions sur la Validite Formelle d'un Commun Pluraliste*, 46 McGill Law Journal 923 (2000). D. L. Donoho, *Relativism Versus Universalism in Human Rights: The Search for Meaningful Standards*, 27 Stanford Journal of International Law 345 (1990).

[28] Terence Turner, *Human Rights, Human Difference: Anthropology's Contribution to an Emancipatory Cultural Politics*, 53 Journal of Anthropological Research 273–291 (1997).

[29] F. Megret, *The Disabilities Convention Human Rights of Persons with Disabilities or Disability Rights?*, 30 Human Rights Quarterly 494–516 (2008).

personal pluralization is a sense of functional pluralization in which international human rights increasingly tackles specific rights phenomena. This was the case with the Convention on torture and is also the case of the Convention on disappearances and the Convention on migrant workers (which tackles, albeit indirectly, the issue of migration). Although these treaties apply to distinct phenomena, they create an extra-layer of legal order that may apply transiently to various individuals or groups, in ways that reinforce the system's inherent sense of legal pluralism.

4.2 International Human Rights Through Legal Pluralism

Legal pluralism is not only, to use Griffiths' categories, an "attribute" of international human rights as a legal system. "Strong" legal pluralism also describes the coexistence of legal orders outside any recognition by the state. International human rights law itself is certainly not legal pluralism in that strong sense, and indeed arguably manifests, like most positive law systems, an aspiration to transcend radical legal pluralism. Clearly the human rights movement has invested considerably in both state and supra-state law in an attempt to be taken seriously as law.

Yet at the same time, the whole corpus of human rights is powerfully dependent on and shaped by partly irreducible legal orders that are themselves manifestations of a deeper legal pluralism. This legal pluralism is based on a challenge of the conventional sources of law production and validation and the idea that, by analogy with state law, international human rights law is first and foremost a product of the structures of international institutions or governance. In this section, I envisage a few axes for the development of a legally pluralist understanding of how international human rights law comes into being.

4.2.1 International Human Rights and New Actors

Some of the most challenging research in human rights has emphasized the extent to which international human rights is perhaps first and foremost increasingly the product of non-traditional actors, particularly non-state actors. The focus on the discipline is still by and large on the institutions of international society specifically designed to promote and articulate human rights, rather than on the strategies put in place by individuals and groups to articulate human rights for themselves. The question of "the relevance of international human rights law and … its impact on those it is designed to benefit" is, arguably, still not raised as directly as it should be.[30]

[30] Ronald C. Slye, *International Law, Human Rights Beneficiaries, and South Africa: Some Thoughts on the Utility of International Human Rights Law*, 2 Chicago Journal of International Law 59, 60 (2001).

Conversely, a critical legal pluralist view would seek to make apparent that non-state actors are using "human rights law" in unexpected and even unorthodox ways. Anthropologists such as Sally Engle Mary have perhaps most significantly contributed to our understanding of the "vernacularization" of human rights, i.e.: their reinterpretation through local appropriation. Under this light, the movement of human rights is seen as involving much more than of "implementation" of internationally promulgated norms. A proper understanding of how human rights evolve would include the extent to which local understandings have historically influenced international formulation. In that respect, a particularly rich subtext in human rights law is how its dialectics are profoundly informed by the relative weight that actors give to certain rights over others, and how particular rights and the rights concept generally are understood. A pluralist human rights agenda would focus less on official declarations by states and more on retracing painstakingly the history of discussions internal to and between constituencies, before, during and after the adoption of, for example, relevant human rights treaties. It would seek to understand how different states or groups within them emphasize different rights (e.g.: freedom of expression v. freedom of religion) and how this creates complex distortions that are as important to human rights as the pursuit of a coherent doctrinal whole.

This would, in turn, command greater attention to how groups and group members frame their rights. For example, women may or may not consider that certain religious practices or laws are a discrimination or a violation of their freedom. One could argue that they are wrong either way, but this misses the point that, at a certain level, concepts such as "liberty" and "equality" only really have meanings within specific worldviews and contexts. Moreover, how these values are ranked will depend on quite profoundly inaccessible reasoning that must be seen as a manifestation of an ability to produce one's own normative views of human rights. Emphasizing the role of the ultimate beneficiaries of human rights as producers of particular human rights "worlds" can help get past some perennial misunderstandings in the international human rights movements. In this section I look at the growing role of a number of intermediary actors, somewhere between the state, the individual, and the international community.

4.2.1.1 Sub-state, Decentralized Entities

It used to be the case that international human rights obligations were mostly to be borne by states. What the state did domestically, in line with its constitutional arrangements and constraints, was the state's exclusive remit. Sub-state entities, such as regions or municipalities were considered largely secondary and irrelevant for the purposes of international human rights, in line with the canons of the law of state responsibility. In practice, however, in addition to the fact that the state has a somewhat waning role when it comes to implementing international obligations,[31]

[31] C. Schreuer, *Warning of the Sovereign State: Towards a New Paradigm for International Law, The*, 4 European Journal of International Law 447–471 (1993).

most human rights issues will hardly ever be taken up as actual matters of state responsibility. Moreover, constitutional issues may arise preventing states from ratifying certain international treaties lest they encroach on sub-state entities' prerogatives.[32] In decentralized or federal states, therefore, international human rights law will often depend for its implementation on its ability to be seized upon by constituent and devolved entities.

At the very least, relevant federal or autonomous entities have been brought into the process of negotiation and eventual ratification of international human rights treaties as is the case, for example, in Canada.[33] Some countries explicitly anticipate human rights functions for sub-state entities.[34] Even in cases where such a role is not envisaged and where sub-state entities cannot formally become bound by international human rights instruments, they may seek to implement customary international human rights obligations, within their sphere of competence. This they may do even in cases where the state has not ratified any corresponding international human rights treaty, or in cases where, for example because of a dualist tradition, the state does not push for implementation by such entities. Some US cities, for example, have gone as far as to "adopt" human rights treaties that the US had not ratified (e.g.: San Francisco and CEDAW). In the US constitutional context, this has led Catherine Powell to argue for a model of shared implementation between the federal state and other entities[35]; Martha Davis has insisted that "State courts have a responsibility to consider international human rights norms (…) even absent a formal mandate"[36] and promoted the idea that "international human rights from the ground up" should seize on the importance of local policy[37]; and Peter Spiro has argued for "the dilution of national control over political subdivisions should find a corresponding dilution of the doctrine of state responsibility", leading to what he calls "condominium responsibility, in which both central and subnational governments are held responsible for the conduct of the latter".[38]

Some sub-state entities have at times taken forceful human rights action to implement human rights on an international basis, at the risk of competing with the

[32] Susan Kilbourne, *Convention on the Rights of the Child: Federalism Issues for the United States, The*, 5 Georgetown Journal on Fighting Poverty 327 (1997).

[33] Koren L. Bell, *From Laggard to Leader: Canadian Lessons on a Role for U.S. States in Making and Implementing Human Rights Treaties*, 5 Yale Human Rights & Development Law Journal 255 (2002).

[34] D. Johnson & R. B. Howe, *Human Rights Commissions in Canada: Reform or Reinvention in a Time of Restraint*, 12 Canadian Journal of Law & Society 1 (1997).

[35] C. Powell, *Dialogic Federalism: Constitutional Possibilities for Incorporation of Human Rights Law in the United States*, 150 University of Pennsylvania Law Review 245 (2001).

[36] M. F. Davis, *Spirit of Our Times: State Constitutions and International Human Rights, The*, 30 NYU Review of Law & Social Change 359, 359 (2005).

[37] M. F. Davis, *International Human Rights from the Ground Up*, Where Human Rights Begin: Health, Sexuality, and Women in the New Millennium 235 (2005).

[38] Peter J. Spiro, *States and International Human Rights, The*, 66 Fordham Law Review 567, 568 (1997).

federal state's monopoly on the conduct of foreign affairs (and human rights dimensions thereof). For example, the Massachussets legislature notably adopted "sanctions" against Burma, by introducing a state agencies' purchasing preference in favor of companies that did not do trade with that country.[39] In some cases, as with the Palestinian Authority, human rights responsibilities are endorsed by entities that are not "sub" or "state" at all.[40] Of course, assumption of human rights functions by sub-state entities, although it may bring human rights closer to their intended beneficiaries, need not be a development for the good, but it is nonetheless an increasingly significant phenomenon that bypasses the state.[41]

4.2.1.2 "Intermediary Bodies", Private Actors and Social Movements

Legal pluralism is an invitation to study the normative regulation, to use Moore's expression, of a number of "semi-autonomous social fields". The attention of legal pluralists in industrialized societies has focused on a variety of private associations below the state: civil society organizations, trade unions, parties, clubs, churches, villages, favelas, prisons, neighbourhoods, tribes. These are areas which at times seem virtually untouched by an excessively centralized and statist view of international human rights,[42] yet which no doubt raise human rights issues. Regardless of the particular answer that the law gives to whether non-state actors can, strictly speaking, violate human rights, such "intermediary bodies" are clearly law producing environments. A better understanding of how human rights can help frame normative problems arising in such environments would go a long way to decentering human rights discourse from the state. There is both a "negative" and a "positive" side to such a program of study.

---

[39] A. Carvajal, *State and Local "Free Burma" Laws: The Case for Sub-National Trade Sanctions.*, 29 Law and Policy in International Business (1998); J. M. Kline, *Continuing Controversies Over State and Local Foreign Policy Sanctions in the United States*, 29 Publius: The Journal of Federalism 111 (1999); D. R. Schmahmann, J. Finch & T. Chapman, *Off the Precipice: Massachusetts Expands Its Foreign Policy Expedition from Burma to Indonesia.*, 30 Vanderbilt Journal of Transnational Law (1997); B. P. Denning & J. H. McCall Jr, *Constitutionality of State and Local Sanctions against Foreign Countries: Affairs State, States Affairs, or a Sorry State of Affairs, The*, 26 Hastings Constitutional Law Quarterly 307 (1998); E. Moritsugu, *Winding Course of the Massachusetts Burma Law: Subfederal Sanctions in a Historical Context, The*, 34 George Washington International Law Review 435 (2002).

[40] Eyal Benvenisti, *Responsibility for the Protection of Human Rights under the Interim Israeli-Palestinian Agreements*, 28 Israel Law Review 310, 310 (1994).

[41] Shannon Speed & Jane F. Collier, *Limiting Indigenous Autonomy in Chiapas, Mexico: The State Government's Use of Human Rights*, 22 Human Rights Quarterly 877–905 (2000).

[42] This leads to conceptual complications, where violations clearly attributable to groups are systematically attributed to the state, through theories of international human rights instruments' "indirect horizontal effect". Whilst this makes sense from the point of view of international law and its particular need to attribute responsibility to states, it makes much less sense from the point of view of human rights law and the need to assess realistically where human rights violations arise primarily.

On the negative side, the issue is not only how non-state actors affect the rights of persons external to them, but also how they may internally compromise those of their members, especially when they act as self-enclosed normative systems. For example, legislation concerning sects in some countries typically criticizes them as leading to rights violations.[43] Corporations also have distinct human rights impact not only as a result of their external practices, as is often emphasized, but also as a result of their internal norms. For example, leaving aside the complex question of how corporations may contribute to rights violations abroad, it has been noted that corporations routinely limit their employees' right to privacy[44] or freedom of speech.[45] The emergence of "corporate codes of conduct" is testimony to the fact that preventing corporations from violating rights is a normative issue, interwoven with issues about the structure of corporations. Finally, guerilla or terrorist groups are a good example of largely autonomous normative fields that produce norms that may be deeply violative of the rights of their members.

On the positive side, the contribution of social movements and their own normative assumptions about rights to an evolving international human rights legal culture is also a fertile terrain of exploration for legal pluralism. By this I do not simply mean the fact that social movements effectively contribute to the development of human rights – something which is by now abundantly recognized – but that they come with normative agendas of their own. There has been much focus on specialized human rights actors and NGOs,[46] but these may not be the most interesting from the point of view of legal pluralism. There is less legal attention to movements that may seem only tangentially related at first to human rights but whose impact is nonetheless very significant. Trade unions and the attempt to impose "corporate

[43] The Declaration of Paris on Sects for example very much emphasizes the working of sects as autonomous – and oppressive – legal orders. Similarly, associations bent on protecting "victims of sects" use the language of human rights to denounce the way in which some groups prey on individuals. See "les sectes et les droits de l'homme" http://www.prevensectes.com/droit1.htm

[44] J. D. R. Craig & H. D. Oliver, *The Right to Privacy in the Public Workplace: Should the Private Sector Be Concerned?*, 27 Industrial Law Journal 49 (1998). Am Everett, Y. Y. Wong & J. Paynter, *Balancing Employee and Employer Rights: An International Comparison of E-Mail Privacy in the Workplace*, 11 Journal of Individual Employment Rights 291–311 (2004). American Civil Liberties Union et al., *Workplace Drug Testing Is Ineffective and Unfair; Random Drug Tests Do Not Ensure a Drug-Free Workplace (From Illegal Drugs, P 62–70, 1998, Charles P. Cozic, ed.-See NCJ-169238)*, (1998). M. L. Rustad & S. R. Paulsson, *Monitoring Employee E-mail and Internet Usage: Avoiding the Omniscient Electronic Sweatshop: Insights from Europe*, 7 University of Pennsylvania Journal of Labor & Employment Law 829 (2004).

[45] M. Becker, *How Free Is Speech at Work*, 29 University of California/Davis Law Review 815 (1995). E. Volokh, *Freedom of Speech and Workplace Harassment*, 39 UCLA Law Review 1791 (1991).

[46] Stephan Hobe, *Global Challenges to Statehood: The Increasingly Important Role of Nongovernmental Organizations*, 5 Indiana Journal of Global Legal Studies 191, 197–198 (1997). J. Smith, R. Pagnucco & G. A. Lopez, *Globalizing Human Rights: The Work of Transnational Human Rights NGOs in the 1990s*, 20 Human Rights Quarterly 379 (1998). A. M. Clark, Diplomacy of Conscience: Amnesty International and Changing Human Rights Norms (2001).

codes of conduct" on multinational companies are an interesting case in point, even if it is one that can be rich with tension with more traditional NGO rights based approaches.[47]

Although I will return to the specific issue of professional ethics, it is worth pointing that professional associations have had a considerable role in the genesis and development of human rights. Scientists, for example, have often been at the forefront of pleading for human rights compatible uses of science.[48] An interesting example is the trajectory of the American Anthropological Association in the twentieth century. Notably, the AAA was one of few voices to challenge the universality or usefulness of the rights concept when the UDHR was adopted. More than 50 years later, in 1999, it adopted a "Declaration on Anthropology and Human Rights" which was seen as much more supportive of human rights,[49] despite some ambiguities.[50] In helping to shape the outlook of an entire profession and, through it, the relationship of the West to the rest of the world, such a declaration can be seen as having a significant impact on both theoretical debates about the nature of rights and concrete dilemmas about the work of anthropology's professionals. Lawyers' professional associations have also obviously had an important role to play.[51]

4.2.1.3 The Private Sphere and Individuals

Thinking about human rights, particularly women's rights, has been a crucial element in the rediscovery of the private sphere as a locus of rights violations but also rights production.[52] This concern with the private sphere is something that meshes well with the study of legal pluralism. An interesting example is the family. Legal pluralism can help construct the family as not only a place of random acts of love and violence but, in many ways, a mini-legal order, one which has considerable significance for the rights experience of, notably, women and children.[53] That legal order is of course in many instances one in which particular religious or cultural values are enforced, typically by men. An understanding of how family normativities

[47] Rainer Braun & Judy Gearhart, *Who Should Code Your Conduct? Trade Union and NGO Differences in the Fight for Workers' Rights*, 14 Development in Practice 183–196 (2004).

[48] L. Rubenstein & M. Younis, *Scientists and Human Rights*, 322 Science 1303 (2008).

[49] http://www.aaanet.org/stmts/humanrts.htm

[50] K. Engle, *From Skepticism to Embrace: Human Rights and the American Anthropological Association from 1947–1999*, 23 Human Rights Quarterly 536 (2001).

[51] Aðalsteinsson Ragnar, *The Role of Bar Associations and Law Societies in the Implementation of Human Rights, dans* International Human Rights Monitoring Mechanisms: Essays in Honour of Jakob Th. Möller (2009).

[52] D. Q. Thomas & M. E. Beasley, *Domestic Violence as a Human Rights Issue*, 15 Human Rights Quarterly 36–62 (1993).

[53] R. J. R. Levesque, *Piercing the Family's Private Veil: Family Violence, International Human Rights, and the Cross-Cultural Record*, 21 Law & Policy 161 (1999).

are constructed by cultural and public normativities which it in turn help mould the state and international human rights agenda should be an aspiration of legal pluralism.

In particular, the typical approach in terms of "indirect horizontal effect" (i.e.: the state is responsible, from the point of view of human rights, for violations occurring in the private sphere that it allowed to happen) seems partial and limited. It fails to bring the human rights fight all the way to culture, to highlight the role of individual agency and patterns of societal oppression in the occurrence of human rights violations. Except in the very limited scenario of international criminal law, it allows individuals a little too easily off the hook in terms of human rights violations. Such violations must be addressed at the source, rather than through rhetorically investing in the reformative prowess of an omnipotent state. A legal pluralist research agenda for international human rights would investigate what might be gained and lost by addressing the whole range of actors involved in human rights violations directly.[54]

4.2.2 New Modes of Norm-Production: Beyond "Bindingness"

The field of international human rights law, no doubt drawing its inspiration from domestic human rights and international law, has been dominated by the idea that what makes norms is that they are binding, that they are authoritatively decided, and that a threat of sanctions exists in case they are violated. In short, notions of adjudication and enforcement dominate the field. Although human rights activists may loath to admit it, power has featured quite conspicuously in these strategies, the goal being typically to accumulate as much of it internationally to be able to back international human rights with credible violence (hence the fact that debates on humanitarian intervention, sanctions and embargoes are never far when dealing with human rights). There has been significant study of how international human rights relies on less formal means of implementation (committees, commissions, rapporteurs, ombudspersons), but this is often seen as a second best. [55] Missing from the mainstream picture are a number of human rights implementation strategies that involve the soft pull of interest or values, which are arguably becoming more prominent in a densely socialized international *milieu*, and which clearly manifest a form of legal pluralism.

Some scholars have clearly taken a step in that direction and laid the bases for a global pluralist research agenda of human rights implementation. For example, Sally Engle Merry has suggested that the formal lawyer of "binding international human rights law" matters less to the implementation of international human rights

[54] C. I. Nyamu, *How Should Human Rights and Development Respond to Cultural Legitimization of Gender Hierarchy in Developing Countries*, 41 Harvard International Law Journal (2000).

[55] C. Peck, *The United Nations as a dispute settlement system: improving mechanisms for the prevention and resolution of conflict* (Martinus Nijhoff Publishers, 1996).

than "transnational consensus building" which "emerges out of specific local interests and concerns".[56] Her work on the "translation" into local vernaculars of international human rights is one of the most striking applications of legal pluralism to the topic.[57] It opens space for an exploration of why, when and how (and at what cost) distinct groups draw on international human rights, rather than simply whether international human rights law "applies" or not.

In what follows I explore a few further characteristic modes of international human rights norm production (needless to say, there are many more) that might inform a legal pluralist agenda and are grounded both in more conventional forms of legal pluralism and evolving notions of global legal pluralism. Typically, mainstream international human rights discourse has been focused on NGOs and civil society as mostly tagging along the inter-state world and, in the best of cases, successfully lobbying governments at international diplomatic conferences. A formalist legal discourse will barely acknowledge not only the contribution of non-state actors, but also the extent to which such actors are "law producing" rather than simply accessories. Legal pluralists however have long observed the tendency of unofficial legal orders to be produced, for example, by merchants. The same can arguably be said of human rights law which is, today, effectively being generated through a growing number of private means.

4.2.2.1 "Codes of Conduct"

A first line of exploration would seek to document the extent to which actors contribute to the formulation of human rights or, more significantly, actually create quasi or significantly "legal" orders through the adoption of "self-binding" codes of conduct. This is the case, for example, when humanitarian organizations develop field rules and standards of conduct,[58] or even when advocacy NGOs do the same in relation to their activism.[59] Another noteworthy example is the adoption by corporations,[60] or indeed entire industries of human rights codes.[61] Even when it

---

[56] Merry, *supra* note_2 at 217. S. E. Merry, *Transnational Human Rights and Local Activism: Mapping the Middle*, 108 AMERICAN ANTHROPOLOGIST 38 (2006).

[57] S. E. Merry, *Rights Talk and the Experience of Law: Implementing Women's Human Rights to Protection from Violence*, 25 HUMAN RIGHTS QUARTERLY 343 (2003); S. E. Merry et al., *The Female Inheritance Movement in Hong Kong*, 46 CURRENT ANTHROPOLOGY 387–409 (2005).

[58] R. Lloyd, *The role of NGO self-regulation in increasing stakeholder accountability*. London, UK: One World Trust (2005). D Hilhorst, *Dead Letter or Living Document? Ten Years of the Code of Conduct for Disaster Relief*, 29 DISASTERS 4 (2005).

[59] The Changing International Legal Framework for Dealing with Non-State Actors August Reinisch, *The Changing International Legal Framework for Dealing with Non-State Actors*, *in* NON-STATE ACTORS AND HUMAN RIGHTS, 48 (2005).

[60] D. Weissbrodt, *Business and Human Rights*, 74 U. CIN. L. REV. 55 (2005). P. Frankental & F. House, *Human Rights Is It Any of Your Business?*, (2000). R Pearson & G Seyfang, "New Hope or False Dawn?: Voluntary Codes of Conduct, Labour Regulation and Social Policy in a Globalizing World" (2001) 1:1 Global Social Policy.

[61] Technology titans to adopt human rights code of conduct, AFP, Octobre 27, 2008.

comes to such unlikely human rights actors as multinational corporations, one could argue that these have become producers of human rights norms in their own right, through a variety of codes of "best practices", many of which emulate the claims of human rights even as they may subtly distort them.[62] Even private military companies have adopted codes of conduct, perhaps largely as a result of being shunned by the interstate world and being deemed beyond the pale.[63] Increasingly it is guerilla groups which are being encouraged by organizations like the Geneva Call to unilaterally subscribe to humanitarian rules, even when they can expect neither recognition nor reciprocity from states.[64]

This increasing infatuation with private self-regulation, which has both its apologists and critics[65] from a human rights point of view, is arguably one of the phenomena legal pluralism can help understand.[66] It can help explain the nature and possible legitimacy of such hybrid normativities, which "while private in nature, … fulfill a public function".[67] Obligation in such contexts is constructed very differently from the way state-centric lawyers would traditionally see it. The commitment is above all the result of a unilateral commitment, one that is made either to self or to a range of diffuse others, with no need for agreement or, even, reciprocity. Reasons for nonetheless becoming bound have to do with the constitutive role of certain norms (I am because I follow a certain rule), or the deeply socialized nature of certain actors. Legal pluralism can also account for some of the ways in which initially voluntary and self-referential commitments become endorsed or implemented by more familiar governmental or inter-governmental emanations.

---

[62] H. W. Arthurs, "7. Private Ordering and Workers' Rights in the Global Economy: Corporate Codes of Conduct as a Regime of Labour Market Regulation" (2005) Ethics Codes, Corporations, and the Challenge of Globalization. As Harry Arthurs notes "TNCs have, in effect, engaged in the reproduction of liberal legality in the transnational economic field".

[63] K. Fallah, *Corporate Actors: The Legal Status of Mercenaries in Armed Conflict*, 88 International Review of the Red Cross 599–611, 3 (2007). A. Forces, *Code of Conduct: Tool for Self-Regulation for Private Military and Security Companies.*

[64] R. Provost, *Asymmetrical Reciprocity and Compliance with the Laws of War.* C. Hofmann, *Engaging Non-state Armed Groups in Humanitarian Action*, 13 International Peacekeeping 396–409 (2006); S. Santos, *A Critical Reflection on the Geneva Call Instrument and Approach in Engaging Armed Groups on Humanitarian Norms: A Southern Perspective, dans* Conference on Curbing Human Rights Violations by Non-State Armed Groups, Armed Groups Project, University of British Columbia. Vancouver 14–15 (2003); A. Clapham, *Human Rights Obligations of Non-state Actors in Conflict Situations*, 88 International Review of the Red Cross 491–523, 291–298 (2007).

[65] Ronen Shamir, *Between Self-Regulation and the Alien Tort Claims Act: On the Contested Concept of Corporate Social Responsibility*, 38 Law & Society Review 635 (2004).

[66] F. Snyder, *Governing Economic Globalization: Global Legal Pluralism and European Law*, Law and Anthropology: A Reader 313 (2005).

[67] H. Keller, *Codes of Conduct and Their Implementation: The Question of Legitimacy.*

4.2.2.2 Professional Ethics

Another very relevant yet little explored domain for the generation of human rights norms is that of professional ethics. It is a well known fact that some of the worst human rights violations to have occurred in the twentieth century have occurred because of the failure by the medical profession, in particular, to uphold the Hippocratic oath.[68] Even though the oath and other professional codes may have traditionally been based mostly on notions of virtue, they have increasingly been framed as involving human rights. Issues such as the "torture debate" in the war on terror have typically focused on the US government, a few leading NGOs, and international experts as the key protagonists. Yet behind the scenes normative orders internal to certain professional practices may have had even more of an impact, both good or bad.[69]

For example, the American Psychological Association, following a report by its Task Force on Psychological Ethics and National Security,[70] once supported member involvement in the interrogation of detainees despite knowledge that some members had been complicit in the design of interrogation procedures that clearly violated the rights of detainees. Manfred Nowak, the UN Special Rapporteur on Torture protested, leading to the creation of a "psychologists for an ethical APA platform" that issued a formal complaint to the organization's president[71] and counseled mass resignation. The debate is still ongoing, but what is interesting for our purposes is that the complaint was framed both in terms of professional ethics and associational governance issues, even as it was in a sense all about human rights. In some cases at least, therefore, issues of professional ethics that may at first sight appear disconnected from issues of international human rights enforcement have in fact become dense arenas of struggle for the upholding of human rights values.

Similar soul searching has occurred in relation to lawyers,[72] particularly advisors to governments.[73] Here, the issue is not so much with the law of human rights as with the ethics of lawyers in general, and how an inability to stand by certain principles of the profession may deeply compromise rights. For example, the US government's "war on terror" decision to authorize the monitoring of attorney-client communications in prison facilities has been resisted by organizations like the American Bar Association as an affront to lawyers' professional ethics that would

---

[68] Michael A. Grodin & George J. Annas, *Legacies of Nuremberg: Medical Ethics and Human Rights*, 276 JAMA 1682–1683 (1996).

[69] George J. Annas, *Unspeakably Cruel – Torture, Medical Ethics, and the Law*, 352 New England Journal of Medicine 2127–2132 (2005).

[70] Report of the American Psychological Association Presidential Task Force on Psychological Ethics and National Security, (2005).

[71] http://www.ethicalapa.com/files/Formal_Complaint.pdf

[72] M. Cheh, *Should Lawyers Participate in Rigged Systems—The Case of the Military Commissions*, 1 Journal of National Security Law & Policy 375 (2005).

[73] Jesselyn Radack, *Tortured Legal Ethics: The Role of the Government Advisor in the War on Terrorism*, 77 University of Colorado Law Review 1 (2006). Richard B. Bilder & Detlev F. Vagts, *Speaking Law to Power: Lawyers and Torture*, 98 The American Journal of International Law 689–695 (2004).

violate the rights of detainees.[74] Professional ethics have thus adroitly been framed as sites of resistance to violence, even as the larger human rights debates (e.g.: security v. liberties) may sometimes seem intractable. Geographers, scientists, nurses and anthropologists have also adopted codes of ethics that emphasize the importance of professional practices that are conducive to human rights, or at least not violative of them. These are arguably all instruments that constitute the practice of human rights in these arenas of practice as much as international human rights law proper.

4.2.2.3 Alternative Dispute Settlement, Mediation, Traditional Justice

Much study of international human rights law is focused on issues of formal adjudication. The risk is that the dialectics of human rights will be conceived essentially in terms of confrontation between parties, as opposed to soft trade-offs, compromises, diffusion, influence, etc. focus on adjudication is a natural byproduct of the legal mind, but adjudication arguably only really accounts for a small, albeit significant, way in which any legal system is enforced. Of notable interest here is the use of new, alternative dispute resolution mechanisms to deal with human rights issues. On the surface, human rights and ADR seem at loggerheads. Human rights often stand for the highest principles in a legal system, and international human rights law certainly makes a claim to rigorous obedience. Dispute resolution, by contrast, seems ideally suited to mediating and accommodating strategies linked to issue areas that are characterized by less principled density. Yet it is already clearly the case that ADR, a conspicuous phenomenon in many advanced industrialized societies and one characteristic of a more post-modern approach to the law, has made significant forays in the area of human rights.

In fact, in addition to its growing domestic uses for human rights,[75] mediation has arguably been a prominent way in which international human rights law has been

---

[74] Ellen S. Podgor & John Wesley Hall, *Government Surveillance of Attorney-Client Communications: Invoked in the Name of Fighting Terrorism*, 17 Georgetown Journal of Legal Ethics 145 (2003). J. M. McCauley, *War on Terrorism and Its Impact on the Ethical Representation of Clients, The*, 4 Richmond Journal of Global Law & Business 37 (2004); K. Ruzenski, *Balancing Fundamental Civil Liberties and the Need for Increased Homeland Security: The Attorney-Client Privilege after September 11th*, 19 . John's J. Legal Comment. 467 (2004).

[75] For example, in the US employers have created internal dispute resolution mechanisms to deal with labor discrimination complaints. Whilst such a process has rightly been criticized as carrying the risk of "recasting discrimination claims as typical managerial problems" and thus "undermining legal rights by deemphasizing and depoliticizing workplace discrimination" (L. B. Edelman, H. S. Erlanger & J. Lande, *Internal Dispute Resolution: The Transformation of Civil Rights in the Workplace,* 27 Law & Society Review (1993).), this is precisely the sort of trade-off and distortion that legal pluralism should seek to elucidate from both a sociological and normative point of view. L. B. Edelman, S. R. Fuller & I. Mara-Drita, *Diversity Rhetoric and the Managerialization of Law 1,* 106 American Journal of Sociology 6 (2001) . At the national level, an institution like the Canadian Human Rights Commission has been at the forefront of using mediation to deal with human rights disputes in relation to discrimination. A. H. Young, *Keeping the Courts at Bay: The Canadian Human Rights Commission and Its Counterparts in Britain and Northern Ireland: Some Comparative Lessons*, 43 University of Toronto Law Journal (1993). For a number of recent examples see http://www.chrc-ccdp.ca/disputeresolution_reglementdifferends/se_2008_ee-en.asp

enforced for a long time, despite the emphasis on formal institutions. Perhaps the better known example is that of regional human rights commissions (European, American, African).[76] For example, the African Commission is to "try through all possible means to reach a peaceful settlement based on the respect for human and peoples' rights".[77] In both the Inter-American and African cases, Commission induced settlements were all there was to theses systems' activity until courts were created. Even though dispute settlement is no longer at the forefront in the European context since the adoption of Protocol XI, it was for many decades one of the defining features of the system. Beyond formalized dispute settlement, there many international human rights related disputes that are settled informally, through tools more familiar to students of international negotiations than domestic human rights, including mediation, investigation, and various forms of negotiations or diplomatic encounters.[78]

Literature on "friendly settlement" is scant compared to the huge amount of attention paid to adjudication,[79] as if this were not a proper area for the study of the law. Indeed, the bias in the discipline seems to be towards an increased judicialization of international human rights disputes, and the ECHR's example of having done away with the Commission is presented as the most "advanced" model, despite the obvious problems that have arisen as a result of the creation of a unitary, highly judicialized system. Apart from the well-known advantages of ADR in terms of rapidity, accessibility, informality and de-clogging of the judicial system, there is no doubt that ADR jurisprudentially represents a different conception of law and justice; it emphasizes, within certain bounds, the transactional and the participatory over authoritative, vertical modes of settlement.[80] It suggests an understanding of

[76] In the universal context, a mediation procedure is anticipated by all treaty bodies when it comes to inter-state disputes, but the latter have never been used making the issue a moot one. Ironically, despite the treaty bodies being in themselves a lot less jurisdictional (and therefore, one might think, more disposed towards ADR), none of them anticipate any form of settlement in the case of individual petitions.

[77] African Convention on Human and Peoples' Rights, article 52.

[78] P. H. Kooijmans, "Inter-State Dispute Settlement in the Field of Human Rights" in M. Brus, A. S. Muller & S. Wiemers, eds., *The United Nations decade of international law: reflections on international dispute settlement* (Martinus Nijhoff Publishers, 1991).

[79] Jeremy McBride, "Friendly Settlement of International Human Rights Claims by Individuals" in C. Samson & J. McBride, eds., *Solutions de rechange au règlement des conflits* (Presses de L'Universite Laval, 1993). C. A. Norgaard, "Reflections Concerning Friendly Dispute Settlement under the European Convention on Human Rights" in F. Matscher & H. Petzold, eds., *Protecting human rights: The European dimension. Protection des droits de l'homme: la dimension européenne; Studies in honour of/Mélanges en l'honneur de Gérard Wiarda* (Carl Heymanns Verlag KG, Köln 1990). Jorge Ulises Carmona Tinoco, *The Peaceful Dispute Settlement of Human Rights at The Universal And Regional Levels, With Special Reference to The Inter-American System,* 6 Mexican Law Review 4 (2006).

[80] It is interesting for example that the ACHR indicates that the Commission "shall be put at the disposal of the concerned parties, in order to reach a peaceful settlement" (article 48.1.f.). This idea of the Commission as being at the disposal of parties suggests that the element of public service dominates over the element of public order.

the law and the consequences to be ascribed to violations that is more rooted in particular solutions freely arrived at between parties than the abstraction of universalizing solutions. It is also perhaps particularly attentive to the role of victims of rights violations.

A legal pluralist agenda to international human rights would link the study of ADR to traditional justice mechanisms that the discipline still has trouble seeing as part of the human rights framework even though, particularly in transitional contexts, they may yield very substantial benefits. The Rwandan Gacaca system, for instance, is still seen largely as one creating *problems* for human rights[81] rather than one addressing, in complex horizontal ways actual dilemmas of justice, forgiveness and truth that clearly have a high incidence on the rights experience of communities.[82]

4.2.2.4 Resistance

A particularly interesting modality of production of human rights law that falls squarely within legal pluralism deals with various forms of resistance which mainstream discourse might not see as typically "legal". On the more "negative" side, an attention to legal pluralism might emphasize the degree of local resistance to international human rights norms, not only from the state as is generally supposed, but from society and groups within it. There is no doubt that international human rights often announce forms of violence specific to a rights culture. Rather than characterize resistance to such processes as inevitably oppressive (when coming from the state) or backward (when coming from society or groups within it), an attention to such resistance would acknowledge the degree to which international human rights also has the potential to cause dislocation, pain and alienation. There is no doubt that certain programs justified in the name of human rights have wrecked havoc in social relations and fragile community compromises. This must surely count as a net cost of international human rights, and a better understanding of logics of normative resistance to their implementation, whether based in religion or tradition for example, can also assist in better understanding the particular connotations that rights discourse sometimes adopts.[83]

On the more "positive" side, there has and certainly continues to be much resistance to the powers that be in the name of human rights, even though this is rarely seen as

---

[81] This "compliance" framework is the one most often used to analyze Gacaca. See L. D. Tully, *Human Rights Compliance and the Gacaca Jurisdictions in Rwanda*, 26 Boston College International & Comparative Law Review 385 (2003).

[82] R. M. Borland, *The Gacaca Tribunals and Rwanda After Genocide: Effective Restorative Community Justice or Further Abuse of Human Rights*, Swords and Ploughshares, A Journal of International Affairs (2003).

[83] Catherine Powell, *Introduction: Locating Culture, Identity, and Human Rights*, 30 Columbia Human Rights Law Review 209 (1998).

belonging to the formal study of human rights law. Resistance might encompass behavior ranging from protest to civil disobedience or armed rebellion. A legally pluralist research agenda for human rights would thus focus on the extent to which international human rights is increasingly serving as a focal point for efforts to assert normativities both against and beyond the state.[84] Balakrishnan Rajagopal, for example, has sought to show how certain social movements engage in "counter-hegemonic globalization" thanks to their ability to play on the diverse registers of "global legal pluralism".[85] In doing so, such movements draw on the language of international human rights, even as they reinvent it for their own purposes of resistance. Indeed Rajagopal has further suggested that the "international human rights movement" should be redefined as a series of resistance struggles, from efforts by slaves to free themselves, to suffragettes, to national liberation movements.[86] Resistance to the law is often a highly normative act, even though it may take forms that international human rights law as such might not directly caution or legitimize. Authors such as Celestine Nyamu-Musembi have emphasized the importance of an "actor-oriented" perspective on human rights as allowing us to transcend the universalist-relativist debate by showing how rights are rooted in struggles against oppression.[87] Indeed, ultimately most significant international human rights advances have been rooted in the struggles of social movements, rather than single-handedly brought about by the "international community".[88]

4.3 Conclusion

This chapter has argued that much can be gained from a broader interaction between international human rights law and the legal pluralist paradigm, in its various forms. International human rights law is, to begin with, legitimizing of certain forms of weak legal pluralism. The emphasis on adherence to an international human rights framework in practice comes alongside considerable tolerance for significant local variation. This is occasionally lost in discourses about "enforcing" human rights against states. It would be wrong and a misunderstanding of the nature of rights to believe that they are constraining in the way rules (particularly international rules) are, and this is even more true of international human rights than it is of domestic

[84] See F. Mégret, *Civil Disobedience and International Law: Sketch for a Theoretical Argument*, Canadian Yearbook of International Law (2009).

[85] B. Rajagopal, *Counter-hegemonic International Law: Rethinking Human Rights and Development as a Third World Strategy*, 27 Third World Quarterly 767–783 (2006).

[86] Balakrishnan Rajagopal, *International Human Rights Movement Today, The*, 24 Maryland Journal of International Law 56 (2009).

[87] C. Nyamu-Musembi, Towards an actor-oriented perspective on human rights in Naila Kabeer (ed), *Inclusive citizenship: Meanings and expressions* (2005) 31–49.

ones. As the Vienna declaration put it, "the significance of national and regional particularities and various historical, cultural and religious backgrounds must be borne in mind".[89] Closer attention to the universalist human rights discourse will find that it sometimes emphasizes a fairly minimalist ambition and its "inherent flexibility" as a normative system, leaving States "maximum room for cultural variation."[90] Of course, this internal normative pluralism is ultimately limited by the constraints of international human rights and the need not to slide into a relativism that would be destructive of the project. Yet it does suggest various overlapping international human rights spheres or orders, and at least an internal pluralism of international human rights law.

Furthermore, international human rights are also constituted by a strong version of legal pluralism, manifested in the increasing diversity of actors and modes of norm production in the rights arena. A legal pluralist research agenda will emphasize the extent to which international human rights is the product of semi-autonomous but constantly intersecting legal orders. This chapter suggested that various non-state actors must be understood not only as contributing (both positively and negatively) to international human rights law as external actors, but actually participating in the genesis of human rights norms through their own internal and external normative frameworks. Moreover, there are new *forms* of human rights production that could be particularly well addressed by a legal pluralist research agenda. We may truly be witnessing a phenomenon of privatization of international human rights production, one that the discipline is barely beginning to comprehend. In the same way Francis Snyder has shown the production of Barbie dolls is dependent on "global economic networks .... Governed by the totality of strategically determined, situationally specific, and often episodic conjunctions of a multiplicity of institutional, normative, and procedural sites throughout the world", much the same could be said of the global production of human rights norms through a "new global form of legal pluralism".[91]

---

[88] Frédéric Mégret, *Le droit international peut-il être un droit de résistance? Dix conditions pour un renouveau de l'ambition normative internationale*, XXXIX ETUDES INTERNATIONALES (2008).

[89] Vienna Declaration, 1993.

[90] D. Ayton-Shenker, *The Challenge of Human Rights and Cultural Diversity. United Nations Background Note. Published by the United Nations Department of Public Information* DPI/1627/HR. In: http://www.un.org/rights/dpi1627e.htm, (1995).

[91] Snyder, *supra* note_66.

Part II
Human Rights Values and Multiple Legal Orders: Connections and Contradictions

Chapter 5
The Protection of Human Dignity in Contemporary Legal Pluralism

Jean-Guy Belley*

Introduction

The concepts of legal pluralism and human dignity are widely endorsed from both a theoretical and practical perspective. In a globalized space where countless economic and social processes traverse national borders on a daily basis, it goes without saying that political and legal regulation is plural.[1] In a global culture dominated by the infinite expansion of material wealth and technological innovation, it seems obvious that respect for human beings can only be assured by the confirmation of the right to protection of human dignity as an eminent value in national and supranational legal orders.[2]

The question this paper seeks to answer is whether the contemporary concepts of legal pluralism and human dignity share an affinity and mutually reinforcing relationship, or whether, on the contrary, they are antonymic or even antagonistic ways of conceiving of law and organizing its operations. Since the beginning of the twenty-first century and in a context of economic globalization and technocratization, is the simultaneous promotion of legal pluralism and respect of human dignity linked to a coherent and common project? Or, on the contrary, do they express the dialectical confrontation of two opposing visions of a desirable future?

---

*This text was translated by Dia Dabby, with the collaboration of Colleen Sheppard.

[1] Christine PARKER, "The Pluralization of Regulation", (2008) 9 *Theoretical Inquiries in Law* 349; Paul SCHIFF BERMAN, "Global Legal Pluralism", (2007) 80 *Southern California Law Review* 1155; Hanne PETERSEN & Henrik ZAHLE, eds, *Legal Polycentricity. Consequences of Pluralism in Law*, Dartmouth, Aldershot, 1995.

[2] Muriel FABRE-MAGNAN, "La dignité en Droit: un axiome", (2007) 58 *Revue interdisciplinaire d'études juridiques* 1; Denise RÉAUME, "Indignities: Making a Place for Dignity in Modern Legal Thought", (2002) *Queen's Law Journal* 63.

J.-G. Belley (✉)
Faculty of Law, McGill University, Montreal, QC H3A 1W9, Canada
e-mail: jean.belley@mcgill.ca

R. Provost and C. Sheppard (eds.), *Dialogues on Human Rights and Legal Pluralism*, Ius Gentium: Comparative Perspectives on Law and Justice 17,
DOI 10.1007/978-94-007-4710-4_5, © Springer Science+Business Media Dordrecht 2013

My answer will unfold in the following manner. First, the meaning afforded to these two concepts will be elaborated and their greater or lesser acceptance in dominant legal thought examined.(1). My hypothesis – that the historical development of legal pluralism has undermined human dignity much more than advancing it – will then be elaborated, highlighting the dynamic conflict between these two key ideas in legal theory. (2). Greater detail will be brought to this hypothesis by pointing out that the political culture of the first modernity enabled the mutual reinforcement of the concepts of legal monism and the protection of human dignity (3); whereas the passage to the second modernity distinctly favoured the concept of legal pluralism, but was detrimental to that of human dignity (4). The discussion will conclude by questioning whether changes could be brought to the current order of things, so that legal pluralism and human dignity would converge instead of clash (5).

5.1 Operational Definitions and Epistemological Statuses

5.1.1 The Concept of Legal Pluralism

Legal pluralism is understood in this chapter to mean the simultaneous existence of a plurality of normative orders having the status of "law" in a given space and time. Such a conception of legal pluralism raises the question inevitably of how we determine which legal relationships (ranging from independence to subordination, including various degrees of autonomy or integration)[3] and which factual relationships (ranging from passive coexistence to active collaboration, including various states of complementarity, competition and conflict),[4] the various recognized legal orders should and do have.

My definition includes, on its face, a considerable variety of different if not opposing conceptions of legal pluralism, according to the space and time considered (i.e. pre-modern/modern; political/economic etc.), according to the manner of distinguishing a legal order from what might simply be a normative order (i.e. is the legal status that makes the difference a socially-recognized attribute or an analytic construct forged by an external observer?), according to whether the theory proposed is meant to be normative (in favour of a particular dogmatic conception of the legal relations between the legal orders), critical (the proposed theory promotes a change in the distribution of status or powers between the orders) or empirical/heuristic (the plurality of legal orders is portrayed as an empirically observable fact or postulated

[3] Georges GURVITCH, *L'Idée du droit social*, Paris, Sirey, 1932, reprinted Verlag 1972, p. 53–95 (typology of the socio-legal orders contemplated in their formal relations with the legal system of the State.)

[4] John GRIFFITHS, "What Is Legal Pluralism?" (1986) 24 *Journal of Legal Pluralism*, 1, p. 2–14 (typology of factual relationships between socio-legal orders participating in a whole that does not necessarily gravitate around a central legal system.)

as an understanding of the actual dynamic of legal regulation which is more adequate than the existing dogmatic representation or than the vision shared by the social actors in the considered space and time).

My purpose here is not to review the diverse theories of legal pluralism that have been formulated up to this point in the science of law and in the social sciences, or to propose a new conception.[5] Rather, I will limit myself to highlighting and illustrating three different epistemological statuses that can be conferred on the notion of legal pluralism.

The concept of legal pluralism benefits from an epistemological status – or perhaps even epistemic privilege when it occupies a key role in the official doctrine espoused by leaders and professionals who are recognized as having the legitimate power to pronounce or apply "the law". One may consider, for example, that the legal orders of churches, cities, traders' guilds, social classes and other groups in medieval Europe enjoyed an independent or autonomous status vis-à-vis the legal order of the State due to a political culture and a legal doctrine privileging the notion of legal pluralism.[6]

When enlisted as a normative justification and theoretical support to counter a decrease or demand an increase in powers, the notion of legal pluralism has a status less socially assured, since it participates in power struggles and becomes the object of doctrinal debates. Illustrations of the notion of legal pluralism serving as social ideology would include, but not be limited to: the invocation of the medieval doctrine of legal pluralism by the Catholic Church to fight the loss of its legal prerogatives that would otherwise benefit the modern State[7]; and the mobilization of an ethnological theory of legal pluralism (persistence of customs; local, ancestral and unofficial law regimes) to support the claim for decolonization against the European colonial powers over the last two or three centuries.[8]

The scientific construct constitutes the third epistemological status. It occurs when the notion of legal pluralism is elevated to the rank of a premise or expressed as one fundamental concept of a scholarly discipline, either within mainstream

[5] See especially Kevin WALBY, "Contributions to a Post-Sovereigntist Understanding of Law: Foucault, Law as Governance, and Legal Pluralism", (2007) 16 *Social & Legal Studies* 551; and also Jean-Guy BELLEY, "L'État et la régulation juridique des sociétés globales. Pour une problématique du pluralisme juridique", (1986) XVIII *Sociologie et Sociétés* 11–32.

[6] André-Jean ARNAUD, *Pour une pensée juridique européenne*, Paris, PUF, 1991, p. 55–100.

[7] A. GIRARD, J. TONNEAU & L. LACHANCE, "La Justice" in *Initiation théologique par un groupe de théologiens*, tome III, *Théologie morale*, Paris, Les Éditions du Cerf, 1952, p. 723–858, p. 779: "Here again, it would be suitable to soften our modern conception of the social life, by renouncing to the fetishism of the State and the written law. One ought to go back to the medieval perspective of a socio-legal pluralism that is extremely complicated and varied, with a multitude of communities enjoying a special law, according to the local customs, the personal statuses and the contracted commitments." [our translation]; Jean-Guy BELLEY, "Une croisade intégriste chez les avocats du Québec: *La Revue du droit* (1922–1939)", (1993) 34 *Les Cahiers de Droit* 183, 195 and following ("Un pluralisme juridique du type théocratique").

[8] Étienne LE ROY, "Sur les chemins de Kahnawake. Décolonisation du droit et mondialisations", in P. NOREAU & L. ROLLAND, eds., *Mélanges Andrée Lajoie. Le droit, une variable dépendante*, Montréal, Ed. Thémis, 2008, p. 493–524.

theory or within a minority current contesting the *a priori* validity of normal science. This status does not confer upon legal pluralism the doctrinal authority of a proposition whose validity is recognized in the dominant legal thought. Nor does it provide the visibility or the legitimacy associated with a social ideology publicly invoked by a more or less powerful group. When acquiring the status of a scientific construct, however, the notion of legal pluralism benefits from a systemization oftentimes more extensive than that of a legal doctrine and, *a fortiori*, of a social ideology. A further advantage associated with this status is the possibility of invoking the particular legitimacy associated with a scientific truth which would impose itself in the name of the reality of things, rather than an ideal vision supported by the official legal dogmatics or by the arbitrary force of a political actor.

Interest in the notion of legal pluralism in the field of "law and society" since 1960 is an obvious illustration of its rise to the status of scientific construct. Espoused at the outset by a minority of scholars, but invoking the prestigious support of predecessors of sociology and anthropology of law,[9] the notion is today squarely rooted in theory and empirical research. What is more, its influence extends now in legal scholarship amongst a rising number of jurists who no longer consider it a heresy coming from the social sciences; they rather perceive it as an adequate representation of the complexity of contemporary law. They call for the development of a pluralist rather than monist organisation of legal regulation in order to meet the challenges of the twenty-first century. It is perhaps premature to claim that legal pluralism henceforth stands as the official doctrine of general legal theory. However, it is certainly plausible that this status will be acquired in the near future, since consensus on this notion has already been reached in many specialized branches of the science of law, where its development and growing influence are encouraged by the current social, economic and political evolution.[10]

[9] Philip SELZNICK, "The Sociology of Law", in *International Encyclopedia of the Social Sciences*, New York, Macmillan & The Free Press, 1968, vol. 9, p. 50–59, p. 50–51. Jean-Guy BELLEY, *Conflit social et pluralisme juridique en sociologie du droit*, doctoral dissertation, Université de droit, d'économie et de sciences sociales de Paris, 1977, p. 43–83.

[10] Jean-Guy BELLEY, "Le pluralisme juridique comme doctrine de la science du droit" in J. KELLERHALS et al., ed., *Pour un droit pluriel. Études offertes au professeur Jean-François Perrin*, Genève, Helbing & Lichtenhahn, 2002, p. 135–165. The rehabilitation of legal pluralism as a doctrine of the science of law is not without relation to the neoliberal critique of State law and the institutions of formal democracy, critique whose primary beneficiaries are the organizations and networks of the globalized economy. See in this way, Laurent COHEN-TANUGI, *Le droit sans l'État: sur la démocratie en France et en Amérique*, Paris, PUF, 1985. For a critique of this very normative version of legal pluralism, see Gad BARZILAI, "Beyond Relativism: Where Is Political Power in Legal Pluralism", (2008) 9 *Theoretical Inquiries in Law* 395; and also Jeremy WEBBER, "Legal Pluralism and Human Agency", (2006) 44 *Osgoode Hall LJ* 167, p. 180–182. The neoliberal rehabilitation of legal pluralism also goes hand in hand with the re-feudalization of legal relations established through contracts of dependence whose primary beneficiaries are large private groups. See on this topic Alain SUPIOT, *Homo Juridicus. Essai sur la fonction anthropologique du droit*, Paris, Seuil, 2005, p. 164–165.

Whatever the case may be, the migration of the premise or concept of legal pluralism from the field of "law and society" into the science of law[11] proves that the three statuses distinguished above are not mutually exclusive and can even combine their effects to maximize the concept's social importance. If it is mobilized as the organizing ideology of an oppressed or a conquering social group, one can easily imagine, for example, the notion finding empathetic or accommodating echoes in one or another learned community; eventually its scientific promotion would end up influencing legal thought by facilitating the task of doctrinal construction. As will be suggested further on, this seems to be the case in the contemporary era of the second modernity. The concept of human dignity will now be addressed, in an effort to show how it also acquires, successively or concurrently, the same three epistemological statuses.

5.1.2 The Concept of Human Dignity

The concept of human dignity refers here to the preeminent value that every human be recognized as a full person, independently of his or her individual characteristics and social relations. This concept has clearly acquired the status of official legal doctrine in modern Western societies and is a central marker of democratic constitutionalism.[12]

---

[11] Jean-Guy BELLEY, "Le droit comme *terra incognita*: Conquérir et construire le pluralisme juridique", (1997) 12 *Revue canadienne droit et société* 1, p. 11–14.

[12] Since the explicit reception of the word "dignity" in the formal language of international law and domestic law, namely since the end of the Second World War, jurists have learnt to distinguish a broad meaning of the concept [equal dignity for all human beings as a general value that is found at the foundation of all freedoms and all constitutionally guaranteed rights] and a narrow meaning [the right to respect of dignity as opposable to a governmental action or a private practice that belittles an individual or a group, that infringes one's self-esteem, perpetuates prejudices or disrespectful stereotypes]. The Québec *Charter of Human Rights and Freedoms*, R.S.Q. c. C-12, for example, has retained these two meanings, respectively at the third paragraph of its *Preamble* ["Whereas respect for the dignity of the human being and recognition of his rights and freedoms constitute the foundation of justice and peace"] and in the fourth section ["Every person has a right to the safeguard of his dignity, honour and reputation"]. In the present paper, human dignity will be understood in its broader sense which makes of it a political-legal transcendant aspiration, rather than in its narrower sense which confers it the status of an autonomous subjective right that, in the same capacity as other rights and fundamental freedoms, protects a patrimonial or specific extrapatrimonial interest, namely physical integrity or reputation. As a democratic aspiration, dignity principally comes from public law. As a protection against a person being discredited, dignity inasmuch comes under the law of civil obligations. On the concept of dignity and the dangers pertaining to legal analyses that do not sufficient distinguish between the broad and narrow meanings, see Daniel PROULX, "La dignité: élément essentiel de l'égalité ou cheval de Troie?", in Barreau du Québec, Service de la formation continue, *Les 25 ans de la Charte canadienne des droits et libertés*, éd. Y Blais, 2007, p. 95–121; also by the same author, "Le concept de dignité et son usage en contexte de discrimination: deux Chartes, deux modèles", (2003) *Revue du Barreau du Québec*, special issue, p. 485–542.

By positing the transcendence of the State as representative of a general interest overriding all private interests, democratic constitutionalism makes possible the affirmation of an equal dignity of all human beings based on their common belonging to the same abstract group, the Nation. Beyond all forms of inequality (social, economical, cultural etc.) that squarely distinguish them, the sharing of a common nationality or citizenship confers to all who hold this status the same formal legal equality. The doctrine of equal dignity of all citizens of a democratic State is the modern legal version of the old Christian doctrine of equal value of all the "Children of God", independently of their social status or wealth.

Before and even after the emergence of the democratic State, the concept of human dignity was at the heart of a great number of social ideologies. It was mobilized in the name of access for all to a full recognition of their citizenship status. Consider the movements advocating legal equality for women, children, and members of all kinds of minorities. This concept was also invoked to justify the extension of the notion of citizenship and its legal effects, either above the standard fundamental rights (i.e. the claims in favour of the constitutionalization of economic and social rights), or above the sphere of relations between the State and its citizens, at the heart of civil society and in the relationships between subjects of law. The most well-known example of this second extension is the working class claim in favour of recognition of an "economic citizenship" or an "industrial democracy" that would affirm the dignity of workers as a limit to owners' prerogatives over the means of production and the holders of capital.[13]

In the social ideologies that have just been evoked, the claims to new rights in the name of human dignity are premised directly on citizenship status of citizens within a democratic State. Citizenship serves here as a lever to demand laws or other interventions from the member State that would protect human dignity while improving the actual condition of the consumers, workers, recipients of social benefits or users of public services.

The same cannot be said in the contemporary ideologies that invoke the respect of human dignity in favour of persons who do not have citizenship in the concerned country, who are citizens of a State that is not officially democratic or who claim a right that even full-fledged citizens cannot claim. These include, for example, social movements in defence of refugees, immigrants, foreigners without papers, the stateless, prisoners of war, civil victims of armed conflicts, and the convicted awaiting execution by capital punishment.

The common element of these various humanitarian or philanthropic claims resides in the invocation of the common humanity of people rather than of a common citizenship. Belonging that is mobilized ideologically understands itself to be

---

[13] Michel COUTU, "Legal Pluralism, Labour Law and the Sovereign State", (2007) 13 *Canadian Labour & Employment Law Journal* 169–185. On the challenges that economic globalization poses in maintaining the legal gains obtained since the middle of the twentieth century in favor of "industrial democracy", see Katherine V.W. STONE, "Flexibilization, Globalization and Privatization: Three Challenges to Labour Rights in Our Time", (2006) 44 *Osgoode Hall Law Journal* 77–104.

universal rather than national. It is as a member of the human genre that a person should benefit from the respect of human dignity. By overstepping the limits of democratic constitutionalism, the humanitarian claim is situated in a philosophical tradition which endorses a conception of human dignity that can be asserted by all human beings – even those who the most democratic of States leave without a voice to express their sufferings and without power to counter the oppression of which they are victims.

It is not surprising that philosophy has been and remains the main source of inspiration for persons and social movements that invoke a universal human dignity. Given that the former abstractions of the "Christian community" or the "Nation" are no longer sufficient to transcend the diversity of religious beliefs and national memberships, it is difficult to assert the pretence of equal dignity of all human beings by virtue of their common belonging to a same abstract group. Accordingly, the theoretical construction of "humanity" as an abstract community on a universal scale could hardly be conducted outside of philosophy and its abstract pretensions to raise itself above the contingencies and actual differences brought to the forefront by the less metaphysical social sciences, such as sociology and anthropology.[14]

Prior and parallel to the legal consecration of Christian and democratic doctrines, the philosophical tradition was used to posit the universality of the human species that would distinguish itself from the world of gods, from the living species of the animal world and from the abstract entities brought to life by the human spirit but lacking a biological substrate (as reflected in the distinction between "legal" persons and "physical" persons). From antiquity to the present, a number of variations of what one could call "philosophical humanism" sought to overcome the limitations of religious doctrine and politics by basing the common belonging to humanity on the universal aptitude of human beings to exercise reflexive reasoning and moral conscience. This aptitude could potentially confer a specific manner of conceiving of the physical world and the relation to the other, of behaving and even suffering within the universe.

Although the source of inspiration for such proclamations of fundamental rights as the *Universal Declaration of Human Rights*, philosophic humanism has not yet attained the status of a legal doctrine that would peremptorily impose itself on the modern doctrine of national sovereignty. The formal recognition of political unity of the world remains insufficient to establish in law the claim of a supranational instance to a universal sovereignty superior to that of Nation States.[15] Even if this

[14] On the evolution of the doctrine of fundamental rights toward the contemporary idea of equal dignity resting on their humanness, see Menachem MAUTNER, "From "Honor" to "Dignity": How Should a Liberal State Treat Non-Liberal Cultural Groups?", (2008) 9 *Theoretical Inquiries in Law* 609; on the possibly negative effects of the reference to a universal culture of human dignity that does not sufficiently take into account the particularities of local cultures, see Sally Engle MERRY, "Human Rights and Transnational Culture: Regulating Gender Violence through Global Law", (2006) 44 *Osgoode Hall Law Journal* 53–75.

[15] As an example, consider the following paragraph from the *Comprehensive and integral international Convention to promote and protect the rights and dignity of persons with disabilities* [E/2003/26]: "Stressing the primary responsibility of Governments in the promotion and protection of all human rights and fundamental freedoms and their full enjoyment by persons with disabilities".

aspiration gains ground thanks to a humanitarian movement on the world scale, the political triumph of this transnational social ideology cannot be taken for granted over the competing movements claiming religious or national identities.

The socio-political and legal destiny of the concept of human dignity is even more uncertain today since it is being played out in the epistemic context of the second modernity, which disrupts the most fundamental of philosophical categories, especially those of reason and moral conscience. In a planetary culture dominated by technology and the presence of machines, whose very functioning escapes common sense although conceived by the human spirit, it cannot be taken for granted that the humans will remain at the centre of the world and their moral pre-eminence uncontested. Overtaken by its own artefacts, the human mind is gradually losing its propensity to uphold the anthropomorphic vision of the world. The technological culture, which insists on the necessary relationship of the human being to machines, confronts philosophical humanism by rendering the hypothesis of the "obsolescence of humanity"[16] more plausible.

5.2 Evolutionary Hypothesis

The hypothesis that will be explored in depth in this text is of a contemporary evolution marked by a conflictual relationship between the promotion of legal pluralism and the protection of human dignity rather than one that is mutually reinforcing. This evolution is integrally linked to the transition from the first modernity (seventeenth to nineteenth century) to the second modernity (twentieth and twenty-first centuries).

From the *Treaty of Westphalia* (1648) up until the end of the nineteenth century, constitutional evolution involved the development of a sovereign State ever more obedient to the standards of a liberal democratic regime. At that stage of modernity, the notion of legal pluralism had lost much of the socio-political importance gained during the Middle Ages. The notion of legal monism, as organised hierarchically under the aegis of the sovereign law of the State, replaced legal pluralism as the general theory of law. From then on, legal pluralism was conceived of as a social ideology of resistance to the rising power of the State as well as a scientific criticism formulated against the official monist doctrine in the name of effective control that many old and new groups wought to retain in relation to the daily ordering of activities and persons falling under their jurisdictions.

---

[16] Aldo HAESLER, "Obsolescence de l'homme", in Yves DUPONT, ed., *Dictionnaire des risques*, Paris, Armand Colin, 2003, p. 282–286. The author outlines philosopher Günther Anders' thesis (1902–1992), to the effect that the contemporary "technomorphism" condemns the human being to "Promethean shame": "Being imperfect and untrustworthy in a universe of objects that are more and more efficient, lacking the imagination to see and foresee the consequences of his or her action, being innocently thrown into a world that he or she must paradoxically destroy in order to survive, the only sentiment corresponding to this series of existential frustrations is shame." (p. 285). [our translation]

Meanwhile, the notion of human dignity had seen its social importance grow as the unity and centrality of the Nation-State were increasingly affirmed, to the detriment of the legal recognition of social diversity and ancient hierarchies. Legal monism and the protection of human dignity found mutual comfort in each other, since the State's aspiration to sovereignty came hand in hand with its constitutional obligation to respect the liberty and ultimately the dignity of citizen partners in the founding social contract.

The transition to the second modernity fundamentally put into question this synergetic equilibrium between legal monism and liberal individualism. The twentieth century witnessed a proliferation of all sorts of legal persons and organizations in law as well as in fact. These distinctive collective entities were situated between the State and individuals; they claimed legal autonomy before the State and demanded the loyalty of their agents, members or beneficiaries. The centrality of the State and the primacy of individual liberty appear to be even more contingent in the beginning of this twenty-first century. Economic globalization required the State to renounce its former legal sovereignty at the same time that transnational or multinational organizations were being recognized as having a greater role in the effective regulation of the globalized world. The practical result of this large scale evolution is the seclusion of human beings from any significant power of initiative and control.

In this context, the table was set for the replacement of the democratic liberal regime by one of corporate liberalism[17] radically changing the respective statuses of the notions of legal pluralism and human dignity. In the organizational society and the corporate economy,[18] as in the sphere of the State, which has itself become a complex conglomerate of specialised and autonomous administrative entities, achieving the rank of official doctrine seems incontrovertible for the notion of legal pluralism. There is no alternative way to adequately translate in legal terms the effective distribution of powers and duties and especially, to increase the advantages of functional specialization and globalization of economic, social and political action.

In order to profit from these advantages, it is necessary that, in return, the freedoms acquired by the organizations or corporate entities vis-à-vis the Nation State not be hindered by the legal autonomy conceded in principle to citizens pursuant to principles of liberal democracy. As a result, the legal status of the concept of human dignity was negatively affected. The official legal discourse, especially that of superior judicial instances invoking the principles of charter rights and freedoms, continues to confer great symbolic value to human dignity. However, the legal rules in force and the daily interventions of public authorities clearly confirm a general legal policy much

[17] On the ideology of "corporate liberalism" and the decisive role played by legal institutions in its triumph in the twentieth century, see Scott R. BOWMAN, *The Modern Corporation and American Political Thought. Law, Power and Ideology*, University Park, The Pennsylvania State University Press, 1996. See also R. Jeffrey LUSTIG, *Corporate Liberalism: The Origins of Modern American Political Theory, 1890–1920*, Berkeley, University of California Press, 1982.

[18] R. PRESTHUS, *The Organizational Society*, New York, Random House, 1962; Claude MÉNARD, *L'économie des organisations*, Paris, La Découverte, 1990.

more favourable to the development of organizational or corporate power than to the protection of individual rights. The invocation of human dignity may serve to limit the organizational powers, but never to the point of hampering their efficiency.

The legal policy of the second modernity is only a particular manifestation of our contemporary culture which generally promotes a technocratic vision of the world and of action. When everything is considered as a potentially useful resource to the transformation of the order of things, not only the material things, but also the human beings and the productions of the human spirit, there is nothing left to prevent the treatment of inventions of legal thought – for instance the category of "legal person" – as techniques to be utilized in the service of efficient action and emancipated from the ancient limitations of individualist humanism. The duty to respect human dignity must then be defined in a way compatible with the promotion of legal technicism for organizational or collectivist usage.

The following two sections will expand on this general hypothesis of evolution at the end of which legal pluralism will become the new legal orthodoxy, whereas the respect of human dignity will only be a subsidiary rather than overriding legal principle and perhaps even more a social ideology of resistance to technicism rather than a preeminent value in law.

5.3 The First Modernity or the Political Episteme of Liberal Democracy

Marking the peak of the doctrinal phase in the nineteenth century, the official legal culture is dominated by the portrayal of an encounter between the State holder of legal sovereignty and the individual considered as citizen and subject of law.

This legal vision of the world is the result of two great historical evolutions. The first is that of *decolonization*, that is to say the attainment of a national system of legal independence vis-à-vis a former imperial or metropolitan legal order. On a worldwide scale, legal pluralism increases by the growing number of sovereign States. On a national scale, which is favoured henceforth by the science of law, decolonization logically strengthens the monist doctrine by virtue of which the sovereign State decides (in relation to external legal orders) upon its degree of participation in the international community and internally, of the degree of independence or autonomy of all normative orders, including the religious ones, operating on the national territory. On an individual scale, legal decolonization liberates the formally colonized self. The resulting self-identity of every citizen will be more or less comfortable depending on whether the individual belongs to the national majority or a cultural minority of that country.

The second historical evolution favourable to the liberal democratic regime is the *delocalization* by which the construction and the legal pre-eminence of a unique national polity is affirmed over the plurality of local spaces. The sources of law and the hierarchy of legal regulations of the monist doctrine assert the primacy of the *common law of the land* over local customs; it confers the status of *higher law* to the legal order of the State against any local or particular normative ordering. The *delocalization* of the dominant legal culture makes the former extra-state legal pluralism disappear. From now on, every manifestation of legal diversity will be portrayed, in the eyes of the law, as conceded or tolerated by the State, integrated or annexed in some way to the State legal order, and subjected to a power of supervision and control rather than independent.[19]

Delocalization, however, including its connection to the national centralisation of law, favours the legal emancipation of individuals. The traditional and communal self is liberated or freed to the advantage of the modern and individualist one. The status of legal person within the law of the State confers political rights (fundamental public freedoms), judicial rights (the right to appear in judicial proceedings before the courts of the State) and civil rights (the right to private property, the right to contract and engage in business, testamentary freedom etc.) that can all be invoked against the traditional culture and opposed to the authority of membership groups. The legal personality of individuals is more strongly affirmed and supported in the law of the liberal State than in the legal orders of groups and communities. The ideal self of the first modernity is the bourgeois one: more national than the ancient aristocratic self; more active and more economically, politically and legally free than the peasant or working-class self.

In order to better identify the constitutive representations and understand the status that they confer on the notions of legal pluralism and human dignity respectively, one must reach deeper into the legal culture of the first modernity.

This new political episteme situates the State at the centre of the society. Through its representative organs, it is conceived as the symbolic body of the Nation gathered in a democratic assembly of equal citizens. It is the legal person *par excellence*, the one that holds the sovereign power to bring into existence or extinguish the legal personality of groups or other entities, irrespective of their claims to social or economic importance.

In this vision of things, the positive law of the State becomes the standard model of juridicity. It is a formalistic law that expresses the sovereign will of the State through legislative enactments or judicial decisions. It is a law of general application. It subdivides itself into a public law regulating the relations between the State and the citizens, and a private law which leads to a decentralization of legal regulation through the totality of individual legal acts, so long as the institutional forms and the substantive rules prescribed by the law of the State are complied with. The ordering logic of the regime is that of a legal system whose operation follows a pyramid-shaped authority. The validity of public and private actions is appreciated from the

---

[19] As an example of this representation of legal pluralism integrated in principle and kept under surveillance within the legal order of the State, see section 33 of the *Code of Civil Procedure*, R.S.Q., c. C-25: "the courts within the jurisdiction of the Parliament of Québec, and bodies politic, legal persons established in the public interest or for a private interest within Québec are subject to the superintending and reforming power of the Superior Court [except for explicit exceptions] ..."

perspective of the State whose prescriptions and symbolic models reach from top to bottom and from the centre to the periphery at all levels and in all manifestations of legal life.[20]

The human being is represented, in this legal culture, as a person endowed with a physical body at the behest of a spirit capable of rationality and civism. This abstract and quasi-metaphorical vision makes each human being a singular individual and a non-decomposable entity that cannot be deprived of its body, which is protected by the right to integrity, or of its spirit, which is protected by the right to dignity; any infringement to these inalienable and imprescriptible attributes of a person will be considered as non-compensable harm.

The legal personality is therefore the additional dimension that the symbolic order of law brings particularly to the humanist conception of human being by substituting itself for the symbolic order of religion. The status of "legal personality" confers all the constitutional and civil rights that enable human beings to satisfy their individual needs while contributing through their rational and civic behaviour to the advent of Reason and Law in political and social affairs. This legal personality occurs by way of principle and is not derived: everyone enjoys it immediately by the simple fact of existing as a human being, independently of the groups to which he or she belongs and of his or her relations with others. The modern conception of the legal personality is atomist and individualistic. It radically distances itself from the communal and relational conception maintained by the traditional normative orders.[21]

In the symbolic encounter where the sovereign State and the free individual are interrelated, there are two main types of infringements of human dignity. First, infringements may be legal ones, if they result from legislative, executive or judicial acts of the State. The "rules of law" regime protects the individual from unconstitutional infringements to fundamental freedoms, since the State is itself submitted to the primacy of Law that guarantees as much the freedom of citizens as the legitimate authority of the sovereign.

The other infringements to human dignity are social in nature. They take root in the culture of groups, in the imposition on individuals of social norms and collective stereotypes. Contrary to absolutist law, liberal law does not condemn or seek to control the authority of private associations and their autonomous management of their internal affairs. The legitimacy of their management is contingent, however, on the initial consent of each individual member and on respect of his or her right of subsequent withdrawal.[22] The freedom of association and the right to withdraw

---

[20] On the religious roots of this intrusive State legality, see Tim MURPHY, *The Oldest Social Science? Configurations of Law and Modernity*, Oxford, Clarendon Press, 1997, p. 8–36 ("Law and Society: The Penetrative Scheme and the Juridical Soul").

[21] For a critique of the atomist and bourgeois conception of the nineteenth century and for a proposition to constitutionalize a relational vision of the legal personality, see Jennifer NEDELSKY, "Reconceiving Rights as Relationships", (1993) 1 *Review of Constitutional Studies* 1–26.

[22] S.J. STOLJAR, "The Internal Affairs of Associations", in L.C. WEBB, ed., *Legal Personality and Political Pluralism*, Cambridge, Cambridge University Press, 1958, p. 66–92. See also by the same author "Developments in the Law. Judicial Control of Actions of Private Associations", (1963) 76 *Harvard Law Review* 983.

freely are legal limits imposed on groups who do not benefit from the prerogatives of unconditional authority as does the State. The very concept of individual right implies that the decision to participate in the activity of social groups, to submit oneself to the demands of a social function, is ultimately left to the arbitrary will of individuals. The only duties that are excluded from an individual's freedom of choice are those of the citizen toward the State.

In the political episteme of liberal democracy, the protection of human dignity logically presents a problem of fact and not a problem of law. In order for this protection to be effective, it is necessary to provide citizens with sufficient resources to defend their constitutional rights effectively against the State and to fully exercise their civil rights against the authority of social groups. Through the supremacy and centrality of the state legal system which protects the fundamental rights of citizens, the issue of human dignity is brought back to a problem of equal opportunity and access to justice for all.

The persistence of ideas of "equal opportunity" and "access to justice" in legal and contemporary political discourse could prompt us to believe that we are still embroiled in the long struggle to obtain respect for human dignity. The key problems would then be the availability of sufficient budgetary resources to insure access to the courts and the promotion of popular educational measures to ensure that all citizens were aware of their rights and aspired to exercise them freely. However, this is an erroneous vision of the problem. It does not take into account the arrival of a second modernity whose culture no longer supports the centrality and primacy of a legal system premised upon individualist liberalism. At this stage, the obstacles to the protection of human dignity are much more legal rather than factual in nature.

5.4 The Second Modernity or the Economic Episteme of Corporate Liberalism

As much as the nineteenth century was one of a law of political inspiration instituting the State as guarantor of the social order and the security of individuals, the twentieth century will have been one of a law of economic inspiration coordinating the interaction between the great corporations that dominate the marketplace and the welfare state that provides protection for individuals against the systemic risks of a society engaged in a continual and rapid self-transformation.

The fundamental logic of this new regime is less political than economic. The priority is not to build a symbolic unity of all citizens and to organize its democratic operations. Instead, it is first and foremost about developing a dynamic and functional network of specialized organizations with their respective strategies, above the formal separation of private and public areas, by articulating as organically as possible their different levels of action and regulation. The main challenge is to maintain the unity of the general system of action and to increase its global performance by building as much as possible on the functional specialization and the strategic intelligence of organizations considered as actors of a superior degree pursuing the achievement of their sectorial objectives as a priority. The efficiency of the economic system, rather than the authority of the State, and the freedom of organizational entities, rather than that of individuals, become the benchmark values that inspire the evolution of social norms and the law.[23]

The social conscience of the swing into the second modernity becomes clearer every day. It has progressed as a result of general ideas such as that of a "mixed economy", "just society" and "economic cooperation". It has advanced even more rapidly since the beginning of the twenty-first century under the influence of discourses advocating the "globalization of the economy", the "openness of borders", the "liberalization of trade" and the "harmonization of norms" to support the systemic performance of the "global village".[24]

Paradoxically, the awareness of the passage to the second modernity has developed perhaps more slowly within the legal community than in the rest of society, despite the clear transformation of positive law throughout the twentieth century. The persistence of classical legal thought may have been favoured by the ideology of globalized neoliberalism espoused by most states over the last three decades. Jurists have undeniably noted the legal and political transformations without which the second modernity could not have occurred. However, they did so in a disorganized manner by forming sub-communities of experts who master a very specialized knowledge of the current legal rules in their respective fields of specialization but who no longer claim adequate knowledge of the other branches of law, nor aspire to a unified understanding of the overall evolution of the legal system. Beyond their field of expertise where they invoke normative and institutional autonomy, most jurists still adhere to the general theory of law of the first modernity, most notably to the idea that public law remains governed by the rule of law and to the idea that private law is still being built on the fundamental rules of classical common law.[25]

---

[23] Peer ZUMBANSEN & Syed Ali AHMED, "The Transnational Law of Transitional Justice: A Bridging Exercise", (2008) 4 *CLPE Research Paper Series* 7, p. 10: "Transnational regulatory fields are characterized by an amalgamation of public and private norm-generating actors that produce sets of norms and regulations, which escape the traditional framework of both public and private international law". Daniel MOCKLE, ed., *Mondialisation et État de droit*, Bruxelles, Bruylant, 2002; Daniel MOCKLE, *La gouvernance, le droit et l'État. La question du droit dans la gouvernance publique*, Bruxelles, Bruylant, coll. "Mondialisation et droit international", 2007.

[24] See, for example, the collective work devoted to the efficiency of legal systems and the transnational harmonization of laws, Jean-François GAUDREAULT-DesBIENS, Ejan KACKAAY, Benoît MOORE and Stéphane ROUSSEAU, eds., *Convergence, concurrence et harmonisation des systèmes juridiques*, Montréal, Les Éd. Thémis, 2009.

[25] It must however be conceded that these two nineteenth century ideas solemnly rest atop the pyramid of the formal sources of state law. The Preamble to the *Canadian Charter of Rights and Freedoms*, Schedule B to the *Canada Act 1982*, (U.K.) 1982, c. 11 states: "Whereas Canada is founded upon principles that recognize the supremacy of God and the rule of law". In the preliminary provision of the *Civil Code of Quebec*, S.Q. 1991, c. 64: "The Civil Code comprises a body of rules which, in all matters within the letter, spirit or object of its provisions, lays down the *jus commune*, expressly or by implication. In these matters, the Code is the foundation of all other laws, although other laws may complement the Code or make exceptions to it."

For this reason, it might appear premature to refer here to a legal culture of the second modernity whose founding ideas are underestimated if not ignored by the general theory of law to which a great number of jurists still adhere. At the risk of taking for granted or exaggerating the ongoing paradigmatic transformation, it is nevertheless appropriate to explain further the main elements of this emerging legal culture, in order to better understand the status that is respectively allotted to the notions of legal pluralism and human dignity.

Even if its doctrinal systemization is still to come, the legal culture of the second modernity is the result of two evolutions under way since at least a century. The first is the growing *de-individualization* of the treatment of problems in the law of the State as well as in the private legal orders submitted to its power of supervision and control. Both in social security law through which the Welfare State is constructed, and business law that recognizes the dynamic role of private organizations while at the same time submitting them to the regulatory power of specialized public agencies, the legal equilibrium of individual versus collectivities now privileges the reinforcement of organizational powers to set objectives and to manage the processual means of achieving those objectives.[26]

The right to social benefits in the field of public law illustrates extremely well how a collective rather than an individual approach to problems and solutions is favoured. The standardized treatment of indemnity claims has replaced the former legal and individual approach of the common law of torts. The law of local self-government has evolved in the same way, shifting away from the customary liberal philosophy of the nineteenth century: the regulatory powers of municipalities and their specialized decision-making bodies prevail, in the name of public order or the efficient administration of public services, over the former scrupulous respect of the individual's right to private property. The decline of an individualist conception of rights and powers to the advantage of a social, collective or corporate vision has been observed in various branches of private law as well. The prerogatives of technocratic governance have been affirmed to the detriment of the individual power of shareholders in the law of business associations and more largely in the law of legal persons.[27]

[26] If we take the development of administrative law in the sphere of public law as a witness, the phenomenon of de-individualization is expressed in the twentieth century by a intra-State legal pluralism, that of the multiplicity of administrative institutions that substitute itself for the extra-State legal pluralism that corresponded to the diversity of local customs up until the end of the nineteenth century. This is the thesis defended with much conviction by Harry W. ARTHURS, *Without the Law. Administrative Justice and Legal Pluralism in Nineteenth-Century England*, Toronto, Univ. of Toronto Press, 1985. In private law, if we take for witness the evolution of the law of contracts, the "collectivization" notably linked to the emergence of private economic powers and to the multiplication of collective contracts could well be the "most remarkable ....legal evolution" according to Gérard FARJAT, *Droit privé de l'économie.2/Théorie des obligations*, Paris, PUF, 1975, p. 57–69, p. 66 [our translation].

[27] After the strong favorable push to managerial technocratism (Adolf A. BERLE & Gardiner C. MEANS, *The Modern Corporation and Private Property*, New York, Macmillan Press, 1939), the law of joint-stock companies is more concerned today with the protection of shareholders. However, this reinforced protection benefits "*institutional*" shareholders and their strategic domination. Hence, the individual shareholders are legally and economically subjected to the control of institutional shareholders *as well as* to that of the managers.

The validity of collective or standard-type contracts whose content prevails over individual wills is now admitted in the common law of contracts (validity of the "adhesion contract") and often developed in a preferential manner in the specialized branches of economic law (especially in labour law, consumer law, and the law of financial institutions). In the law of successions, the individual exercise of testamentary freedom is practically constrained by the substantive and procedural regulations of the public and private systems of insurance, retirement, social security, and protection of family patrimony.

As a result, the evolution of the law of the State over the twentieth century has followed a recurrent and general pattern: the individual oftentimes retains the legal right to adhere and to withdraw from the programmes or services offered by public and private organizations (rights of *opting in* and *opting out*), but if he or she adheres, the right of initiative and control over the determination of goals and means is legally lost. In the law of the twentieth century, the social law of organizations endowed with legal personality acquires precedence as a matter of principle over individual free will, just as big organized capitalism imposes itself on small independent capitalism in the market economy, just as national public policies impose themselves on the autonomy of local institutions in the sphere of public law.

The de-individualization of law frees or liberates the corporate self of legal persons to the detriment of the individual self of human beings. The individual who is insured, represented, a member, an employee, a client, a user, a mandatory or even a leader must bend before the requirements of the legal person's institutional self. The individual loses the quality of a subject of law enjoying inalienable prerogatives. The exercise of his or her economic and social rights must conform to a regime of rights whose purpose and scope are determined by their social function; these entitlements do not follow the former logic of subjective rights left to the arbitrary will of individuals. Adhesion to institutional strategies, programmes and rules is the incontrovertible counterpart of individual entitlement to the advantages derived from collective action.

In the new social contract of corporate liberalism, the State is no longer the sovereign power or the only "Subject of History" (Hegel). The State shares its status of great organizer of law with all other legal persons to which the citizens-beneficiaries submit themselves by voluntary or forced servitude: "I consent, therefore I am."[28] The legal prerogatives that nineteenth century liberalism guaranteed to individuals in the sphere of private law, and even most of their constitutional rights, are now claimed by each legal person as their own: "I organize, therefore I hold the legal powers required by the production of expected advantages".[29]

---

[28] M. MARZANO, *Je consens, donc je suis ...*, Paris, PUF, 2006. Cited by M. FABRE-MAGNAN, *op. cit.*, *supra*, note 2, p. 6.

[29] On the fundamental importance of the concept of "power" and its radical distinction with the classical notion of "subjective right", since the legal power enables a private actor, very often an organization endowed with or without legal personality, to impose a decision or a legal act to other actors without their consent, see Emmanuel GAILLARD, *Le pouvoir en droit privé*, Paris, Economica, 1985. Organic in nature when resulting from the legal person's internal constitution, the legal powers oftentimes have contractual origin and nature. See Pascal LOKIEC, *Contrat et pouvoir. Essai sur les transformations du droit privé des rapports contractuels*, Paris, LGDJ, 2004.

De-territorialization is the second general evolution that must be acknowledged. The legal regulation of action is no longer submitted to the strict respect of borders and formal jurisdictions. The former legalist doctrine of *ultra vires* has been overshadowed by the *leitmotiv* of a functional law that develops the networking and synergy of all institutions (local, national and supranational; public and private; general and specific) that can and must contribute to the development of the economy, social solidarity, learning, health, entertainment, communication, and culture, etc. Thus, transboundary systems of action and regulation can legitimately invoke a functional law whose effectiveness requires the self-limitation of territorial rights of States, of the powers of legal persons and of individual rights of human beings.[30]

The emerging legal culture that accompanies this evolution of positive law fuels itself on exogenous ideas drawn from the sciences of organizational systems and cybernetic regulation of action, from the ideologies of participative management and from the network logic imposed by the systemic nature of things, if not by the requirements of a common good: "Since we are all in the same boat, let us put aside our formal identity and pool our respective resources in favor of general functional efficiency".[31]

When considered from the point of view of a citizenship linked to the territoriality of the State within the culture of the first modernity, the new legal functionalism frees or liberates the self-rooted in national belonging in favour of a more cosmopolitan self. However, this uprooted self is not – or at least not yet – the "citizen of the world" envisioned by the activists who are opposed to dominant global neoliberalism. The self that is liberated is rather an instrumental self, preoccupied with the rational and systematic pursuit of a common goal.

This comes as no surprise since the general culture of the second modernity no longer rests on a personal and anthropomorphic vision of the world, one that suited a society of individuals, but on an impersonal and technical metaphysic befitting of a universe of machines and a society of organizations. Given their inherently instrumental nature, organizations require their individual members to develop a one-dimensional self that maximizes collective efforts and ultimately brings individual benefits.

---

[30] On the pluralist and functional regulation in contemporary transnational law, see especially Gunter TEUBNER, ed., *Global Law Without a State*, Dartmouth, Aldershot, 1997; Georges A. BERMANN, Matthias HERDEGEN & Peter L. LINDSETH, eds, *Transatlantic Regulatory Cooperation. Legal Problems and Political Prospects*, Oxford, Oxford Univ. Press, 2000; Rodney Bruce HALL & Thomas J. BIERSTEKER, eds, *The Emergence of Private Authority in Global Governance*, Cambridge, Cambridge Univ. Press, 2002; Christian JOERGES, Inger-Johanne SAND & Gunther TEUBNER, eds, *Transnational Governance and Constitutionalism*, Oxford, Hart, 2004. On the difficulties of maintaining the coherence and minimal normative unity of globalized legal pluralism, see Andreas FISCHER-LESCANO & Gunther TEUBNER, "Regime-Collisions: The Vain Search for Legal Unity in the Fragmentation of Global Law", (2004) 25 *Michigan Journal of International Law* 999–1046.

[31] Céline LAFONTAINE, *L'empire cybernétique. Des machines à penser à la pensée machine*, Paris, Seuil, 2004; Patrick BESSON, ed., *Dedans-dehors. Les nouvelles frontières de l'organisation*, Paris, Librairie Vuibert, 1997; Etienne TASSIN, *Un monde commun. Pour une cosmo-politique des conflits*, Paris, Seuil, 2003.

The new legal functionalism is not the transposition of the former national citizenship to the supranational or global level. Rather, it is the substitution of a cybernetic logic to the former humanist ideal. The ideal self of the second modernity is not the multidimensional self that individuals can cultivate and protect against the encroachment of organized power. It is rather the one-dimensional self-fostered by the conscience of belonging to a system of action and regulation that covers all levels and spheres of existence from now on. The ideal self, promoted as much by the law as by cybernetics, is a fundamentally technocratic self: more enlightened than the layman since he knows how the system functions; more loyal than the bourgeois self of the nineteenth century, since he does not pretend to control the goals of the system, but only to manage its operations or to submit to it effectively. This ideal self is within the reach of legal persons and is in keeping with their aspirations since it comes from their universe. But it is not within the reach of human beings and cannot be sustained by them unless under the mode of alienation.[32]

The representations constitutive of the legal culture of the second modernity will now be clarified.

How does the State conceive of itself? It is no longer understood to be an abstract entity – the incarnation of the idea of the "politically organized society". Nor is it viewed as the metaphysical expression of the democratic ideal entertained by citizens, as the "State subject to the Rule of Law". In a more prosaic and concrete way, the State now sees itself as a vast bureaucratic and technocratic organization that administers the public domain, that manufactures or contracts out goods and services, to the general benefit of its citizens-users.[33]

In order to achieve its objectives, the State is less inclined to assert symbolic monopoly over legal sovereignty than to enter into terms of exchange and cooperation with other organizations controlling resources or possessing a useful expertise. This is how, in theory as well as in practice, the State becomes operator or stakeholder

[32] Herbert MARCUSE, *One Dimensional Man*, Boston, Beacon Press, 1964.

[33] The passage from the traditional metaphysics of a State unified on the basis of the general principles of public law to a new culture of legal functionalism invoking advantages of organizational specialization is clearly noticeable in the evolution of the law of judicial review exercised by the courts of common law on the decisions and legal interpretations of multiple administrative tribunals whose creation in the twentieth century rendered the administration of the state justice system much more complex. A striking synthesis of this evolution in Canadian administrative law can be found in the work of Suzanne COMTOIS, *Vers la primauté de l'approche pragmatique et fonctionnelle. Précis du contrôle judiciaire des décisions de fond rendues par les organes administratifs*, Cowansville, Éd. Yvon Blais, 2003. As underlined by the author, this evolution is not without certain ambivalence. The decline of the former legal doctrine of *ultra vires* established on a hierarchical conception of judicial review is carried out to the advantage of a policy of deference of superior courts before the expertise of specialized tribunals. However, in parallel, the courts of common law have demonstrated themselves more open than before to control the rationality and the legitimacy of the executive power's decisions. Narrowly tied to the constitutional politics of the protection of rights and freedoms of individuals against the intrusive interventions of an omnipresent executive power, this second evolution suggests that the intra-organizational dynamic of the contemporary State could be considered as the expression of a legal mono-pluralism that recognizes a new and more complex version of the dialectics between unity and diversity.

within a multitude of systems of action and regulation, in cooperation with other organizations that have attained, in every sector of relevant intervention and at each pertinent operational level, the organizational quality and the strategic importance that enable them to present themselves as incontrovertible interlocutors and desirable partners of the public authority. The other states of the international community, the large-scale organizations of the national and world economy, the NGOs of the supranational civil society and the non-profit associations of the country – all these legal persons henceforth have a privileged vocation to play. They have a significant role in the system of action and regulation that the state creates or to which it adheres as a result of a pragmatic calculation. This new regime of public/private action is not constrained by the former dogmatic mythology of a sovereign State that can do anything and negotiates with no one.

The State now conceives of itself in necessary or useful relationships of interconnection with a wide range of other organizations in its environment. The primary concern is no longer to mobilize its legislative power to edict the applicable law nor the judicial power to impose respect for the law, but rather the executive power to orient its strategic behaviour according to the well-understood interest of citizens, through a general policy of inter-organizational cooperation. Achieving these strategic objectives requires putting the political representation of the unity of the State above that of a plural society ("*E Pluribus Unum*") on the backburner in order to highlight the economic representation of the intra-State and the extra-state organizational pluralism that must be mobilized in the best interest of citizens (*"One Among Many"*).[34]

Since it is first and foremost about inserting the State at the centre or periphery of the organizational pluralism that *de facto* prevails in each sector of intervention, the notion of what kind of law is adequate to the society of organizations can only align itself with the idea of legal pluralism. The paradigm of law that fits the ideal of the second modernity is no longer that of a homogenous and hierarchical pyramid, but rather of a heterogeneous and functional network.[35] The model of reference of the legal order to be put into place and operated efficiently is that of the multinational corporation, whose organization is transnationally-based, or perhaps more abstractly, whose system of action, coordination and regulation spans the world.

The ideal legal system is the one that recognizes, protects and mobilizes the diversity of actors and stakeholders all at once. It is a law of functional integration, differentiated in many levels and segments, dynamically managing the network of multiple operational units that are more or less autonomous according to the requirements of their respective duties. It is a composite and vague legal regime, at times

[34] On the new political culture claimed by the holders of executive powers to bring about a genuine "denationalization" of the state legal system in favor of a functional openness to the norms and practices of "good" transnational governance, see Saskia SASSEN, "The State and Globalization", in R.B. HALL et al., *op. cit.*, *supra*, note 30, p. 91–112.

[35] Karim BENYEKHLEF, *Une possible histoire de la norme*, Montréal, Éd. Thémis, 2008; François OST & Michel van de KERCHOVE, *De la pyramide au réseau? Pour une théorie dialectique du droit*, Bruxelles, Publications des Facultés universitaires Saint-Louis, 2002.

formal and at other times informal, rigid or supple, constantly reshuffling in favour of desirable adjustments in the exchanges between the system of action and its environment. In each subfield and in the general configuration of the interactions between various systems of action, the legal pluralism evolves while counting on the normative value of "best practices" as much as on the established rules, while respecting useful autonomies, but projecting over borders that detract from efficiency.

In formerly airtight but now porous spheres of public and private law, of national and supranational law, of political and economic action, the new ideal of law is embodied in the dynamic harmonization of rights that are open to each other rather than enclosed in their own internal logic. The passage from law as imperial force to law as useful resource in all these sectors and partial legal cultures brings with it the ideal that conformity to the law should be utilized to enhance rather than limit performance.[36]

In the legal culture of the second modernity, the human being is no longer conceived as the irreducible and sacrosanct unity of a body and soul, but as a decomposable and mobilizable set of physical, psychological and intellectual resources potentially useful if not necessary to the efficacy of the systems of action and regulation. According to the functional needs, the body can be here or there, the soul may be elsewhere and the spirit nowhere.

The paradigmatic encounter is no longer the social contract between the citizen and the State or the economic exchange of the subject of law with another subject of law, but rather the interaction between the human being and the machine or the technology with which everyone must become familiar in order to better serve it. The supervisor of an industrial robot, the pilot of a supersonic plane, the Internet user plugged into his computer, the virtual character displayed on the portrait gallery of Facebook or Twitter, is not a body governed by its own soul, but an individual resource put to the service of a machine animated by the logic of an organizational system or rather a borrowed subjectivity under the direction of a transpersonal system of representation.

The body of the postmodern person unites with the body of the machine. The human soul connects systemically with the culture of the organization and network. The dissociation and dispersion of the individual self echoes the diversity and the multiplicity of systems that mobilize everybody. The person can no longer aspire to

---

[36] The economic analysis of law played a predominant role in this evolution of the legal culture by promoting the idea that legal institutions must be analyzed from the point of view of actors-consumers looking for products offering resources and imposing constraints to be appreciated on the sole decisive criterion of economic efficiency. The normative products offered by national legal systems should compete within a transnational marketplace to the benefit of global players opting for the most attractive legal regimes. The *Doing Business* reports published by the World Bank since 2004 are the most questionable instrumentalization of this ideology. See on this topic Bertrand DU MARAIS, ed., *Des indicateurs pour mesurer le droit? Les limites méthodologiques des rapports Doing Business. Études du programme de recherches sur l'attractivité économique du droit*, Paris, Documentation française, 2006. For a more academic but no less reductionist version, see Roberta ROMANO, "Law as Product: Some Pieces of the Incorporation Puzzle", (1985) 1 *Journal of Law, Economics & Organization* 225.

a strong and unified subjectivity, since the achievement of the organizational goal or the individual pleasure of the fantasy sustained by the system of action is only possible through the symbiosis of the human being and the machine. The thought, will and singular affectivity of the individual are disqualified by the complexity of the system, by the opacity and the rapidity of its operations. The individual self is maintained in a physical and symbolic relationship with the things and technologies that can only reflect a person's materialist or technical image. The machine, the organisation, the system, are no longer the tools that extend the hand or thought of the human being. The body, the spirit, the individual's personality, are rather the extension of the machine, of the instrumental rationality of the organization and the impersonality of the system.[37]

What is the present dominant representation of legal personality? It is no longer the immediate and irrevocably added value provided to each person by virtue of his or her symbolic belonging to an all-inclusive legal order mythically produced by and for the human being. It is more prosaically the legal resource made available, optionally and for a discretionary time, to any entity (a human being, an animal, a group, a business, an organization, a system, a thing, an idea, an aspiration, a feeling etc.) to which it seems appropriate to confer the symbolic shape or mask of a person in the eyes of one or many legal systems. These legal systems in turn conceive of themselves as providers of resources which could be useful to the functioning of all other social systems of action and regulation.

The typical legal personality of the second modernity is that of an impersonal entity rather than of a human being: it is an optional status, replaceable, with variable geometry, revisable, eventually cumulative, whose ascription and withdrawal can be decided by others. Let us think, for example, of the legal personality that may or may not be ascribed to the subsidiary of a multinational firm operating in one or another national jurisdiction. The enjoyment of the legal personality is not an essential quality, but only accidental or at best circumstantial to the considered entity. It comes to existence or ceases at the behest of a utilitarian calculation and often as the result of a power struggle between interested players. It no longer has the automatism of a dogmatic *a priori*, of a metaphysical necessity, as was the case in the anthropomorphic legal culture of the first modernity.

The legal personality of human beings was conceived in a humanist perspective, as the necessary attribute of a person of needs that will enjoy its quality as subject of law to legally guarantee the satisfaction of his or her needs and the protection of his or her interests. In contrast, the legal personality of impersonal entities is conceived as the technical appendix that is added or not to the entity according to

---

[37] On the decentering and instrumentalization of the human being in the theories of cybernetics, of communication, of structuralism, of systemism and postmodernism, which have keenly attracted the favour of scientists and intellectuals alike since the middle of the twentieth century, see the far-reaching synthesis of Céline LAFONTAINE, *op. cit.*, *supra*, note 31. The title of the book by the father of cybernetics is ingenuously illustrative: Norbert WIENER, *The Human Use of Human Beings: Cybernetics and Society*, Boston, Houghton Mifflin, 1954.

the needs of the system that mobilise it. Seen in this way, the legal person has no other needs than those necessary to its useful and preferable optimal functioning.[38]

The legal culture of the second modernity operates a reversal of paradigmatic status between the legal personalities of the human being and the impersonal entity. In the classical culture, the legal personality of the human being imposed itself first in the legal mind. It served as the model of reference for the conception of the legal personality of other entities, precisely designated as "persons", but only "moral" or "legal" since their legal existence did not repose in the possession of a human body, but came from the official legal recognition of the moral value that they embodied or, more prosaically, resulted from a fiction created by a state enactment.[39] In the new legal culture, it is rather the legal personality of the organizational entity that comes to mind first and serves as model for a renewed vision of the legal personality of human beings. The day is not so far where the former "law of persons" subdivided into "law of human beings" and "law of legal persons" will be replaced in the legal dogmatics by the "law of legal entities", subdivided into "law of organizational entities" and "law of human entities". As much as the first dogmatics was governed by the idea of the "person", the second will be governed by the idea of "function".[40]

My objective is not to recapitulate the shift that has taken place from the fundamental idea of the "person" to that of the "function" in positive law and in the general theory of legal personality. For the purposes of the present discussion, I will limit myself to indicating what is changing fundamentally in the law of persons within the paradigm of legal pluralism and, in consequence, what becomes of the idea of human dignity when transposed in the conceptual universe of a general law of legal entities whose uppermost priority is to respond to the needs of a material and technical civilization.

In the context of the first modernity, the awarding of legal personality was considered as one of the powers held in monopoly by the State. It was, amongst others, an exclusive power that resulted from its legal sovereignty. At the outset, the exercise of this power was absolutist, authoritarian and discretionary: the status of legal personality would only be granted to the organisational entity judged useful to the pursuit of the State's goals and to human beings judged worthy of engaging in and creating legal relations. Under the cover of liberal and democratic ideologies, the exercise of this monopoly was increasingly submitted to the values of liberty and equality, in this area as in others: so long as they respect the formal laws of general incorporation, all organizational entities that choose to adopt this status become legal persons; all human beings become legal persons as soon as the requirements of biological existence are met.

---

[38] On the technical character of the legal personality within a system of law that has taken leave of philosophical and political foundations of the former anthropomorphic legal thought, see Charlaine BOUCHARD, *La personnalité morale démythifiée. Contribution à la définition de la nature juridique des sociétés de personnes québécoises*, Québec, Les Presses de l'Université Laval, 1997, p. 127 and following.

[39] T. BATY, "The Rights of Ideas – and of Corporations", (1919–1920) 33 *Harvard LR* 358.

[40] Reiner KRAAKMAN et al., *The Anatomy of Corporate Law. A Comparative and Functional Approach*, Oxford, Oxford Univ. Press, 2004.

The emergence of the pluralist and technical legal culture enables one to foresee a third fundamental evolution in the exercise of the power of attribution of the legal personality. Even from a strictly formalist view, this power will no longer be exclusively exercised by the State, but shared with other enabling organizations. It is already the case when a State recognizes in fact if not in law the legal personality conferred by another State to an organizational entity that has come to act and invest on its territory.[41] It will become more often the case when the State treats entities created by interlocutors and partners as legal persons, either on the strength of a formal delegation by the State or in an independent manner. For all intents and purposes, the recognition of the legal personality conferred privately is set out as an imposed condition by the organization whose cooperation is actively sought by the State. The pluralist paradigm of juridicity logically and practically commands the pluralist ascription of the legal personality.

By assigning the power to attribute legal personality in a plural manner, the law of the second modernity opens the door wide to a new way of understanding legal status, whether it is a question of allocating or refusing it to interested entities. Echoing general legal culture, the new conception is economic rather than political, technical rather than humanist. Before the advent of the second modernity, when exercising its monopoly over the creation of legal persons, the State modeled the legal status on its own image. Each legal person would be like the State, but on a smaller scale, a political body unified and independent, benefiting from freedom of will. In its internal workings, the legal person subscribes to the ethic of a representative democracy within which the leaders must periodically respond, in the exercise of their delegated powers, before the general assembly of members, shareholders, contributors or partners. With the advent of the second modernity, organizations impose their own way of conceiving an entity's personality as soon as their legitimate possession of the power to attribute legal personality is firmly entrenched. Like the organization itself, the entity is personified in exclusive relation to the goal that has been assigned to it within a larger system. In the uniqueness of its place within a group, the functional entity thus recognized does not consider itself as independent, but as interdependent with the other components of the system of reference to which it is organically tied. Rather than a free person in voluntary interaction with other free persons, it is the equivalent of a link inserted in a chain, of a box drawn in the chain of command or amongst the functional divisions of an organizational chart, or of a sub-programme operating within a computer programme. Rather than a legal person equal to all other legal persons, it benefits from a status specifically tailored to the efficient exercise of its functions: its abilities, powers, the breadth of its freedom of action and its discretionary decision-making, its democratic or autocratic internal structure according to its needs, make up a specific and contingent personality rather than espousing a uniform and egalitarian model of the legal personality.

[41] See Cynthia DAY WALLACE, *The Multinational Enterprise and Legal Control. Host State Sovereignty in an Era of Economic Globalization*, The Hague, Martinus Nijhoff Pub., 2002, esp. p. 101–158; Peter MUCHLINSKI, *Multinational Enterprises and the Law*, Oxford, Blackwell, 1995, esp. p. 57–120.

From its conception, the legal personality continually evolves in direct relation to the organisational system of reference. Its function, from beginning to end, is determined according to the needs of the system rather than to its own. Its attributes will be variable in quantity and in quality, temporary or durable, equal or unequal to that of other entities. The granting of legal personality is removed or refused according to the possibilities of procuring the same functional attributes through alternative techniques borrowed from property law, contract law or the law of organizations not endowed with legal personality. Just as the machine owes its existence to the will of someone else, the legal personality is controlled by a will outside of its own.

In the society of organizations and systems of action, in the culture of cybernetic regulation, we are no longer concerned with the legal recognition of citizens of the political society or agents of civil society, but of entities that could and will have to behave as useful cogs in the working wheel of their respective systems of belonging. Let us think again of the exemplary status of a subsidiary company integrated within a group of multinational businesses. Its personality is decided by another person, the parent company. Its political and strategic decisions are controlled (legally, contractually or *de facto*) by external authorities. Its abilities, its powers, its real autonomy depend on the internal dynamic and strategic positioning of a macro-organizational group that presides over the destinies of a considerable number of legal persons. All these legal persons are directly or indirectly controlled by a decisional centre that may well not have itself a legal personality, but that holds in fact the master keys to the general system and the ultimate control over its operations.[42]

What will become of the dignity of human beings in this universe dominated by organizations in law and in fact? Since the general coherence of the legal order is one of a functional law, given that the personality of organizations is the archetype of any legal personality, the status of human beings cannot be different than that of all other recognized entities: at best, the status of a function that is more or less ranked and promoted; sometimes the status of a more or less central link; often times, the status of a simple peon on the chessboard. The expected dignity of each human being will consist of standing at the height of the function, the task or the subaltern if not sacrificial role that is allocated to him or her within the system of belonging or perhaps the multiple systems that assign him or her a place. If an individual is not offered a place within this or another system of action, or if individuals exclude themselves from a system that is offered to them, those individuals can still assert a biological and psychological existence, a social existence outside of organizations, but they will not have access to the most significant sources of

[42] For a theorization of the multinational business as a transnational interorganizational network, see Sumantra GHOSHAL & D. Eleanor WESTNEY, eds, *Organization Theory and the Multinational Corporation*, New York, Palgrave, 2005. For a legal analysis of the upheaval brought about in the law of the legal personality by the contemporary phenomenon of transnational businesses, see Philip I. BLUMBERG, *The Multinational Challenge to Corporation Law. The Search for a New Corporate Personality*, New York, Oxford Univ. Press, 1993; and also José ENGRÁCIA ANTUNES, *Liability of Corporate Groups. Autonomy and Control in Parent-Subsidiary Relationships in US, German and EU Law*, Deventer, Kluwer, 1994.

legal personality and consequently will no longer have a legally guaranteed aspiration to dignity. Human dignity, just as the dignity of a machine or any other entity, will no longer be conceived and no longer recognized without its necessary subordination to the organizational authority and to the operational rules of systems whose existence is the only one that is seen, from the perspective of legal pluralism, as indispensable to the life of an organizational society.

In the mature second modernity, the attacks on human dignity will not be of a different nature or of a greater gravity than the infringements to the dignity of any other recognized entity. They will be physical or symbolic attacks on the function, the role or technical capability of a systemic component rather than a fully-fledged being. Excluding or destroying a human being will be neither more nor less wrongful, legally and socially, than the exclusion or destruction of a useful thing, a high-performance machine or a profitable idea. Each entity, human or not, will only purport to being respected in its fundamental right to usefulness.[43]

5.5 Toward a Pluralist and Humanist Third Modernity

Given that the game has not decisively been played out, how can we imagine a reversal of tendencies to make it possible for the contemporary concepts of legal pluralism and human dignity to mutually reinforce each other rather than act in opposition to each other? This exercise of imagination, which goes against the grain of corporate liberalism and the technical episteme that dominates today, needs not be apologetic about its necessarily utopian character. Indeed, it is rooted, on the one hand, in social realism because it requires a willingness to recognize the tragic consequences of the present situation. On the other hand, it appeals to a legal idealism anchored in the experience of modernity, since it envisions a solution that is premised upon a commitment to the constitutional principle according to which individual fundamental rights must prevail over the legal powers of organizations each time that the standard of minimal impairment and proportionality is not met by a practice unilaterally inspired by the pursuit of organizational efficiency.[44]

---

[43] Under the paradigm of usefulness, there is no longer a decisive reason to limit the ascription of legal personality to human beings and to their various types of groupings. Extending this attribution to non-human entities, for instance to purely technical instruments of communication, seems imperative as soon as these entities would gain in functional utility if they are recognized as legal persons. See Gunter TEUBNER, "Rights of Non-Humans? Electronic Agents and Animals as New Actors in Politics and Law", (2006) 33 *Journal of Law and Society* 497.

[44] The criterion of minimal impairment and proportionality was notably retained by the Supreme Court of Canada to determine whether a legal rule or decision that infringes a fundamental freedom can nonetheless be considered valid because it proves to be within of "such reasonable limits prescribed by law as can be demonstrably justified in a free and democratic society" (*Canadian Charter of Rights and Freedoms,* L.R.C. (1985), App. II, n° 44, art. 1). This criteria finds its roots in *R.* v. *Oakes*, [1986] 1 R.C.S. 103.

The tragedy of the situation should be acknowledged by recognizing the theoretical and practical triumph of the concept of legal pluralism that is carried out at the cost of an alienated conception of human dignity brought to a technical rather than humanist common denominator. Does the vision of things explained in the previous section prevail? Is it reflective of a deeply embedded and factual reality of our current situation? For the purposes of our reflection, it is possible to admit that reasonable doubts can still be entertained and that the readings of facts are ultimately commanded by the reader's optimistic or pessimistic inclination. Admittedly, any interpretation remains dependent on either wonder or dismay in the face of both the magical or grievous techniques now prevalent in the lived world.

Rather than claiming illusory factual truth, let us presume the equal likelihood of the two readings and consider instead the stakes of the present situation in order to determine whether it would be better to reflect from the best or the worst hypothesis. The second option seems, in this respect, to impose itself in the name of caution and of wisdom. It also seems to be preferable as a principle of precaution dictated by the gravity and irreversibility of the violations that will be imposed on human dignity if the growth of organizational power is not curbed by a broadened legal protection and more stringent vindication of fundamental rights of the human being.

The ultimate risk, given contemporary trends, is, on the one hand, an organizational terrorism that forces the individual to choose between alienating inclusion and marginalizing exclusion[45] and, on the other hand, a systemic totalitarianism that condemns the persons most devoted to their multiple functions to be subjected to the impossible reconciliation of increasingly onerous demands that each organization or each sub-organization makes on their bodies and their souls, without paying attention to the physical and mental limitations of the individual who is the common target of all these demands.[46] In language used as early as 1943 by Simone Weil, the ultimate risk of contemporary legal pluralism is the radical negation of the aspiration to responsibility of the human being and of his need for order.[47]

Is it realistic to believe that the law in force today, with its old and new solutions, offers sufficient protection against the advent of this ultimate risk of the society of organizations? The caselaw of national and supranational jurisdictions provides a growing number of much publicized examples of victorious invocations of human rights

[45] Jean-Guy BELLEY, "Gouvernance et démocratie dans la société neuronale", in Linda CARDINAL and Caroline ANDREW, *La démocratie à l'épreuve de la gouvernance*, Ottawa, Les Presses de l'Université d'Ottawa, 2001, p. 153–171, p. 165–169.

[46] Vincent de GAULEJAC, *La société malade de la gestion: Idéologie gestionnaire, pouvoir managérial et harcèlement social*, Paris, Seuil, 2005. As excessive as it may seem in theory, the totalitarian and organizational terrorism thesis already finds empirical illustrations in current affairs. See in this way Dominique NORA, "L'homme qui fait trembler France Télécom", *Le Nouvel Observateur*, n° 2342, 24–29, septembre 2009, p. 38–40 (24 suicides by this company's employees since the beginning of 2008; 22 suicides in 2003 and 29 in 2002 …).

[47] Simone WEIL, *L'Enracinement. Prélude à une déclaration des devoirs envers l'être humain*, Paris, Gallimard, 1949, p. 25 (crucial need for initiative and responsibility) and p. 18 ("that no one be forced to breach rigorous obligations in order to fulfill others" – need for order).

to invalidate the rules or practices of organizations. The idea of constitutionalizing the internal functioning of private as much as public organizations, transnational as much as national, for-profit as much as charitable, on the model of liberal democracy is gaining ground in general legal theory.[48] The idea that the very dynamic of economic globalization will lead sooner or later to the construction of a world legal order is spreading. As a result, a sort of federalist mono-pluralism on the world scale would emerge, within which the eminent value of a cosmopolitan humanism[49] could be opposed to the world government and all national governments.

Yet the historical and sociological lessons of the past suggest that these current and foreseeable progressions in contemporary legal culture stem dialectically, under the mode of resistance or anticipation, from the very rise in power and hegemony of organizations over the last two centuries and in all societies of advanced modernity. Practical wisdom requires us to recognize that the principles of individual freedom, of democracy and of humanism are and can only be secondary and not paramount legal principles so long as the evolution of the economy, politics and social life continue to be driven by the primary logic of material growth and technological progress. This logic places the organizations and the systems at the forefront, both ahead and above individuals. As observed many decades ago by Julien Benda, the principles of liberal democracy that protect the person can only be practiced and oftentimes are considered dysfunctional in a civilization that places its hopes of progress in the dividends that are procured by organizational power. The primacy of human principle over that of the functional principle is only possible at the cost of a firm option in favour of freedom of the individual and of democracy, even when they are an impediment to general efficiency.[50]

The guiding principle that will offer solutions to conflicts between the promotion of legal pluralism, of which organizations are the first beneficiaries, and the respect of human dignity, to the exclusive benefit of human beings, must be identified in order for this option to become conceivable and credible. This preeminent principle should be conferred fully and with the rigor that is required by the tragic nature of the current situation. Which principle, of what breadth, can we imagine at the centre and at the summit of the pluralist and humanist legal order that we dream of emerging within an utopist third modernity?

To act as a counterweight to and impose itself on the law of functionalism and efficiency that organizations are claiming, we would turn to the right to life – a right

---

[48] C. JOERGES et al., *op. cit., supra*, note 30; Christopher D. STONE, "Corporate Vices and Corporate Virtues: Do Public/Private Distinction Matters?", (1982) 130 *Pennsylvania Law Rev.* 1441.

[49] Etienne TASSIN, *op. cit., supra*, note 31; Ignacio RAMONET, *Géopolitique du chaos*, Paris, Gallimard, 1999.

[50] Julien BENDA, *La grande épreuve des démocraties. Essai sur les principes démocratiques*, New York, Éditions de la Maison Française, 1942, p. 211: "By affirming the superior value of the freedom of human beings and their dignity over the pursuit of organizational goals, the democratic regime makes clear the fundamental issue of deciding if humanity wants to be moral or powerful." [our translation].

that can already be constitutionally invoked by citizens of democracies.[51] But, we would confer an expanded scope upon this fundamental right given the seriousness of the current situation. For the same reason, we would of course retain all meanings and dimensions that have already been recognized by the national and supranational jurisdictions that have been most sensitive to the humanist rhetoric.

The first prerogative that would be retained as a postulate is the affirmation that the fundamental right to life, contrary to most other modern constitutional rights, can only be claimed by human beings. Legal persons would never be allowed to claim this fundamental prerogative in their own right.[52] This constitutes a clear and concise affirmation of the exclusion of organizational entities, whose power one precisely wants to counter,[53] from this right.

---

[51] "Everyone has the right to life, liberty and security of the person and the right not to be deprived thereof except in accordance with the principles of fundamental justice" (*Canadian Charter of Rights and Freedoms*, L.R.C. (1985), App. II, n° 44, art. 7). Current Canadian case law is to the effect that the guarantee to the right to life is only opposable to acts of governmental nature and does not apply in the context of private litigation (*RWDSU* v. *Dolphin Delivery Ltd.*, [1986] 2 S.C.R. 573). It goes without saying that, within the present framework of the defended thesis, this inherited restriction of classical constitutional law would not be maintained. Luckily, other constitutional instruments protecting fundamental freedoms have a field of application that encompasses private law relations as well as the relations between the State and individuals. It is the case for the Québec *Charter of Human Rights and Freedoms*, R.S.Q., c. C-12 and notably for its first article: "Every human being has a right to life, and to personal security, inviolability and freedom". For an analysis of the effects, at least indirect, of the constitutionalization of human rights on the law of private relations, see France ALLARD, "L'impact de la *Charte canadienne des droits et libertés* sur le droit civil: une relecture de l'arrêt *Dolphin Delivery* à l'aide d'une réflexion sur les sources du droit civil québécois" (2003) *Revue du Barreau*, special number, 1–72, esp. 44 and following.

[52] On the advantages that legal persons of private law have drawn from most rights and freedoms constitutionally guaranteed by charters of rights, see Thom HARTMAN, *Unequal Protection. The Rise of Corporate Dominance and the Theft of Human Rights*, Rodale, 2002; Carl J. MAYER, "Personalizing the Impersonal: Corporation and the Bill of Rights", (1990) 41 *Hastings L.J.* 664; Jean-Philippe GERVAIS, "Les personnes morales et la *Charte canadienne des droits et libertés*", (1993) 38 *Revue de droit de McGill* 263. For a critique of this phenomenon, see Meir DAN-COHEN, *Rights, Persons, and Organizations. A Legal Theory of Bureaucratic Society*, Berkeley, Univ. of California Press, 1986. This mobilization of fundamental rights by legal persons has found itself accelerated by the propagation of a neoliberal paradigm of human rights that increasingly imposes itself on the humanist paradigm of the *Universal Declaration of Human Rights*. See on this topic Oche ONAZI, "Towards a Subaltern Theory of Human Rights", (2009) 9 *Global Jurist Advances* 1, p. 11: "… this TRMF [trade-related market-friendly human rights regime] paradigm prioritizes the collective (human) rights of global capital over those of "flesh and blood" human beings". The author borrowed this thesis from Upendra BAXI, *The Future of Human Rights*, Delhi, Oxford Univ. Press, 2002.

[53] Understood in the narrow sense of biological life, it goes without saying that the right to life cannot be extended to organizations and legal persons since they only have a metaphorical body. The discrimination advocated here takes all its value as soon as the right to life is extended to a meaning that greatly boils over the narrow sense that has been proposed. Alternatively, a less radical discrimination could be imagined that would leave room for the recognition of a limited legal personality and a limited right to life to the legal persons. In counterpart, the latter will be imposed with, just as the modern State, the responsibility of guaranteeing and promoting the respect of the fundamental rights of human beings. See in this way David KINLEY & Dunko TADAKI, "From Talk to Walk: The Emergence of Human Rights Responsibilities for Corporations at International Law", (2004) 44 *Virginia Journal of International Law* 931, p. 945–946.

The dimensions of the right to life that have already been recognized in modern law, at least in a declaratory if not operational manner, would also be added to this postulate: the basic right to life that protects the existence of every human being against capital punishment and other unusual treatment, even those allegedly justified in the name of imminent justice or in the public interest[54]; the right to subsistence, to a materially decent life, even if this requires that the collectivity provide a distributive justice that today is being eroded even within richer nations and which is still a long way from realization on a planetary scale; the right to ecological life, to a sustainable environment, in absence of which human existence is only maintained by respite, as an endangered species amongst others; the right to intellectual life and to cultural diversity for affirming the value of different human souls in contrast to the materialist and technicist homogenization accelerated by globalization[55]; and lastly, the right to democratic life, so that human beings remain, both in principle and in practice, at the centre of strategic decisions through protective clauses that would firmly exclude the political free speech of organizations and confine them to a strictly operational role.[56]

Admittedly, it will take a long time before the dimensions of the right to life that are already affirmed enjoy full protection in existing law and concrete effectiveness in the functioning and regulation of organizations and systems. In a paradoxical manner, it is possible that by demanding even more, in the name of an extended right to life beyond its current legal recognition, the humanist social conscience will best succeed in upholding the legal advances of modernity in favor of the preeminence of the human over the functional principle.

Let us enter into utopist thought and imagine two new legal dimensions of the right to life that would have to prevail upon the law of usefulness and organizational efficacy. First, the right to *affective* life, that is the right to maintain meaningful relationships with other human beings, the right to live within a specific natural environment and a determined place, to sustain a traditional way of life, the right to prefer a firmly rooted mode of existence to a nomadic one, to choose the status quo in lieu of progress, to opt for economic decline instead of material growth, in a word the right to the preservation of a simple life rather than a fully developed one. Second, we would recognize the right to *useless* life, the right to human detachment, the right to escape and to solitude, the right to the voluntary dissolution of the

[54] Amitai ETZIONI, "Life: The Most Basic Right" (2010) 9 *Journal of Human Rights* 100.

[55] Saptarishi BANDOPADHYAY, "Fighting Homogenization: The Global Infiltration of Technology and the Struggle to Preserve Cultural Distinctiveness" (2010) 10 *Global Jurist* 1.

[56] The right to democratic participation and the control of human beings on collective decisions cannot logically and practically be opposed to only state organizations. The junction of legal pluralism and the promotion of human rights assumes that human beings benefit from a democracy animated by them within private organizations as well, including for profit organizations, at both the global and local levels. In a legal pluralism that is favorable to the rights of human beings, democratic participation presides over the creation and the management of the inner order of any organization. See in this way O. ONAZI, *op. cit.*, *supra*, note 52, p. 16–22.

individual self, the right to break the mirror that reflects the image of its masks of social use to the human being and ultimately, because it is fatally included in the right to life, the right to die voluntarily to oneself and consequently to others, the right to risk the final jump into a cloud where the human soul abandons itself to a cosmos that transcends its individual existence.

Legally and socially guaranteeing, with a right of withdrawal and financial compensation, the freedom to prefer affection to function, inalienability to useful exchange, such would be the ultimate condition to satisfy so that all other dimensions of the right to life take their full meaning and are confirmed without compromise in their normative authority. This utopist but necessary dream participates in the fundamental right to life. Without this first imperative, it is illusory to hope that the respect of human dignity will impose itself on the promotion of legal pluralism.[57]

[57] I dedicate this paper in my father's memory. Loyal agent of a great insurance company, he was a kind-hearted man, however, rather than a "man of the organization".

Chapter 6
Equality Through the Prism of Legal Pluralism

Colleen Sheppard*

6.1 Introduction

Exploring equality through the prism of legal pluralism means examining the effects of multiple, overlapping and plural normative orders embracing formal and informal legal regimes, customs and practices. Legal protections for equality are found in a plurality of legal instruments, including international, regional, national, state and municipal human rights documents and institutional codes of conduct. Moreover, formal equality rights operate in social and cultural contexts that are deeply influenced by the customs, norms and social practices of everyday life. In assessing the role of law in advancing equality, it is critical to examine the interaction between different sources of formal human rights protection and diverse, overlapping and coexisting social and cultural orders – or regimes of informal law. Such an exploration provides important insights into systemic, structural and social obstacles to effective enforcement of formal anti-discrimination and equality rights protections – obstacles institutionalized and embedded in both official and unofficial law and custom. Moreover, an appreciation of the intersections and interactions between a plurality of legal orders (both formal and informal) illuminates how strategic reliance on different sources of protection may advance the effective enjoyment of the right to equality.

In this chapter, I highlight three lenses for examining the influences of a plurality of formal and informal legal orders on equality rights. The first lens is an institutional one – focusing on mainstream and dominant societal institutions such as the

*I wish to thank Sarah Goldbaum and Dia Dabby for their research assistance on this chapter. I also wish to thank participants in the workshop "How Can the Law Help Reduce Group-Based Inequalities?" organized by the Centre for Research on Inequality, Human Security and Ethnicity (CRISE) at Oxford University, 14–15 May 2009, where I first presented this paper. An earlier version was published online at: http://www.crise.ox.ac.uk/pubs/workingpaper75.pdf.

C. Sheppard (✉)
Faculty of Law, Centre for Human Rights and Legal Pluralism, McGill University, Montreal, QC H3A 1W9, Canada
e-mail: colleen.sheppard@mcgill.ca

R. Provost and C. Sheppard (eds.), *Dialogues on Human Rights and Legal Pluralism*, Ius Gentium: Comparative Perspectives on Law and Justice 17,
DOI 10.1007/978-94-007-4710-4_6, © Springer Science+Business Media Dordrecht 2013

workplace and educational institutions. Building upon the concept of systemic or structural discrimination, it highlights how, to be effective, anti-discrimination law must address institutional relationships, practices, norms, policies, and cultures within the mainstream institutions of society. We cannot assume that a formal legal command not to discriminate will operate effectively to reduce group-based inequalities because the exclusions and harms of discrimination are often embedded in seemingly neutral institutional practices, policies and norms. We need to assess, therefore, how formal anti-discrimination law may be relied upon to raise questions about, and change institutional cultures of exclusion and the inequitable distribution of societal privileges. Using law in this way is a much more complex process than the traditional, retroactive, command and control paradigm of legal intervention. It is a process that occurs outside of the formal channels of law enforcement; it engages internal institutional change-makers rather than simply external lawmakers.

The second lens is a community one – focusing on how equality rights affect minority ethnic, religious, language, and indigenous communities that operate in "semi-autonomous spheres" separate from the mainstream institutions of the majority.[1] Two key questions arise with respect to this second lens. Firstly, to what extent does the advancement of group-based equality rights require greater legal recognition of collective autonomy and self-governance? Second, how do state-based equality rights protections affect communities governed by informal laws based on custom, tradition, and religion, particularly with respect to vulnerable individuals and groups within minority communities?

The third lens is transnational – examining the growing intersection between international, regional, national, municipal, local and customary legal regimes. Scholars of what some have called "new legal pluralism" highlight an "emerging field of global legal pluralism."[2] From this perspective, international sources of legal protection for equality are utilized at the local and domestic level to advance legal rights. The plurality of formal law has meant that increasingly, courts and tribunals are turning to international human rights law to assist in their interpretation and application of domestic laws. The elaboration of legal rights at the domestic level is also informing the content of international legal norms.[3] Moreover, in an era of increased global communication, we are witnessing new patterns of international solidarity and local engagement with international norms.[4] One manifestation of this shift is the growing reliance by civil society organizations and community-based groups on formal human rights norms emanating from multiple sources, ranging from international covenants and conventions to local codes of conduct. International sources of equality rights reinforce the normative starting point of domestic

---

[1] Sally Falk Moore, "Law and Social Change: The Semi-autonomous Social Field as an Appropriate Subject of Study" in *Law as Process* (London: Routledge, 1978), at 54.

[2] Paul Schiff Berman, "The New Legal Pluralism" (2009) 5 Annual Review of Law and Social Science 225, 226.

[3] See, for example, UN General Assembly, *Convention on the Rights of Persons with Disabilities: Resolution/adopted by the General Assembly*, 24 January 2007, A/RES/61/106, available at: http://www.unhcr.org/refworld/docid/45f973632.html [accessed 29 October 2010].

[4] Arjun Appadurai, "Deep Democracy: Urban Governmentality and the Horizon of Politics" (2001) 13 Environment and Urbanization 23.

engagement with litigation, law reform and social transformation. When local laws do not provide sufficient protection, recourse to protections included in international human rights laws can be of significant strategic importance. Similarly, where political will is lacking, the effects of international norms may be important for obtaining legal and policy change. Moreover, it is through the advocacy and mobilization of social movements that legal protections begin to be realized and lived in the context of everyday realities and social relations. This informal practice of global human rights engagement represents an alternative vision of understanding access to justice.[5] It is useful, then, to reflect upon how a plurality of sources of law is used strategically (both in formal legal processes and in social struggles) to reinforce equality.

6.2 The First Lens: Institutional and Systemic Contexts

The first wave of legal reform to advance equality rights in the post-World War II era was premised upon an instrumentalist vision of law.[6] Legislators and government policy-makers enacted anti-discrimination laws which prohibited discrimination based on specific grounds, such as race, national or ethnic origin, sex, religion, disability (and subsequently sexual orientation and social condition) in specific contexts, including employment, housing, education and services normally offered to the public.[7] Individuals who experienced discrimination were entitled to file a complaint with government-funded commissions and seek redress retroactively. Such a system was based on the assumption that discrimination was generally exceptional or aberrant in society, caused by individual behaviour based on discriminatory attitudes and negative stereotypes about certain groups in society. However, by the 1980s, the underlying premises of this regulatory model were being questioned. Tribunals, courts and legislators had begun to identify adverse effects or indirect discrimination.[8] Such discrimination occurred as a result of the negative

[5] See Roderick Macdonald's contribution to this volume, as well as: Roderick A. Macdonald, "Access to Civil Justice" in P. Cane & H. Kritzer (eds.), *Oxford Handbook of Empirical Legal Research* (Oxford: Oxford University Press, 2010) at 492–521; Roderick A. Macdonald, "Access to Justice and Law Reform #2" (2001) 19 Windsor Yearbook of Access to Justice 317–326.

[6] This chapter highlights legal developments in the Canadian context; however, a fairly similar law reform trajectory occurred in many countries. For a review of anti-discrimination law in the employment context in a number of jurisdictions, see International Labour Organization, *Equality at Work – The Continuing Challenge,* Global Report under the Follow-up to the ILO Declaration on the Fundamental Principles and Rights at Work (Geneva: ILO, 2011); International Labour Organization, *Equality at Work: Tackling the Challenges*, Global Report under the Follow-up to the ILO Declaration on Fundamental Principles and Rights at Work (Geneva: ILO, 2007) & ILO, *Time for Equality at Work*, Global Report under the Follow-up to the ILO Declaration on Fundamental Principles and Rights at Work (Geneva: ILO, 2003).

[7] Walter S. Tarnopolsky & William F. Pentney, *Discrimination and the Law* (Toronto: Carswell, 2001).

[8] Colleen Sheppard, "Of Forest Fires and Systemic Discrimination: A Review of British Columbia (Public Service Employee Relations Commission) v. BCGSEU" (2001) 46 McGill L.J. 533.

effects of apparently neutral institutional rules, policies and practices. Adjudicators recognized that discrimination could occur even in the absence of an overt intent to discriminate – when policies, rules, or practices developed for the dominant majority groups in society had detrimental effects on the life chances, opportunities and well-being of minorities and women.

Building upon legal recognition of adverse effects discrimination, the concept of systemic or structural discrimination also emerged. Systemic discrimination occurs when discrimination goes beyond discrete or individual instances of prejudice or wrongdoing to encompass more widespread problems of inequality in society generally or within specific societal institutions. It often includes both direct and adverse effects discrimination and it is reproduced in the institutional and social relations of everyday life. One of the most difficult dimensions of systemic discrimination is its tendency to be reinforced over time. Inequitable privileges mean that those who enjoy such privileges have access to more resources and support and consequently often perform better – thereby seemingly justifying the initial inequitable distribution of privileges. The cyclical and relational dimensions of systemic inequalities are difficult to reverse.[9]

A growing recognition of systemic discrimination prompted a rethinking of the legal regulation of equality. It became apparent that a retroactive, individual complaints-driven approach to remedying discrete acts of discrimination was insufficient for problems of discrimination and exclusion that are deeply embedded in institutions, structures and systems. As a result, a number of proactive policy initiatives, such as affirmative action, employment equity, contract compliance, procurement policies and pay equity, were introduced in many jurisdictions.[10] While some of these proactive measures have produced important results, they continue to be quite limited and often very poorly enforced.[11] Moreover, these proactive initiatives are often grafted onto an unchallenged institutional status quo – thus failing to address the underlying sources of exclusion and inequality. For example, affirmative action will secure access most effectively for the most privileged members of historically underrepresented minority groups because it is those individuals who can best assimilate into dominant societal institutions. The institutional policies and practices tied to historical exclusions are not revisited or revised; instead exceptional individuals from minority communities gain expedited access. The kind of social and institutional transformation required to address the underlying causes of systemic and structural inequities has not occurred in the wake of proactive anti-discrimination initiatives. Remedying the institutionalized dimensions of exclusion and discrimination,

---

[9] For a review of these developments, see Rosalie Silberman Abella, *Report of the Commission on Equality in Employment* (Ottawa: Ministry of Supply and Services, 1984); see also, Susan Sturm, "Second Generation Employment Discrimination: A Structural Approach" (2001) 101 Columbia Law Review 458.

[10] Elaine Kennedy-Dubourdieu (ed.), *Race and Inequality: World Perspectives on Affirmative Action* (Ashgate Press, 2006).

[11] Carol Agócs (ed.), *Workplace Equality: International Perspectives on Legislation, Policy and Practice* (The Hague: Kluwer Law International, 2002).

therefore, presents an ongoing challenge for those committed to advancing equality rights in the mainstream institutions of everyday life.

It is in confronting this challenge that the lens of legal pluralism becomes very instructive for it teaches us to be attentive to how formal anti-discrimination protections must operate in institutional contexts governed by a complex array of rules, norms, customs, traditions, and practices. Scholars of legal pluralism have highlighted important ways in which formal and informal normative orders intersect and interact.[12] As Sally Engle Merry describes it, "state law both constitutes and is constituted by" other normative orders.[13] Her work also examines facilitative law "that functions not by imposing obligations but by providing individuals with facilities for realizing their wishes through conferring legal powers on them."[14] Gunther Teubner has also explored what he calls "policies of proceduralization;" whereby the "legal system concerns itself with providing the structural premises for self-regulation within other social subsystems".[15] Increasingly, there is recognition of the hybridity of legal systems, embracing both state and non-state legal regimes.[16] To stop the reproduction of exclusion and inequality embedded in the non-state law of institutions – that is in the structures, relationships, traditions and practices of social and institutional life – we need to analyse how formal laws affect or fail to affect the social and institutional decision-making, policies and practices.

Susan Sturm's important work on structural discrimination explores how the legal norm of equality affects decision-making processes in the workplace. She suggests that one of the most effective ways to implement anti-discrimination protections is to integrate them into day-to-day employment policies, practices and decision-making processes. According to Sturm, "Legal norms play the role of opening spaces for ongoing engagement about current practice in relation to aspirations that have been identified to be of public significance".[17] She explores the role of law in terms of its function in creating "occasions for analysis, reflection, relationship building, boundary negotiations and institution building".[18] Such an integrated approach to enforcing anti-discrimination norms is considered particularly important with regard to systemic or structural discrimination, which is not easily redressed through retroactive complaints processes that tend to focus on discrete and severe incidents of discrimination. From this more pluralist perspective,

[12] Sally Engle Merry, "Legal Pluralism" (1988) 22 Law & Society Review 869; S.F. Moore, *supra* note 1; Roderick A. Macdonald, "Metaphors of Multiplicity: Civil Society, Regimes and Legal Pluralism" (1998) 15 Arizona Journal of International & Comparative Law 69.

[13] S.E. Merry, "Legal Pluralism", *supra* note 12, 883.

[14] Ibid., 885.

[15] Gunther Teubner, "Substantive and Reflexive Elements in Modern Law" (1983) 17 Law & Society Review 239, 283.

[16] Paul Schiff Berman, "Global Legal Pluralism" (2007) 80 Southern California Law Review 1155.

[17] Susan Sturm, "Owen Fiss, Equality Theory, and Judicial Role" (2003) Issues in Legal Scholarship: The Origins and Fate of Antisubordination Theory (Berkeley Electronic Press) article 18, p. 7.

[18] Ibid.

the legal norm of equality is subject to interpretation and application by numerous institutional actors; legal interpretation and enforcement are not the exclusive domain of lawyers and adjudicators. Indeed, legal norms will be most effectively enforced when they form the normative backdrop for institutional decision-making. In such a context, anti-discrimination law operates indirectly as facilitative law. Law enforcement does not simply refer to formal, state-based processes. Rather, legal norms and principles become embedded in the institutional culture and practice of everyday life.

While this vision suggests that the public law norms of equality may infuse institutional practice and decision-making in multiple and myriad ways, in many cases, the opposite occurs. Rather than transformative public law norms being incorporated into institutional cultures and decisions, institutions resist and reassert traditional and exclusionary practices and norms. Linda Hamilton Kreiger, for example, documents socio-legal institutional resistance to the transformative agenda of anti-discrimination laws, including the phenomena of what she calls "capture" and "backlash".[19] Capture refers to the subtle ways in which traditional norms and values resist new directions in law and public policy. Backlash occurs when there is open, vocal and direct rejection of legal reforms. For example, affirmative action initiatives may be rejected as unfair forms of reverse discrimination. Or pay equity reforms may be challenged as impermissible interference with the free market. Thus, pre-existing social and institutional norms persist and may even be inadvertently reinforced in the face of challenges to their validity or fairness by state-based equality rights initiatives. For those concerned with advancing the equality goals included in anti-discrimination laws and policy initiatives, it is necessary to be aware of the risks of institutional resistance, and to take it into account in implementation strategies. The difficulty of reducing institutionalized group-based inequalities, however, should not prevent us from developing new approaches and strategies that take these systemic realities into account.

Some of the most promising strategies contest traditional channels of institutionalized power and privilege by insisting that anti-discrimination law empower those situated at the bottom of organizational hierarchies. Developing safe mechanisms for enhancing more participatory forms of governance within mainstream societal institutions such as workplaces and educational institutions is one critically important strategy. Imagining how to use state-based legal norms to move in this direction is a further challenge. Autonomous trade unions have been one important vehicle for enhancing democratic participation of workers and promoting more equitable workplaces.[20] Student democracy is another mechanism for hearing the voices of those with less power in the institutional structures in which we live. There remains much work to be done in thinking about how to use

[19] Linda Hamilton Kreiger, "Afterword: Socio-Legal Backlash" (2000) 21 Berkeley Journal of Employment & Labor Law 476, 484.

[20] Adelle Blackett & Colleen Sheppard, "Collective Bargaining and Equality: Making Connections" (2003) 142 International Labour Review 419.

law to restructure institutional relationships towards more equitable and democratic participation.[21]

6.3 The Second Lens: Customs, Traditions and Self-Governance

Another important way of thinking about legal pluralism and equality concerns self-governing communities within larger state structures. Indeed, early work on legal pluralism emerged from the observations of legal anthropologists regarding the persistence of customary legal regimes following the imposition of colonial rule.[22] While statutory anti-discrimination laws have tended to focus on ensuring the integration of individuals from socially-disadvantaged groups into mainstream institutions, such as workplaces, educational institutions and public spaces, law may also advance group-based equality by giving legal recognition to the traditions, customs and laws of minority communities. Group-based equality may be enhanced, therefore, when formal state law takes into account, validates, or endorses the separate institutions and practices of minority communities. This connection has been recognized most clearly in relation to indigenous peoples and minority linguistic communities.[23] It has also arisen in more controversial ways with respect to religious communities and religious-based family arbitration.[24]

In terms of indigenous peoples, James Anaya maintains that self-determination is integrally linked to the idea that all peoples are equally "entitled to control their own destinies".[25] Greater political autonomy, through self-governance and self-determination, therefore, "tear[s] at the legacies of empire, discrimination, suppression of democratic participation and cultural suffocation".[26] From this perspective, equality rights for oppressed indigenous communities are integrally linked to providing separate political spaces that will allow them to govern themselves pursuant to their own laws, traditions and customs.[27] Support for the legal pluralism inherent in self-governance,

---

[21] For an extended discussion of democracy and equality, see Colleen Sheppard, *Inclusive Equality – The Relational Dimensions of Systemic Discrimination in Canada* (Montreal: McGill-Queen's University Press, 2010), ch. 6. See also, Iris Marion Young, *Inclusion and Democracy* (New York: Oxford University Press, 2000).

[22] P.S. Berman, "Global Legal Pluralism", *supra* note 16, 1171.

[23] Colleen Sheppard, "Constitutional Recognition of Diversity in Canada" (2006) 26 Vermont Law Review 463.

[24] Ayelet Shachar, "Religion, State, and the Problem of Gender: New Modes of Citizenship and Governance in Diverse Societies" (2004–2005) 50 McGill L.J. 49.

[25] James S. Anaya, *Indigenous Peoples in International Law*, 2d (New York: Oxford University Press, 2004), p. 97.

[26] Ibid.

[27] Val Napoleon, "Aboriginal Self Determination: Individual Self and Collective Selves" (2005) 29(2) Atlantis: A Woman's Studies Journal 31.

therefore provides a structural means to advance group-based equality. It gives oppressed communities greater political and legal control over their destinies. While constitutional and international law have often been the focus of legal claims to self-government by indigenous communities, recognition of autonomous indigenous legal orders has also been implicit in some private law contexts.

In the Canadian context, dating back to the late 1800s, there have been judicial decisions affirming the legality of marriages and adoptions carried out pursuant to indigenous legal regimes.[28] More recently, Aboriginal peoples in Canada have turned to constitutional protections and international law to assert their right to self-governance. Since 1982, Aboriginal rights have been accorded express constitutional protection (Constitution Act, 1982, s. 35).[29] The scope and meaning of these constitutional rights have been the subject of extensive debate and litigation. To date, Canadian courts have taken a case-by-case and piecemeal approach to aboriginal rights, affirming the right to engage in the traditional practices and customs that characterized pre-colonial indigenous life.[30] Such an approach appears to be somewhat limited and inadequately cognizant of the need to redress the deleterious legacy of colonization. It has, however, provided concrete benefits in some cases. The courts, moreover, have been reluctant to endorse a full right to self-government, given the potential impact on non-Aboriginal communities. At the international level, both the Covenant on Civil and Political Rights and the Covenant on Social, Economic and Cultural Rights affirm the right of self-determination for peoples.[31] Canada is a signatory to both, as well as the Optional Protocol of the Covenant on Civil and Political Rights. Aboriginal communities in Canada have used the Optional Protocol to claim rights to self-determination in the international arena.[32] Indigenous communities in Canada have also engaged in global efforts to protect the rights of

[28] John Borrows, *Recovering Canada: The Resurgence of Indigenous Law* (Toronto: University of Toronto Press, 2002), p. 4. For an early decision recognizing the validity of a marriage between a Cree woman and non-Cree man, conducted in accordance with Cree customary law, see Connolly v. Woolrich and Johnson (1867) 17 R.J.Q. 75 (Q.S.C.), affirmed [1869] 1 Revue légale 253 (C.A.).

[29] The Constitution Act, 1982 provides:

35. (1) The existing aboriginal and treaty rights of the aboriginal peoples of Canada are hereby recognized and affirmed.

(2) In this Act, "aboriginal peoples of Canada" includes the Indian, Inuit, and Metis peoples of Canada.

(3) For greater certainty, in subsection (1) "treaty rights" includes rights that now exist by way of land claims agreements or may be so acquired.

(4) Notwithstanding any other provision of this Act, the aboriginal and treaty rights referred to in subsection (1) are guaranteed equally to male and female persons.

[30] Early leading cases on the constitutional interpretation of Aboriginal rights include: *R. v. Sparrow,* [1990] 1 S.C.R. 1075; *R. v. Van der Peet,* [1996] 2 S.C.R. 507. See also, John Borrows, "The Trickster: Integral to a Distinctive Culture" (1997) 8:2 Constitutional Forum 27.

[31] J.S. Anaya, *supra* note 25.

[32] See *Lubicon Lake Band v. Canada, Communication No. 167/1984* (26 March 1990), U.N. Doc. Supp. No. 40 (A/45/40) at 1 (1990).

indigenous communities around the world, including participation in the drafting of the *Declaration on the Rights of Indigenous Peoples*.[33]

Minority linguistic communities in Canada have also sought to ensure the survival of their language through separate cultural, social and educational institutions. Educational policy has been a critical strategic terrain in this regard. Understanding that integration into the majority language educational system would spell assimilation, there has been a long and continuing struggle for publicly-funded French language schools outside of Quebec. The importance of the historical and contextual realities of specific struggles is highlighted by this story. Whereas in the United States, one of the most important civil rights struggles of the twentieth century revolved around efforts to integrate racially segregated public schools, in the Canadian context, forced integration into English public schools for the francophone minorities would have spelt assimilation and the demise of their communities.[34] Indeed, up until the 1970s, there were legal reforms that undermined the rights of francophone minority groups outside of Quebec by eliminating French language public schools.[35] These anti-French policies deeply damaged the survival of the French language outside of Quebec. When constitutional protection for minority language education was finally entrenched in the Constitution in 1982, there was a significant risk that the constitutional reforms were too little and too late.[36] Nevertheless, courts have accorded a generous interpretation to minority linguistic education rights, recognizing the urgency of securing vibrant French language schools.[37] Despite efforts by the judiciary to give a broad interpretation to these language rights, assimilation continues to pose a significant challenge to the survival of francophone minority linguistic communities outside of Quebec.

Thus, francophone minority linguistic communities in Canada have tried to advance equality by maintaining separate institutions rather than being integrated into majoritarian institutions. This choice of equality through separation parallels the efforts of many indigenous communities to reduce group-based inequalities through separate autonomous institutions. Of significance in the minority language education cases is judicial recognition that protecting the rights of a linguistic minority requires an affirmation of a right (where numbers warrant) to participate in the management

[33] *Declaration on the Rights of Indigenous Peoples* (UN GA Resolution 61/295, 13 September 2007): Canada was one of four countries to vote against the resolution. The others included the United States, Australia and New Zealand. Canada eventually endorsed the Declaration in November, 2010.

[34] Colleen Sheppard, "Equality in Context: Judicial Approaches in Canada and the United States" (1990) 39 University of New Brunswick Law Journal 111.

[35] Michael Behiels, *Canada's Francophone Minority Communities: Constitutional Renewal and the Winning of School Governance* (Montreal: McGill-Queen's University Press, 2005).

[36] See *Canadian Charter of Rights and Freedoms*, Section 23.

[37] See, for e.g. *Mahe v. Alberta* [1990] 1 S.C.R. 342; *Arsenault-Cameron v. Prince Edward Island*, [2000] 1 S.C.R. 3; *Doucet-Boudreau v. Nova Scotia (Minister of Education)*, [2003] 3 S.C.R. 3.

and control of minority language education.[38] Participation is considered essential to ensure that the needs, concerns and interests of the linguistic minority are reflected in educational policy decisions. The Supreme Court of Canada has recognized that "the majority cannot be expected to understand and appreciate all of the diverse ways in which educational practices may influence the language and culture of the minority".[39] In a subsequent decision, the Court added, "Empowerment is essential to correct past injustices and to guarantee that the specific needs of the minority language community are the first consideration in any given decision affecting language and cultural concerns."[40] Thus, although the minority language education context addresses schooling exclusively, it reinforces the idea that self-governance, affirmed and protected through law, may be a critical pathway to equality.

While self-governance is an important and promising strategy for advancing substantive group-based equality, it also presents significant challenges, complexities and difficulties. First, it is necessary to delineate the legal boundaries of the group – a task which risks resulting in the congealing of group-based identities and the construction of categories of essentialist and homogeneous group difference.[41] Second, according legal recognition to semi-autonomous communities raises complex and difficult questions about representation of the community. Who speaks for the group and what should we do in the face of conflict and dissent within the community? Moreover, how do we insure that more vulnerable individuals within the community are adequately protected?[42] Numerous scholars are endeavouring to understand how to advance group-based claims for autonomy and self-government while being attentive to the risks of a divergence between community-based religious or cultural norms and state-based human rights.[43] Increasingly, courts are also navigating the complex waters of the intersections between customary law and human rights. In some cases, state-based equality rights protections provide necessary protection from inequitable community-based customs or practices.[44] In other cases, customary law is being interpreted and applied to advance human rights.[45]

---

[38] *Mahe v. Alberta, supra* note 37. On the right of English minority education in Québec, see most recently *Nguyen v. Québec (Minister of Education, Recreation and Sport)*, [2009] 3 S.C.R. 209.

[39] *Mahe v. Alberta, supra* note 37, 372.

[40] *Arsenault-Cameron v. Prince Edward Island*, [2000] 1 S.C.R. 3 at para. 45.

[41] Nitya Iyer, *Categorical Denials: Equality Rights and the Shaping of Social Identity* (1993) 19 Queen's L.J. 179 (1993); Angela Harris, "Race and Essentialism in Feminist Legal Theory" (1980) 42 Stanford Law Review 581; James Tully, *Strange Multiplicity: Constitutionalism in an Age of Diversity* (Cambridge: Cambridge University Press, 1995).

[42] See Val Napoleon's contribution to this volume; Vrinda Narain, *Gender and Community – Muslim Women's Rights in India* (Toronto: University of Toronto Press, 2001); Ayelet Shachar, *Multicultural Jurisdictions: Cultural Differences and Women's Rights* (Cambridge: Cambridge University Press, 2001).

[43] Will Kymlicka, *Politics in the Vernacular – Nationalism, Multiculturalism & Citizenship* (Oxford: Oxford University Press, 2001); P.S. Berman, "Global Legal Pluralism", *supra* note 16.

[44] V. Narain, *Gender and Community, supra* note 42.

[45] Jewel Amoah, "Equality Rights for the Girl Child under the South African Constitution Watch GRACE grow: African Customary Law in the Constitutional Garden" Conference Presentation, International Feminist Constitutionalism Conference, Queen's University, Kingston, 2009.

In an important South African example, elders in the community had interpreted traditional customs to allow a young woman to assume a leadership role – a conclusion that was contested in court by a young man who believed he was entitled to become the community's chief. In the ensuing legal challenge, the courts deferred to the elders' dynamic interpretation of their customary law – an interpretation that embraced gender equality.[46]

6.4 The Third Lens: Global Legal Pluralism

One final lens through which to examine legal plurality and equality rights focuses on the intersection of international and local formal and informal sources of protection for group-based equality, ranging from customary law, institutional or municipal codes of conduct, national laws and international conventions. This global legal pluralism is distinctive for its transnational character.[47] International and regional human rights conventions are often raised in litigation to reinforce claims for equality at the national, provincial/state, or municipal level. Indeed, judges increasingly rely on international human rights norms as interpretive aids in domestic litigation. Beyond a vertical and formal reliance on international law, the rise of international conventions and declarations on human rights has also nurtured a robust global movement of civil society organizations. Transnational convergence of human rights norms promotes "horizontal learning" between those engaged in struggles for social justice and enhances their recognition by local governments and institutions.[48] Arjun Appadurai, who describes the emergence of transnational networks of solidarity as "globalization from below", suggests that it contributes to new forms of global democratic engagement.[49] Merry refers to the "vernacularization of international human rights concepts" – a paradoxical process drawing on universal human rights norms, but reshaping them to resonate with local cultural frameworks.[50]

---

[46] *Shilubana and Others v. Nwamitwa*, [2008] ZACC 9.

[47] P.S. Berman, "Global Legal Pluralism", *supra* note 16. On the ambiguities surrounding "global" legal pluralism, see William Twinning, "Normative and Legal Pluralism: A Global Perspective" (2010) 20 Duke Journal of Comparative & International Law 473, esp. at 504–517.

[48] A. Appadurai, "Deep Democracy: Urban Governmentality and the Horizon of Politics", *supra* note 4, 39. Boaventura De Sousa Santos' speaks of "subaltern cosmopolitan legality", which "calls for a conception of the legal field suitable for reconnecting law and politics and reimagining legal institutions from below." See Boaventura De Sousa Santos & César Rodríguez-Garavito, "Law, Politics, and the Subaltern in Counter-Hegemonic Globalization" in Boaventura De Sousa Santos & César Rodríguez-Garavito (eds.), *Law and Globalization from Below: Towards a Cosmopolitan Legality* (Cambridge: Cambridge University Press, 2005), p. 1 at p. 15.

[49] A. Appadurai, "Deep Ddemocracy: Urban Governmentality and the Horizon of Politics", *supra* note 4, 42.

[50] See Sally Engle Merry's contribution to this volume.

To illustrate this final lens, it is useful to highlight three examples where the plurality of law has functioned to enhance the promotion of equality rights. The first entails reliance on international human rights norms by domestic courts and tribunals. In the Canadian context, there are numerous cases where the Supreme Court cites international human rights conventions to inform the interpretation of domestic law. For example, in *Baker v. Canada (Minister of Citizenship and Immigration)*,[51] a Jamaican woman who was residing illegally in Canada was facing deportation. During her time in Canada, she had given birth to four children, all of whom were Canadian citizens by virtue of their birth in Canada. The Supreme Court of Canada stayed her deportation because the immigration official failed to take into account the impact of her pending deportation on the best interests of her children as required under the *Convention on the Rights of the Child*, to which Canada is a signatory. Thus, the protection of children's rights at the international level was used to reinforce their protection domestically. The plurality of laws protecting children helped to secure their protection and to protect a vulnerable racialized mother facing deportation from Canada.

The second example involves a use of international human rights complaints processes to bring global attention to domestic violations of rights. There are numerous examples of reliance on such processes. One very significant and historical example involved a complaint against the Canadian government under the *Optional Protocol of the International Covenant on Civil and Political Rights*. An indigenous woman, Sandra Lovelace, lost her status as a Maliseet Indian pursuant to federal legislation upon marriage to a non-Indian man.[52] Indigenous men did not face any loss of their Indian status upon marriage to non-Indian women. The federal law, in effect, imposed a patrilineal approach to indigenous status in Canada. An earlier challenge in Canadian courts had failed at the Supreme Court of Canada.[53] Accordingly, Lovelace was allowed to proceed with her complaint before the Human Rights Committee set up under the Optional Protocol. The Committee concluded that Canada was in violation of the Covenant, focusing on minority rights, and her entitlement to continue to be part of her minority community. One of the adjudicators also concluded that the provisions discriminated against indigenous women. Reforms were made to eliminate the most overt discrimination, and to reinstate women who had lost their status into their communities. The legislative reforms, however, have not addressed all of the problems linked to this historical denial of rights to indigenous women, their children and grandchildren in Canada and legal challenges continue.[54]

Beyond the critical role of litigation that engages with legal protections from a plurality of sources, organizations of civil society are increasingly drawing on

---

[51] *Baker v. Canada (Minister of Citizenship and Immigration)*, [1999] 2 S.C.R. 817.

[52] Sandra Lovelace v. Canada (adopted on 30 July 1981 at the Committee's thirteenth session). Communication No. 24/1977, reproduced in Human Rights Committee 1981 Report to the General Assembly, Annex XVIII; Selected Decisions, Vol. I, pp. 83 et seq.

[53] *Attorney General of Canada v. Lavell*, [1974] S.C.R. 1349.

[54] See *McIvor v. Canada (Registrar of Indian & Northern Affairs)* 2009 BCCA 153 (application for leave to appeal to the Supreme Court of Canada dismissed, No. 33201 (05.11.2009)). See also, R. L. et al. v. Canada, Communication No. 358/1989, U.N. Doc. CCPR/C/43/D/358/1989 at 16 (1991).

multiple sources of law in their advocacy and work for social change at local, national, regional and international levels. A third example, therefore, is reliance on international protections by civil society organizations working through global solidarity networks to address human rights violations. To highlight a concrete example, there have been important developments in the domain of violence against women. Carolyn Andrew outlines how women's organizations draw on global legal pluralism in seeking to secure safe and secure living environments for women. She outlines how civil society organizations use "global links in their local or municipal work, the links to the global being a resource in local activity".[55] Indeed, once an issue gains recognition at the global level, local authorities are much more inclined to acknowledge the importance of the issues and concerns in their own communities. Bringing women's urban safety into the international arena, not only puts the issue of gender and security in everyday life on the agenda of the global community, but also enhances its legitimacy as a pressing social issue in the eyes of local authorities.[56] According to Sally Engle Merry, the city takes on a distinct legal space with its own relationship to international law; city ordinances are used as vehicles for incorporating international conventions. International conventions, such as CEDAW, the ICCPR, the ICESR and the CERD are being introduced through city ordinances in the United States[57]; similar trends in this regard can be observed in Canada.[58] The Stolen Sisters campaign of Amnesty International provides another important example of efforts to forge global solidarity to raise awareness about violence against indigenous women in Canada as a human rights abuse.[59] Despite the

---

[55] Carolyn Andrew, "Women in Cities International: A Case Study in Knowledge Transfer", Seminar Presentation, Faculty of Law, McGill University (2008), p. 20.

[56] See http://www.femmesetvilles.org/english/index_en.htm. The Femmes et villes organization has a current project entitled "Gender Inclusive Cities: Increasing Women's Safety by Identifying and Disseminating Effective and Promising Approaches that Promote Women's Equal Access to Public Spaces (GICP)". Its purpose is to enhance women's inclusion and "right to the city", see Baseline 2010 Report: http://www.femmesetvilles.org/pdf-general/gicp_baseline.pdf

[57] Sally Engle Merry, "International Law and Sociolegal Scholarship: Toward a Spatial Global Legal Pluralism" (2008) 41 *Studies in Law, Politics and Society* 149, 163–164. See also Stacy Laira Lozner, "Diffusion of Local Regulatory Innovation: The San Francisco CEDAW Ordinance and the New York City Human Rights Initiative" (2004) 104 Columbia Law Review 768.

[58] See the *Montreal Charter of Rights and Responsibilities*, adopted in 2005 and effective as of 2006: http://ville.montreal.qc.ca/pls/portal/docs/page/charte_mtl_en/media/documents/charte_droits_en.pdf (site accessed 08.06.2011). In 1999, the city of Toronto adopted a Charter that focuses on children's rights, entitled the *Toronto Children's Charter*: see http://www.toronto.ca/children/pdf/charter.pdf (site accessed 08.06.2011).

[59] See Amnesty International, *Stolen Sisters: A Human Rights Response to Discrimination and Violence Against Indigenous Women in Canada* (October 2004), online: http://www.amnesty.ca/campaigns/resources/amr2000304.pdf. On the 2009 follow-up report by Amnesty International, see *No More Stolen Sisters: The Need for a Comprehensive Response to Discrimination and Violence Against Indigenous Women in Canada*, online: http://www.amnesty.ca/amnestynews/upload/AMR200122009.pdf. Amnesty International concluded at page 25 that "[i]mportant gaps in available statistical data need to be filled in order to ensure that social policy is based on sound information. The need for further research, however, is not an excuse for inaction."

difficulties civil society organizations face in securing long-term financial support, there is widespread consensus about the importance of developing links between social movements on a global scale. In thinking about the role of law in reducing group-based inequalities, therefore, it is critical to examine how law is being used in multiple, creative and diverse ways, globally and locally by social actors seeking to foster a more equitable and inclusive world.

6.5 Conclusion

There is little doubt that we live in an era of legal hybridity characterized by a plurality of intersecting and overlapping legal regimes. Human rights laws, however, including anti-discrimination and equality rights have often been understood as creating universal norms that should effectively trump local laws, practices and customs. Legal plurality, from this perspective, is in tension with the universalism of human rights. It is this vision of legal plurality as oppositional to legal equality that I have tried to interrogate in this chapter. Rather than viewing legal plurality as a threat to equality in all instances, the plurality of law can be understood as an important resource for enhancing the effective implementation of group-based equality in some contexts. Building upon an enlarged vision of law that embraces both formal state-based and informal non-stated based laws, legal plurality may operate to promote more effective enjoyment of equality in three ways.

First, the informal law of social institutions must be taken into account in developing effective mechanisms for implementing equality norms. When group-based inequalities in the mainstream institutions of society are embedded in systemic and structural norms, traditions and practices that are reproduced, entrenched and legitimated over time, it is necessary to develop regulatory approaches that transform institutional relationships and processes of decision-making. Reducing group-based inequalities requires institutional transformation – a change in institutional cultures and practices. It is not enough to provide retroactive relief to isolated individuals who manage to pull together the resources, evidence and strength to contest discrimination. More transformative, proactive and preventive strategies are needed that grapple with both the positive and negative dimensions of informal institutional law.

Second, group-based equality may be advanced in some contexts by legal affirmations of cultural and community autonomy and self-governance. By allowing local communities to govern themselves, in ways that respect their traditions, customs and practices, substantive equality and respect for diversity are often enhanced. Ensuring equitable representation and the protection of vulnerable individuals within minority communities are necessary corollaries to self-governance as a pathway to equality.

Third, when group-based equalities are recognized in multiple and overlapping sources of formal law at multiple levels of governance, legal plurality reinforces the pursuit of equality. A global plurality of sources of equality protection has been successfully used in the formal processes of adjudication. The interplay between local, regional and international legal regimes has also nurtured new global social movements around issues of common concern, influencing mobilization strategies, political struggles and social transformation. Asserting the right to equality and inclusion, therefore, engages both law and politics. And the key actors in the political struggle for equality are the myriad groups and organizations of civil society.

Chapter 7
Labour Law in Canada as a Site of Legal Pluralism

Guylaine Vallée*

In a pluralism perspective, legal regulation arises from the plurality of legal orders but also from their "cohabitation",[1] competition and coexistence. The workplace is particularly interesting in this regard, given that it is governed by a plurality of rules belonging to different spheres of state law (including civil and common law, legislated labour law, criminal law and fundamental human rights) and emanating from non-state actors in the workplace (i.e. collective agreements, individual employment contracts, enterprise policies and customs). [2] From this perspective, to understand legal regulation of labour requires an appreciation of the plurality of these intra-state

* The present chapter is a translation of an updated version of a text that first appeared in French in 2006 in honour of the great professor and sociologist of law Guy Rocher: Guylaine VALLÉE, "Le droit du travail comme lieu de pluralisme juridique", in C. SAINT-PIERRE and J.P. WARREN, *Sociologie et société québécoise. Présences de Guy Rocher*, Montréal, Presses de l'Université de Montréal, 2006, p. 241. The author would like to thank the McGill Centre for Human Rights and Legal Pluralism and Dia Dabby, with the collaboration of Colleen Sheppard for the translation of this paper.

[1] Guy ROCHER, "Les fondements de la société libérale, les relations industrielles et les Chartes", in R. BLOUIN, G. FERLAND, G. LAFLAMME, A. LAROCQUE and C. RONDEAU, *Les Chartes des droits et les relations industrielles*, Québec, Département des relations industrielles, Université Laval, Les Presses de l'Université Laval, 1988, p. 12.

[2] Guy ROCHER, "Les avenues de la déréglementation" in M. BROSSARD (ed.), *La déréglementation des relations du travail. Le pour et le contre*, Montréal, École de relations industrielles, Université de Montréal, 1987, p. 150.

G. Vallée (✉)
École des relations industrielles, Université de Montréal,
Montréal, QC H3C 3J7, Canada
e-mail: guylaine.vallee@umontreal.ca

R. Provost and C. Sheppard (eds.), *Dialogues on Human Rights and Legal Pluralism*, Ius Gentium: Comparative Perspectives on Law and Justice 17,
DOI 10.1007/978-94-007-4710-4_7, © Springer Science+Business Media Dordrecht 2013

and extra state legal orders.[3] Legal pluralism, therefore, has an important *explanatory dimension*.

There is another, perhaps even more fundamental, reason that justifies appealing to legal pluralism when thinking about labour law. Contrary to other branches of law where legal pluralism has largely remained the "business of sociologists", the labour law environment is distinctive.[4] In the case of labour law, legal pluralism has a *constitutive dimension*. To illustrate this constitutive dimension of legal pluralism in labour law at both the historical and contemporary levels, I draw on the sociology of law of Guy Rocher. On the one hand, I emphasize how collective social phenomena are taken into account as sources of law that accompany the emergence of labour law and structure the relationship between the plurality of workplace rights. On the other, I demonstrate that this particular reading of the plurality of rights affects how actors in labour law – most particularly adjudicators and judges – think about its transformation.

7.1 The Historical Perspective: Collective Autonomy and the Emergence of Labour Law

The emergence of labour law rests on a pluralist reading of the sources that govern labour and on the importance of collective action – in particular trade unionism, collective bargaining and the collective agreement – as mechanisms to balance power in the workplace. These autonomous sources of law – developed outside of state law – in fact have a preponderant impact compared to other sources of applicable law.

7.1.1 The Particular Legitimacy of Collective Labour Relations Institutions in the Heart of the Emergence of Labour Law

Labour law was historically constructed upon two observations: the inequality of powers put into evidence by industrialization and the deplorable living conditions that resulted therein for the worker, inequalities that contradicted the liberal principles and values of the times. It is important to remember that liberal individualism predominated the legal framework governing new social relationships that emerged

[3] Guy ROCHER, "Pour une sociologie des ordres juridiques", (1988) 29 *Les Cahiers de droit* 91–120.

[4] Pierre VERGE and Guylaine VALLÉE, *Un droit du travail? Essai sur la spécificité du droit du travail*, coll. "Le droit aussi", Cowansville, Éditions Yvon Blais, 1997, p. 26–30. The practise of labour law reflects this distinctiveness. For example, university research and teaching in labour law take place as much as in the faculties of law as in the schools of industrial relations. The practitioners of labour law and in particular the people sitting within the various specialized labour tribunals or those who plead before them, are not obligatorily members of the Bar.

with the industrialization of the late 1800s.[5] It recognized formal equality between individuals and posited that all free and equal individuals were capable of concluding contracts whose content was just and fair and that it was necessary to protect the exercise of this contractual freedom from any interference from State or from coalitions that could interfere with the result. In accordance with this concept, the State was not perceived as the best guarantor of just and fair working conditions. The same could also be said about workers' organizations and concerted action aimed at improving working conditions, since they were considered as illegal phenomena that could lead to civil and criminal sanctions.[6]

This background is important for understanding the context in which labour law emerged. Labour law participates in a global movement involving the assertion of economic and social rights of a new collectivity[7]: the working class. These rights are fundamentally different from the individual liberal rights affirmed up until then for two reasons. First, their "objective is to ensure a decent quality of life to each citizen, basic security and protection against the unexpected incidentals of life".[8] Secondly, they assume that the State has a role to play in promoting the well-being of individuals in society.[9] The affirmation of these economic and social rights has been done in two ways. One approach has been direct intervention by the State in numerous industrialized countries to insure basic working conditions guaranteeing the physical and economic security of workers.[10] The key justification for direct regulation of the contract of employment is to "counteract the inequality of bargaining power [...] inherent in the employment relationship"[11] by controlling its effects. A second approach has involved the gradual recognition by states of the legitimacy of trade unionism, collective bargaining and collective agreements which first were appeared outside state law.[12] This recognition was gradual in

[5] Marie-France BICH, "Droit du travail québécois : genèse et génération", in H.P. GLENN (ed.), *Droit québécois et droit français : communauté, autonomie, concordance*, Cowansville, Éditions Yvon Blais, 1993, p. 520–531.

[6] Guylaine VALLÉE and Julie BOURGAULT, "Cadre juridique de la convention collective", in P. JALETTE and G. TRUDEAU (eds), *La convention collective au Québec*, 2e ed., Montréal, Gaëtan Morin Éditeur, 2011, p. 18–20.

[7] Guy ROCHER, *supra*, note 1, p. 7.

[8] *Ibid*, p. 7–8 [our translation]. The original, in French: "ont pour but d'assurer à chaque citoyen et citoyenne des conditions de vie qui soient relativement bonnes, une certaine sécurité, la protection contre les imprévus de la vie"

[9] *Ibid*, p. 8.

[10] Alain SUPIOT, "Pourquoi un droit du travail?" (1990) *Droit social*, p. 485, 487–489.

[11] Paul DAVIES and Mark FREEDLAND, *Kahn-Freund's Labour and the Law*, 3e éd., London, Stevens & Sons, 1983, p. 18 cited in *Slaight Communications Inc.* v. *Davidson*, [1989] 1 S.C.R. 1038, 1052.

[12] Hugo SINZHEIMER, "La théorie des sources et le droit ouvrier", dans *Le problème des sources en droit positif*, (1934). *Annuaire de l'Institut international de philosophie du droit et de sociologie juridique*, p. 73–74; P. VERGE and G. VALLÉE, *supra*, note 4, p. 27.

both Quebec and Canada.[13] As of 1944, under the influence of developments in the United States, the Canadian jurisdictions promoted a new model of collective organization deployed at a decentralized level, that of the workplace. Public certification of labour unions in particular workplaces afforded such unions an exclusive right of representation of the workers and resulted in the negotiation of workplace-based collective agreements. This remains the dominant model today.

This model radically transforms the regulation of workplaces. In fact, state law does not limit itself to acknowledging any manifestations of collective phenomena. Instead, it favours the development of a particular form of collective action in the system of industrial relations.[14] In this regard, in unionized workplaces, collective bargaining becomes the primary means of elaborating not only collective rights, but also individual rights of workers in the workplace. The role of the State is limited to setting out the processes for recognizing trade unions and establishing collective bargaining in workplaces.[15] At the same time, this model of collective labour relations is perceived as the privileged instrument of a democratization project in the workplaces, since it enables a certain *equality of powers* to be accomplished at the heart of the enterprise, between a group of workers represented by a union and their employer. It is no longer about "neutralizing" the effects of inequality of power between workers and employers, but rather correcting it by providing to the worker "the possibility of acting collectively to oppose a force akin to that of employer power".[16] Lastly, this model's objective is to guarantee veritable industrial peace by favouring understanding and compromise between parties with opposing interests.[17]

---

[13] On the "negative" then "positive" recognition of unionism by the state law, see: Robert P. GAGNON, L. LEBEL and Pierre VERGE, *Droit du travail*. 2e éd. Sainte-Foy, 1991, Les Presses de l'Université Laval, p. 17–29.

[14] Judy FUDGE and Eric TUCKER, *Labour Before the Law: The Regulation of Workers' Collective Action in Canada, 1900–1948,* Toronto, Oxford University Press, 2001, p. 1–15.

[15] Katherine VAN WEZEL STONE, "The Legacy of Industrial Pluralism: The Tension between Individual Employment Rights and the New Deal Collective Bargaining System", (1999) 59 *The University of Chicago Law Review* 575, 623: "The industrial pluralist vision is not merely a neutral description of the workplace. It is a description with a normative message about how collective bargaining should be structured. The picture of the workplace as an autonomous, self-sufficient, democratic realm suggests that the conditions inside the workplace are fair and just. The normative message is that all is well, and that outsiders, such as legislatures, should not intervene".

[16] Ulrich ZACHERT, "La légitimité des rapports juridiques de travail. À propos de la conception de la légitimité chez Max Weber et Hugo Sinzheimer", dans M. COUTU and G. ROCHER (eds.), *La légitimité de l'État et du droit. Autour de Max Weber*, coll. "Pensée allemande et européenne", Québec, Presses de l'Université Laval, 2005, p. 301, 313 [our translation]. The original, in French: "au travailleur la possibilité d'opposer une puissance correspondante à celle de l'employeur". Unlike other systems of industrial relations, it is at the heart of the enterprise and not at the sectorial or interprofessional level that this ideal of equality is sought in the North American industrial pluralism. [our translation]

[17] This finality of the regime of collective labour relations instituted in 1944 was particularly important in Canada: Daphne Gottlieb TARAS, "Collective Bargaining Regulation in Canada and the United States. Divergent Cultures, Divergent Outcomes", in B. KAUFMAN (ed.), *Government Regulation of the Employment Relationship*, IRRA Series 1997, 50th Anniversary Volume, p. 295–341.

This model gave birth to the doctrine of "industrial pluralism". In accordance with this doctrine, when collective relations are established in a workplace, the working environment is no longer governed exclusively by the legal order of the enterprise,[18] the employer's regulatory power and by individual negotiation: it is endowed with joint instances of elaboration, application and interpretation of rules that develop a form of "industrial citizenship".[19] Union representation thus becomes a legitimate force of opposition in the enterprise; negotiation of a collective agreement, a privileged site of elaboration of norms relative to labour; and grievance arbitrator, as a specialized adjudicator, the interpreter of this negotiated "charter" of the workplace.

This historical context explains why the rules issued from the regime of collective labour relations enjoy a particular legitimacy within labour law. In a context where the intervention of the State was reduced, it is primarily through these collective labour relations that workers had access to just and reasonable working conditions as well as equitable treatment, free from discrimination or the arbitrary abuse of power on the part of the employer.[20] In the Canadian context, it was primarily through collective labour relations that economic and social rights were accessed for workers. This particular historical legitimacy of collective relations institutions explains the predominant status of collective bargaining law in relation to the other applicable legal orders in the workplace.

7.1.2 A Principle of Articulation of the Plurality of Applicable Rights in the Labour Context

In theory, the organization of collective relations can be viewed as radically transforming the nature of the enterprise. Such was the vision that Bora Laskin, the former Chief Justice of the Supreme Court of Canada, held when he was

---

[18] On the enterprise as legal order, see : G. ROCHER, *supra*, note 2, p.150 ; Jean Marcel LAPIERRE, Guy ROCHER and Guylaine VALLÉE, "Légitimités et légitimations de l'arbitrage de griefs et discrimination dans les milieux de travail syndiqués", dans M. COUTU and G. ROCHER (eds.), *La légitimité de l'État et du droit. Autour de Max Weber*, collection "Pensée allemande et européenne", Québec, Presses de l'Université Laval, 2005, p. 360–361.

[19] See the classical statements of this approach that constitute the founding postulates of the field of study of industrial relations and labour law: Neil W. CHAMBERLAIN, *Collective Bargaining*, First ed., New York, McGraw-Hill Book Company, 1951, esp. p. 125–139; Allan FLANDERS, "Éléments pour une théorie de la négociation collective", (1968) *Sociologie du travail*, p. 13–35; Harry W. ARTHURS, "Developing Industrial Citizenship: A Challenge for Canada's Second Century". (1967) *The Canadian Bar Review* 786. On the distinctive traits of the Canadian model of industrial citizenship, see : Judy FUDGE, "Au-delà de la citoyenneté industrielle : la citoyenneté marchande ou du travail ?" in COUTU and G. MURRAY (eds.), *Travail et citoyenneté : quel avenir ?*, Québec, Presses de l'Université Laval, 2010, p. 421.

[20] This is the case for stipulations subjecting the dismissal of an employee to a just and sufficient cause or imposing the taking into account of the seniority of an employee with regards to promotion, transfer, lay-off or termination of employment. These stipulations limit the employer's discretionary power by imposing criteria that must be taken into account in the management of personnel.

grievance arbitrator. Recognized as one of the chief defenders of industrial pluralism in Canada, he wrote in 1954:

> The change from individual to Collective Bargaining is a change in kind and not merely a difference in degree. The introduction of a Collective Bargaining regime involves the acceptance by the parties of assumptions which are entirely alien to an era of individual bargaining. Hence, any attempt to measure rights and duties in employer-employee relations by reference to pre-collective bargaining standards is an attempt to re-enter a world which has ceased to exist. Just as the period of individual bargaining had its own "common law" worked out empirically over many years, so does a Collective Bargaining regime have a common law to be invoked to give consistency and meaning to the Collective Agreement on which it is based.[21]

This conception, which effectively excludes the common law as a source of law if the workplace is unionized, represents a radical re-reading of the articulation of the plurality of rights applicable in the workplace. Pursuant to this vision, collective labour relations prevail over the individual negotiation of an employment contract between an employee and an employer (1) but also over the unilateral determination of working conditions by the employer (2). Such a re-reading of the power relationships enabled the democratization project of the workplace to be manifested through the doctrine of industrial pluralism.[22]

7.1.2.1 The Private Contractual Order

Consistent with Justice Laskin's vision, the Supreme Court of Canada has taken the view that the common law governing the private contractual order inspired by economic liberalism is inapplicable as soon as the collective relations are established in a workplace.[23] *Individual freedom of contract* that was otherwise recognized by the common law with respect to individual employees and employers disappears upon unionization. An employee's freedom of contract is thereby replaced with a collective freedom belonging to the certified union. Moreover, an *individual contract of employment* that was negotiated prior to unionization no longer constitutes an *active* source of determination of working conditions when a collective agreement exists, even if it survives as the original source of the employment relationship. No space is left for individual negotiation between an employee and an employer as soon as a certified association exists within a workplace.

---

[21] *United Electrical, Radio & Machine Workers of America, Local 527 in re Peterboro Lock Mfg. Co. Ltd.*, (1954) 4 L.A.C. 1499–1506, 1502, February 27 1954 (B. Laskin, adj.).

[22] *Supra*, notes 15–19.

[23] *Syndicat catholique des employés de magasins de Québec Inc.* v. *La Cie Paquet Ltée*, [1959] S.C.R. 206; *McGavin Toastmaster Ltd* v. *Ainscough*, [1976] 1 S.C.R. 718; *St. Anne Nackawic Pulp & Paper* v. *CPU*, [1986] 1 S.C.R. 704; *CAIMAW* v. *Paccar of Canada Ltd.*, [1989] 2 S.C.R. 983; *Hémond* v. *Coopérative fédérée du Québec*, [1989] 2 S.C.R. 962; *Noël v. Société d'énergie de la Baie James*, [2001] 2 S.C.R. 207. It must be noted that the labour law doctrine in Québec is very divided on the opportunistic character of this approach: G. VALLÉE and J. BOURGAULT, *supra*, note 6, p. 40–45.

7.1.2.2 The Legal Order of the Enterprise and the Employer's Managerial Rights

Another important dimension of the doctrine of industrial pluralism is that the arrival of a union introduces a new order into the enterprise and requires an employer, henceforth, to share decision-making power concerning labour with the union. The employer's managerial rights are circumscribed: the employer can no longer make major decisions without consulting the union, or potentially obtaining its approval.

This dimension of the industrial pluralism doctrine has remained largely marginal in Canada.[24] The courts have rather considered that the employer, as owner of a business, possesses all the rights related to the management of the enterprise, subject only to the rights that have been assigned in collective bargaining and the limits that have been *expressly* articulated in the current collective agreement.[25] Unlike individual contractual freedom, the employer's managerial rights subsist when the collective labour relations are installed in an enterprise in this thesis of *residual rights*. Rights not addressed by the collective agreement come under the employer's jurisdiction, subject to applicable laws; the employer does not have to negotiate with the certified union even if the unionized workers' working conditions are affected. The democratization project of the enterprise, which is integral to the doctrine of industrial pluralism, is not completely achieved: the collective agreement represents, to borrow the metaphor of an American critical labour scholar, "a miniature island of democracy in an otherwise autocratic ocean".[26]

Even if born of a pluralist reading of the law governing workplaces – which acknowledges the role played by collective autonomy – the doctrine of industrial pluralism within labour law does not provide a complete account of the plurality of legal orders that compete to effectively regulate workplaces. Although the doctrine of industrial pluralism does not explain all of Canadian labour law, it has had an undeniable normative impact since it characterizes the representation that actors make of the relations between the various norms that govern the workplaces, particularly between norms emanating from collective agreements and those emanating from state law.

---

[24] Examples of this minority position: *United Electrical, Radio and Machine Workers of America, Local 527 in re Peterboro Lock Mfg. Co. Ltd.*, *supra*, note 21. See also Justice Wilson's dissenting opinion in *CAIMAW* c. *Paccar of Canada Ltd.*, *supra*, note 23, 1024, who wrote: "Must we conclude that in the absence of a specific provision in the Code the employer is free to do anything which he is not specifically prohibited from doing? This seems to be the underlying premise of the appellant's position. Nothing in the Code, they say, prevents the employer from unilaterally imposing new terms. Or do we in filling the legislative vacuum take guidance from the legislative scheme? It seems to me that the latter must be the proper course."

[25] For a presentation of these two approaches, that of *implicit limitations* and that of *residual rights*, see: G. VALLÉE and J. BOURGAULT, *supra*, note 6, p. 36–39. Moreover, the collective agreements routinely contain stipulations explicitly recognizing the employer's power.

[26] Katherine VAN WEZEL STONE, "The Post-War Paradigm in American Labor Law", (1981) 90: 7 *The Yale Law Journal* 1509, 1557.

7.2 The Contemporary Perspective: Collective Autonomy and State Law

The doctrine of industrial pluralism was developed and asserted in a context where the State was relatively absent in protecting individual rights of employees.[27] Even if this period was marked by the adoption of certain laws by the State, intervening in the determination of minimal working conditions which guaranteed a certain amount of physical and economic security to employees, these laws were characterized by a limited scope of application, orders specifically destined to certain sectors, a reduced range of minimal norms or application mechanisms that were either lacking or dependent on political power.[28] This situation begins to change in the mid-1970s in jurisdictions across Canada. Increasingly, labour law was no longer focused on the creation of favourable legal conditions for the establishment of collective bargaining. In recognition of the fact that the majority of workers were not unionized – and therefore left by and large only with the applicable common law in contractual matters – the State intervened directly to establish public order provisions giving individual rights for all employees. Many important laws bear witness to this changing role of the State. Such was the case when adopting the Québec *Charter of Human Rights and Freedoms* in 1975, which contains an assertion of fundamental human rights and freedoms as well as important dispositions on equality, particularly in employment.[29] Other labour laws were also adopted during this period. In Quebec, the *Act Respecting Labour Standards*[30] and the *Act respecting Occupational health and safety*[31] were passed in 1979 and the *Act respecting industrial accidents and occupational diseases*[32] in 1985. It also bears mentioning the entry into force of a complete chapter dedicated to the contract of employment in the *Civil Code of Québec* in 1994; this chapter also contains some public order dispositions.[33]

This situation modified the plurality of rights governing the workplace. Aside from "private interest individual rights", that is to say those developed by the employer or from an individual negotiation framed by the common law, and "collective interest individual rights" established by the collective agreement, we now find "general interest individual rights,"[34] whose combination with collective labour relations

[27] It is the case in Québec and in Canada, but also in the United States. See: Katherine VAN WEZEL STONE, *supra*, note 15, 631.

[28] On the subject of Québec législation, see: Christian DESILETS et Denis LEDOUX, *Histoire des normes du travail au Québec de 1885 à 2005 : de l'*Acte des manufactures *à la* Loi sur les normes du travail, Québec, Publications du Québec, 2006.

[29] *Charter of Human Rights and Freedoms*, R.S.Q., c. c-12.

[30] R.S.Q. c. N-1.1.

[31] R.S.Q., c. S-2.1.

[32] R.S.Q., c. A-3.001.

[33] S.Q. 1991, c. 64, art. 2085–2097.

[34] To resume this interesting typology employed by Diane VEILLEUX, "L'arbitre de grief face à une compétence renouvelée…", (2004) 64 *Revue du Barreau* 217 [our translation]. The original types in French are: "droits individuels d'intérêt privé", "droits individuels d'intérêts collectifs" and "droits individuels d'intérêt général".

institutions have not been clearly established. How are these sources combined in the workplace? More particularly, how are the rules and institutions of collective labour relations understood to relate to rules of state law?

The courts constitute a privileged scope of observation of this legal pluralism in action since they are asked more and more regularly to deal with questions involving the relationship between these distinct legal orders. Two examples will be given. The first is drawn from a research study of the adjudication of grievances[35] and deals with the manner in which grievance arbitrators conceive of the relationship between rights protected by the Quebec *Charter of Human Rights and Freedoms* and those secured by collective labour relations institutions (Sect. 7.2.1). The second example is drawn from three important decisions of the Supreme Court of Canada that put into question the relationship between state law and the institutions governing the collective labour relations (Sect. 7.2.2).

7.2.1 Grievance Arbitration and Statutory Human Rights

Grievance arbitration is a central institution of the law of collective labour relations. It involves a specialized tribunal that handles, to the exclusion of all other tribunals, disputes relating to the application and interpretation of a collective agreement. The decision is final, without appeal and binds the parties.[36] In exercising its jurisdiction, the grievance arbitrator has the power to apply or interpret a law insofar as it is necessary to resolve the grievance.[37] This power, enshrined in the collective bargaining legislation, after having been recognized by the Supreme Court of Canada in the mid-1070s,[38] "signaled a rupture with 30 years of a legislative scheme resting on the quasi indelible principle of the contractual autonomy of the parties."[39] It represented an important shift, since it clearly authorized arbitrators to search for the solution to a grievance not only in the collective agreement but also in state law. This transformation was also "cultural", since it "put into question the fundamentally "contractual" fibre of the collective labour relations world."[40] It remained to be

[35] The study was part of a greater study whose theme was the *Implementation of the norm of equality in the workplace, human rights and collective labour relations* (Social Sciences and Humanities Research Council of Canada, 2000–2003, Guylaine VALLÉE, Michel COUTU and Guy ROCHER, Jean Marcel LAPIERRE and Jean Denis GAGNON).

[36] *Labour Code*, R.S.Q. c. C-27, art. 101.

[37] *Ibid*, art. 100.12 (a).

[38] *McLeod* v. *Egan*, [1975] 1 S.C.R. 517.

[39] Denis NADEAU, "L'arbitrage de griefs : vecteur d'intégration des droits de la personne dans les rapports collectifs du travail", dans Tribunal des droits de la personne et Barreau du Québec, *La Charte des droits et libertés de la personne : pour qui et jusqu'où?*, Cowansville, Éditions Yvon Blais, 2005, p. 157 [our translation]. The original, in French: "marquait une rupture avec trente années d'un régime législatif reposant sur le principe quasi indélébile de l'autonomie contractuelle des parties"

[40] *Ibid*, p. 157 [our translation]. The original, in French: "remettait en cause la fibre foncièrement "conventionnelle" du monde des relations collectives du travail."

seen how arbitrators would conceive of the relation between these various sources of law since they come from different legal universes – negotiated agreements and the state – when a grievance had to be resolved. To establish this, the jurisdictional activity of arbitrators was examined when grievances involved a problem of discrimination in the workplace. An arbitrator seized by a grievance of this nature may not only resolve it by relying upon the collective agreement but also based on the interpretation and application of the *Charter of Human Rights and Freedoms.*[41] This plurality of sources of law provided an ideal context in which to observe empirically how arbitrators combined state law and norms contained in collective agreements.

An analysis of the contents of 137 arbitration decisions rendered between 1992 and 1999 revealed that the collective agreement constituted the most commonly employed source used by arbitrators to adjudicate grievances related to discrimination during this period.[42] A certain transformation was however perceptible in the arbitral jurisprudence starting from 1999, when recourse to the *Charter of Human Rights and Freedoms* and to associated jurisprudential notions appeared to become more important, at least with respect to certain grounds of discrimination.[43] For jurists, the tendency for arbitrators not to rely on state-based human rights laws for a number of years is surprising: how could one explain that the *Charter of Human Rights and Freedoms*, that enjoys a preeminent legal status – even a quasi-constitutional status – in the hierarchy of formal sources of law, has been used so rarely in disputes where it was potentially applicable? And why is it only as of 1999 – and not since 1976, the year that the Charter entered into force – that it became more widely used by arbitrators? What explains such a prudent and belated integration?[44] On a theoretical level, these results demonstrated once again that the legal rule does not necessarily have a widespread effect simply by virtue of its legislative creation or even by its preeminent status in positive law.

In spite of the fact that the data was meant to be descriptive,[45] some saw an indication of the incapacity of arbitrators to apply a law as important as the *Charter.*[46] Other "contextual" explanations have since surfaced. It was put forward that the incertitude as to the sense and the scope of the rules prohibiting discrimination in the workplace could explain the prudence exhibited by arbitrators with regard to the

[41] *Supra*, note 29.

[42] Guylaine VALLÉE, Michel COUTU and Marie-Christine HÉBERT, "La norme d'égalité en milieu de travail : étude empirique de la mise en œuvre de la norme d'égalité par le Tribunal des droits de la personne et les tribunaux d'arbitrage", in G. VALLEE, M. COUTU, J. D. GAGNON, J.M. LAPIERRE AND G. ROCHER (eds.), *Le droit à l'égalité : les tribunaux d'arbitrage et le Tribunal des droits de la personne*, Montréal, éd. Thémis, 2001, p. 43–45. See a similar finding in D. NADEAU, *supra*, note 39, p. 161.

[43] G. VALLÉE, M. COUTU and M.-C. HÉBERT, *supra*, note 42.

[44] See also in this way: D. NADEAU, *supra*, note 39, p. 158.

[45] G. VALLEE, M. COUTU and M.-C. HÉBERT, *supra*, note 42, p. 21–28.

[46] See the contrasting reactions that these data produced in the following consolidated collection: G. VALLEE, M. COUTU, J. D. GAGNON, J.M. LAPIERRE and G. ROCHER (eds.), *Le droit à l'égalité: les tribunaux d'arbitrage et le Tribunal des droits de la personne*, Montréal, éd. Thémis, 2001.

Charter.[47] It had also been recalled that the *Charter of Human Rights and Freedoms* was not widely utilized in many tribunals and that it was not only labour arbitrators who hampered its implementation.[48] Drawing on a stance inspired by Max Weber, we chose to locate part of the explanation in the manner in which the actors – namely the unions, the employers and the adjudicators themselves – would conceive of their own role and that of the adjudicator with regard to this plurality of rules.

Interviews conducted with arbitrators between 2001 and 2002 revealed the logic they applied in combining internal law (emanating from the parties and the collective agreement) and external law (arising from the law or judges) when they had to resolve a grievance that concerned discrimination in the workplace.[49] A first finding was identified: an exclusive focus on the perceptions arbitrators had of the Charter would not explain their reticence to integrate the Charter into their decisions. For example, all or substantially all adjudicators interviewed did not adhere to the discourse that suggested that the individual values embedded in the *Charter* were irreconcilable with the collective values embodied in collective labour relations law. The prudence exhibited by arbitrators with regard to the *Charter* could not be attributed, therefore, to their perception of the legitimacy of the Charter.[50] A second finding could also be identified: *the Charter, even when perceived as being legitimate, coexisted with other sources that were equally legitimate in the eyes of the arbitrators.*[51] The majority of arbitrators found themselves to be competent to apply the *Charte*r only when the parties consented to it, explicitly or implicitly, by referring to it in the collective agreement or during the grievance hearings (arguments presented, remedies requested). In a similar spirit, they were also sensitive, most notably in the choice of remedies, to the impact of their intervention on the ongoing relationship of the parties.[52] Other arbitrators said that they looked for the foundation of their decision in the workplace, thereby applying their specialized expertise in this area; one even admitted that he had recourse to external sources only after the fact, in order to validate his decision.[53] Lastly, other adjudicators declared themselves competent to directly apply the *Charter*, even in the absence of implicit or explicit consent on the part of the parties to the collective agreement, by taking into account its hierarchical status in the legal order of the state.[54]

In short, these are the constitutive principles of the arbitral institution's legitimacy in the legal scheme – respect for the relatively equal will of the parties, the fairness of the rules emanating from the workplace, concern with maintaining less conflictual labour relations – that guided the manner in which the majority of arbitrators

[47] D. VEILLEUX, *supra*, note 34, p. 231–232.

[48] D. NADEAU, *supra*, note 39, p. 159–160.

[49] J.M. LAPIERRE, G. ROCHER and G. VALLÉE, *supra*, note 18.

[50] *Ibid*, p. 362–364; p. 369–370; p. 377. See also: D. NADEAU, *supra*, note 39, p. 159.

[51] J.M. LAPIERRE, G. ROCHER and G. VALLÉE, *supra*, note 18, p. 378.

[52] What we have called "relational logic": *Ibid*, p. 370–374.

[53] What we have called "situational logic": *Ibid*, p. 374–375.

[54] What we have called "legislative rule logic": *Ibid*, p. 375–376.

combined, at the time of the interviews, the collective bargaining law and the "external" law of which the *Charter* is part. These constitutive principles of industrial pluralism are intrinsically tied to the history of labour law.[55] Arbitrators who employed these principles in order to apprehend a changing context display a remarkable institutional coherence. In this way, their approach is quite similar to that of the one held by the Supreme Court in more recent cases, which have also put into question the articulation of collective labour relations institutions and state law in the workplace.

7.2.2 Supreme Court Jurisprudence, Collective Relations and State Law

The Supreme Court of Canada has been called on to intervene in three cases concerning the jurisdictional competence of grievance arbitrators to apply, in addition to the rights resulting from the collective agreement, the norms of state law. In all these decisions, the Supreme Court of Canada was divided but the majority clearly relied on the fundamental values of industrial pluralism to address the new context created by the development of state law. It is not my objective to offer a detailed commentary of these cases, but rather to demonstrate what they reveal about the actual stakes involved in the articulation of a plurality of sources that govern the workplace, particularly when collective labour relations and state sources are both invoked.

7.2.2.1 State Law as the Implicit Content of Collective Agreements

In *Parry Sound*,[56] rendered in 2003, the Court had to determine if a board of arbitration duly constituted by the [Ontario] *Labour Relations Act*[57] could apply an existing section of a code protecting human rights. In the case at bar, a probationary employee, whose terms of employment were governed by the collective agreement, was discharged a few days before the end of her probationary period and a few days after her return from maternity leave. The grievance alleged that the discharge was discriminatory, that it contravened the [Ontario] *Human Rights Code*[58] and that the board of arbitration had jurisdiction to resolve this dispute. The employer argued that the collective agreement included a clause that gave him the discretionary right to discharge a probationary employee and that such an action by the employer would

---

[55] *Supra*, notes 15–20 and corresponding text.

[56] *Parry Sound (District) Social Services Administration Board* v. *O.P.S.E.U., Local 324*, [2003] 2 S.C.R. 157, 2003 SCC 42.

[57] *Labour Relations Act*, 1995, S.O. 1995, c. 1, Sch. A.

[58] R.S.O. 1990, c. H.19, art 5 (1).

not be subject to grievance or arbitration procedures.[59] The board of arbitration found that the law recognized its authority "to interpret and apply human rights and other employment-related statutes, despite any conflict between those statutes and the terms of the collective agreement."[60] It thus concluded that it had the power and the responsibility to hear the dispute. The Supreme Court of Canada considered that the board of arbitration did not commit an error. Aside from sections in the collective agreement that were explicitly negotiated by the parties, the collective agreement also contained implicit content that included substantive rights and obligations of employment-related and human rights statutes.[61] A dispute on the application or interpretation of these implicit dispositions could be the focus of a grievance falling within the board of arbitration's jurisdiction.

This decision established an *implicit incorporation approach,* which confirmed the mixed public and private function of the collective agreement. The Court did not consider that the rights and obligations borne of state law were simply part and parcel of the general legal context within which the collective agreement operated. Rather, it went much further by integrating these rights and obligations <u>into</u> the collective agreement. Simply put, the collective agreement was interpreted to include statutory protections that were not agreed to expressly by the parties, as required pursuant to a vision based purely on private contracts.[62] The same can also be said about the adjudication function of grievances arbitration: since the rights and obligations flowing from the laws are explicitly contained in the collective agreement, any dispute on their application or interpretation can be the basis of a grievance and a matter for which the arbitrator has jurisdiction. The arbitrator can no longer be considered simply a private judge for the parties.[63]

At first glance, this decision would appear to be inconsistent with industrial pluralism, where the collective agreement is seen as the primary source of workplace regulation, operating in a self-sufficient manner, without state intervention.[64] Upon closer examination, however, the widening of the scope of the collective agreement and the issues subject to adjudication through the grievance procedure affirmed in this decision was completely coherent with the legitimacy that these institutions have in contemporary labour law. It is particularly clear that the Supreme Court considered the arbitration of grievances as a privileged instrument for guaranteeing

---

[59] *Parry Sound (District) Social Services Administration Board* v. *O.P.S.E.U., Local 324, supra*, note 56, par. 3.

[60] *Labour Relations Act, supra*, note 57, art. 48 (12) (j).

[61] *Parry Sound (District) Social Services Administration Board* v. *O.P.S.E.U., Local 324, supra*, note 56, par. 28 and 55.

[62] *Ibid*, par. 30 and 36.

[63] However, the expansion of this jurisdiction does not modify the essentially private nature of the functioning of the institution: Gilles TRUDEAU, "L'arbitrage des griefs au Canada : plaidoyer pour une réforme devenue nécessaire", (2005) 84 *La Revue du Barreau canadien* 249, 253 and 265–274.

[64] *Supra*, note 15 and corresponding text.

justice in the workplace, insuring peace in industrial relations and protecting the employees against an abusive use of managerial powers.[65] It is for this reason that the integration of new workplace rights – even those included in preeminent human rights legislation – had to be channeled through the grievance process where it exists (in unionized places). Any other conclusion, according to the Court, "would lessen human rights protection in the unionized workplace by allowing employers and unions to treat such protections as optional, thereby leaving recourse only to the human rights procedure".[66]

Despite the emergence of new statutory individual rights for employees, this decision ensured that collective labour relations remained at the heart of labour law in unionized workplaces. The challenges of articulating these emerging statutory rights with other employment collective rights and obligations are to be addressed within the current processes of collective labour relations and not outside of them.

7.2.2.2 Is State Law Compatible with Collective Labour Relations?

In *Isidore Garon*,[67] rendered in 2006, the Supreme Court of Canada had to determine whether arbitrators had jurisdiction to determine whether the notice given upon termination met the requirements established in the *Civil Code of Québec*.[68] In two separate cases, employees had lost their jobs following the closing of the enterprise where they worked. The collective agreements did not contain clauses governing the length of the notice to which they were entitled in such circumstances.[69] The employees had received a notice that complied with the time requirement established by the *Act Respecting Labour Standards*[70] and demanded through the grievance

[65] *Parry Sound (District) Social Services Administration Board* v. *O.P.S.E.U., Local 324, supra*, note 56, par. 51. The Court expressly draws on the analyses of Paul WEILER, important labour jurist embodying this perspective of industrial pluralism in Canada and the United States.

[66] *Parry Sound (District) Social Services Administration Board* v. *O.P.S.E.U., Local 324, supra*, note 56, par. 36. This solution makes it possible for unionized workers to benefit from individual State rights that have emerged in the last few years, contrary to the situation that prevailed in the American law, a solution strongly criticized by K. VAN WEZEL STONE, *supra*, note 15, esp. 593–620.

[67] *Isidore Garon ltée v. Tremblay; Fillion et Frères (1976) inc.* v. *Syndicat national des employés de garage du Québec*, [2006] 1 S.C.R. 27, 2006 SCC 2.

[68] The *Civil Code of Québec* sets out that a party to a labour contract of indeterminate term "may terminate it by giving notice of termination to the other party [...] [This notice] shall be given in reasonable time, taking into account, in particular, the nature of the employment, the special circumstances in which it is carried on and the duration of the period of work." (*Civil Code of Québec, supra*, note 33, art. 2091) and that "[t]he employee may not renounce his right to obtain compensation for any injury he suffers where insufficient notice of termination is given..." (*Ibid*, art. 2092).

[69] In one of the two cases, the collective agreement simply set out that the *Act Respecting Labour Standards* was applicable in the case of a layoff that was for six or more consecutive months: *Isidore Garon ltée v. Tremblay; Fillion et Frères (1976) inc.* v. *Syndicat national des employés de garage du Québec, supra*, note 67, par. 67.

[70] *An Act respecting Labour Standards, supra*, note 30, art. 82.

process, the right to a notice of reasonable delay in accordance with the *Civil Code of Québec*. In a divided decision (four versus three), the Supreme Court quashed the arbitrators' decisions to accord the notice required by the *Civil Code of Québec*, on the grounds that they did not have jurisdiction to make such a ruling.

This decision adhered to some of the principles set out in its earlier *Parry Sound* decision. Both the majority and minority justices concluded that the substantive rights and obligations set out in statutory laws are part of the implicit content of a collective agreement and subject to arbitral jurisdiction.[71] Statutory provisions, however, are not to be read into a collective agreement when they are incompatible with the collective labour relations regime.[72] It was on the question of incompatibility that the Court was deeply divided, and most particularly on the *method* that should be used to determine incompatibility between the statutory and collective labour relations norms.

The majority held that the arbitrators did not have the requisite jurisdiction in these two disputes to apply the reasonable notice provided by the *Civil Code of Québec*. This codified norm was not part of the implicit content of the collective agreement because it was incompatible with the collective labour relations regime for three reasons.[73] First, the notice, as it is exists in common law, is negotiated at the moment of termination of employment by the employee by taking into account individual circumstances. This would be incompatible with the collective relations regime where "this condition of employment is negotiated with the union, not the employee, is negotiated for all employees or for various classes of employees, not individually, and is agreed on when the collective agreement is entered into, not when the employment is terminated".[74] Second, the reasonable delay set out in the *Civil Code of Québec* is the counterpart to the employer's right to terminate the employment relationship, which would be incompatible with the collective regime where the employer's right to dismiss is substantially limited.[75] Lastly, the legislative history of this specific provision in the *Civil Code of Québec* demonstrates that it is meant "to protect employees who are in an inferior bargaining position."[76] Unionized workers are not considered to be in such a vulnerable state.[77] Nevertheless, this reading was contradicted by the factual situation at the outset of the dispute: the employees, albeit unionized, had been victims of a unilateral termination of the employment relationship following the closure of the enterprise, and found themselves in a situation where the collective agreement did not provide any protection.

[71] *Isidore Garon ltée v. Tremblay; Fillion et Frères (1976) inc.* v. *Syndicat national des employés de garage du Québec, supra*, note 67, par. 24 (for the judges of the majority) and par. 141–151 (for the judges of the minority).

[72] *Ibid,* par. 24–31 (for the judges of the majority) and par. 177–181 (for the judges of the minority).

[73] *Ibid,* par. 9 and 32–61.

[74] *Ibid,* par. 47.

[75] *Ibid*, par. 51 and 53.

[76] *Ibid*, par. 58.

[77] *Ibid*, par. 59.

The judges of the majority situated their analysis in continuity with historic judgments of the Supreme Court affirming the principle that the common law governing the private contractual order is inapplicable once a workplace becomes unionized. These are constitutive decisions, as we have seen, of the doctrine of industrial pluralism.[78] Nevertheless, and despite this position of principle, their analysis could have led to the marginalization of collective labour relations institutions. If this method had been applied more widely – that is to say to laws other than the *Civil Code of Québec*[79] -, important rights created by state law and involving individualized measures that take into account an employee's particular circumstances would have been deemed incompatible with collective labour relations regimes. Different statutory obligations individual in nature, as the obligation to accommodate an employee who has been a victim of discrimination, can require adjustments, or even exceptions to general rules contained in a collective agreement. In many instances, these individualized measures are inconsistent with the terms of the collective agreement, but they are not necessarily incompatible. The approach taken by the majority of Court in *Isidore Garon* could have resulted in a conclusion that there is an *incompatibility* whenever individual rights are juxtaposed against collective representation.

The minority opinion also situated its analysis in continuity with prior jurisprudence of the Court.[80] A much more restricted conception of the *incompatibility*

---

[78] *Ibid*, par. 10–16 and 24. In doing so, it is considered that the freedom to contract is abrogated once a collective agreement is concluded (*Ibid*, par. 11 and 27) and that the individual labour contract does not constitute an *active* source of determination of working conditions when a collective agreement exists, even though it can subsist as the creator of the individual employment link (*Ibid*, par. 27). See also: *Supra*, note 23.

[79] Did this method affect all rights of State source or only those born from the *Civil Code of Québec*? The answer was far from clear. In fact, the method stated by the judges of the majority did not seem to be limited to common law, even if in the case at bar, it was applied to common law stipulations. Paragraph 24 of the decision states: "*Parry Sound* did not reverse *Paquet*, *McGavin*, *Hémond* or *Noël*. The principle that emerges from that case is that, if a rule is incompatible with the collective labour relations scheme, it cannot be incorporated and must be disregarded, as was the case in *McGavin*, *Hémond* and *Noël*. If the rule is found to be compatible and if it is a supplementary or mandatory norm, as in *McLeod*, *Weber* and *Parry Sound*, the arbitrator will have jurisdiction to apply it. [...] Before determining whether the norm is supplementary or mandatory, its compatibility must be ascertained. How do we determine whether a provision or rule is compatible? What rights are supplanted by the collective scheme? Underlying the first line of cases is the desire to give precedence to collective bargaining for all conditions of employment. If the right claimed can be characterized as a condition of employment, it cannot be negotiated individually by the employer and the employee. The union alone performs this task, and it must do so for the employees collectively." In accordance with this approach, *Civil Code of Québec* norms are not necessarily implicitly incorporated into the collective agreement; only those compatible will be (*Ibid*, par. 30).

[80] *Ibid*, par. 116–133. Justice LeBel deemed, as did the judges of the majority, that the principle of freedom of contract disappears when a union is certified in a enterprise (*Ibid*, par. 128 and 135) and that the effect of the collective agreement on the individual contract is "considerable", though "there remains, at the very least, an individual act under which the employee is hired, and its effect, in any case, survives should the certification and the collective agreement cease to have effect." (*Ibid*, par. 133). Justice LeBel also seems to see the survival of the individual employment contract as the foundation of certain obligations that employees and employers for which they still remain accountable (*Ibid*, par. 139, 140 and 165), even if he later affirms that these obligations are part of the implicit content of the collective agreement (*Ibid*, par. 167 and 175).

between state norms and the collective labour relations regime, however, is articulated. A legislative disposition would be judged incompatible with the collective regime only if it is susceptible of "jeopardiz[ing] the integrity of the principle that the certified association is the employees' sole representative."[81] This was not the case at bar, since the unions – and not the individual employees – demanded the right to reasonable delay for the employees they represented.[82] The minority held that "the collective labour relations scheme was created to equalize the balance of power in negotiating conditions of employment, not to require that those conditions be identical for all employees."[83] The minority opinion also noted "a union often has to negotiate on behalf of an employee on an individual basis."[84] Such an approach affirms a vision that suggests that individual rights and collective representation are not in opposition to each other, but rather, can complement and reinforce each other.

7.2.2.3 Collective Agreements and the Hierarchy of Relevant Sources of Labour Law

In the 2010 decision, *Syndicat de la fonction publique du Québec v. Quebec,*[85] the Supreme Court had to determine whether two arbitrators, appointed in accordance with the [Quebec] *Labour Code,*[86] had jurisdiction to hear dismissal grievances of a casual and of a probationary employees. Pursuant to the collective agreement, these employees had no access to grievance arbitration to contest their dismissal. Following the approach developed in *Parry Sound*, the union argued that the arbitrators had jurisdiction to adjudicate the grievances on the basis of section 124 of the *Act Respecting Labor Standards*, a public order provision which the union maintained was implicitly incorporated into the collective agreement. Section 124 recognizes that a unionized employee or non-unionized employee credited with 2 years of uninterrupted service in the same enterprise may not be dismissed without good and sufficient cause. It also creates a special recourse before the Commission des relations du travail for the employee who does not have access to an equivalent remedial procedure provided for elsewhere in legislation or in agreement. The employer, in contrast, argued that the Commission des relations du travail should have exclusive jurisdiction over the employees' complaints rather than grievance arbitrators, since the collective agreement excluded them from the grievance procedure.

The Supreme Court sought to address this question by elaborating a new approach to jurisdictional issues arising when a collective agreement as well as legislative provisions are potentially applicable. The Court unanimously rejected the *implicit incorporation approach* that it had elaborated in *Parry Sound* and which had been

---

[81] *Ibid*, par. 181.

[82] *Ibid,* par. 181.

[83] *Ibid*, par. 179.

[84] *Ibid*, par. 180.

[85] Syndicat de la fonction publique du Québec v. Québec (Attorney General), [2010] 2 SCR 61.

[86] Labour Code, *supra*, note 30, art. 100.

reaffirmed in *Isidore Garon*: the integration of legislative norms in the implicit content of a collective agreement must result from the expressed will of the legislator or the parties in their collective agreement. The majority of the Court nevertheless recognized the arbitrator's jurisdictional competence by relying on an approach that considered "how the hierarchy of relevant sources of labour law affects the content and implementation of such agreements."[87] According to this approach, an arbitrator *must examine the effect of the legislative public order provision on the content of the collective agreement* when faced with a grievance of this nature. When a section of the collective agreement is incompatible with a public order protection, the content of the collective agreement must be modified. It is up to the grievance arbitrator to determine whether he still retains jurisdiction to hear the grievance, by reviewing the collective agreement, as modified by the legislative provision.[88]

Despite the changes introduced with regard to previous Supreme Court decisions, this approach – based on a *hierarchy of sources of law* – remains faithful to the postulates of industrial pluralism. It affirms that the content of the collective agreement must be examined at the outset, an approach which reaffirms and reinforces the principle of the parties' autonomy.[89] Yet the collective agreement is not entirely self-sufficient and can be modified if it appears to be incompatible with external norms of public order. For Professor Denis Nadeau, this approach reconciles "the contractual essence of collective labour law to the legal system as a whole"[90] while avoiding "the route of automatic and integral migration of a corpus of external norms towards the collective agreement",[91] as well as compatibility problems raised by, as notably illustrated in *Isidore Garon*, the coexistence of intra- and extra- State norms within the same normative instrument. This approach also reaffirms the grievance arbitrator's central role and importance within the framework of industrial pluralism, in ensuring the application of public order provisions in unionized work environments. Under this approach, grievance arbitrators must take the hierarchy of labour law sources into account and the public order norm should prevail when a provision in a collective agreement is incompatible. In short, the relationship between negotiated and legislative sources is determined within the current processes of collective labour relations and not outside of them.

[87] Syndicat de la fonction publique du Québec v. Québec, *supra*, note 85, par. 39.

[88] The Québec Court of Appeal has applied this approach in: *Syndicat des métallos, section locale 2843 (Métallurgistes unis d'Amérique, section locale 2843)* v. *3539491 Canada Inc.*, 2011 QCCA 264.

[89] Denis Nadeau, "La perméabilité du droit au sein des rapport collectifs de travail et la compétence arbitrale : nouveau regard sur la valse hésitation de la Cour suprême du Canada" (2010) 69 *Revue du Barreau* 219, par. 33.

[90] Ibid, par. 36 [Our translation]. The original, in French: "l'essence contractuelle des rapports collectifs du travail à l'ensemble de l'ordonnancement juridique"

[91] Ibid, par. 32 [Our translation]. The original, in French: "la voie de la migration automatique et intégrale d'un corpus de normes extérieures vers la convention collective"

7.3 Conclusion

The doctrine of industrial pluralism that appeared in the 1940s still constitutes the point of reference from which actors of the collective labour law world understand the transformation of employment law and in particular the emergence of statutory protections designed to protect basic human rights and employment standards over the past 30 years. It is for this reason that it is possible to conclude that the doctrine of industrial pluralism has an ongoing *normative impact*, even if it is not unequivocal. Various interpretations have been extrapolated and are premised on different ways of understanding the cohabitation of the plurality of legal orders governing labour and the role that the collective labour relations institutions play in this scheme. These interpretations embody two visions of the sources in labour law.

For some, the project of democratization embedded in the doctrine of industrial pluralism has been realized: the establishment of collective relations in an enterprise truly enables the attainment of equality between employees and employers. Did the majority of the Court in *Isidore Garon* not write that: "[t]o say that an employee is isolated or vulnerable when he or she is represented by a union would be an affront to organized labour"?[92] This understanding would suggest that the collective labour regime is self-sufficient and that State, as well as judges, should not intervene into collective labour relations institutions.[93]

Others reach different conclusions, despite their common affirmation that collective representation in the workplace puts employees in a better position to durably transform the power relationships at work. Pursuant to a second vision of how to approach the plurality of sources of labour law, collective relations institutions are seen as the best way to ensure the effective implementation of rights conferred on employees, irrespective of whether these rights emanate from the collective agreement or state law.[94] This reading, also inspired by industrial pluralism, contains

[92] *Isidore Garon ltée v. Tremblay; Fillion et Frères (1976) inc.* v. *Syndicat national des employés de garage du Québec*, *supra*, note 67, par. 59.

[93] The policy of judicial reserve with respect to the legal order constituted by collective labour relations is well expressed, in another context by Justice McIntyre who wrote in *Reference Re Public Service Employee Relations Act (Alta.)*, [1987] 1 S.C.R. 313, par. 182: "Labour law, as we have seen, is a fundamentally important as well as an extremely sensitive subject. It is based upon a political and economic compromise between organized labour – a very powerful socio-economic force – on the one hand, and the employers of labour – an equally powerful socio-economic force – on the other. The balance between the two forces is delicate and the public-at-large depends for its security and welfare upon the maintenance of that balance. One group concedes certain interests in exchange for concessions from the other. There is clearly no correct balance which may be struck giving permanent satisfaction to the two groups, as well as securing the public interest. The whole process is inherently dynamic and unstable. Care must be taken then in considering whether constitutional protection should be given to one aspect of this dynamic and evolving process…"

[94] In this way, individual and collective rights do not oppose each other. If the "tendency toward individualization […] can be analyzed as a loosening of the constraints that are exercised by the group on the individual", it can also be seen as "the risk of a lessening in the protection of the individual by the group" (A. SUPIOT, *supra*, note 10, 490) [our translation]. The original, in French : "[Si] la tendance à l'individualisation […] peut être analysée comme la chance d'un desserrement des contraintes que le groupe exerce sur l'individu", elle peut aussi être vue comme "le risque d'une réduction de la protection de l'individu par le groupe".

within it fundamental changes in the operation of collective labour relations institutions. From this perspective, unions may not be viewed only as "co-legislators" of labour conditions by collective bargaining. Their role includes ensuring respect for the rights contained both in collective agreements and in the state laws, namely laws relating to human rights that are guaranteed to each employee.[95] It also behooves arbitrators – previously perceived as interpreters of the will of the parties to a collective agreement – to be the guarantors of the implementation of the rights of employees in the unionized workplace, whether these rights emanate from the collective agreement or enacted laws. These changes could even contribute to the realization of the initial project of industrial pluralism by authorizing a certain arbitral control in the exercise of managerial rights not limited by provisions in a collective agreement.[96] In this way, the distinctive legitimacy of collective labour relations could be reaffirmed rather than threatened by the emergence of statutory norms.[97]

These contrasting visions of industrial pluralism are apparent not only in the decisions of judges and arbitrators; they also impact upon the understanding that all of the various actors in labour law, including union representatives, workers, employers, and researchers, have of their roles. In that sense, even if the doctrine of "industrial pluralism" does not perfectly reflect the plurality of legal orders in the workplace revealed by a broader comprehensive legal pluralism perspective[98], it can explain, from a normative perspective, the recognition of the centrality of collective autonomy and the values and principles behind the institutionalization of a particular form of collective labour relations institutions.

---

[95] Simon DEAKIN, "L'évolution de la relation d'emploi", in Peter AUER and Bernard GAZIER (eds.), *L'avenir du travail, de l'emploi et de la protection sociale: dynamique du changement et protection des travailleurs*, Genève, Institut international d'études sociales (B.I.T.), 2002, p. 224.

[96] See in this way: *Parry Sound (District) Social Services Administration Board* v. *O.P.S.E.U., Local 324, supra*, note 56, esp. par. 23 and 36.

[97] J.M. LAPIERRE, G. ROCHER and G. VALLÉE, *supra*, note 18, p. 379–382. More generally on the paradoxal effect of constitutionalization on the autonomy of labour law, see: Michel COUTU, "Le droit du travail comme ordre légitime", dans M. COUTU and G. ROCHER (eds.), *La légitimité de l'État et du droit. Autour de Max Weber*, collection "Pensée allemande et européenne", Québec, Presses de l'Université Laval, 2005, p. 353.

[98] Michel COUTU, "Crise du droit du travail, pluralisme juridique et souveraineté", *Lex Electronica*, vol. 12 n°1 (Printemps / Spring 2007), in part. par. 13.

Chapter 8
The Rigidity and Density of Discipline in Youth Rehabilitation Centres … Or Rules That Counter Rights

Julie Desrosiers*

8.1 Introduction

The starting point of State intervention in youth protection is the violation of a child's rights. Children in need of protection have difficult life stories. They are stories of abandonment, neglect, physical and psychological abuse. The line between these populational groups is often blurred since many children who have been abused or neglected at a young age develop serious behavioural problems as adolescents.[1] Their most fundamental rights have been infringed, including their most basic right to security of the person. The State intervenes when parents fail to provide or undermine the fundamental and basic needs of their child – that is to say, in legal terms – when there is a failure to ensure respect for the physical and psychological integrity, health and education of the child.[2] Accordingly, it is the violation of a child's fundamental rights that constitutes the foundation for State intervention. And it is respect for those basic rights that both *legitimizes* and *governs* the kind of responses that the State may take. State intervention loses its legitimacy if it reproduces the violence or the violations suffered by the child; furthermore, any decisions or

*This paper draws on a chapter from my doctoral dissertation entitled *Isolement et mesures disciplinaires dans les centres de réadaptation pour jeunes* (Montréal: Wilson & Lafleur, 2005). This text was translated by Dia Dabby with the collaboration of Colleen Sheppard.

[1] On any average year, the population in rehabilitation centres for youth is composed of young offenders (about 25%) and youths in need of protection (about 75%).

[2] *Youth Protection Act*, S.R.Q., c. P-34.1, s. 38; see also the *Convention on the Rights of the Child*, G.A. res. 44/25 (1989), s. 19.

J. Desrosiers (✉)
Faculty of Law, Université Laval, G1V 0A6, Québec, QC, Canada
e-mail: julie.desrosiers@fd.ulaval.ca

R. Provost and C. Sheppard (eds.), *Dialogues on Human Rights and Legal Pluralism*, Ius Gentium: Comparative Perspectives on Law and Justice 17,
DOI 10.1007/978-94-007-4710-4_8, © Springer Science+Business Media Dordrecht 2013

interventions of the State must be governed by the principle of the best interests of the child and respect for his or her rights.[3]

This chapter draws on the experiences of youth in Quebec rehabilitation centres and assesses the extent to which the fundamental rights of youth are protected and advanced in this institutional context.[4]

In terms of the most basic of rights, it is clear that the young people who stay in youth rehabilitation centres do not go hungry. The food is abundant and generously offered. They attend school, unless confined to their room for disciplinary reasons. Yet, their leisure activities are carefully controlled; sports are often mandatory, as are library visits. Their choice of personal forms of expression is also controlled. Room decoration, music, telephone conversations, personal movements, and personal hygiene – are equally controlled. There are rules for everything in a rehabilitation centre. So numerous are the prescriptions that it is practically illusory to hope to escape from the authoritarian controls and constraints. At any moment, the youth may find him or herself in violation of some particular institutional rule or regulatory detail. Given the restrictions on freedom, the omnipresence of regulations and time spent in their rooms, youths experience rehabilitation centres as something akin to prison.[5] Such experiences raise critical questions about whether such rehabilitation centres actually advance the best interests of young people? Do they respect and enhance their rights?

The rigidity of the institutional framework can be explained, at least in part, by the "characteristics of the clientele", to employ an expression often used in health and social services. The youth that inhabit the rehabilitation centers have histories of not respecting authority. Many have violated laws or school rules. They have often been left to themselves or run away from home. The institutional framework offered by rehabilitation centres is seen as a way to counter, or at least control, these past patterns of behaviour. The disciplinary measures participate in a vast educational program that is aimed at promoting self-discipline and compliance with institutional rules and social norms.

Educators at rehabilitation centres who confine a youth to his or her room do so with rehabilitation in mind. To the extent that the disciplinary measures interfere with the youth's freedom, they are thought to be justified as measures designed to

[3] *Youth Protection Act,* S.R.Q., c. P-34.1, s. 3. In the same way, see s. 33 of the *Civil Code of Québec,* S.Q. 1991, c. 64.

[4] In Québec, there are approximatively 50 youth rehabilitation centres. The vast majority of these centres receive adolescents between the ages of 12 and 18, who are sent pursuant to the *Health and Social Services Act,* the *Youth Protection Act* or the *Youth Justice Criminal Act* (S.C. 2002, c. 1): see Julie Desrosiers and Lucie Lemonde, "Les centres de réadaptation : protéger les uns et punir les autres (1869–)" (2000) 34 *R.J.T.* 435, 469 and more generally at pages 469–478.

[5] The research report by the Conseil permanent de la jeunesse [Permanent Counsel on Youth] largely canvassed youths' comments on the dullness of the premises, the fences and gridded windows, the restrictions on freedom, the omnipresence of regulations and time spent locked up in their room. For youths, a rehabilitation centre was akin to prison. See Conseil permanent de la jeunesse, *Les jeunes en centres jeunesse prennent la parole!*, Research report, July 2004, especially pages 16–21.

insure the security and individual development of the youth. The educators hope that the youth will learn from the disciplinary measures, acquire new relationship skills and social abilities that will allow for successful rehabilitation. In reality, however, the juvenile rehabilitation universe is coercive and adolescents are often remanded to their rooms because they are not behaving in a way that the educators approve. Although educators may isolate and effectively lock-up youth for clinical and educative ends, their interventions enter a disciplinary logic that the youth perceive as punitive. To put it another way, the professional culture that impregnates human relations in rehabilitation centres contributes to the rigidity of the system; educator-youth interactions become occasions first and foremost, to discipline.

The authoritarianism that pervades youth rehabilitation centres can also be explained drawing on the work of sociologist Erving Goffman on total institutions.[6] His work casts an interesting light on the role and exercise of discipline in youth rehabilitation centres. It brings to light a recurring institutional paradox between the stated therapeutic aims and the real effects of the rules in force, namely to maintain order through the oppressive and bureaucratic treatment of particular groups.

It is useful to explore the normative universe of rehabilitation centres and in particular the institutional codes of conduct in different rehabilitation units through the lens of Goffman's analysis, and in this way highlight the effects on the daily lives and fundamental human rights of youths.

8.2 A Goffmanian Analysis of Code of Conduct

According to Goffman, one of the essential characteristics of total institutions is the organization of all aspects of an individual's life, including work, home and leisure within the walls of the institution. Consolidated in such a manner, each of these spheres are organized using the same organizational framework, which includes a complete lack of privacy of the large number of institutionalized individuals and adherence to strict and predetermined rules and programs.[7]

Since life in a total institution operates within an entirely closed universe, it is life in a parenthesis, a detached episode, artificial, alien to the "real" life that is unfolding outside. The total institution is built on an inside/outside opposition, where the institutional universe counter-reflects that of civil society. Goffman analyzed administrative admissions processes as rites of passage from the outside to the inside, demarcating the split with one's previous life. Once inside the institution, the individual is deprived of his or her personal effects and relations, resulting in the partial atrophy of his or her identity.

[6] Erving Goffman, *Asylums: Essays on the Social Situations of Mental Patients and Other Inmates* (Chicago: Aldine Publishing, 1961).

[7] *Ibid*, p. 5.

Goffman describes the omnipresence of discipline in total institutions and reveals the functioning of a system of privileges and sanctions, whose first instrument is that of the internal regulation, prescribing in detail the conduct and austerity of daily life of the "shut-ins". These multiple prescriptions allow for constant and fastidious control of all aspects of existence, from the way to dress, speak and eat.[8]

According to Goffman, regardless of the official purposes of an institution, total institutions seek to reduce differences between individuals through identical treatment for all. In principle, the spirit of rehabilitation goes against this totalizing and universalizing tendency because it aims for the individualization of measures. In rehabilitation centres, however, all youth must walk to the same rhythm, follow the same strict and obligatory programming, move in small packs, do the same thing at the same moment and are treated in the same manner. Could this constitute what Goffman describes as a recurring institutional paradox? By focusing on the methodic description of daily life in a psychiatric hospital, Goffman remarkably illustrated the gap between the official objective of an institution (in this case, to care for patients) from the real effects, enabling us to gauge the "permanent divorce, or at least the constant tension, between the therapeutic activity and the security demands and social safeguards of the hospital."[9] In a rehabilitation centre, the distance that separates the rehabilitation project from the institutional treatment of the youths is significant.

We can debate the appropriateness of the total institution's characteristics and those of a rehabilitation centre, namely at the level of the impermeability of the "inside" and "outside" universes. In fact, whereas the youths in the secure rehabilitation units live, eat, sleep, work and go to school within the same walls, the youths in regular rehabilitation units can have regular contact with the outside. Moreover, all of these youths can benefit from outings and leaves of absences on weekends. The current tendency is also resolutely edging towards the reduction and decentralization of rehabilitation centres. However, the analytical grid proposed by Goffman is still relevant in institutions for minors,[10] particularly in secure rehabilitation units, where the omnipresent breadth and rigidity of discipline is striking.

[8] *Ibid*, pp. 38–39 and 41.

[9] See "Foreword" by Robert Castel in the French translation of Erving Goffman's *Asylums*: Erving Goffman, *Asiles: études sur la constitution sociale des malades mentaux et autres reclus* (trans. by Liliane and Claude Lainé, Paris: Les Éditions de Minuit, 1968), p. 25.

[10] This position is defended by Lorraine Green and Wendy Parkin, "Sexuality, Sexual Abuse and Children's Homes – Oppression or Protection?" in The Violence Against Children Study Group, *Children, Child Abuse and Child Protection: Placing Children Centrally* (Chichester: Wiley, 1999), pp. 115–192, at pp. 186–189. Closer to home, the Law Commission of Canada in Restoring Dignity, Responding to Child Abuse in Canadian Institutions (Ottawa: Minister of Public Works and Government Services, March 2000), p. 22, referred to reformatories, child protection institutions and residential schools for Aboriginal children (from the end of the nineteenth century up until the 1960s) as total institutions, that is to say "institutions that seek to re-socialise people by instilling them with new roles, skills or values." Given that "it believes that the abuse of children in out-of-home care settings continues to this day" (p. 347), the Commission suggests to counter the institutional totalitarianism by openness to the outside. Accordingly, "Total institutions (…) must also take steps to minimise their own isolation from society. They must become less "total" by welcoming interaction with, and the involvement of, community members." (p. 361).

Respect for codes of conduct occupies a preponderant place in rehabilitation centre units. According to our observations, most youths receive discipline, including isolation in their rooms following a breach of the code of conduct. It is easy to violate one or another of the multiple rules and prescriptions in the codes: too much timein the shower, an improper tone of voice, tardiness and the list goes on. It is only by looking more closely at these codes of conducts that one can begin to appreciate the density and rigidity of the rules they prescribe.

A comprehensive review of codes of conducts in Quebec youth rehabilitation centres revealed significant similarities.[11] Accordingly, eight sample rehabilitation centres (both regular and secure male and female unit) and their respective codes of conduct were relied upon in our study.[12] Four axes of analysis were identified: "admission", "re-engineering identity", "absence of intimacy" and the "minute control of daily life".

8.2.1 Admission

According to Goffman, admission into a total institution is the first step in the individual's degradation process. Deprived of his or her personal effects, forced to wear the anonymous clothing of the institution, cut from the rest of the world and especially from those who give meaning to his or her existence, individuality is reduced. As Corinne Rostaing comments, in her work on women's prisons: "even if the admissions ceremonies have changed (...), even if the mandatory haircut or the wearing of the drugget no longer exist, the obligatory shower, the

[11] In October 2000, we wrote to all youth centers in Québec asking them to send us their internal rules regarding disciplinary measures as well as their current codes of conduct in rehabilitation units. After a few reminders, we were able to obtain all the internal rules, but had mitigating success for the codes of conduct. Only the Centre jeunesse du Bas St-Laurent et le Centre jeunesse de Québec responded entirely to our request, however.

[12] The selected centres included: secure rehabilitation units for girls (Centre jeunesse de Québec, Campus adolescentes Escale, *Unité Perce-Vent, Code et procédures de l'encadrement intensif*, April 1998, 23 pages and the Centre jeunesse du Bas-Saint-Laurent, *Unité l'Anse. Code et procédures,* March 2000, 18 pages); regular rehabilitation units for girls: (Centre jeunesse de Québec, *Code et procédures de l'unité multiprogramme La Nacelle*, June 1999, 8 pages & Centre jeunesse du Bas-Saint-Laurent, *Unité La villa Dion. Code de vie,* October 2000, 12 pages); secure rehabilitation units for boys: (Centre jeunesse de Québec, Le Gouvernail, *Codes et procédures de l'Unité Foyer,* Janurary 2000, 13 pages & Centre jeunesse du Bas-Saint-Laurent, *Unité Le Quai, Code et procédures,* July 2000, 25 pages); and regular rehabilitation units for boys: (Centre jeunesse de Québec, *Unité Le Rivage. Codes et procédures,* September 5, 2000, 9 pages & Centre jeunesse du Bas-Saint-Laurent, *Unité L'Ancrage. Code de vie et normes et procédures,* January 2000, 19 pages). The relevant excerpts from the codes of conduct are reproduced in Desrosiers., *Isolement et mesures disciplinaires dans les centres de réadaptation pour jeunes* (Montréal: Wilson & Lafleur, 2005), at Annex 3, at the corresponding heading. The annex contains, for example, under the "admission" section, all passages from the codes of conduct that address this theme.

body search, the sorting of personal objects, fingerprinting, the anthropometric photos still subsist ..." She continues by stating that the "entrance into the total institution marks the split with their previous life, the breaking of habits, the loss of their former social status. It forces the individual to undo their former self rendering her vulnerable."[13]

This extraction phenomenon exists in youth rehabilitation centers. The sorting of personal clothes, obligatory showers, kwellada treatment, mandatory isolation periods, are all palpable signs of a break with the youth's previous life. Particular attention is paid to the clothing that a youth will be allowed to wear in his or her "new life". It comes as no surprise that adolescents place particular importance on their body image and clothing, an incarnation of their budding identity. By parsing the clothing and accessories from which they draw a part of their identity's strength, one can perhaps think that this makes them more malleable or flexible to change.

The searching of a youth's luggage, clothing and personal effects are an integral part of the admissions process (which can double as a body search if deemed necessary). It becomes a sorting between what is permitted and what is forbidden – all objects and clothing labeled as not conforming to the "values of the environment" will be confiscated. With the girls, the list of forbidden objects generally includes clothing and accessories that have a sexual connotation or simply sexy: jewelry, leather items, shirts that leave shoulders or midriffs uncovered, mini skirts, boots and so forth. With the boys, the forbidden items relate more to the theme of violence: knives, army boots and clothing suggestive of physical violence will be confiscated.

A segue way is addressed here. In 1979, Cesari wrote that "what determines the minor woman's conduct's antisocial character is rarely in the ordinary sense of delinquency given to the male homologue (theft in the bulk of the cases) but the pure and simple use of her body – the sexualized body – outside of the codes established by the male society."[14] The conveyed values by the codes of life of rehabilitation centers are a magnifying mirror of social stereotypes, a caricature of sexual organization that prevails in the global society. With the girls, for example, the dress code is subject to much stricter attention than with the boys. The code of conduct has more to do with hygiene, make-up, hairstyling, and jewelry. A rehabilitation unit can even go as far as regulating tanning sessions. Caressing and tickling amongst adolescents is forbidden, just as loving gestures during visits. There is nothing similar

[13] Corinne Rostaing, *La relation carcérale. Identités et rapports sociaux dans les prisons pour femmes* (Paris: PUF, 1997), p. 144. [Our translation] The original, in French: "même si les cérémonies d'admission ont changé (...), même si la coupe obligatoire ou le port du droguet n'existent plus, il subsiste la douche obligatoire, la fouille corporelle, le tri des objets personnels, la prise d'empreintes, les photos anthropométriques... [...] l'entrée dans l'institution totale marque la coupure par rapport à la vie précédente, la rupture des habitudes, la perte de son ancien statut social. Elle force l'individu à se défaire de son moi antérieur ce qui le rend vulnérable."

[14] Giorgio Cesari, *Psychiatrie et pouvoir* (Paris: Éd. Anthropologie, 1979), p. 125 [Our translation]. The original, in French: "ce qui détermine le caractère antisocial du comportement de la femme mineure est rarement d'ordre de la délinquance au sens ordinaire que l'on donne à ce mot quand il s'agit de son homologue mâle (vol dans la plupart des cas), mais l'utilisation pure et simple de son corps – le corps sexué – en dehors des codes établis par la société des mâles."

with the boys. The difference in treatment is not at the heart of the subject at hand, but certainly does influence the use of discipline in a rehabilitation centre.

The mandatory shower is also instrumental to the admissions process. With the girls, this washing (passage from the outside, where the youth is dirty and stained to the inside, where he is cleaned and purified) can include a treatment against parasites. "The Kwellada or Nix (for a young pregnant girl) treatment is *obligatory* for any youth arriving at Perce-Vent (…) The clothing in the youth's luggage will [also] be put in a bag for Kwellada treatment."[15] The treatment against parasites is an implicit reference to young girls' sexual depravation; boys do not appear to be submitted to such treatment.

Mandatory search and shower can be repeated each time one returns from an outing. For example, at the Anse unit, the section 4.3 of the code of conduct provides: "after returning from your outing, the content of your luggage will be checked by an educator or guardian before you reclaim possession. It is to be noted that you are to take a shower when you return from sleeping outside of the centre".

After the mandatory shower, the youth must put on "clean clothes". In certain units, notably the secure units for girls, these clothes are provided by the unit. At the Perce-Vent unit, much emphasis is placed on carrying out a triage of an adolescent's personal clothes with care: "there is no urgency in proceeding to [the verification of personal effects] especially since a basic trousseau will be supplied at her arrival". The youth will therefore use the clothing put at her disposal by the institution while waiting to recover her own clothes, or at least those judged adequate and washed with Kwellada. In the Anse unit, the adolescent must "put on pajamas and a bathrobe" after having a shower, regardless of the time of day. At the Foyer unit, devoted to intensive monitoring of youth under protection and to open custody of young offenders, a youth's personal objects judged consistent with the values of the environment "will be returned according to [this] process".

The first moments following initial contact between the youth and the institution generally include a spatial-temporal isolation. At the Le Quai unit, the adolescent must retire to the assigned room in order to take notice of the unit's code of conduct; he will only leave when he receives permission.[16] During the first 5 days, he will not be able to circulate inside the rehabilitation centre, "no gymnasium, and no all-purpose room". Instead of these activities, he will be confined to his room, where he will be able to "read, write or take the time to reflect on his situation."[17]

---

[15] Centre jeunesse de Québec, Campus adolescentes Escale, *Unité Perce-Vent, Code et procédures de l'encadrement intensif*, April 1998 [Our translation].

[16] It is the same at the Anse unit, where the adolescent must stay in her room to take notice of the code of conduct until she receives permission to step out. *Unité l'Anse. Code et procédures,* March 2000: "This arrival time gives you time to install yourself and take notice of the code and procedures. A questionnaire will be given to you after having read the code of conduct and procedures to make sure that you have understood." [Our translation]

[17] It is also the same for the Le Foyer unit, where the "first five days, [the adolescent will have to] have reflection periods. [There will be] a reflection period in the afternoon and another at night. If [attending] school, [he will only have] one reflection period at night. The reflection period last an hour and is during a structured activity." (Le Gouvernail, *Code et procédures de l'Unité Foyer,* January 2000). [Our translation]

The schism with youth's former life is also felt in the communications by telephone during the admission process to the rehabilitation centre. At Perce-Vent, the adolescent is not allowed to call anybody but her parents for the first 72 h of her arrival. At La Nacelle, the same goes for the first 48 h.

On occasion, it happens that a newly arrived youth must live in "proximity", which is a perfect illustration of the loss of privacy incurred when living in the centre. "Proximity" can also be understood as promiscuity. For example, the code of conduct at the La Nacelle unit states: "During the first 48 h, [w]e ask that you be in the same room as an educator. Following that, we will establish together what best suits you (it is proximity)."

8.2.2 *Re-engineering Identity*

Goffman did not speak of re-engineering, but rather of identity deprivation. According to him, the total institution deprived the individual of his personal culture by using various techniques of degradation of his personality, including that of "stripping" of his clothes and belongings to replace them with anonymous and undifferentiated ones from the institution.[18] The expression of "re-engineering identity" translates better the effect, at the same time real and sought, of the rules that prevail in rehabilitation centers, where the youth is not deprived of all that belongs to him or her, but only what is deemed contrary to the "values of the environment".

"Image" is a frequently used expression in the rehabilitation centre. "Negative image" is the one that refers back to the schemes of delinquent behaviors, is that of the hardened youth, squatter, criminal biker or drug dealer, and that of the young prostitute. It is the image that must be deconstructed. "Positive image", is the other, the one that is "adequate" and "respectful". It must be encouraged. The rules that follow are supposed to reinforce the rehabilitation project of the centre; they were designed to encourage and promote respect of self and others. Disciplinary sanctions can be incurred by the youth who violates them.

8.2.2.1 Dress Code, Jewelry, Tattoos, Body Piercing

The rehabilitation centre does not divest youths of *all* of their personal belongings. They are still allowed to wear some of their own clothes, and keep some of their personal belongings to which they are emotionally attached. However, there are significant limits. They are prohibited from displaying certain widespread symbols of American adolescence, such as bare midriffs and tattoos, mini skirts and form-fitting tank tops, which are seen as celebrations of the condemnable body

[18] Goffman, *supra* note 6, pp. 18–21.

from within the walls of the institution. The symbols of juvenile marginality, of the underground culture of the youth, or even a new aesthetic are also banned: no belly-button, nose or eyebrow rings, no holed or otherwise altered clothing, no hoodies, no "bizarre" haircuts ...

Girls are first and foremost subjected to the constraints of sexual decency. The forbidden list is long and the effort to asexualize is obvious. "The wearing of the mini-skirt, the belly shirt [and] the boot"[19] is barred, the "shirt without sleeves and leaving shoulders uncovered is not permitted outside of the summer period", the "bra is mandatory" and the "3/4 Bermuda shorts are authorized."[20] The adolescent "must demonstrate restraint in her makeup and hairstyle" and should were "discreet" jewelry. In secure units, control is consolidated and regulates all vestiges of femininity: all jewelry, mirrors and razors will be confiscated, "even electric razors".[21]

For male youth, codes require that boys avoid looking unkempt. Nor are they to wear t-shirts decorated with "skulls, bloodied faces, etc. ..."[22] All "clothing of a pornographic, morbid, violent or drug-related character"[23] are forbidden, as are those that are "torn, scribbled on or patched."[24] "Pants are to be worn at the hip" and caps are only allowed outside.[25] Adolescents must avoid walking around bare-chested and are not allowed to wear undershirts outside of sports practices.[26] As with the girls, tattoos and body piercing jewelry are forbidden.

In addition to the provisions to desexualize girls' dress, most of the prohibitions addressed to boys are also applicable to girls. For example, at La Nacelle, a regular unit for girls, risky clothing is forbidden, as are caps, hats, hoodies, as well as any clothing that is torn or a symbol of degrading, violent or pornographic inscriptions. In the clothing restrictions, girls are doubly regulated.

8.2.2.2 Corporal Posture, Language and Manners

What is "decent" is what is "is appropriate", according to the Oxford English Dictionary. What is "adequate" is "what is proportionate to the object and adapted to its objective". This vast and vague world of unruly behavior carries these two adjectives. Appropriate posture, adequate dress, decent language ... There are as many requirements that permit intervention at any moment to remodel the youth's

[19] *Code et procédures de l'unité multiprogramme La Nacelle*, June 1999 [Our translation].

[20] *Unité l'Anse – Code et procédures*, March 2000 [Our translation].

[21] *Unité Perce-Vent – Code et procédures de l'encadrement intensif,* April 1998 [Our translation].

[22] *Codes et procédures de l'Unité Foyer,* January 2000, p. 11 [Our translation].

[23] *Unité Le Rivage – Code et procédures,* 2000, p. 6 [Our translation].

[24] *Id.*

[25] *Id.*

[26] *Id.* In the same way, see, *Unité l'Ancrage – Code de vie et normes et procédures*, January 2000; and *Codes et procédures de l'Unité Foyer*, January 2000 [Our translation].

behavior in accordance with a certain idea of what is correct. Here, as elsewhere, the youth risks disciplinary sanctions:

> Posture and dress: For the well-being of your body, you must adopt a decent posture (example: a chair has four feet…). Your clothes must also be adequate with the objective of respect for each person's vital space.
>
> Language, gestures and conversations: Your language and gestures must be respectful. No vulgarity, swearing, use of surnames, etc. will be tolerated. At all times, the tone and content of your conversations must be decent. The regulation on disciplinary measures will be applied when there is a failure in respecting this article.[27]
> [author's emphasis]

All processes of socialization include the integration of social norms that are difficult to define with precision. An adolescent can be extremely arrogant while using the most polite langue; another can be very respectful without, however, having said thank you. All educational enterprises rest on words that mean nothing in and of themselves, aside from referring back to a soft corpus of social conventions to be integrated.[28] Being polite or nice is always a question of context, tonality and expression. In that regard, the rehabilitation centre does not use a language that is different from that of the school or of the family. However, within the rehabilitation centre, the globalizing potential of the "adequate" qualifier is deployed to counter certain manifestations of youth culture and participate in the re-engineering of identity: for example, having adequate language entails avoiding vulgarities and abstaining from swearing, but it is also proscribing the use of surnames.

8.2.2.3 Reading, Music

Popular music groups, particularly those valued by youth, often sing about sex, drugs and alcohol. The musical universe of youth profoundly defines them. In the centre, the choice of readings and music is part of the youth's re-engineering project and is a part of the rehabilitation approach. At the Villa Dion, therefore, "[a]ny object, video, music, reading or other conveying morbidity, aggressiveness, drugs, alcohol, pornography, indecency or spiritualism" are forbidden "since they do not correspond to the values of our environment." At the Quai centre, the "books, journals and newspapers with a violent or indecent character" are forbidden, as is heavy metal music.

8.2.3 *The Absence of Privacy*

Individuals living in a total institution see their sphere of privacy considerably reduced, first by the promiscuity of a great number of other people and then by the institutional propensity to control their complete existence. In a total institution, all

---

[27] *Unité l'Ancrage - Code de vie et normes et procédures*, January 2000 [Our translation].

[28] Paul Amselek, "La teneur indécise du droit" (1992) 26 *R.J.T.* 1.

relationships are public and are open to the scrutiny of the administration, whether it is relationships between "lock-ins" or with the outside.

It is true of the rehabilitation centre, where a number of rules attempt to create obstacles to the development of close relationships or intimacy between youths in the same unit. Whispering, secrets, giggling, visits from one room to another … there are as many grey zones that are potentially dangerous for the educator. A planned escape staged here, an attempt to sell drugs there … The organization of a rehabilitation centre tends to neutralize these attempts by minimizing occasions to meet and freely discuss among the youth. Even if the stakes are low, even if it is not a case of escape or drugs, but rather detailed narration of a sexual experience, the educator must know, hear and perhaps intervene immediately to re-balance the statement or perhaps come back to it when having a face-to-face discussion with the youth. It is by the same logic that both visits and mail are controlled: monitoring the "security" of the environment (avoiding escapes, consumption of alcohol and drugs, sexual relations between youths and so forth) and promoting the youth's rehabilitation.

8.2.3.1 Conversations and Relationships Between Youths of a Same Unit

In the rehabilitation centers, the interpersonal relationships between youths are organized and managed in such a way that the educator is aware of the substance. Any zone of relational intimacy is eliminated through the organization of the space. Aside from the rooms, all the spaces are common. Moreover, codes of conducts prohibit youths from visiting each other's rooms: "You do not visit any other youth in their room and do not entertain any in yours. Your room will be checked routinely."[29] It is therefore impossible to use one's own room or have a private conversation outside of the regulatory gaze of the educators.

Youth can however communicate among each other in the common rooms, during the meals or cigarette breaks. The conversations, however, must be "frank and amicable, and out loud,"[30] so that the educator can hear them and control the content. For example, during the cigarette break at the Perce-Vent unit, "the conversations (…) must be addressed to the whole group in order to avoid one-on-one discussions. Educators must be present in order to monitor the content of conversations."[31]

Other rules also reflect a high degree of control over interpersonal relationships, for example: silence during showers and during the "tanning period" at the Perce-Vent unit; prohibition on caressing hair, kissing or tickling at the Villa Dion unit or writing to each other at La Nacelle unit.

---

[29] *Unité Le Quai - Code et procédures*, July 2000 [Our translation]; *Unité l'Anse - Code et procédures,* March 2000; *Unité La villa Dion - Code de vie,* October 2000 [Our translation].

[30] *Unité l'Anse - Code et procédures,* March 2000 [Our translation].

[31] *Unité Perce-Vent, Code et procédures de l'encadrement intensif,* April 1998 [Our translation]

8.2.3.2 Loans, Donations and Exchanges

Offering a cigarette, lending money, exchanging clothes – while these gestures seem natural to adolescents – they are prohibited in rehabilitation centres. All loans, donations, exchanges or sales are prohibited across the board, whether they are clothing, money or cigarettes. These rules are routinely challenged during cigarette breaks, or "transitions". Many youths in rehabilitation centres are, in fact, smokers. It often happens that one of them is missing cigarettes, either because he or she was recently admitted to the unit or because his or her supply is exhausted. In such a case, the individual must watch the others smoke and no one is allowed to share their cigarettes.

8.2.3.3 Mail and Visits

Two rationales are behind the verification of the mail: (a) insuring that the youth's correspondent is not the object of a contact prohibition; (b) verifying whether the envelope contains money, drugs or other prohibited objects. In principle, the letters are not read. Nevertheless, the educator must seal those sent by the youth and those received will be opened before being handed over:

> *You have the right to receive your mail; however, if they are personal letters, the educator will ask you to open them in front of him and after having verified the content of the envelope, will give it back to you.*
>
> *It is a similar process to send mail. Before sealing the envelope, you must present it to the educator, who verifies the address of your correspondent and the content of the envelope; if done in accordance, he will take care of mailing it. You must assume the costs of your correspondence.*[32]

Visits are held once a week, generally on Sunday afternoons. As in the case of interpersonal relationships between youth, relations with people from the outside are closely monitored. Visits are effectively "public visits." Such supervision is an intrusion on intimacy paralleling Goffman's observation that in a total institution outsiders are brought into contact "with the individual's close relationship to significant others."[33] In addition to the intrusiveness of institutional observation, other rules also infringe on the free flow of these encounters:

- *During the visits [of friends], your attitude, speech and comments as well as your dress must illustrate the respect of others as well as the premises; no contact is allowed aside from a embrace at arrival and departure.*[34]
- *During visits to the unit, it is essential that visitors retain correct speech. Amorous gestures are not permitted.*[35]
- *The attitudes that perturb either a youth, or the group, will be signaled to the concerned persons and immediate collaboration to remedy the situation should be sought out.*[36]

---

[32] *Unité l'Ancrage - Code de vie et normes et procédures*, January 2000 [Our translation].

[33] Goffman, *supra* note 6, p. 31.

[34] *Unité l'Anse - Code et procédures,* March 2000 [Our translation].

[35] *Unité La villa Dion - Code de vie,* October 2000 [Our translation].

[36] *Unité l'Ancrage – Code de vie et normes et procédures*, January 2000 [Our translation].

8.2.4 *The Minute Regulation of Daily Life*

It has been established that the total institution deprives the individual of his or her previous identity references. The "structure of his new personality" must be edified on the basis of an institutional system of privileges and sanctions.[37] This system rests on "house rules" that "spell out the austere round of life of the inmate."[38] Youths who respect the regulation receive awards and favours; however, these are always subject to being denied if a regulation is contravened. Disciplinary sanctions would also ensue.

Goffman defines the "house rules" as a "relatively explicit and formal set of prescriptions and proscriptions that lays out the main requirements of inmate conduct."[39] The codes of conduct elaborate the minutia of scheduling, timing and procedures for each aspect of life: sleeping, waking up, getting dressed, smoking, showering and so on. These codes are generally long; between ten (10) and twenty-five pages (25) devoted to the multiple rules that elaborate the daily routine of the unit. The points addressed as well as the writing style are similar from one unit to another, although secure units employ a more stringent style. Selective excerpts, taken from both of the codes in effect in both regular and secure units, for both girls and boys, provide a better understanding of the nature and extent of the monitoring to which youths are subject.

Wake up (Le Rivage unit, CJ Quebec, regular monitoring, boys):
On school days, wake up is between 6 h30 and 8 h00 (the hour varies according to your school schedule). Procedures are accomplished in a low voice (respect for others).

When I am authorized by the educator to get up, I must:

- Make my bed.
- Get dressed.
- Clean up my room.
- Wash my face and comb my hair.
- Ask that these routines be checked.

Meals (Perce-Vent, CJ Quebec, secure monitoring, girls):
Each youth must take the place that has been attributed to her, as indicated on the seating plan for the table on the billboard. Only the adolescent responsible for setting the tables is allowed to walk around; the others must remain seated at their place. The educator will help the adolescent who is attending to the table. Service must be carried out in silence and no walking around will be tolerated until the very end of the meal service. Conversations with girls at other tables are not permitted, to ensure a climate of tranquility. At the end of the meal, each youth will do her own dishes and only one girl at the time will be allowed in the kitchenette. When the educator

---

[37] Goffman, *supra* note 6, pp. 48–51.

[38] *Ibid*, p. 48.

[39] *Ibid*.

has all cutlery in his possession, they must be meticulously counted (15 of each as well as a "snip pit" to open the milk). When assured of the number of utensils, the educator will distribute the cigarettes and insure the cleanliness of the premises. At that point, the youth can leave the meal room.

Showers (Le Quai, CJ Bas-St-Laurent, secure monitoring, boys):
You are to be respectful of your body and we ask you to always be clean: hair, personal hygiene and dental. Grooming must be done at the indicated moments on the schedule. A shower must be taken after every activity or at night.

You must take one shower per day and in silence. A reasonable time period is set aside for each youth. The door to the shower room must stay open.

The educator will open your cupboard and you will take all that you need and then retire to your room. You will hand over your bathrobe, put on your slippers and wait for the educator's signal.

Cigarettes (La Nacelle, CJ Quebec, regular monitoring, girls):
You must manage your consumption and cost of cigarettes. You can only smoke outside and there are specific moments in the schedule that are set aside for smoking. If you smoke inside, a fine will be imposed. You must keep your cigarettes in a cubbyhole and you must use a lighter and not matches. Only pre-made or "easy-roll" cigarettes are accepted at the unit. No educator or girls from the units can buy you cigarettes. You must obtain your parents' authorization to smoke.

Telephones (La Villa Dion, CJ Bas-St-Laurent, regular monitoring, girls):
A telephone is at your disposal; it is the educator who will dial the number. Personal telephone calls are made during the weekdays at night and on afternoons and at night during the weekend. You can make a call at any point during office hours to your social worker, lawyer, clerk, judge and the Commission des droits de la personne et des droits de la jeunesse. This period is not included in the allocated time. Since your phone calls are personal, we ask you to be discreet in the subject of your call and to maintain a reasonable tone of voice. (…) It is important that you respect the telephone time of others, by the tone of your voice and the volume of the music, given the time allotted (10 min).

Bedtime (Le Foyer, CJ Quebec, secure monitoring, boys):

- Go to your room.
- Close the door.
- Put your clothes in your cupboard.
- We will turn off the light in your room at 10 h45.

Each moment of the day is detailed in this way, so that the code of conduct literally covers a period of 24 h. Everything is considered, even down to piggy-backed details (i.e.: "when the snack of choice is popcorn, you must put on the butter and salt at the educator's signal"[40]). Everything becomes a "procedure" – a procedure to

[40] This example is drawn from the *Interlude* (girls) unit's code of conduct, Centre jeunesse de Laval, undated, p. 11 [Our translation].

get up, a procedure to shower, a procedure to go to bed and so on. The typical schedule of a day in a rehabilitation centre set out below illustrates the ways in which institutional life is regulated and repetitive:

Typical schedule of a weekday and weeknight (Le Quai, CJ Bas-Saint-Laurent, secure monitoring, boys)

Daytime	
07 h45:	Wake-up
08 h10 to 08 h35:	Breakfast
08 h35 to 08 h45:	Cigarette break
08 h45 to 09 h35:	School
09 h35 to 09 h45:	Break
09 h45 to 10 h35:	School
10 h35 to 10 h45:	Cigarette break
10 h45 to 11 h35:	School
11 h35 to 12 h00:	Occupied Free Time (O.F.T.)[41]
12 h00 to 12 h35:	Lunch
12 h35 to 12 h45:	Cigarette break
12 h45 to 13 h00:	Hygiene
13 h00 to 13 h50:	School
13 h50 to 14 h00:	Cigarette break
14 h00 to 14 h50:	School
14 h50 to 15 h00:	Break
15 h00 to 15 h50:	School
15 h50 to 16 h00:	Preparing for nap
16 h00 to 17 h00:	Nap
Night time	
17 h00 to 17 h35:	Supper
17 h35 to 17 h45:	Cigarette break
17 h45 to 18 h00:	Hygiene
18 h00 to 18 h30:	Preparing for activity
18 h30 to 19 h30:	Activity
19 h30 to 20 h15:	Shower
20 h15 to 21 h00:	Tasks
21 h00 to 22 h00:	Snack and television
22 h00 to 22 h15:	Hygiene
22 h15:	Bedtime

Activities in the programming are mandatory. If a youth does not participate, he risks disciplinary sanctions. It should also be noted that youths spend time in their room on a mandatory basis; it could be a daily nap of an hour, a daily period of

[41] *Unité Le Quai - Code et procédures*, July 2000, p. 13: "Occupied free time means that you must decide on the activity that you want to do during a given period of the day as defined in the program. If you are unable to make a choice, it is the educator that will make the decision and you will have to respect his choice. The permitted activities during occupied free time are as follows: board games, cards, checkers, reading or others. All games are in the library, you must only make a choice. When you have finished, you must put it back in its place." [Our translation]

reflection or study, a "down time" or a "transition time" where youths have to go back to their room for 15 min. The time spent in their room is earmarked in the code of conduct and easily add up to an hour per day.[42] In this context, it is easy to understand that the addition of withdrawal hours and deprivation of outings are greatly resented by the youths; as stated by one of them, "we are already stuck in our rooms, if we have to do even more, it is exceedingly boring."[43]

8.2.5 A Sample Disciplinary File

To understand how institutional codes of conduct – as sources of informal law setting out rigid and extensive regulations – contribute to human rights violations, it is necessary to understand how violations result in extensive and recurrent discipline. The form of discipline often takes the form of isolation in one's room, or the denial of basic freedoms in everyday living.

Below is a sample disciplinary file, as compiled by the educators. No compiled statistics in disciplinary matters exist, but educators take down the daily measures imposed on a youth in his or her personal file.[44] The file reproduced here was identified as "medium" by the personnel of the unit, that is to say a file in which the youth involved had accumulated neither the most nor the least disciplinary interventions. Given the secure character of the facility in Stéphane's case, all withdrawals are carried out behind locked doors. The following excerpt covers a period of 2 months and all names are fictitious:

Stéphane's Disciplinary File

February 2: While I gave 1 h of withdrawal to Jean, Stéphane accused me of an "abuse of power" – he also received 1 h of withdrawal.

February 6: Stéphane is facing the table behind us in the cafeteria and exchanges glances with a youth. Stéphane had been warned about this attitude, and also received a measure of withdrawal. When I intervened, he continued to look at the other youth. He received a withdrawal measure of 3 h with reflection.

---

[42] See Desrosiers, *supra* note 12, Annex 3, at heading 3.4.6.

[43] See the Conseil permanent de la jeunesse, *Les jeunes en centre jeunesse prennent la parole!*, *supra* note 5, p. 67.

[44] We had the privilege of consulting these files within the framework of a 30 day *in situ* observation conducted in the spring of 2002 in three secure rehabilitation units of the Centres jeunesse de Montréal [Youth Centers of Montreal], Unité d'arrêt d'agir l'Intervalle, Centre de réadaptation Dominique-Savio-Mainbourg; Unité d'encadrement intensif Inouik, Centre de réadaptation Cité-des-Prairies; Unité de garde fermée l'Épisode, Centre de réadaptation Cité-des-Prairies. We were three observers sharing the task. During those 30 days, we shared the daily life of the youths, 8 h a day, distributed over different moments of the day, in order to observe the whole day, from morning to night.

February 8: When inspecting the room for cleanliness, I notice a bag of candy on his table. I therefore advised him that he must assume (1) hour of withdrawal in his room following his breach of the code of conduct. He has already completed 45 min of his retreat. Therefore 15 min left.

I had already advised Stéphane this week that telephone calls are 10 min. He stayed on the phone for over 15 min tonight. As he was exiting the telephone room, I call him on the length of his call and the code of conduct regarding telephone calls. He answered me by saying, "what are you doing there" in an arrogant manner and then said, "Hey Man"; he went to his room and will have a 3 h disciplinary measure for his lack of respect. I told him about his disciplinary measure.

February 11: Supper. Stéphane is hiding behind his hand to speak to a guy from another unit. 3 h of disciplinary measures.

February 18: Stéphane is speaking loudly in the showers … I ask him to be quiet. 2 min later he starts to sing = 1 h of disciplinary measures.

February 20: Stéphane is sent to his room at 5 pm following a grave insult towards Sébastien. He denies everything – reflection to be done. [After meeting with the educator, he ends up admitting to having lied.] (…) Therefore: complete withdrawal for the evening for Stéphane, meeting with Sebastien and apologized (…), will have to give in a problem-solving resolution on this situation, will have to turn off his light at 9:30 tonight for lost sleep.

February 21: Stéphane put the Cheese Whiz in the pantry. He starts to argue when I ask him to put it in the fridge. "Marie told me that it went there". I then asked him to read the instructions on the cap. (…) He continues to argue with me, so I take him out for an hour. When I go meet him, he tells me that all is well. I ask him the reasons why he behaved like that. He responds by: "And for what reasons do you speak to me like that." 3 more hours. He misses the problem-solving activity = 1 1/2 h more; he misses French class = 1 h more.[45] At lunchtime, I inform him that he is missing out on the unit. He said that he has reflected. I hold my stance. He tells me he doesn't want to eat. After lunch, I meet up with him. We go over the situation from this morning #1. I have big doubts about his sincerity. He seems "to conform."[46] I give him his problem-solving for yesterday's situation plus his problem-solving resolution work for today. After the homework period, he still has 2 h [to do].

February 22: Eating candies in his room. Withdrawal from 6:15 to 7:15 pm.

[45] The educator will make the sanction override the hours of class so that the boy will stay in his room rather than go to the "problem solving" and to his French class. So as to not be too delayed when compared to the rest of his group and so as to avoid that a withdrawal becoming the equivalent to a school break, he will nevertheless have to take up the activity and French class in his room. He will have to do the required homework during a period of time that is equivalent to the one that he would have normally spent devoted to those tasks.

[46] "To conform," means that the adolescent will say what he thinks his educator wants to hear, in order to avoid further problems, but is not sincere.

February 23: A situation between Christian and another youth [from another unit] brings Stéphane to intimidate the youth with a very insistent expression, leading to Stéphane finding himself in his room with a problem-solving grid that he does very well. Following his reflection, we meet with the youth [from the other unit]. Stéphane participates very well in the meeting, recognizes his gestures and finds ways to settle the problem (…). Following this meeting for Stéphane, the problem has been settled and the situation of bullying will not reproduce itself. Considering the seriousness of his efforts, I authorize the end of his withdrawal at 9 pm.

February 28: (1) Stéphane decides that he will not help to clean up [during the workshop consisting of packing up screws]. I tell him: "It's your choice but don't expect that I will offer you my help in the next contract". He answers: "You just don't have to help me". (2) When coming back [from the workshop] he leaves his room without authorization. "Where are you going Stéphane?" "I am going to see Marcel." "Marcel is busy, go back to your room." He passes next to me and holds my stare. He is very, very intimidating. I follow him back to his room and tell him to quit that look. He keeps it anyway. I tell him in a loud voice that he has 3 h of disciplinary measures and that it is in his interest to change that look because he will go and do it elsewhere (I have to "threaten" him with going to the Relance,[47] for him to stop). Finally he understands and changes his tune. 20 min later, I give him a written reflection to do and advise him that as long as his reflection is not satisfactory, he will remain in his room, including for school periods that he will have to retake. His eyes stay glued to floor.

March 1: Meeting with Stéphane. Revisiting yesterday's situation. Stéphane recognizes his menacing look all the while telling me that his attitude comes from rancor from past situations. He excuses himself and cries. I share my clear expectations with him. He still has 2 h to go.

March 13: Arrives 15 min late following his weekend. I ask him to empty his pockets, which he categorically refuses to do. If he has nothing to hide, I tell him that he should opt for openness instead of refusing. I am within my rights to make my call to the Relance given his refusal to empty his pockets. Following the search, we find two big screws fused with the help of a large elastic band (homemade weapon). Following this, he is sent to the Relance. [Sent to the Relance at 5:30 pm until the following afternoon at 1:15 pm, for a total of 19 h and 45 min in the withdrawal room.]

March 19: Simon and Stéphane are telling each other that "I'll fuck your mother". 3 h of withdrawal. Unacceptable speech.

March 21: Deals well with his withdrawal during the time [of the workshop], given that he cannot attend for the moment (consequence of having made a weapon).

[47] It is a unit devoted to off-duty withdrawal and is managed by security agents. The withdrawal rooms are concrete, completely empty and without windows. Efficient monitoring of the lock-up of youths is ensured by video cameras.

March 22: Shows his bulldog collar despite the prohibition. 3 h.

March 24: Following the note [from another educator] I check and the radio is still stuck on Stéphane's bed.[48] Will have 3 h when he wakes up. When announcing it to Stéphane, he denies it – said he listened to it this morning – not true since he was sleeping when I arrived = 3 h.

March 27: Stéphane answers Max that he has all the time to complete his task because he doesn't smoke.[49] I spoke to Stéphane on that point and took him out for 1 h because his gesture was unacceptable (speech). Lack of consideration for another.

8.3 Conclusion: Rights Violations and Institutional Culture

The normative universe within rehabilitation centres and the density of disciplinary rules are potential sources of violation of adolescents' rights. These include violations of their right to freedom of movement,[50] since any violation of the code of conduct can lead to a spatial-temporal isolation, whether in the youth's own room or in a specially designated room for this purpose. Their right to know clearly which behaviours are forbidden and a youth's entitlement to protection from arbitrary treatment[51] are also infringed, since the rules are so numerous and oppressive that it is impossible to know which will be sanctioned. Their right to an education and to flexible rules developed to advance their best interests[52] are also undermined, since the blanket application of rigid prescriptions considerably reduces the flexibility required for an individual approach to each youths needs and circumstances.

Nevertheless, the disciplinary processes within the rehabilitation centres are supposed to respect the rights of adolescents and to protect them against the arbitrary. More than 30 years ago, the Batshaw Committee, preoccupied by the abuse of

---

[48] It is prohibited to listen to the radio before going to bed.

[49] When all youths have completed their chores, the educator decrees a cigarette break. Under current circumstances, Stéphane answered Max, who seems to hurry through his task so that he could go smoke, whereas he had no reason to hurry since he did not smoke.

[50] *Canadian Charter of Rights and Freedoms*, S.R.C. (1985), app. II, no. 44, s. 7; *Charter of Human Rights and Freedoms*, S.R.Q., c. C-12, s. 1 and s. 24; see also the *United Nations Rules for the Protection of Juveniles deprived of their Liberty* ('the Havana Rules') 1990, G.A. res. 45/113 (1990) and the *United Nations Guidelines for the Prevention of Juvenile Delinquency* ('Riyadh Guidelines'), G.A. res. 45–112 (1990), s. 21 and 54.

[51] *Canadian Charter of Rights and Freedoms*, S.R.C. (1985), app. II, no. 44, s. 7; *United Nations Standard Minimum Rules For the Treatment of Prisoners* (1975), adopted by the First Congress of the United Nations for the prevention of crime and treatment of delinquents (Geneva, 1955), applicable to minors deprived of freedom through the *UN Standard Minimum Rules on the Administration of Juvenile Justice* ('the Beijing Rules'), G.A. res. 40/33 (1985); *UN Rules for the Protection of Juveniles deprived of their Liberty* ('the Havana Rules') 1990, G.A. res. 45/113 (1990).

[52] *Convention on the Rights of the Child*, G.A. res. 44/25 (1989), ss. 3, 28, 39; *Youth Protection Act*, S.R.Q., c. P-34.1, s. 3 and s. 10. *Civil Code of Québec*, S.Q. 1991, c. 64, s. 33.

power within youth detention centres, recommended that legislation be introduced to regulate the management of discipline in rehabilitation centres.[53] Indeed, the subsequent inclusion of section 10 in the Quebec *Youth Protection Act* responded to this recommendation. It affirms that "[e]very disciplinary measure taken by an institution operating a rehabilitation centre in respect of a child must be taken in the child's interest and in conformity with internal rules that must be approved by the board of directors and posted in a conspicuous place in the facilities of the institution."[54]

The board of directors of the youth centre adopts the internal rules on disciplinary measures. In a typical fashion, these internal rules set out the expected behaviours in terms of the basic values that must be respected: respect of self, of others, of the environment and so on. These values flow from a series of behavioural prescriptions: being discreet about one's private life, being polite, keeping one's room clean, participating to the best of one's abilities and so forth. These prescriptions resemble those found in a great number of families and seem reasonable despite their vagueness, since they refer back to widely accepted social values. A careful examination of the internal rules on disciplinary measures, however, also reveals that under the heading of "respect for others", a youth must respect the code of conduct of the rehabilitation unit.

However, as we have just seen, the code of conduct puts into place a normative universe that is much closer to that of incarceration than family life. The codes of conduct diverge from their initial goals by operationalizing the values of self-respect, respect of others, and of the environment as promoted by the internal rules on disciplinary measures in the youth centre. Ironically, the codes of conduct erode the rights of the child, while multiplying the normative prescriptions that are supposed to protect the rights of the youth with the rehabilitation centres. A review of the operational realities in rehabilitation centres reveals that the discretionary application and meting out of disciplinary punishments, including isolation, creates a reality starkly divergent from the spirit that was supposed to inform the rehabilitation centre's project.

A first critique takes aim at the largesse attributed to administrative discretion and the important leeway in the educators' decisions in managing internal discipline. It seems clear that fear of creating obstacles to the rehabilitation project, the legislator did not want educators and administrators of rehabilitation centres to feel overly constrained by legislative regulations. Indeed, adolescents are harmed

[53] Comité d'étude sur la réadaptation des enfants et adolescents placés en centre d'accueil, Québec, Minister of Social Affairs, 1976 (better known as the Batshaw Committee), Principles 14–16 : "Principle 14. The child has the right to know the regulations that apply at the youth shelter, and a copy must be handed over and explained when admitted to the center. Principle 15. No disciplinary measure must be taken against a child unless it is for an infraction to the institution's regulations. Principle 16. The child has the right to be protected against humiliating, excessive and cruel punishments." [Our translation]

[54] *Youth Protection Act,* S.R.Q., c. P-34.1, s. 10.

by the weight of prohibitions and arbitrary discipline, and the educators' power is experienced as quasi total.[55] The discretion granted by the legislator to the administrative authorities is translated by a quasi-absolute control of the youth's behavior, which multiplies the personnel's possibilities of intervention, while not limiting them. The result: multiple withdrawal measures and disciplinary penalties that do not always appear to be fair to those observing their application. Further modifications are required to constrain the exercise of institutional discretion and set out guidelines for interventions designed to promote rehabilitation.

The analysis of code of conducts reveals that the effect of legal texts depends not only on its formal words and provisions but also the institutional culture and intervention philosophy that exist within rehabilitation centres. The rights, rules and obligations of codes of conduct can be applied in an extremely formalistic and legalist manner, and yet be completely out of sync with their underlying objectives. Consider, for example the right to be informed of forbidden behaviours. For example, in one case, a youth who arrived at a centre was brought to his room, where he was asked to read the code of conduct. Did he have questions? No. He is now considered informed of behaviors that are susceptible to being sanctioned. This manner of proceeding is possibly not in the spirit of the right to education of the child, where rules should be learning occasions and disciplinary measures are considered steps towards the acquisition of self-discipline, but it is nonetheless consistent with the strict letter of the code of conduct law.

Of course, an educator could proceed otherwise and explain the code of conduct over time, in a period of a few days. However, it is unlikely that individual actions of those in charge will ensure respect for the rights of the youth who find themselves in rehabilitation centres. Individual choices are critical important, but they are but one component that operates in conjunction with many other influences in an institution. As wisely noted by one youth, "all of the educators working in youth centres arrive with a spirit of aid. But over time and as part of a greater system, these are very disciplinary rules and they do not have free reign."[56] The nearly crushing power of the institution cannot be obscured when reflecting on the respect of youths' fundamental rights in rehabilitation centres. To enhance protection for youth rights within rehabilitation centres, therefore, beyond law reform, there is a need to transform professional and institutional cultures.

---

[55] This reality is expressed many times in the Conseil permanent de la jeunesse, *Les jeunes en centre jeunesse prennent la parole!*, *supra* note 5. See especially the following comment at page 46: "It is the educators, it is them who decide. If you say anything, whether you are right or not and they tell you: *Go to your room!*, you go to your room. If they find that you move too much or speak too loudly: *Go relax in your room* followed by a reflection period. And if they are not satisfied with what is on the page, they will slide back under the door and will make you work until you admit that you are the problem." [Our translation]

[56] Conseil permanent de la jeunesse, *Les jeunes en centre jeunesse prennent la parole!*, *supra* note 5, p. 47 [Our translation].

Chapter 9
Reconceptualising Social and Economic Rights: The Right to Housing and Intersecting Legal Regimes

Jane Matthews Glenn*

Economic and social rights are increasingly under threat worldwide as a result of government retrenchment in social spending for both pragmatic and philosophical reasons. Government indebtedness increased rapidly during the 1980s and early 1990s, and the response was to cut deeply into social programmes. And further government retrenchment would seem inevitable in the coming decade, as the recession – and the massive stimulus spending to counter it – has pushed governments back into deficit positions. In many countries, the earlier cuts in social programmes were imposed by the international financial institutions (notably the International Monetary Fund and the World Bank) through structural adjustment programmes that became part of every loan package.[1] In some countries, such as Canada, the cuts were voluntary and flowed from a general recognition that the country could not sustain its then high rate of indebtedness without sacrificing its advantageous credit rating on loans from the international banking sector. In Canada, the resulting cuts in spending meant restrictions on unemployment insurance, "clawback" of benefits paid to children and seniors, elimination of national standards for provincial welfare programmes and services, and cuts in the level of social assistance. The cumulative effect of these changes on the social safety net as a whole compounded the effect of cuts to individual strands.[2] Current recession-imposed cuts can only exacerbate this situation.

---

*I am grateful to the Dobson Fund of the Faculty of Law, McGill University, for its financial support while researching this topic, and to the direction and staff of the Netherlands Institute for Advanced Study (NIAS) for their warm hospitality while writing this chapter.

[1] E.g. John Pender, "From 'Structural Adjustment' to 'Comprehensive Development Framework': Conditionality transformed?" (2001) 22 Third World Quarterly 397–411.

[2] Judith Keene, "Claiming the Protection of the Charter: Charter litigation arising from government 'restraint'" (1998) 9 National J. of Constitutional Law 97–116 at 102.

J. Matthews Glenn (✉)
Faculty of Law, McGill University, H3A 1W9 Montreal, QC, Canada
e-mail: jane.glenn@mcgill.ca

R. Provost and C. Sheppard (eds.), *Dialogues on Human Rights and Legal Pluralism*, Ius Gentium: Comparative Perspectives on Law and Justice 17,
DOI 10.1007/978-94-007-4710-4_9,

Philosophically, a neoliberal, or market-based, approach to governance has been promoted by international lending institutions and others since at least the late 1980s,[3] and is now followed in many countries. In Canada, governments took up this approach in the housing field (e.g., facilitating insurance-backed private-sector mortgages rather than providing government mortgages; providing rent subsidies rather than public housing). And the election of conservative governments, at various levels, had led to further and deeper cuts in social spending, with more to be expected in the future.

The effect of this two-pronged approach – imposing social spending cuts in the context of a market-based governance strategy – on the economic and social rights of the most vulnerable is increasingly questioned.[4] But how to protect economic and social rights is difficult to conceptualise, as their legal effect is a matter of debate. The debate focuses mainly on the *recognition* of rights (i.e. their source and content) and their *enforcement* (i.e. justiciability), and the relationship between the two. However, this focus tends to leave out an interim step, that of the *implementation* of rights. Can social and economic rights be reconceptualised in a way that places more emphasis on implementation and thus attenuates perceived problems of justiciability?

9.1 Recognition

Economic and social rights are recognised, either explicitly or implicitly, at both the international and domestic levels. Explicit recognition is found in a variety of international instruments ranging from hard-law treaties through to soft-law documents. Treaty examples of recognition of the right to housing include, at the universal level, the *International Covenant on Economic, Social and Cultural Rights* (ICESCR)[5] and, at the regional level, the *European Social Charter*.[6] The ICESCR recognises the right to housing in the following terms:

> Art. 11 (1) The States Parties to the present Covenant recognize the right of everyone to an adequate standard of living for himself and his family, including adequate food, clothing

[3] E.g. Gareth Jones & Peter M. Ward, "The World Bank's 'New' Urban Management Programme: Paradigm shift or policy continuity?" (1994) 18:3 Habitat International 33–51.

[4] E.g. Mary Dowell-Jones, *Contextualising the International Covenant on Economic, Social and Cultural Rights: Assessing the economic deficit* (Leiden: Nijhoff, 2004); Gail Fawcett & Katherine Scott, *A Lost Decade: Urban poverty in Canada, 1990–2000* (Ottawa: Canadian Council on Social Development, 2007); National Council on Welfare, *Welfare Incomes 2009* (Ottawa: National Council of Welfare, 2010).

[5] *International Covenant on Economic, Social and Cultural Rights* (1966), United Nations, Treaty Series, vol. 993, p. 3, art. 11(1). See also e.g. *Convention on the Elimination of All Forms of Discrimination against Women* (1979), United Nations, Treaty Series, vol. 1249, p. 13, art, 14(2)(h); and *Convention on the Rights of the Child* (1989), United Nations, Treaty Series, vol. 1577, p. 3, art. 27(3).

[6] *European Social Charter (revised)* (1996), Council of Europe, European Treaty Series, No. 163, Part I (31) & Part II, art. 31 (although right to housing not included amongst core rights binding on all Parties: see Part III, art. A(1)(b)). See also e.g. *Protocol to the African Charter on Human and Peoples' Rights on the Rights of Women* (2003), African Union, art. 16.

and *housing*, and to the continuous improvement of living conditions. The States Parties will take appropriate steps to ensure the realization of this right, recognizing to this effect the essential importance of international co-operation based on free consent.

Soft-law documents are legion, and housing examples chosen at random from three decades are the United Nations General Assembly resolution on the *Realization of the right to adequate housing* (1987), the *Istanbul Declaration on Human Settlements* (1996) and the U.N. Commission on Human Rights resolution on *Adequate housing as a component of the right to an adequate standard of living* (2004).[7]

Implicit recognition occurs through a process by which economic and social rights are "read into" international instruments dealing with civil and political rights.[8] This is notably the case with the *European Convention on Human Rights*, where, for example, the right to adequate housing has been read into the right to protection against inhuman and degrading treatment and the right to respect for private and family life.[9] It is also the case with the *African Charter on Human and People's Rights*, where a right to housing or shelter has been read into the combined effects of the rights to property, health and protection of the family.[10]

Economic and social rights, including the right to housing, are also recognised explicitly and implicitly at the domestic level. This recognition is strongest when it is found in constitutional documents, as in the 1996 South African constitution,[11] but it might also be found in ordinary legislation although this is more vulnerable to changing political agendas. A recent legislative example is France's *Loi instituant le droit au logement opposable*, which recognises a right to "decent and independent" housing guaranteed by the State and enforceable by mediation and court action.[12]

---

[7] *Realization of the right to adequate housing*, U.N. General Assembly Res. A/RES/42/146 of 7 December 1987; *Istanbul Declaration on Human Settlements*, U.N. General Assembly Res. 51/177 of 16 December 1996 & 53/242 of 28 July 1999; and *Adequate housing as a component of the right to an adequate standard of living,* U.N. Commission on Human Rights Res. 2004/21.

[8] William A. Schabas, "Freedom from Want: How can we make indivisibility more than a mere slogan?" (2000) 11 National J. of Constitutional Law 187–209 at 205.

[9] Adopted as *Convention for the Protection of Human Rights and Fundamental Freedoms*, Council of Europe, European Treaty Series No. 5, arts. 4 & 8. See e.g. *Connors v. United Kingdom* (2004) 40 European Human Rights Report 9 (Eur. Ct. H.R.); *Doherty et al. v. Birmingham City Council* [2009] A.C. 367 (H.L.).

[10] (1981) Organisation of African Unity [now African Union], OAU Doc. CAB/LEG/67/3 rev. 5, 21 I.L.M. 58 (1982), arts. 14, 16 & 18(1). See e.g. *Social and Economic Rights Action Center (SERAC) v. Nigeria*, African Commission on Human and Peoples' Rights, Communication 155/96, 1996.

[11] *Constitution of the Republic of South Africa*, Act No. 108 of 1996, art. 26. For other examples, see Christopher Golay & Melik Özden, *The Right to Housing: A fundamental human right affirmed by the United Nations and recognized in regional treaties and numerous national constitutions* (Human Rights Programme of the Europe-Third World Centre (CETIM)) [http://www.cetim.ch/en/documents/bro7-log-A4-an.pdf].

[12] Loi no. 2007–290 du 5 mars 2007, Journal Officiel de la République française du 6 mars 2007, adding a new art. L. 300–1 to the *Code de la construction et de l'habitation*; other examples include England and Scotland. See e.g. Marie Loison-Leruste & Deborah Quilgars, "Increasing Access to Housing: Implementing the right to housing in England and France" (2009) 3 European J. of Homelessness 75–100; Eric Tars, "Great Scot! The Scottish plan to end homelessness and the lessons for the housing rights movements in the United States" (2009) XVI Georgetown J. on Poverty Law & Policy 187–216.

And Canada's proposed *Secure, Adequate, Accessible and Affordable Housing Act* will, if adopted, require the Minister responsible for the Canada Mortgage and Housing Corporation to establish a national housing strategy designed to "respect, protect, promote and fulfil the right to adequate housing as guaranteed under international human rights treaties ratified by Canada"; however, this Private Member's Bill has been before the federal Parliament in one form or another since 2001, and its adoption under the present government is unlikely.[13] Nevertheless, the various provincial human rights codes offer Canadians a limited protection of the right to housing through their focus on non-discrimination.[14]

"Reading in" also occurs at the national level, either constitutionally as in India where a right to adequate housing has been read into the constitutional guarantees of the right to life and mobility rights, or legislatively as in the United Kingdom where the *Human Rights Act* gives domestic effect to the *European Convention*.[15] Reading economic and social rights into the *Canadian Charter of Rights and Freedoms*, notably sections 7 and 15, is a recognised possibility.[16]

These legal regimes – international and domestic – can and often do intersect in two different ways. A first is in regard to content, as international rights are often incorporated into domestic legislation either by reference to the international instrument (as in the Argentine constitution which provides that some nine international agreements "are at the same level as the Constitution … and should be considered as complementary to the rights recognised by the Constitution") or in identical or substantially similar terms to it (as in the UK *Human Rights Act* which reproduces the substantive articles of the *European Convention of Human Rights* in an annex).[17] A second is in regard to enforcement, as domestic courts often have regard to international instruments either to enforce them directly in monist jurisdictions where this is permitted or to use them as aids in interpreting and applying domestic rules in dualist jurisdictions such as Canada where direct enforcement is not permitted.[18]

---

[13] Presently House of Commons Bill C-400, 1st Sess., 41st Parl., s. 3(1).

[14] E.g. *Human Rights Code*, R.S.O. 1990, c. H.19, s. 2 & 4; *Charter of Human Rights and Freedoms*, R.S.Q. c. C-12, Part I, Chap. I.1.

[15] E.g. S. Muralidhar, "India: The expectations and challenges of judicial enforcement of social rights", 102–124 in Malcolm Langford, ed., *Social Rights Jurisprudence: Emerging trends in international and comparative law* (Cambridge: Cambridge University Press, 2008); *Human Rights Act 1998*, c. 42 (U.K.); and e.g. *Doherty*, supra note 9.

[16] E.g. Martha Jackman & Bruce Porter, "Canada: Socio-economic rights under the Canadian Charter", 209–229 in Langford, supra note 15; Jane Matthews Glenn, "Enforceability of Economic and Social Rights in the Wake of *Gosselin*: Room for cautious optimism" (2004) 83 Can. Bar Rev. 929–957; and A. Wayne MacKay & Margaret Holgate, "Fairness in the Allocation of Housing: Legal and economic perspectives" (1983) 7 Dalhousie Law J. 383–446.

[17] Golay & Özden, supra note 11 at 18; *Human Rights Act*, supra note 15, Schedule 1.

[18] René Provost, "Judging in Splendid Isolation" (2008) 56 American J. of Comparative Law 125–172.

9.2 Enforcement

The enforceability of economic and social rights is hotly contested and is intertwined with the issue of recognition. Rights are often regarded in black and white terms, as being either fully justiciable or simply aspirational. Because economic and social rights are justiciable with difficulty at best, they are often placed in the aspirational category and thus not recognised as "rights".

The justiciability of economic and social rights, such as the right to adequate housing, is questioned on the grounds that they are too vague to have clear legal content, too costly to implement and thus too political for judicial decision, and too positive to be amenable to court supervision. These are the reasons why economic and social rights are recognised e.g. "to the extent provided by law" in Quebec's *Charter of Human Rights and Freedoms.*[19] And these are the reasons why both the ICESCR and the *European Social Charter* were, for so long, monitored through State reporting procedures rather than complaints procedures like their sister treaties, the *International Covenant on Civil and Political Rights* and the *European Convention on Human Rights.*[20]

The U.N. Committee on Economic, Social and Cultural Rights (CESCR), the monitoring body of the ICESCR, has responded to the enforcement critique in a number of ways. One response has been to modify the enforcement mechanisms so that judiciarisation can now be said to be supplementing dialogue. One change was to sharpen the reporting system itself to make it more adversarial in nature. It did this by encouraging the submission of "shadow reports" from national non-governmental organisations[21] and by issuing rather pointed public "Concluding Observations" on the individual national reports. Canada has not been treated gently by the Committee, and inexistent or inadequate housing is one of its clear concerns: in its most recent assessment of Canada's reports, for example, the Committee "reiterates" its recommendations made in earlier assessments that federal, provincial and territorial governments "address homelessness and inadequate housing as a national emergency by reinstating or increasing, where necessary, social housing programmes for those in need, improving and properly enforcing anti-discrimination legislation in the field

---

[19] Quebec *Charter*, supra note 14, Part I, Chap. IV.

[20] Complaints procedures were adopted for the *European Social Charter* in 1995 (*Additional Protocol to the European Social Charter Providing for a System of Collective Complaints*, European Treaty Series No. 158; see now revised *Charter*, supra note 6, Part IV, art. D) and the ICESCR in 2008 (*Optional Protocol to the International Covenant on Economic, Social and Cultural Rights*, U.N. General Assembly Res. A/RES/63/117 of 10 December 2008).

[21] Committee of Economic, Social and Cultural Rights (CESCR), *Substantive Issues Arising in the Implementation of the International Covenant on Economic, Social and Cultural Rights: NGO participation in the activities of the Committee on Economic, Social and Cultural Rights: Note by the secretariat*, ECOSOC Doc. E/C.12/2000/6. On the role of Canadian housing NGOs in this development, see Bruce Porter, "Claiming Adjudicative Space: Social rights, equality and citizenship" in Margot Young, Susan B. Boyd, Gwen Brodsky & Shelagh Day, *Poverty: Rights, social citizenship, and legal activism* (Vancouver: UBC Press, 2007) 77–95 at 77–78.

of housing, increasing shelter allowances and social assistance rates to realistic levels, and providing adequate support services for persons with disabilities".[22] Another change was to supplement the reporting system with a complaints procedure. This was realised in 2008 with the adoption of an *Optional Protocol*[23] providing for Committee jurisdiction to receive and consider individual and inter-State complaints ("communications"). A complaints procedure sends a clearer signal than a reporting system that economic and social rights are "rights" and not simply aspirations.

A second response has been to counter the objection of vagueness by issuing a number of documents clarifying the content of rights. In this vein, the Committee has issued General Comments on various rights guaranteed in the ICESCR (e.g., *The right to adequate housing*, General Comment No. 4, 1991); it has had Special Rapporteurs named to study particular rights, particularly the right to adequate housing;[24] and it has held "days of general discussion" on individual rights.

A third response has been to address justiciability arguments based on cost and positive nature by clarifying the nature of State obligations under the Covenant. In its General Comment No. 3 (*The nature of States parties' obligations*, 1991), the Committee defined them as comprising obligations to take steps towards realising the rights (albeit progressively), to avoid any unjustifiable backsliding (i.e. "deliberately retrogressive measures") in their realisation, and to assume a minimum core obligation in regard to each right. The Committee has also endorsed a "typology" of State obligations which disaggregates them into (1) the obligation to *respect* (i.e. to refrain from interfering with the rights of individuals), (2) the obligation to *protect* (i.e. to protect individuals from interference with their rights by others), and (3) the obligation to *fulfil* (i.e. to provide the object of the right, such as adequate housing).[25] This well-known typology goes some way to responding to objections of justiciability: an obligation to respect is essentially negative in nature and does not require the use of State resources; an obligation to protect might require State action (such as adopting legislation) but does not place undue strain on State resources; it is only the obligation to fulfil that raises the two objections – costliness and positive nature – most acutely.

[22] CESCR, "Consideration of Reports Submitted by States Parties under Articles 16 and 17 of the Covenant: Concluding observations of the Committee on Economic, Social and Cultural Rights: Canada", ECOSOC Doc. E/C.12/CAN/CO/4 & 5 (on Canada's 4th and 5th reports, which were submitted almost simultaneously)

[23] *Optional Protocol*, supra note 20.

[24] Special Rapporteurs on "adequate housing as a component of the right to an adequate standard of living" have included Rajindar Sachar (1991–1994) (final report: E/CN.4/Sub.2/1995/12), Miloon Kothari (2000–2008) (final report: A/HRC/4/18), and Raquel Rolnik (2008–). Kothari also reported on particular countries, including Canada in 2007 (Preliminary note: A/HRC/7/16/Add.4; Mission report: A/HRC/10/7/Add.3).

[25] E.g. Ida Elisabeth Koch, "Dichotomies, Trichotomies or Waves of Duties?" (2005) 5 Human Rights Law Rev. 81–103.

The Committee's typology disaggregates State obligations as a way of responding to the enforceability critique of economic and social rights. This suggests that it might be possible to conceive of the rights themselves in a disaggregated way – as consisting of a number of discrete elements, each of which is recognised and enforced in its own way – rather than thinking of it solely in an aggregated manner as a composite whole (i.e. the "right to adequate housing") to be recognised and enforced as such. The right to adequate housing, for example, can be thought of as consisting of such component rights as a right to a mortgage on affordable terms, a right to salubrious rental accommodation at a fair rent, a right to equal consideration for access to social housing or, at the very least, a right to sleep somewhere if one is homeless. To disaggregate rights in this way highlights implementation rather than enforcement, and brings to the fore a number of intersecting domestic legal regimes.

9.3 Implementation

Another way of phrasing the Committee's typology is in terms of State roles rather than State obligations. In this way, the obligations to respect, protect and fulfil suggest that the State can play a negative role as *perpetrator* of a violation of a right, and positive roles as *enabler* and as *provider* of the subject of a right, such as the right to adequate housing. Focusing on the roles a State plays emphasizes the implementation of rights, and provides a framework through which to analyse rights in a disaggregated way. This is best tested by looking at the possibilities available under one legal system, and Canada's has been chosen for obvious reasons.

9.3.1 The State as Perpetrator

The State as perpetrator of a violation is not as important in Canada as it is in some developing countries, where destruction of squatter settlements on government land, clearing of pavement dwellers and so on occur regularly. An equivalent Canadian example might be the adoption and enforcement of municipal bylaws prohibiting the homeless from sleeping in public spaces. In *Victoria (City) v. Adams,* enforcement of such a bylaw was challenged on constitutional grounds, whereupon the city amended the bylaw to allow sleeping but prohibit "tak[ing] up a temporary abode overnight;" this prohibition was understood to prevent the homeless from erecting temporary overhead shelter, such as tents, tarpaulins attached to trees, boxes and so forth. The British Columbia Court of Appeal held that this prohibition constituted a violation of homeless people's rights to life, liberty and security of the person under section 7 of the *Charter* but was careful to circumscribe this holding to the situation where "homeless people are not prohibited from sleeping in public parks, and the number of homeless people exceeds the number of available shelter beds". The first caveat reflects the facts in *Adams* but should not be taken as an endorsement of bylaws that prohibit sleeping in parks where the homeless have no other option: if being forced to sleep under the stars constitutes a violation of their *Charter* rights, surely not being allowed to sleep at all constitutes a more serious violation.[26]

A second possible example might be government civil liability for actions adversely affecting the adequacy of housing. In *Kamloops v. Nielsen,* a well-known illustration, the Supreme Court of Canada held a municipality responsible in negligence for damages resulting from its failure to enforce its building construction bylaw: the relevant legislation imposed a private law duty of care on the municipality in favour of the homeowner, and there were no overriding policy reasons not to enforce this duty.[27] On the other hand, several B.C. courts have declined to hold public authorities responsible for damage caused by using a construction method that trapped moisture within the building envelope (i.e. "leaky condo" cases). In *Kimpton v. Canada (Attorney General),* the British Columbia Court of Appeal denied the responsibility of either the federal or the provincial government, even though the construction method was contained in the *National Building Code* published by the National Research Council and incorporated by reference in the *British Columbia Building Code* enacted by regulation adopted under the *Local Government Act* (making it mandatory). The Court held that the relationship between the National Research Council and the condo owners was not sufficiently proximate to give rise to a private law duty of care, and that the adoption of the *British Columbia Building Code* was an act of law-making and thus immune from the application of tort law.[28] However, there are now signs in other areas that the courts might be more open to the possibility of sanctioning what might be termed "tortious law-making", at least at the regulatory level.[29]

What is interesting about the government wrongs cases, for present purposes, is the extent to which the analysis deals with issues similar to those raised about the justiciability of economic and social rights. The common law's historical position was to hold the Crown immune from civil liability actions (i.e. to deny the justiciability of such actions); however, in the 1950s, Canada, like other common law jurisdictions, recognised the unfairness of this historical position and adopted legislation subjecting governments and government agencies to the same rules, generally

[26] *Victoria (City) v Adams* (2009) 313 D.L.R. (4th) 29 (B.C.C.A.); see also *Johnston v. Victoria (City)* 2010 BCSC 1707 (*Adams* protects only nighttime shelters as prohibiting daytime shelters constitutes reasonable limit under s. 1 of *Charter*; burden of proving inadequacy of number of shelter beds rests on homeless). See also *R. v. Tanton* 2006 BCPC 0226 (Provl Ct) (municipal seizure of homeless person's shopping cart, his "home", violates *Charter* rights to protection against abuse of process (s. 7) and unreasonable seizure (s. 8)).

[27] *Kamloops v. Nielsen* [1984] 2 S.C.R. 2.

[28] *Kimpton v. Canada (Attorney General)* (2004) 236 D.L.R. (4th) 324 (B.C.C.A.); see also *McMillan v. Canada Mortgage and Housing Corporation* [2009] 2 W.W.R. 405 (B.C.C.A.).

[29] E.g. *Sauer v Canada (Attorney General)* (negligent regulation of animal feed, causing outbreak of "mad cow" disease): motion to strike pleadings (2007) 225 O.A.C. 143 (C.A.), leave to appeal refused [2007] S.C.C.A. No. 454; certification of class action 2008 CanLII 43774 (Ont. S.C.), leave to appeal refused (2009) 246 O.A.C. 256 (Ont. Div. Ct.)

speaking, of tortious liability as private persons.[30] But a major concern with enforcement has been to balance the State's private law duty of care, owed to private individuals, against its public law responsibility to govern effectively, owed to the general public. In the common law provinces, the balance is struck in the way courts apply a two-stage test, applicable in negligence actions generally, to determine whether a duty of care exists.[31] The first stage looks at factors arising from the relationship between the parties to see if they show the requisite foreseeability and proximity to give rise to a prima facie duty of care. A key proximity requirement in actions against the government is to distinguish between duties owed to the public as a whole and those owed to private individuals. Private duties must be grounded in the legislative intention of the governing statute, although this intention need not be express. This is explained succinctly in *Williams v. Canada (Attorney General) et al.,* one of several class actions arising out of the 2003 SARS (severe acute respiratory syndrome) outbreak in Toronto:

> … although the starting point in a case like this must be the statute that imposes duties, or confers powers, on the Crown, this issue of proximity is not dependent on finding a specific legislative intention to impose a private law duty of care owed to the plaintiffs. If, on the construction of the statute, such an intention appears, that will be the end of the inquiry but proximity will not be excluded by the fact that the statute is silent on the question. Similarly, a legislative intention to create duties owed to the public will not necessarily preclude a finding of proximity unless … it appears that only such duties were intended to be imposed. Even where legislation imposes duties that are owed only to the public – or confers powers exercisable only in the public interest – a relationship of proximity may arise from the manner in which the duties or powers are exercised …[32]

The second stage looks at factors outside this relationship to see whether there are any residual policy considerations that negate the imposition of a duty of care. An important policy consideration in actions against a public authority is the general principle of maintaining separation between the activities of the legislature and the judiciary, coupled with the inherent difficulties of having judges decide questions involving the allocation of scarce resources. This has led the courts to distinguish between "policy" decisions, immune to judicial scrutiny, and "operational" decisions, subject to government liability. However, the boundary between the two categories has shifted back and forth over time, and courts now appear to move consideration of it from the less justiciable policy-oriented second stage to the more justiciable fact-oriented first stage, and to use it to reinforce decisions about proximity.[33] The government wrongs cases are interesting models for two reasons. One is the way in which the two-pronged test allows the courts to adjudicate rights claims

---

[30] E.g. *Crown Liability and Proceedings Act*, R.S.C. 1985, c C-50 (adopted as S.C. 1952–53, c. 30). Similar legislation has been adopted by the provinces.

[31] Test set out by House of Lords in *Anns v. Merton London Borough Council* [1978] A.C. 728 and refined by Supreme Court of Canada in *Cooper v Hobart* [2001] 3 S.C.R. 537 and *Edwards v Law Society of Upper Canada* [2001] 3 S.C.R. 562.

[32] *Williams v. Canada (Attorney General) et al.* (2005) 257 D.L.R. (4th) 704 at para. 72.

[33] See e.g. Jane Matthews Glenn, "'Government Wrongs': Civil liability for GMO regulation in Canada" (2008) 18 J. of Environmental Law and Practice 169–193.

against the government without overstepping appropriate separation of powers boundaries. The other is fact that the courts' jurisdiction to order the government to pay damages is not questioned even though the claims are often brought as class actions and the amount of damages accordingly high.

These several illustrations of the State in its role as perpetrator involve different legal regimes. The homeless example is based mainly in public law, notably constitutional and human rights law but also some municipal law; the leaky condos example is based mainly in private law, notably torts law, although statutory and procedural laws also play a role.

9.3.2 The State as Enabler

The State as enabler of the provision of adequate housing by the private sector is the most extensive of the three roles that the State plays in the housing field in Canada, and this will undoubtedly continue to be the case. A rough-and-ready breakdown indicates that about 70 % of Canadian housing stock is owner-occupied and 30 % non-owner-occupied (rental, cooperatives and the like), and the private sector provides almost all of both types. The "for-profit" private sector provides virtually all of the owner-occupied housing and about five-sixths of the non-owner-occupied, with the "not-for-profit" private sector (also called the third sector) providing most of the remaining one-sixth (social housing) as well as shelter space for the homeless.[34] The amount of public sector (provincial and municipal) housing stock is thus low, and falling further as governments sell off existing stock for fiscal and philosophical reasons.

A rights-based analysis focuses on the ways in which the State encourages, enables or requires the private sector to provide adequate housing to the lower-income sectors of the population. A main policy objective is to have the for-profit sector provide adequate housing as far down the income ladder as possible, and mortgage financing, residential tenancies and municipal land use policies are well-known examples of how this is done in Canada. Affordable mortgage financing is an important component of affordable home ownership and the federal government plays a key role in this regard, not just because of its regulatory jurisdiction over the banking sector[35] but also as an exercise of its spending power. The Canada [formerly Central] Mortgage and Housing Corporation (CMHC), set up in 1945, initially granted mortgages directly to borrowers. However, it gradually withdrew from direct lending after the chartered banks were authorised to enter the mortgage field in 1954, and now

[34] Canada Mortgage and Housing Corporation, "2010 Housing Observer" [http://www.cmhc-schl.gc.ca/en/corp/about/cahoob/cahoob_001.cfm]; Federation of Canadian Municipalities, *Quality of Life in Canadian Communities: Trends and issues in affordable housing and homelessness*, Theme Report #4 (2008) [http://www.fcm.ca/CMFiles/qol20081VVM-3272008-3162.pdf]

[35] *Constitution Act, 1867*, 30 & 31 Victoria (U.K.), c. 3, s. 91 (15), (16) and (18)–(21)

plays a more indirect role of providing government-backed mortgage insurance for "non-conventional" mortgages (that is, mortgages with lower down payments and longer amortisation periods than banks are otherwise authorised to grant). This makes home ownership more affordable for low income buyers, as lower down payments mean they need to save less before purchasing and longer amortisation periods reduce their monthly payments – although care must be taken to find the right balance, as the recent sub-prime mortgage crisis illustrates. Mortgage law involves several different public and private legal regimes, ranging from administrative law (protecting the borrower's right to a fair assessment of eligibility for a mortgage at the beginning of the process) through to equity law (recognising a right to be credited with a fair market price in the event of foreclosure and sale at the end).[36]

Residential tenancy legislation is important because lower income households rely principally on rental accommodation to house themselves. Every province now has residential tenancy legislation protecting tenants against such things as inadequate maintenance, unjustifiable increases in rent and unjustifiable terminations of tenancy[37] – although care must be taken to find the right balance here as well, as private sector landlords cannot be expected to provide rental housing without a reasonable possibility of profit.[38] Public sector landlords can be exempted from these legislative provisions, but only if this meets the constitutional test of being "reasonable and demonstrably justifiable in a free and democratic society". In *Sparks v. Dartmouth/Halifax County Regional Housing Association*, for example, the Nova Scotia Court of Appeal held that a provision denying security of tenure to public housing tenants contravened section 15 of the *Charter* and was not saved by section 1 as it impaired the tenants' rights "to such an extreme extent that the sections cannot be said to be a minimal or reasonable impairment so as to achieve the objectives of making sure that public housing is available for only those persons who qualify".[39] Tenants' rights under residential tenancy legislation are based in both private law (notably contracts and property) and public law (statutory, administrative and constitutional) and are enforceable before specialised administrative tribunals as well as courts of general jurisdiction.[40]

---

[36] See generally Virginie Traclet, "Structure of the Canadian Housing Market and Finance System", background paper for Committee on the Global Financial System, *Housing Finance in the Global Financial Market*, CGFS Paper No. 26 (Bank for International Settlements, 2006) [http://www.bis.org/publ/wgpapers/cgfs26traclet.pdf]; see also *Royal Bank of Canada v. Marjen Investments Limited* (1998) 155 D.L.R. (4th) 538 (N.S.C.A.) (right to fair sale price).

[37] E.g. *Residential Tenancy Act*, S.B.C. 2002, c. 78; *Residential Tenancies Act*, S.O. 2006, c. 17; *Civil Code of Quebec*, R.S.Q., c. C-1991, s. 1892 f. and *Act respecting the Régie du logement*, R.S.Q., c. R-8.1

[38] E.g. Federation of Canadian Municipalities, Theme Report #4, supra note 34 at ii ("construction of new rental housing lagged far behind historical levels. While one-third of all households rent, fewer than 9 % of all housing units completed in Canada's largest cities between 2001 and 2006 were rental suites.")

[39] *Sparks v. Dartmouth/Halifax County Regional Housing Authority* (1993) 119 N.S.R. (2d) 91 (N.S.C.A.) at para. 36.

[40] *Reference re Amendments to the* Residential Tenancies Act *(N.S.)* [1996] 1 S.C.R. 186.

Finally, municipal land use policies can play an important role in ensuring the availability of affordable housing. Some policies may be broad brush, such as Ontario's identification of the "adequate provision of a full range of housing" as being a "matter of provincial interest": this means that all planning authorities (including municipal councils, the Ontario Municipal Board and the Minister of Municipal Affairs and Housing) must "have regard to" such matters in carrying out their responsibilities under the *Planning Act*; and if the matter has also been the subject of a Cabinet-approved policy statement, all decisions of planning authorities must "be consistent with" the policy statement.[41] The policy statement currently in force requires planning authorities to "provide for an appropriate range of housing types and densities to meet projected requirements" by, inter alia, "establishing and implementing minimum targets for the provision of housing which is *affordable* to *low and moderate income households*".[42] Whether or not a planning authority, including the Ontario Municipal Board, has respected these obligations can be challenged before the courts.[43] Other land use policies may be fine brush, and examples include encouraging the private sector to provide affordable housing through bonus and other inclusionary zoning tools[44] and allowing homeowners to create secondary suites in their dwelling or on their property.[45] Members of the public have the right to participate in public hearings on adoption of land use plans and their implementing by-laws, to challenge the validity of both plan and by-laws before the courts, and to enforce the by-laws themselves if need be even in the absence of specific statutory authorisation to do so.[46] These rights are based mainly in public law (municipal, administrative and sometimes constitutional).

However, there comes a point where the for-profit private sector cannot or does not meet the housing needs of the population, and this is the case for people who are

---

[41] *Planning Act*, R.S.O. 1990, c. P.13, s. 2 & 3.

[42] Ontario, Ministry of Municipal Affairs and Housing, *Provincial Policy Statement* (Toronto: Queen's Printer for Ontario, 2005) 9 [emphasis in original].

[43] E.g. *Toronto (City) v. R&G Realty Management Inc.*, 2009 CanLII 42397 (Ont. Sup. Ct.) (holding that OMB erred in law by applying "have regard to" and not stronger "be consistent with" legal test to policy statement and by inadequately considering condominium conversion provisions of City's Official Plan). See also, re condominium conversion, *Toronto (City) v. Goldlist Properties Inc.* (2003) 232 D.L.R. (4th) 298 (Ont. C.A.).

[44] E.g. *Planning Act* (Ont.), supra note 41, s. 37 (authorising height and density bonusing in return for provision of e.g. social housing). See also Nellie Chang, "Inclusionary Zoning for the Provision of Affordable Housing: A comparative analysis of Vancouver and San Francisco", Proceedings of Symposium on Affordable and Sustainable Housing, University of British Columbia, 2009 [http://www.scarp.ubc.ca/content/symposium-proceedings].

[45] British Columbia, Ministry of Community, Aboriginal and Women's Services, *Secondary Suites: A guide for local government* (2005); see also *Planning Act* (Ont.), s. 16 (3) ("secondary units") and s. 39.1 ("garden suites"). See also *Tenants' Rights Action Coalition et al. v. Corporation of Delta et al.* (1997) 151 D.L.R. (4th) 729 (B.C.C.A.) (by-law limiting secondary suites to "in-law suites" discriminatory under municipal law).

[46] *Association des Propriétaires des Jardins Taché Inc. et al. v. Entreprises Dasken Inc. et al.* [1974] S.C.R. 2.

inadequately housed (i.e. in accommodation that is inadequate for reasons of either cost or condition), at risk of homelessness (i.e. in accommodation that is inadequate for reasons of both cost and condition), and homeless (i.e. in shelters or on the street). In this event, the State can provide fiscal incentives such as grants, subsidies and tax advantages to encourage the private sector (both for-profit and not-for-profit) to participate in the lowest income segments of the housing market. This is closely related to the State's role as provider of affordable housing and is discussed in the next section.

9.3.3 The State as Provider

The State as provider of adequate housing is based principally on the spending power and includes direct provision of public housing, on the one hand, and indirect provision through housing-related fiscal incentives such as grants, subsidies and tax advantages, on the other.[47] In Canada, the role of the State has evolved from direct to indirect provision and devolved from federal to provincial, even municipal, responsibility.[48] The change from direct to indirect provision dates mainly from the 1970s, with the development of CMHC programmes to provide financial assistance to the non-profit housing sector, including cooperatives: public housing became social housing. Devolution of responsibility from the federal to provincial governments dates from the 1990s, when the federal and provincial governments entered into "Social Housing Agreements" transferring administrative and financial responsibility for social housing programmes from CMHC to the provinces, in return for which CMHC agreed to provide the provinces with annual funding (capped at the mid-1990 level) for the duration of existing agreements (i.e. until about 2035). In other words, federal financial obligations were capped and are now diminishing, whereas provincial obligations are open-ended as they must make up any shortfalls in subsidies payable to social housing providers under existing operating agreements.[49] Devolution of responsibility from the provinces to municipalities dates from the late 1990s and 2000s, notably in Ontario following the election of a Conservative government with a strong neoliberal agenda (the "common sense revolution"). The province's *Social Housing Reform Act* devolved responsibility for the financing and management of social housing onto designated municipalities – or

[47] Tax advantages are particularly important for the charitable organisations that provide the bulk of shelter accommodation for the homeless. See generally e.g. David G. Duff, "Tax Treatment of Charitable Contributions in Canada: Theory, practice, and reform" (2004) 42 Osgoode Hall Law J. 47–98.

[48] See Jeanne M. Wolfe, "Canadian Housing Policy in the Nineties" (1998) 13 Housing Studies 121–133; see also Yvon Chouinard & Robert Gagnon, *Inventaire des programmes provinciaux et territoriaux en habitation au Canada* (Québec: Société de habitation du Québec, 2006).

[49] See e.g. Co-operative Housing Federation of Canada, "Critique of the Federal/Provincial Social Housing Agreement" (1997) [http://www.chfcanada.coop/eng/pages2007/docs_002.asp].

"service managers", in the language of the Act – and this devolution will continue under the newly adopted *Housing Services Act*.[50] In other words, and somewhat perversely, the State's role as provider has devolved from the level of government with the largest purse to those with the smallest.[51]

Broadly put, social housing subsidies are provided to pay down non-profit housing providers' expenses (e.g., operating cost subsidies) and to top up occupants' rent (e.g., "rent-geared-to-income" assistance). The operator's subsidy rights are set out in its operating agreement with the State, and are enforceable principally through private law (contract law). The occupants' rights to financial assistance are set out in the relevant legislation. On occasion, these rights are substantive in the sense that occupants enforcing their rights have successfully attacked the legislative provisions themselves. For example, the "spouse in the house" rule, which presumes that an occupant living with someone of the opposite sex is in a spousal arrangement and entitled to less State support as a result, has been held to affect women and particularly single mothers disproportionately and declared invalid under section 15 of the *Charter*. The decision of the Ontario Court of Appeal in *Falkiner v. Ontario (Minister of Community and Social Services)* to this effect is particularly noteworthy, as it held that "receipt of social assistance" is an analogous ground under section 15.[52] Similarly, substantive rules dealing with welfare fraud, and the disproportionate effect their strict application can have on access to housing and other basic necessities, have been accepted as justiciable by the courts. For example, although a *Charter* challenge to Ontario's lifetime ban on further social assistance (the "zero tolerance" rule) was settled out of court after the newly elected government repealed the ban, the Ontario Divisional Court awarded the applicants their

---

[50] *Social Housing Reform Act*, S.O. 2000, c. 27; *Housing Services Act*, S.O. 2011, c. 6, Schedule 1. See also e.g. Jason Hackworth & Abigail Moriah, "Neoliberalism, Contingency and Urban Policy: The case of social housing in Ontario" (2006) 30 International J. of Urban and Regional Research 510–527.

[51] *Constitution Act, 1867*, supra note 35, ss. 91(3) (empowering federal government to raise money "by any Mode or System of Taxation") & 92(2) (limiting provinces to "Direct Taxation" only); as creatures of the province, municipalities are similarly limited to direct taxation, and rely mainly on property taxes. See e.g. Federation of Canadian Municipalities, *Quality of Life in Canadian Communities: Mending Canada's frayed social safety net: The role of municipal governments*, Theme Report #6 (2010) [http://www.fcm.ca//CMFiles/QofL6En_Embargp1KGE-3242010-6436.pdf] at 37 (50 % of Canadian taxes paid to federal government, 42 % to provincial governments and mere 8 % to municipalities; moreover, property taxes regressive as poorest 20 % pay 10 % of income in property taxes and wealthiest 20 % pay 2 %).

[52] *Falkiner v. Ontario (Minister of Community and Social Services)* (2002) 212 D.L.R. (4th) 633 (Ont. C.A.) (disagreeing with oft-cited *Masse v. Ontario (Ministry of Community and Social Services)* (1996) 134 D.L.R. (4th) 20 (Ont Div. Ct.), leave to appeal refused without reasons: [1996] O.J. No. 1526 (Ont. C.A.) [1996] S.C.C.A. No. 373 (S.C.C.)); but see *Boulter v. Nova Scotia Power Incorporated* (2009) 307 D.L.R. (4th) 293 (N.S.C.A.) ("poverty" not analogous ground.). See also Murray Wesson, "Social Condition and Social Rights" (2006) 69 Saskatchewan Law Rev. 100–117; David Wiseman, "Competence Concerns in *Charter* Adjudication: Countering the anti-poverty competence argument" (2006) 51 McGill Law J. 503–546.

costs in the proceedings on the grounds that their claim was *prima facie* meritorious and the issue raised was of public importance.[53] And the Nova Scotia Supreme Court has commented upon the inappropriateness of bringing the full weight of the criminal law to bear on welfare fraud, suggesting that its penalties may be too stringent for courts to apply in practice.[54]

More often, occupants' rights to financial assistance are more procedural than substantive in the sense that they require that occupants be treated fairly and with dignity throughout. Fairness implies full and complete application of statutory requirements – such as accurately stating the grounds of termination in an eviction notice[55] – but it implies more than this. A good example is *Jung v. Toronto Public Housing Corporation*, an eviction case, in which the Ontario Divisional Court stressed that administrative tribunals must apply the rules of natural justice at all stages of the procedure and held that the hearing officer had violated "virtually all of the rules of natural justice" and demonstrated an apparent "lack of understanding of those fundamental principles".[56] Another example is *Iness v. Caroline Co-operative Homes Inc.*, an occupancy charge case, in which the Human Rights Tribunal of Ontario held that the occupant had been discriminated against because she received social assistance, receiving a treatment that was disrespectful and undermined her sense of personal dignity.[57] These various examples of occupants' substantive and procedural rights rely mainly on public law (constitutional, statutory and administrative).

But what if the financial assistance provided by the State is, by any measure, manifestly inadequate to provide access to acceptable housing? What rights do people

---

[53] *Broomer v. Ontario (Attorney General)* (2004) 187 O.A.C. 192 (Ont. Div. Ct.) (ban had been set out in regulations adopted under neoliberal *Ontario Works Act*, S.O. 1997, c. 25, Sched. A); see also *Rogers v. Sudbury (Administrator of Ontario Works)* (2001) 57 O.R. (3d) 460 (Ont. Sup.Ct.) (granting interim relief reinstating benefits pending decision in *Charter* challenge to regulations; applicant died before trial).

[54] *R. v. Rehberg* (1994) 127 N.S.R. (2d) 331 (N.S.S.C.) at paras. 61 & 105 (single mother charged under Criminal Code with fraud, an indictable offence carrying up to 10-year sentence, for minor violation of then "man-in-house" rule; rule held discriminatory under *Charter*). See generally Dorothy E. Chunn & Shelley A.M. Gavigan, "From Welfare Fraud to Welfare as Fraud: The criminalization of poverty", 217–235 in Gillian Balfour & Elizabeth Cormack, eds. *Criminalizing Women: Gender and (in)justice in neo-liberal times* (Halifax: Fernwood Publishing, 2006).

[55] *Courtland Mews Co-operative Homes Inc. v. McKay* 2008 CanLII 5583 (Ont. Sup. Ct.) (amount of arrears overstated in notice of eviction).

[56] *Jung v. Toronto Community Housing Corporation* (2008) 228 D.L.R. (4th) 225 (Ont. Div. Ct.) at paras. 25 & 26 (see also 2008 CanLII 1538 (Ont. Div. Ct.) (costs)). See also *Dubajic v. Regional Municipality of Peel* (2008) 240 O.A.C. 199 (Ont. Div. Ct.) (revocation of rent-geared-to-income subsidy; need for fairness).

[57] *Iness v. Caroline Co-operative Homes Inc.* (2006) 57 Canadian Human Rights Report 1 (Human Rights Tribunal of Ontario); see also *Canada Mortgage and Housing Corporation v. Iness* (2004) 236 D.L.R. (4th) 241 (Ont. C.A.) (CMHC not subject to provincial human rights codes). Note that s. 4(1)(f) of newly enacted *Housing Services Act*, supra note 50, provides that it is a matter of provincial interest that the system of housing and homeless services "treats individuals and families with respect and dignity".

have to contest this? One possibility is to argue that this constitutes an unjustifiable infringement of the right to "life, liberty and security of the person" guaranteed by section 7 of the *Charter*. This was argued in *Gosselin v. Québec (Attorney General)*, and a close reading of the case suggests that this remains a possibility: only one judge, Bastarache J., was of the view that a right to social assistance is, by its very nature, outside the scope of section 7, and all judges accepted the possibility that the section could impose positive obligations on the State in appropriate circumstances.[58] This question is again before the courts in the recently filed *Tanudjaja et al. v. Canada (Attorney General) and Ontario (Attorney General)*, and this is a case to watch.[59]

Another possibility might be to argue that the government is guilty of a civil wrong, as discussed above.[60] After all, if governments can be held civilly responsible for damage caused to individual houses through their failure to enforce building construction by-laws, can they not also be held responsible for damage caused to many people by making housing inaccessible through their radical cuts to social assistance in a time of rising prices?

A third possibility could be to argue that the government is liable for breach of fiduciary duties. Although governments are not typically held subject to such duties in the exercise of their functions, the courts have nevertheless accepted the possibility of doing so in appropriate cases. The Crown's fiduciary duties to Aboriginal peoples have been recognised for some time, and the Supreme Court of Canada has now provided guidelines for recognising them more widely. In *Alberta v. Elder Advocates of Alberta Society*, the Court accepts, albeit cautiously, that governments can owe fiduciary duties outside recognized categories, and that this is determined in the same way for State and private actors ("although they may play out differently where the alleged fiduciary is a public authority"). In the Court's view, "vulnerability alone is insufficient to support a fiduciary claim"; rather, the claimant must also show:

> 1) an undertaking by the alleged fiduciary to act in the best interests of the alleged beneficiary or beneficiaries; 2) a defined person or class of persons vulnerable to a fiduciary's control ...; and 3) a legal or substantial practical interest of the beneficiary or beneficiaries that stands to be adversely affected by the alleged fiduciary's exercise of discretion or control.[61]

The application of each of these elements to a situation of manifestly inadequate financial assistance for housing will require careful consideration. At first blush, the

---

[58] *Gosselin v. Québec (Attorney General)* [2002] S.C.R.429; Matthews Glenn, supra note 16.

[59] *Tanudjaja et al. v. Canada (Attorney General) and Ontario (Attorney General)* (Ont. S.C.) (notice of application filed 26 May 2010) [http://www.socialrights.ca/litigation/homelessness/Notice%20of%20Application%20Amended.pdf].

[60] See supra, the text at note 27 f.

[61] *Alberta v. Elder Advocates of Alberta Society* [2011] 2 S.C.R. 261 at paras. 26, 28 & 36 (alleged overpayment of accommodation charges in long-term care facilities; motion to strike pleadings: breach of fiduciary duty and several others struck; unjust enrichment and s. 15 of *Charter* not struck).

requirement to show an "undertaking" to act in the beneficiary's best interest appears the most difficult to argue. Perhaps one might argue that Canada's ratification of international human rights treaties such as the ICESCR supplemented by assurances it has given in the monitoring process constitutes such an undertaking. Or maybe that an initial grant of financial assistance constitutes an undertaking, so that subsequent cuts at least – particularly cuts as draconian as Ontario's 21.6 % cut to social welfare benefits in 1995 – are in breach of fiduciary duty: this would respect the "no back-sliding" obligation under the ICESCR;[62] it would also be consistent with the law's general preference for sanctioning acts of misfeasance over acts of nonfeasance. Or possibly that the approach of courts in the government wrongs cases to the requirement that private law duties be grounded in legislation provides a useful analogy.

These three examples – section 7, government wrongs, and breach of fiduciary duties – of possible challenges to inadequate financial assistance are based in public law (constitutional) and private law (torts, equity).

9.4 Concluding Observations

The enforceability of economic and social rights is a matter of on-going concern. They are said to be too vague to litigate, too political to judge, too costly to implement, and too positive to enforce. In short, they are said to be non-justiciable. This chapter has sought to respond to the justiciability critique by reconceptualising economic and social rights in a disaggregated way, as consisting of a number of discrete rights enforceable in their own ways. The right to housing was chosen as illustration for three reasons: it cuts vertically through all levels of jurisdiction: international, national, provincial and municipal; it involves multiple actors: governments, administrative tribunals, courts, the private sector (both profit and non-profit), and individuals; and it engages a wide range of intersecting forms of normativity: hard law and soft law; international treaties and declarations; domestic legislation, regulations and policy documents; public and private law; and informal rules. The sampling of cases chosen to illustrate the disaggregated approach demonstrates the wide range of rights – both substantive and procedural – available to protect different elements of the right to housing. More generally, it also shows a willingness on the part of the courts to hear, at least, cases that affect government policy decisions and the use of public resources. The government wrongs and fiduciary duties cases are particularly interesting on this score.[63] Bruce Porter emphasizes the symbolic impor-

[62] See supra, the text following note 24.

[63] It is also interesting to note, for example, that the Canada Assistance Plan (CAP) – the federal/provincial framework agreement governing social assistance for some 30 years (1966–1996) – has been before the Supreme Court of Canada on seven different occasions, ranging from *Alden v. Gagliardi* [i.e. Minister of Rehabilitation and Social Improvement] [1973] S.C.R. 199 through to *Québec (Attorney General) v. Canada* [2011] 1 S.C.R. 368. One case, *Reference re Canada Assistance Plan (B.C.)* [1991] 2 S.C.R. 525, specifically addressed the issue of justiciability.

tance of opening "adjudicative space" for economic and social rights regardless of the outcome of the particular case, and Alana Klein speaks evocatively of "judging as nudging".[64]

However, adjudicative space costs money, money which those who are unable to house themselves adequately can ill afford to spend. Some of the court decisions used as examples in this chapter attempt to address this problem in the way they award costs – in awarding, for example, interim costs to an impecunious party to enable it to continue a prima facie meritorious action[65] or final costs calculated on a solicitor-client basis to a successful impecunious party to encourage lawyers to accept such cases on a pro bono basis.[66] Others attempt to address the problem by recognising that groups or individuals have public interest standing to bring an action with or instead of someone directly affected.[67]

In short, problems of access to housing intersect with issues of access to justice. But this is too wide a topic to examine further here.

[64] Porter, supra note 21; Alana Klein, "Judging as Nudging: New governance approaches for the enforcement of constitutional social and economic rights" (2007–2008) 39 Columbia Human Rights Law Rev. 351–422.

[65] E.g. *Rogers v. Sudbury (Administrator of Ontario Works)* (2001) 57 O.R. (3d) 467 (Ont. S.C.); see also supra note 53. See generally *British Columbia (Minister of Forests) v. Okanagan Indian Band* [2003] 3 S.C.R. 371 (discussing criteria for awarding interim costs in public interest litigation).

[66] *Victoria (City) v. Adams*, supra note 26.

[67] *Tenants' Rights Action Coalition*, supra note 45; see also *Finlay v. Canada (Minister of Finance)* [1986] 2 S.C.R. 607 (recognising public interest standing to bring CAP challenge).

Part III
Communities, Human Rights and Local Practices

Chapter 10
Transnational Human Rights and Local Activism: Mapping the Middle

Sally Engle Merry[*,†]

10.1 Introduction

How do transnational ideas such as human rights approaches to violence against women become meaningful in local social settings? How do they move across the gap between a cosmopolitan awareness of human rights and local sociocultural understandings of gender and family? Ethnographic studies suggest that human rights ideas, including ideas of women's human rights, are spreading to many urban and even rural areas around the world. They are appropriated by groups such as indigenous peoples, ethnic minorities, and women[1] as well as military officials and government employees in Columbia and the US.[2] For example, Mark Goodale describes a local activist in rural Bolivia who delivers a long lecture on women's

*This chapter first appeared as an article in the *American Anthropologist* in 2006; see volume 108(1), at pages 38–51. I am grateful to the Cultural Anthropology Program and Law and Social Sciences Program, National Science Foundation, BCS-9904441, for support for this research. I am also grateful for research support from Wellesley College and the Mellon New Directions Fellowship. I also benefited from a fellowship year at the Carr Center for Human Rights Policy at the Kennedy School, Harvard University. Mark Goodale, Richard Rottenburg, and Aradhana Anu Sharma provided helpful comments on an earlier draft.

[1]Jane K. Cowan, Marie-Benedict Dembour & Richard Wilson (eds.), *Culture and Rights* (Cambridge, Cambridge University Press, 2001).

[2]Winifred Tate, "Counting the Dead: Human Rights Claims and Counter-Claims in Columbia" (Ph.D. dissertation, Department of Anthropology, New York University, 2004).

S.E. Merry (✉)
Department of Anthropology, New York University, 10003 New York, NY, USA
e-mail: sally.merry@nyu.edu

R. Provost and C. Sheppard (eds.), *Dialogues on Human Rights and Legal Pluralism*, Ius Gentium: Comparative Perspectives on Law and Justice 17,
DOI 10.1007/978-94-007-4710-4_10, © Springer Science+Business Media Dordrecht 2013

human rights to each couple he marries.[3] Celestine Nyamu-Musembi argues that promoting women's human rights to land ownership can affect local administrative forums in Kenya,[4] while Hussaina J. Abdullah describes the growth of human rights and civil liberties activism in Nigeria along with a simultaneous religious revivalism.[5] This increasing 'religiosity,' along with authoritarian state feminism, has reinforced patriarchal structures so that even the explosion in human rights activism has not significantly challenged them.

On the other hand, some local justice officials find that human rights ideas undermine their capacity to deliver justice in ways that they find reasonable. For example, Jane Collier and Shannon Speed describe the conflicts between understandings of justice shared by judges in an indigenous community in Mexico and those of human rights advocates who criticize local justice.[6] Marilyn Strathern discusses a similar conflict in Papua New Guinea, in which a woman was willing to be given to another kin group to create peace between villages but human rights activists objected.[7] Even women's groups in Northern Nigeria that talk about implementing women's rights increasingly refer to women's rights under Shari'a rather than under international law. Although this formulation talks about rights, it does not challenge gender inequality.[8] Local leaders in many parts of the world resist the human rights claims of subordinated groups by asserting that this is an alien, Western import not suited to local normative systems, a position framed most strongly in the claim that Asian values are distinct from human rights.[9]

Human rights ideas are created in transnational conferences and meetings of UN commissions such as the High Commission on Human Rights or the Commission on the Status of Women. The 1993 world conference on human rights in Vienna articulated for the first time that women's rights are human rights. The Fourth World Conference on Women in 1995, often called the Beijing Conference, produced a policy document called the Platform for Action that has been very influential in

---

[3] Mark Goodale, "Legal Ethnography in an Era of Globalization: The Arrival of Western Human Rights Discourse to Rural Bolivia" in June Starr and Mark Goodale (eds.), *Practicing Ethnography in Law: New Dialogues, Enduring Methods* (New York, Palgrave Macmillan, 2002), pp. 50–72.

[4] Celestine Nyamu-Musembi, "Are Local Norms and Practices Fences or Pathways? The Example of Women's Property Rights" in Abdullahi An-Naim (ed.), *Cultural Transformation and Human Rights in Africa* (London, Zed Books, 2002), pp. 126–150.

[5] Hussaina J. Abdullah, "Religious Revivalism, Human Rights Activism and the Struggle for Women's Rights in Nigeria." pp. 151–191 in Abdullahi An-Na'im, *supra* note 4, p.151 at 152–153.

[6] Shannon Speed and Jane Collier, "Limiting Indigenous Autonomy in Chiapas, Mexico: The State Government's Use of Human Rights" (2000) 22 *Human Rights Quarterly* 877–905.

[7] Marilyn Strathern, "Losing (Out on) Intellectual Resources" in Alain Pottage and Martha Mundy (eds.), *Law, Anthropology, and the Constitution of the Social: Making Persons and Things* (Cambridge, Cambridge Univ. Press, 2004), pp. 201–234.

[8] H.J. Abdullah, "Religious Revivalism, Human Rights Activism and the Struggle for Women's Rights in Nigeria", *supra* note 5, pp. 169–171.

[9] Joanne R. Bauer and Daniel A. Bell (eds.), *The East Asian Challenge for Human Rights* (London and New York, Cambridge University Press, 1999).

defining a set of policies for improving women's status around the world. The Platform focuses on 12 areas of particular urgency that require strategic action from governments, the international community, and civil society, including non-governmental organizations (NGOs) and the private sector.[10] One of these is violence against women, a second is a "lack of respect for and inadequate promotion and protection of the human rights of women." During the 1990s and 2000s, violence against women became the centerpiece of women's human rights, fundamental to these documents and incorporated within the major women's human rights convention, the Convention on the Elimination of all Forms of Discrimination Against Women (CEDAW) by a new general recommendation.

Ideas about women's human rights are developed in global conferences and commission meetings with wide participation by all the countries of the world, not just by those of the global North – the countries of Europe and North America. Despite vast inequalities in wealth and power among these countries, the documents take into account a wide variety of national perspectives.[11] Although the idea of human rights originated in the West in the eighteenth and nineteenth centuries, its recent development has been global. There is now considerable support for human rights ideas in parts of Latin America, Africa, Asia, and the Pacific. In the same period, the resistance to applying human rights at home has been growing in the US, particularly to ratifying and implementing human rights conventions.

During the 1990s and 2000s, core human rights principles concerning women spread from their global sites of production in New York and Geneva to local settings around the world. But how did these ideas travel? What are the paths by which human rights ideas become relevant to local settings? The intense debates between universalists and relativists of the 1990s highlighted the question of how human rights ideas move across cultural contexts. Universalists claimed that human rights are powerful because of their universality and should be adopted in all cultural contexts despite differences from local normative systems, while relativists argued that human rights ideas should not be imposed on societies with different value systems. Pragmatically, some argue, human rights will spread more effectively and with greater legitimacy if they are adapted to local cultural contexts and systems of law.[12]

---

[10] UN 1996. *The Beijing Declaration and the Platform for Action*. United Nations, New York: Department of Public Information, pp. 33–34.

[11] See Annelise Riles, "Infinity within the Brackets" (1998) 25 *American Ethnologist* 378–9; and Sally Engle Merry, *Human Rights and Gender Violence: Translating International Law into Local Justice* (Chicago, University of Chicago Press, 2006).

[12] See Abdullahi An-Na'im, "Toward a Cross-Cultural Approach to Defining International Standards of Human Rights: The Meaning of Cruel, Inhuman, or Degrading Treatment or Punishment" in Abdullahi Ahmed An-Na'im (ed.), *Human Rights in Cross-Cultural Perspectives: A Quest for Consensus* (Philadelphia, University of Pennsylvania Press, 1992), pp. 19–44; Abdullahi An-Na'im and Jeffrey Hammond, "Cultural Transformation and Human Rights in African Societies" in Abdullahi An-Na'im (ed.), *supra* note 4, pp. 13–38; and Radhika Coomaraswamy, "To Bellow like a Cow: Women, Ethnicity, and the Discourse of Rights" in Rebecca J. Cook (ed.), *Human Rights of Women: National and International Perspectives* (Philadelphia, University of Pennsylvania Press, 1994), pp. 39–57.

Yet, there has been relatively little anthropological attention to the process by which universal human rights ideas are adopted and applied locally, particularly in areas other than indigenous rights.[13] This article theorizes this process by focusing on forms of appropriation and the role of intermediaries. Theorizing the cultural translation process is an old anthropological problem, but the globalization of human rights discourse raises it in a new guise.

The theoretical question, how do human rights ideas become adopted in a wide variety of culturally distinct communities, is one instance of a broader question about how ideas and institutions move from one sociocultural setting to another. It raises the question of how concepts can be translated between social and cultural contexts. Understanding when and how cultural translation is possible has long been an issue in anthropology. The famous Gluckman-Bohannan debate in legal anthropology was ostensibly about how to do comparative research but was fundamentally about the difficulties of translation. Max Gluckman argued that it was possible to interpret the legal behavior of the Barotse people through the categories of Western law in order to make comparisons between Lozi and Western law.[14] He identified broadly similar features of legal reasoning between Barotse and European law such as the idea of the "reasonable man." Paul Bohannan countered, on the basis of his research on the Tiv, that legal categories are folk categories that should be understood in their own terms.[15] He peppered his ethnography of Tiv law with Tiv words, arguing that translating them into English terms in order to make comparisons distorted their meaning.[16] Although he envisioned a time when computer language would provide a culture-free set of categories for analysis, at this point the English language and its legal categories were not culture neutral. He accused Gluckman of doing "backward translation" by reading Lozi law through Western legal terms instead of translating Lozi terms into English[17] This backward translation process enabled Gluckman to show that the Lozi judicial process was similar to that of Western society, but Bohannan claimed that these similarities appeared because Gluckman had used Western law to understand Lozi law in the first place.[18] As anthropologists recognized the difference between folk terms and analytic terms and that comparison relies on analytic categories, the debate subsided.[19]

---

[13] But see J.K. Cowan, M.-B. Dembour & R. Wilson, *supra* note 1.

[14] Max Gluckman, The judicial process among the Barotse of Northern Rhodesia (Manchester, Manchester University Press for the Rhodes-Livingston Institute, 1955); Max Gluckman, "Concepts in the Comparative Study of Tribal Law" in Laura Nader (ed.), *Law in Culture and Society* (Berkeley, University of California Press, 1997), pp. 349–373.

[15] Paul Bohannan, "Ethnography and Comparison in Legal Anthropology" in L. Nader, *supra* note 14, pp. 401–418.

[16] Paul Bohannan, Justice and Judgment among the Tiv of Nigeria (London, Oxford University Press, 1957).

[17] P. Bohannan, "Ethnography and Comparison in Legal Anthropology" *supra* note 14, p. 411.

[18] *Ibid.*

[19] Laura Nader (ed.), *Law in Culture and Society* (Berkeley, University of California Press, 1997).

The underlying question of how translating one set of cultural categories and meanings into another transforms them remains. Nevertheless, ideas now circulate globally at a dizzying speed, and translations and mistranslations are constant.

This essay will use empirical examples of the localization of women's human rights to highlight some important dimensions of the process. It considers scholarship from development studies to social movement studies to studies of colonial rule. I argue that analyzing the process of translating between global and local systems of meaning is critical to understanding the making of human rights in the vernacular. Translators play a critical role in vernacularizing human rights by refashioning global rights agendas into local contexts and reframing local grievances in terms of global human rights norms. Their strategies fall along a continuum from the local replication of global forms to the hybrid merging of distinct local and global institutions and ideologies. It appears that globally connected translators tend to replicate global forms while more locally rooted ones develop more hybrid institutions.

The term "local" is of course deeply problematic here, as is its oppositional twin "global." In the context of discussions of transnationalism, local tends to stand for a lack of mobility, wealth, education, and cosmopolitanism as well as recalcitrant particularity, while global encompasses the ability to move across borders, to adopt universal moral frameworks, and to share in the affluence, education, and cosmopolitan awareness of elites from other parts of the world. Thus social class, education, travel, and transnational consciousness blend with geography in defining these terms. Clearly, the cluster of ideas evoked by local and global goes far beyond spatial referents. Their wider array of meanings is relevant to understanding the process of localizing human rights. Despite considerable critique of the use of the terms global and local and numerous studies that show that things we call global are often circulating locals, these terms have a recalcitrant tendency to shape discussions of transnational phenomenon.[20]

As global ideas appear in local communities, they are typically *vernacularized*, or adapted to local institutions and meanings. The concept of vernacularization was developed to explain the nineteenth-century process by which national languages in Europe separated, moving away from the medieval transnational use of Latin and creating a new and more differentiated sense of nationhood in Europe.[21] Human rights language is similarly extracted from the universal and adapted to national and local communities. The term *indigenization* focuses on shifts in meaning, on the

---

[20] Kim Berry discusses the way Indian policies toward women's development were shaped by the US emphasis on the woman as housewife, an idea that conformed to the ideas of local elites in some parts of India that a family's honor is connected to a woman's confinement to the home. American ideas of female domesticity also conformed to Indian nationalist representations of women as mothers of the nation: Kim Berry, "Developing Women: The Traffic in Ideas about Women and Their Needs in Kangra, India." in K. Sivaramakrishnan and Arun Agrawal (eds.), *Regional Modernities: The Cultural Politics of Development in India* (Stanford, Stanford University Press, 2003), p. 75 at 84–85.

[21] Benedict Anderson, Imagined Communities: Reflections on the Origin and Spread of Nationalism (London, Verso Books, 1983).

way new ideas are framed and presented in terms of existing cultural norms, values, and practices. For example, when a violence against women initiative developed in the US is presented in India by using stories of a powerful Hindu female deity, it is indigenized. Indigenization is the symbolic dimension of vernacularization.

Social movement theorists have developed the concept of framing as a way to understand what makes an idea persuasive in a social movement. The idea of framing is also valuable for understanding indigenization. Frames are not themselves ideas but ways of packaging and presenting ideas that generate shared beliefs, motivate collective action, and define appropriate strategies of action.[22] Snow uses the term "framing" to refer to the signifying work of social movement activists: "they frame, or assign meaning to and interpret relevant events and conditions in ways that are intended to mobilize potential adherents and constituents, to garner bystander support, and to demobilize antagonists."[23] The frame is an interpretive package surrounding a core idea.[24] It can produce significant change in individual consciousness about an issue or problem or more broadly in a wider domain in a manner similar to religious conversion.[25] Indigenization occurs when an innovation is framed in terms of local symbols and terminology.

In social movements, the products of this framing activity are called "collective action frames." These frames can have powerful effects on the way situations are understood and on the tactics their supporters deploy.[26] Collective action frames are not static, reified entities but dynamic, recursive processes that organize talk within specific interaction contexts and are continuously revised in response to confrontations with issues and events.[27]

Social movement theorists point out that the frame needs to be resonant with cultural traditions and narratives to be appealing.[28] Snow et. al. argue that the higher

[22] David A. Snow, E. Burke Rochford, Jr., Steven K. Worden, Robert D. Benford, "Frame Alignment Processes, Micromobilization, and Movement Participation" (1986) 51(4) American Sociological Review 464–481; Sidney Tarrow, *Power in Movements: Social Movements and Contentious Politics*, 2nd ed. (Cambridge, Cambridge University Press, 1998).

[23] David A. Snow and Robert D. Benford, "Ideology, Frame Resonance, and Participant Mobilization" (1988) 1 International Social Movement Research 197 at 198 as quoted in David A Snow, "Framing Processes, Ideology, and Discursive Fields" in David A. Snow, Sarah A. Soule, and Hanspeter Kriesi (eds.), *The Blackwell Companion to Social Movements* (Malden, MA, Blackwell, 2004), p. 380 at 384.

[24] Myra Marx Ferree, "Resonance and Radicalism: Feminist Framing in the Abortion Debates of the United States and Germany" (2003) 109(2) *American Journal of Sociology* 304, 308.

[25] D.A. Snow, *supra* note 23, at p. 394.

[26] Sanjeev Khagram, James V. Riker, and Kathryn Sikkink (eds.), *Restructuring World Politics: Transnational Social Movements, Networks, and Norms* (Minneapolis, University of Minnesota Press, 2002), pp. 12–13.

[27] Marc W. Steinberg, "The Talk and Back Talk of Collective Action: A Dialogic Analysis of Repertoires of Discourse among Nineteenth-Century English Cotton Spinners" (1999) 105 *American Journal of Sociology* 736–780; D.A. Snow, *supra* note 23, at p. 403.

[28] D.A. Snow, *supra* note 23, at p. 401.

the degree of frame resonance, the greater the likelihood it will be successful, all else being equal.[29] However, Ferree counters that resonant discourses are less radical than non-resonant ones, and that some movement leaders may chose the non-resonant approach in order to induce greater social change in the long run.[30] Indeed, resonance is a costly choice since it may limit the possibility of long-term change. Choosing resonance requires sacrificing ideals, limiting demands on authorities, and possibly excluding significant groups and their demands from the movement.[31]

This is precisely the problem human rights activists confront: If they present human rights as compatible with existing ways of thinking, these ideas will not induce change. It is only their capacity to challenge existing power relations that offers radical possibilities. For example, the success of the battered women's movement in the US depended on fundamentally changing the way women understood violence from their partners, shifting it from discipline to abuse. On the other hand, to be adopted, human rights ideas must be framed in indigenous cultural categories. Translators must assess to what extent they can challenge existing modes of thinking and to what extent they must package radical ideas in familiar boxes.

The process of vernacularization depends on translation. National and middle-level social activists appropriate ideas from human rights and feminist discourse and translate them into local terms. They show how the human rights framework offers them a new perspective on their everyday problems. I saw this translation process happening in a support group for battered women in a small town in Hawai'i a few years ago. When one of the participants described her misery when her partner forced her to have sexual relations, the leader of the group pointed out that this was a case of rape. The speaker paused, then said with some surprise in her voice that it had felt like rape, so that must be what it was. She saw the act differently when it was called rape. It became a violation of her body and her rights rather than a performance of wifely duty. Similarly, in a social movement against male-only inheritance of family land in the New Territories of Hong Kong in 1993, Hong Kong feminist activists persuaded a group of indigenous women to see their exclusion from houses and land as gender discrimination and a human rights violation rather than only as poor treatment by their male kin.[32]

Yet, battered women and others who experience injuries that can be defined as rights violations tend to adopt this new framework in a limited and contingent way.[33] Human rights add a new interpretation but rarely displace older ones. Instead, the human rights perspective is typically layered over other frameworks, such as fair

[29] D.A. Snow et al., "Ideology, Frame Resonance, and Participant Mobilization", *supra* note 23, 477.

[30] M.M. Ferree, "Resonance and Radicalism: Feminist Framing in the Abortion Debates of the United States and Germany", *supra* note 24, 305.

[31] *Ibid*, 340.

[32] Sally Engle Merry and Rachel Stern, "The Female Inheritance Movement in Hong Kong: Theorizing the Local/Global Interface" (2005) 46(3) *Current Anthropology* 387–409.

[33] Sally Engle Merry, *Human Rights and Gender Violence: Translating International Law into Local Justice* (Chicago, University of Chicago Press, 2006).

treatment by kinsmen. Just as battered women in Hawai'i came to see themselves as badly treated by their partners as well as having the right to take their batterers to court, so the indigenous women in Hong Kong came to see themselves as abused by their male kin who failed to care for them as well as endowed with the right to inherit land equally with male relatives. Whether the rights layer of understanding endures or not depends in part on the institutional response claimants receive. My research on battered women showed that these women try out a rights subjectivity but drop it if the courts, police, and prosecutors trivialize and ignore their problems.[34] In Hong Kong, the indigenous women's enthusiasm for rights activism dropped off after they discovered that the new inheritance law did not benefit them personally.[35]

Thus, for global human rights concepts to be adopted locally, they must be presented within familiar symbolic frameworks and treated as serious violations by local legal institutions. The role of intermediaries is essential. These intermediaries do the work of translation: they put global human rights ideas into local terms and use stories of local indignities and violations to give life and power to global movements. They hold a double consciousness, combining both human rights concepts and local ways of thinking about grievances. They may be local activists, human rights lawyers, feminist NGO leaders, academics, or a host of other people who have one foot in the transnational community and one at home.

Translators negotiate the middle. On one hand, they have to speak the language of international human rights preferred by international donors in order to get funds and global media attention. On the other hand, they have to present their initiatives in cultural terms that will be acceptable to at least some of the local community. As they scramble for funds, they need to select issues that international donors are interested in, such as female genital cutting, women's empowerment, or trafficking, and connect these agendas to problems that interest local populations, such as clean drinking water, jobs, or good roads.

These people translate up and down. They reframe local grievances in global human rights terms and human rights language in local terms. They take ideas from larger systems and remake them in local terms. At the same time, they reinterpret local ideas and grievances in the language of national and international human rights. The groups occupying this space are no longer the village headmen of colonial indirect rule but, increasingly, activists providing services and advocacy to local communities. They are aware of national and transnational movements and discourses of justice while they seek to develop ideas that make sense to the everyday lives of poor people in urban and rural areas.

This process of cultural translation is familiar to anthropologists, who typically translate the cultural worlds of the people they study into the cultural worlds of their readers and students. As anthropologists have paid increasing attention to the

---

[34] Sally Engle Merry, "Rights Talk and the Experience of Law: Implementing Women's Human Rights to Protection from Violence" (2003) 25(2) *Human Rights Quarterly* 343–381.

[35] S.E. Merry and Rachel Stern, "The Female Inheritance Movement in Hong Kong: Theorizing the Local/Global Interface", *supra* note 32.

inequalities in power involved in this process, they have become more reflexive about their own practice.[36] As Talal Asad notes, languages themselves are unequal in power, as a result of global inequalities of wealth and power. Translating from a "weaker" language into a "stronger" one, such as from a "third-world" into a "first-world" language, means translating from a less powerful to a more powerful language.[37] Because of these differences among languages, determined by professional, national, and international factors, the process of "cultural translation" can be an act of power, especially when it means reinterpreting one set of experiences and categories in terms of another, more powerful one. Just as anthropologists translate local experiences into written texts or films in dominant global languages, so human rights translators take local grievances and translate them "up" into the more powerful language of transnational human rights. This usually means framing the stories differently than the victims themselves do.[38]

The translator occupies a position of both power and vulnerability. She has the power to define and articulate issues for audiences beyond the local community. Yet, as she struggles to satisfy the expectations of people in different and possibly incompatible worlds, she risks appearing as a traitor or collaborator with one side rather than the other. Anthropologists have long been fascinated with people who occupy middle positions, translating between worlds above and worlds below. Max Gluckman's analysis of the position of the village headman in British Central Africa under British colonial governance is a classic example.[39] After delineating the importance of the village headman in many societies of Central Africa, he notes that there is a tension between the headman's position in the village, which uneasily pairs his leadership in a web of kinship ordered by diffuse moral sanctions with his political power supported by legal and political authority. The latter includes his role as a key (although unpaid) official in the British colonial administration. The headman and his followers in the village share a common set of values but do not accept those of the British. Nevertheless, the headman is held responsible by the

[36] See for example: James Clifford and George E. Marcus (eds.), *Writing Culture: The Poetics and Politics of Ethnography* (Berkeley, University of California Press, 1986); Lila Abu-Lughod, *Writing Women's Worlds: Bedouin Stories* (Berkeley, University of California Press, 1993).

[37] Talal Asad, "The Concept of Cultural Translation in British Social Anthropology" in James Clifford and George E. Marcus (eds.), *Writing Culture: The Poetics and Politics of Ethnography. School of American Research Advanced Seminar* (Berkeley, University of California Press, 1986), p. 141 at 163–164.

[38] Studies of the dilemmas activists face in trying to win asylum status for their clients underscore this dilemma. Both McKinley (1997) and Ticktin (1999) show, in different cases, how an African or South Asian woman's story of abuse had to be reframed as one in which she has been victimized by custom in order to win asylum status in the US and the UK: Michelle McKinley, "Life Stories, Disclosure, and the Law" (1997) 20(2) *PoLAR: Political and Legal Anthropology Review* 70–83; Miriam Ticktin, "Selling Suffering in the Courtroom and Marketplace: An Analysis of the Autobiography of Kiranjit Ahluwalia" (1999) 22(1) *PoLAR: Political and Legal Anthropology Review* 24– 42.

[39] Max Gluckman, "The Village Headman in British Central Africa: Introduction" (1949) 19(2) *Africa* 89, 93–94.

British for reporting suspicious deaths, illnesses and strangers and for making sure that his villagers keep the village clean, hoe paths, use latrines, follow agricultural and veterinary regulations, and pay taxes, etc. Gluckman notes that the headman is no more ready than the villagers are to accept these as good practices, but he must nevertheless enforce the rules since if he does not, he is liable to be punished by fining, imprisonment, and ultimately deposition. "As he applies these unwelcome and unaccepted rules, his position becomes subject to still greater strains."[40] Thus, Gluckman's analysis of the headman provides insight into the dilemma of intermediaries more generally: they hold power by virtue of their ability to look both ways and work with conflicting value systems yet are vulnerable because the power delegated by higher authorities demands translation into terms that may not be welcome to subordinates and the subordinates make demands that may not be acceptable to higher authorities.

Ethnographic studies of development projects offer insight into the translation process. In development as in human rights implementation, competing ideas of action, objectivity and value coexist and must be translated in situations of substantial inequality. In his fascinating study of an organizational improvement project in Ruritania, an unnamed African country, funded by Normland, an unnamed European country, Richard Rottenburg describes the tensions created by differences in perspectives, classifications and priorities that various actors and organizations bring to the project.[41] The development bank, the national development ministry, the Normland consultant, the water ministry, the regional and urban administration, and finally the management of the Ruritanian urban water utilities all held differing expectations. After 20 years of investing in the country's water supply system, Normland's development bank wanted to solve the water system's lack of economic viability rather than building new capacity. The key problem was the small percentage of consumers who actually paid for their water, a figure of about 30 %. However, generating an accurate list of customers proved a political as well as administrative nightmare, for which the language of technical development was completely inadequate. Nevertheless, the demands of a structure that required collaboration between the African water engineers and the development consultants meant that this issue remained the subject of a purely technical conversation. A "metacode" based on ideas of development, progress, and technical expertise dominated discussions although the problems were largely based in political and organizational arrangements, not the technologies of water production.[42]

In his analysis of this development project, Rottenburg describes chains of translation (*Uebersetzungsketten*) along which interpretations of situations and facts are developed at various stages of reporting results that then become the basis for further interpretations. These chains stretch from the situation in the urban water utilities

[40] *Ibid.*

[41] Richard Rottenburg, *Weit hergeholte Fakten: Eine Parabel der Entwicklungshilfe* [Far-fetched facts: A parable of development] (Stuttgart, Lucius und Lucius, 2002).

[42] R. Rottenburg, *supra* note 41, p. 232.

ministry of Ruritania to the headquarters of the development bank to the political process in Normland where politicians must justify the expenditure of tax money on development projects.[43] At each point, facts are gathered, classified, and separated into individual units that have been delineated in the project documents, subject always to further subdivision and reclassification within a particular context. As data is subdivided and reclassified, its underlying fragility and unreliability are converted into an appearance of stability and solidity. This leads in some cases to a transformation of the data into forms that promote the ultimate goal of the project and avoid the appearance of mistakes.

Rottenburg's study highlights the creative work of intermediaries navigating between different and incompatible perspectives on a shared task. They rely on a subtly hegemonic structure of information analysis and presentation despite the framework of collaboration and joint decision-making.[44] His analysis highlights the power of those who are able to make these translations, at the same time as it underscores their vulnerability as they sift and sort flawed data to fit into predetermined goals. Ironically, the African managers are the strongest advocates of a universal approach to water utility management and standards of objectivity. This allows them to present themselves as worthy partners in development yet insulates them from the European managers by assuring them they are carrying out the work according to universal principles so that further intervention and inspection are unnecessary. The universalist façade obscures the fact that things are still being done in local ways. There are clear parallels with the translation of human rights ideas from a transnational metacode of human rights law to local situations. Local leaders are often eager to appear compliant with human rights expectations while continuing to act in non-compliant ways. Following the form and language of human rights while ignoring local violations is a common practice. Human rights translators, like development consultants, are often caught in the middle.

10.2 Processes of Vernacularization

Vernacularization includes a variety of processes that fall along a continuum from replication to hybridity. These processes differ in their inclusion of local cultural forms and institutions. At one end of the continuum is replication, a process in which the imported institution and its forms of authority and practice remain virtually unchanged despite superficial, decorative changes such as new names or icons. At the other end is the process of hybridization, in which local and global institutions and symbolic structures merge, sometimes uneasily. These variations are a matter of degree and are not sharply bounded. At both ends of the continuum, the translator

[43] *Ibid*, pp. 228–229.

[44] *Ibid*, pp. 15–16.

seeks to conceptualize problems in terms that will resonate with local populations and at the same time satisfy global expectations.

Remaking imported ideas and institutions such as human rights commissions or battered women's centers in the vernacular can satisfy two quite different political agendas. One is to make the new institution appealing to consumers. In this market-driven process, vernacularizers frame their services in familiar symbols and terminology to increase their program clientele or customer base. A second agenda is to promote cultural nationalism. Indigenizing an imported institution asserts the value of local cultural forms and practices. The leaders of a project to diminish violence against women in China developed curricular materials aimed at the culture of Han people, for example. Conservative Islamic women's groups in Nigeria talk about rights under Shari'a rather than international law when they want to encourage women to seek medical care for protracted labor and cannot get permission from their husbands to leave the home. Market and nationalist objectives are not mutually exclusive, of course. When Chinese lawyers adopt traditional Chinese names for their new law firms, for example, they seek to attract a local market for legal services as well as to show that they are fundamentally Chinese and not simply replicating the West.[45]

10.2.1 Replication

In translation by replication, the transnational language sets the overall organization, mission, and ideology of an intervention while the local context provides its distinctive content. The transnational idea remains the same, but local cultural understandings shape the way the work is carried out. Of course, any global prototype has been developed in another local situation before being launched into global circulation. Some of its original content is stripped away in the process, although some remains. I discuss how a U.S.-style batterer's treatment program was adapted to Chinese concepts of masculinity in a Hong Kong women's center to illustrate replication in the field of violence against women.

A key strategy in global feminists' efforts to address violence against women is the creation of women's centers. These centers replicate local models developed in the late 1970s and early 1980s in North America and Europe. They typically use human rights language to encourage women to resist violence and stand up for themselves. Most provide counseling for women, legal assistance, and in some cases temporary housing. Some also offer training programs for the men who are violent. The technology of batterer treatment programs comes from Euro-American traditions of therapeutic intervention in family situations and from law: men are taught how to recognize their anger and identify their feelings and are told that their

[45] Ethan Michelson, "Global Institutions, Local Meaning: Appropriation and Indigenization in the Chinese Legal System" [2005, on file with author].

partners have rights to equality and freedom from violence.[46] They are told that their violence is a crime.

By 1985, Hong Kong had its first center for battered women, called Harmony House. It was started by Americans and Britons using models from the US and UK as well as Hong Kong residents with North American experience. Thus, its origins were local Euro-American practices for dealing with gender violence. When I interviewed the executive director in 2002, she told me that she had spent 10 years in Canada working on family violence before coming to Harmony House. At first, the center described its program as counseling and sheltering abused women rather than promoting women's human rights in order to deflect the opposition a human rights approach would evoke (interview March 2002). By 2002, three other centers had opened in Hong Kong offering shelter, hotlines, counseling, legal, financial, and housing assistance, and support groups plus tutorial groups for children.[47]

In 1995, one of these centers initiated a treatment program for men who batter their wives. The idea of training men who batter not to use violence against their spouses is again a local development, taking place in several locations in the US in the early 1980s following somewhat different models. Some of the best known are Emerge in Boston and the Duluth, Minnesota Domestic Abuse Intervention Program.[48] US programs for batterers focus on teaching anger management, violence control, and gender equality and use feminist theories of domestic violence as an expression of patriarchy to treat battering as a form of asserting power and control. They teach men how to avoid using power and control tactics against their partners and that their violence may succeed in the short run but alienate and ultimately drive partners away in the long run.

In 1997, Chan Ko Ling, a graduate social work student at the University of Hong Kong, did research on this center's programs for batterers. His goal was to develop an indigenous batterer treatment program grounded in the values of Chinese masculinity. He hoped this approach would help social workers understand why men had such difficulty talking about their problems with violence and suggest a more culturally appropriate strategy for working with these men. He was, in other words, transplanting a local North American program into the Hong Kong context, a practice moving transnationally between two local sites. His dissertation describes his research and his exploration of Chinese conceptions of honor, family, relationships, and achievement,

[46] Sally Engle Merry, "Rights, Religion, and Community: Approaches to Violence against Women in the Context of Globalization" (2001) 35 *Law and Society Review* 39–88.

[47] Ella Lee, South China Morning Post, Feb. 16, 2002, p. 4; Caroline Yeung,"Wife Abuse: A Brief Historical Review on Research and Intervention" (1991) 25 *Hong Kong Journal of Social Work* 29, at 35; Catherine So-Kum Tang, Antoinette Lee, and Fanny Mui-Ching Cheung "Violence against Women in Hong Kong" in Fanny M. Cheung, Malavika Karlekar, Aurora De Dios, Juree Vichit-Vadakan, and Lourdes R. Quisumbing (eds.) (Hong Kong, Equal Opportunities Commission in collaboration with Women in Asian Development and UNESCO National Commission of the Philippines, 1999), pp. 38–58.

[48] Ellen Pence and Michael Paymar, *Education Groups for Men Who Batter: The Duluth Model* (New York, Springer Publishing Company, 1993).

then explains how these ideas prevent men from talking to others about their problems and seeking help for their violence.[49] Both in the dissertation and in an interview in 2002, Chan talked about how hard it is to persuade men to participate and the value of making the program mandatory through the courts, as it is now in many parts of the US.

Chan participated with two social workers in running two groups, each of which had a 2-h session once a week for 8 weeks. He interviewed 19 men before and after the program. The men were mainly working class, but a few were middle class. Most reported significant job stress and financial difficulties.[50] Chan argues that it is very difficult for these men to talk about their violence given Chinese conceptions of gender, face, and marital relationships. When men refuse to talk about their violence in the North American programs, this is interpreted as justification, denial, and minimization of the violence, but he suggests that accepting men's stories in their own terms, which include ideas of face and *yi,* rather than reacting in a judgmental way, encourages them to talk.[51]

Chan explores Confucian, Taoist, and Buddhist traditions of family life, emphasizing the importance of the concept of *yi* or rightness as the place where a program should begin.[52] He describes the widespread idea of a "*yi* husband and following wife," meaning that men are to be committed to and responsible for the marriage relationship and expect their wives to be obedient and submissive. When marital relations do not follow this pattern, men sometimes become violent.[53] The concept of "face," the public representation of one's self, is also important since personal success is linked to face.[54] Since an individual receives help from others depending on how they perceive his power and status, maintaining face in front of others is critical.[55] A man's face is affected by the performance of his wife, whose actions can diminish his face and therefore his power in social relationships. Aggression is the strongest form of face saving strategy. Interpreting domestic violence in this way shifts responsibility for the violence to the woman, who is viewed as responsible for the loss of face.[56] This model of Chinese masculinity explains why Chinese men have difficulty seeking help. To talk about their violence is to disclose family secrets and personal weaknesses, leading them to feel embarrassed and to lose face.

Chan theorizes that the Chinese batterers suffer from an impaired ability to differentiate the self. He cites an American text on family therapy for the concept of the

---

[49] Chan Ko Ling 2000 Unraveling the Dynamics of Spousal Abuse through the Narrative Accounts of Chinese Male Batterers. Ph.D. dissertation (publication no. 61332), Department of Social Work and Social Welfare, University of Hong Kong.

[50] *Ibid*, p. 195.

[51] *Ibid*, p. 166.

[52] *Ibid*, p. 146.

[53] *Ibid*, p. 318.

[54] *Ibid*, p. 130, 148.

[55] C.K. Ling, *supra* note 49, p. 144.

[56] *Ibid*, pp. 148–153.

undifferentiated self (again, importing a localism transnationally) while defining it in the Chinese context as the product of rigid cultural beliefs of *yi* and putting the pursuit of *yi* over the fulfillment of personal needs.[57] He concludes: "The more rigid the definition of masculinity in *yi*, the more serious the *undifferentiation of self*, and thus the lower is the capacity of conflict resolution. As a result, the higher will be the probability of using violence against their female partners."[58] Thus, he imports Western therapeutic ideas that the self must be disentangled from others in order to deal with conflict, even as he incorporates Chinese conceptions of masculinity. Chan advocates making programs mandatory given these men's unwillingness to seek help. He concludes, "Mandatory counseling for batterers, aimed at managing the emotions, anger control and abusive beliefs of batterers, should be encouraged by the government."[59] He also recommends temporary shelters for men so that they can leave their spouses during conflicts.

This is an example of a program locally tailored in cultural content but unchanged in its fundamental structure, aims, and methods from its transnationally derived local prototype. This is still a group therapy program with 2-h weekly meetings that focus on talking about feelings. Despite references to Chinese conceptions of masculinity and marital relationships, the approach relies on theories drawn from psychology and social work developed in the U.S. Chan's dissertation is theoretically grounded in American literature on domestic violence. The program is indigenized in that its substantive content focuses on Chinese masculinity and ideas of face, masculinity, and norms of marital relationships to inform the practice and understanding of why men refuse to talk about their violence, but the underlying ideas of improving safety for women, holding men responsible for their violence, the value of talking about feelings, and the socially derived understanding of violence are replicated from the transnationally circulating prototype.

Chan, the doctoral student, was a translator. Fluent in both English and Cantonese and in US theories of psychology and domestic violence as well as Chinese conceptions of masculinity, he developed a program that reached out to both worlds. When I met him in 2002, he was a professor of Social Work at the University of Hong Kong. His educational level was well above that of the men in the program even at the time of the research. Yet, he says in his dissertation acknowledgements that the sharing of the men in the program brought him to reflections on being a man in his social context: "Surprisingly, I found that we shared common beliefs of masculinity, though we acted out differently"[60] In addition to thanking his advisors at the University of Hong Kong, he thanks his wife and says he has learned how to be non-abusive and non-dominating in their relationship. Thus, he is situated between U.S. feminist and Chinese conceptions of masculinity and violence.

[57] *Ibid*, p. 387.

[58] *Ibid*, p. 421 [emphasis in original].

[59] *Ibid*, p. 430.

[60] C.K. Ling, *supra* note 49, v.

The women's center I studied in Hilo, Hawai'i made similar efforts in the late 1990s to develop a batterer treatment program designed specifically for Hawaiian men, again focusing on using words and images from the Hawaiian language and culture within a program structure modeled after the Duluth prototype. At the same time, a Native Hawaiian Christian pastor developed a more radical departure from this model. By 2000, when I visited his program, he had been offering anger management programs since 1995 and taking referrals from the courts. I visited the program twice, sitting with the men in his kitchen next to the large room that served as the church meeting room. His program combined prayer, singing, and discussions of sin and forgiveness with an analysis of the way Native Hawaiians have been oppressed by colonialism. At one meeting, the pastor pointed out that Hawaiians have legitimate reasons to be angry about the way they have been treated, but that it is wrong to take that anger out on loved ones. He talked about the ideal of the warrior as a person violent in war but not at home.

His theory is that domestic violence occurs because local men are caught between two cultural worlds, Hawaiian and white, and face difficult questions about who they are and what masculinity means. The pastor was skeptical about the feminist approach to batterer treatment of the local women's center. The center used the Duluth power/control wheel and grid-like violence control logs developed on the U.S. mainland.[61] The pastor complained that the feminist program tries to do healing through learning pie charts (a reference to the power/control wheel) and producing a school-like environment in which the men have to fill out lots of forms. Like school, the program uses too many big words and expresses too much hostility to its clients. The pastor said he prefers to frame his discussions of male violence in the ideas from the Hawaiian sovereignty movement as well as Christian ideas that every person is worthy in the eyes of God and can change given enough time, prayer, and the power of God. Of course, his models come from Pentecostal Christian churches elsewhere as well as the global indigenous rights movement.

His approach departs farther from the feminist model than the Hong Kong program does, but still retains the 2-h weekly group meeting format and takes referrals from the courts. Despite resisting the court's control and oversight, the pastor must take attendance and inform the probation officer when he thinks a person is finished. These examples are all close to the replication end of the continuum. The US model of batterer treatment programs is retained although its content is symbolically indigenized. It is a local creation circulating transnationally and superficially adapted to a new context.

10.2.2 Hybridity

At the other end of the continuum, local and global symbols, ideologies and organizational forms mesh to produce a new, hybrid institution differing in ideology and

[61] Sally Engle Merry, "Gender Violence and Legally Engendered Selves" (1995) 2 *Identities: Global Studies in Culture and Power* 49– 73.

organization from either parent prototype. An example of a hybrid institution are the *nari adalats* or women's courts that emerged in India in the mid-1990s to promote women's human rights, particularly in situations of domestic violence. These courts merged ideas of women's human rights, Indian feminism, women's empowerment and development, and traditional local governance by councils. They were formed by local women leaders paid a stipend by a women's empowerment program to develop community development programs. After some consultation concerning local needs, the village women organized women's courts to help with domestic violence, negotiating divorce, and returning dowry. Although the ideology and training offered by the development program was empowerment and human rights, the women who developed and maintained these courts joined local norms, government authority, and references to human rights to settle everyday problems.

Nari adalats developed in Gujarat, Uttar Pradesh, and a few other states from a government-initiated program to develop women's collectives in villages. They were also shaped by a long tradition of women's movement activism against violence against women. Although I have not done ethnographic research on these courts, I have relied on ethnographic research on the courts and on the development program. The parent program, called *Mahila Samakhya,* is a national-level rural women's "empowerment" program started by the Department of Education of the Government of India in 1989 with funding from the Dutch government.[62] Mahila Samakhya endeavored to promote gender equality, development, and social change by empowering poor women and providing them the knowledge and self-confidence to make changes.[63] The program introduced human rights ideas to its clientele of poor, illiterate women, many of whom are tribals or dalits, low-caste people.[64] Domestic violence was a core concern.[65]

The philosophy of the MS program is that decision making should rest with local level collectives. The program depends on a cadre of women activists, or *sahyoginis*, who develop and encourage *sanghas,* or women's collectives, in each village. Each sahyogini works with a cluster of ten villages. The MS program straddles the government/NGO divide, claiming whichever identity seems most helpful at the moment.[66] It functions in the autonomous fashion of a non-governmental organization

---

[62] International Center for Research on Women (ICRW) (1999–2002), Domestic Violence in India, vols. 1–5. Washington, DC: USAID/India, p. 49; Aradhana Sharma, "Cross-breeding Institutions, Breeding Struggle: Women's "Empowerment," Neoliberal Governmentality, and Engendered Statehood in India" (2006) 21 *Cultural Anthropology* 60–95.

[63] Veena Poonacha, and Divya Pandey *Responses to Domestic Violence in the States of Karnataka and Gujarat* (Mumbai, Research Centre for Women's Studies, SNDT Women's University, 1999), p. 161; A. Sharma, *supra* note 62; International Center for Research on Women (ICRW) (1999–2002), Domestic Violence in India, vols. 1–5 (Washington, DC, USAID/India, 1999–2002), pp. 32–65.

[64] It promoted women's equality along with health, literacy and non-formal education, savings, political involvement, and community development initiatives. The program uses "conscientization" and "empowerment" to describe the process by which women collectively become aware of their situations and take action to address their problems (A. Sharma, *supra* note 62).

[65] International Center for Research on Women (ICRW) (1999–2002), *supra* note 63, p. 70.

[66] A. Sharma, *supra* note 62.

in some contexts and as a government program in others. Personnel are paid by the government but are not government employees and receive less than government workers.[67] The largely female work force lacks job security, pensions and health benefits and is poorly paid.[68]

During the first 4 years of the MS program, participants were trained by Jagori, a feminist resource and training center in Delhi.[69] Seventeen women were trained as paralegals with a feminist critique of the legal system and alternative definitions of violence against women and divorce.[70] When I visited Jagori in 2001, the director said that the program puts a strong emphasis on women's rights but that their concepts are inspired more by national than international law. They sometimes refer to international conventions and treaties but Indian sources are more important.

Since violence in the home was a major concern to many of the village women, the women's collectives developed a system of women's courts to handle domestic violence, divorce, and other family conflicts. The system of *nari adalats* emerged in Gujarat in 1995 and in Uttar Pradesh in 1998.[71] These were informal courts intended to handle women's legal problems. A 2001 study reported that in the 6 years since they were initiated, the four *adalats* in the Vadodara district handled about 1,200 cases of marital violence, harassment, divorce, maintenance, property, and child custody and successfully resolved a majority of these. The clients were mostly low caste and tribal women.[72]

The *nari adalat* consists of a core team of *sahyoginis* and selected *sangha* women, most of whom have poor literacy skills and many of whom are *dalits*, people of low caste status.[73] The members of the *nari adalat* tour the district, meeting at regular days and times in public places near government offices to dispense legal advice and settle marital disputes.[74] They are not paid nor is their transportation covered. They have no legal authority but rely on pressure and shaming. Like the parent MS program, they straddle the government/NGO divide, claiming either identity as it seems helpful.[75]

Krishnamurthy's ethnography describes how *nari adalats* move creatively between community and state to gain recognition in the villages and access to formal institutions.[76] The women meet in government compounds close to police and local government offices, assert their status as part of the official MS program, use state symbols such

[67] *Ibid.*

[68] In 1998 they received only slightly above the government-stipulated minimum wage for skilled work (A. Sharma, *supra* note 62, at footnote 42).

[69] Mekhala Krishnamurthy, *In the Shadow of the State, in the Shade of a Tree: The Politics of the Possible in Rural Gujarat* (BA thesis, Department of Social Sciences, Harvard University, 2002), p. 42.

[70] International Center for Research on Women (ICRW) (1999–2002), *supra* note 63, p. 49.

[71] International Center for Research on Women (ICRW) (1999–2002), *supra* note 63, p. 34.

[72] M. Krishnamurthy, *supra* note 69, p. 3, based on Annual MS Reports.

[73] International Center for Research on Women (ICRW) (1999–2002), *supra* note 63, p. 36.

[74] V. Poonacha and D. Pandey, *supra* note 63, pp. 161–178.

[75] A. Sharma, *supra* note 62.

[76] M. Krishnamurthy, *supra* note 69, pages 12 and 51.

as files, stamp paper, and seals, call on the police for protection, and cite formal laws to support their decisions as they were trained to do by urban activists. At the same time, they reflect the communities they come from. They use humor and shaming to pressure litigants, adjust their meeting times to the rhythms of village life, and use their knowledge of local practices, customs, and social networks to gather evidence and negotiate agreements. They do not try to end marriages but emphasize the rights of the woman within marriage.[77] Their authority is limited, and they seem to be most successful in helping women arrange divorces and escape violent marriages, particularly among poor families. They are less successful with wealthy families and with cases of rape and molestation, which require greater evidentiary effort.[78]

Nevertheless, an ICRW study in 1999–2000 indicated that the operation of these courts and the closely related *mahila panch* (Women's Councils) made violence in the home a more open and public offense. ICRW evaluations of these programs indicate that *sangha* and *sahyogini* women and those who experienced the *nari adalats* were more aware of their rights and better able to speak up.[79] A counter-culture based on resisting violence in terms of the intrinsic rights of women is developing slowly, largely in local terms: "Research documented the innovative ways in which activists use their local knowledge to reshape and reinterpret community idioms, phrases and beliefs to create and persuade the community to adopt new perspectives."[80] As they promote the ideology of human rights, some women say they have learned to stand up for themselves.

Although the MS program was a new initiative, it built on a familiar political structure, the panchayat. Panchayats for castes or villages are widespread in India and have deep historical roots.[81] A women's court is therefore an adaptation of an existing structure. In this hybrid example, the basic structure came from the local community and was overlaid with ideas of empowerment, development, and women's rights of both national and transnational origin. To what extent core ideas of human rights, such as equality among all people, the importance of making choices for oneself, and the integrity of the body became part of the practices of the nari adalats is hard to determine without further research. Ideas such as a woman's right to the return of some of her dowry at divorce and not to be treated cruelly have become more widespread, but these are notions already embedded in Indian law. Other ideas grounded in the human rights regime, such as gender equality, are probably far less widely accepted. Nevertheless, to some extent these courts did bring ideas of human rights to a grassroots legal institution.

The nari adalats relied on three levels of translation: the grassroots samgha women leaders, the sahyoginis, and the more educated and cosmopolitan Indian feminists who occupied leadership roles in the program and carried out the paralegal

[77] International Center for Research on Women (ICRW) (1999–2002), *supra* note 63, p. 51.

[78] *Ibid*, p. 99.

[79] *Ibid*, pp. 40–41, 54.

[80] International Center for Research on Women (ICRW) (1999–2002), *supra* note 63, p. 72.

[81] See Marc Galanter, *Law and Society in Modern India* (Delhi, Oxford University Press, 1989).

and human rights training. Many came from NGO backgrounds.[82] My recent research in Gujarat suggests that some of these innovative leaders have subsequently left the MS program and taken up leadership roles in independent NGOs promoting women's human rights. Both levels of translators were more educated and globally focused than the client population, but the sahyoginis were closer to the local communities they served than the NGO leaders. In contrast, in the Hong Kong batterer treatment program, the translator was an academic in the field of social work who had traveled in the US and was very familiar with the American literature on domestic violence interventions. In each case, the translator was socially and culturally intermediate, but the hybrid organization relied more on grassroots-level translators while the replication depended largely on an elite, cosmopolitan intermediary. Although I was not able to observe the training process, Berry's description of an Indian NGO focusing on women's development offers an instructive example. She describes how staff members use slides of pre-Aryan goddesses to develop a concept of *shakti*, or feminine spiritual power, as an image for Indian to think about their power to contest all forms of oppression against women.[83] Thus, it combines local practices and discourses drawn from elsewhere, including feminist discourses inside and outside India, to produce a hybrid feminist discourse of shakti. Her account of the activities of these village women's organizations, which include resolving conflicts over harassment and rape, concludes that this discourse produces new subjectivities which are embraced by members, but negotiated long with prior ones.[84] Thus, Berry offers another example of such a hybrid institution and delineates the multiple subjectivities which it evokes.

Unlike replications, which are thinly adapted to local circumstances, hybrids such as the nari adalats are thickly shaped by local institutions and structures. Replications retain the basic structure of the imported institution, such as a therapy groups for batterers, but overlay them with local symbols such as ideas of yi and face. Hybrids merge local structures such as councils with imported ideas such as women's human rights. It is likely that the different positioning of the intermediaries shapes the nature of vernacularization in each case. Hybrid adaptations draw more heavily on local institutions, knowledge, idioms, practices, and leaders than replications.

10.3 Conclusion: The Power and Vulnerability of the Translator

These examples show the power and vulnerability of the translator. The power of the translator is her ability to set the terms of the exchange and to channel it, but her vulnerability is in the limits she faces in her ability to persuade people with

[82] A. Sharma, *supra* note 62.

[83] K. Berry, *supra* note 20, at pp. 86–87.

[84] K. Berry, *supra* note 20, at pp. 94–96.

grievances to accept her interpretation and to induce elites to provide financial, social, and political support. The translator must walk a fine line between too much replication, in which case the new ideas will lose their appeal to local communities, and too much hybridity, in which case the reforms will lose the support of the global community, including its funding and publicity. There are, in other words, constraints on either end of the replication/hybridity continuum.

Moreover, intermediaries are always somewhat suspect since they are not fully in one world or the other. They could be traitors to either one, much as the village headman in British Central Africa was forced to serve two masters and pleasing neither. The Normland consultants in Ruritania were forced to rely on flawed information for their development planning, while the African managers used their mastery of technical language to avoid scrutiny. Of course, as in social movements generally, there is a continual processes of backtalk and reformulation in response to events and opportunities which redefines both the power and the limits of translation.[85]

The larger structure of economic and political power that surrounds human rights activism means that translation is largely a top-down process from the transnational to the local and the powerful to the less powerful. Local programs developed in affluent nations such as the US are more likely to circulate transnationally to poorer ones than vice versa. This uneven circulation is driven by funders. Since NGOs and social service programs are usually dependant on international foundations or foreign government funding, they need to present their work in a way that inspires these funders. Transnational human rights principles are effective in attracting international funding and garnering media attention. Organizations may adopt international human rights language even when this is not the most effective approach. Despite arguments that human rights must be translated into local webs of meaning based on religion, ethnicity, or place in order for them to appear both legitimate and appealing, translators must please their donors.

Consequently, human rights ideas are not fully indigenized, even though this might make them more readily accepted. They are embedded in a distinctive vision of the good society that envisions the state as the provider of social justice and the individual as responsible for making rights claims on the state. This vision assumes that all people have equal rights, although all do not have equal needs. As human rights are vernacularized, these conceptions of person, state, and community remain the same. The failure to fully indigenize these ideas impedes their spread, yet to do so would undermine their potential for change. Of course, these transnational imports are local conceptions from elsewhere that have been powered into the transnational domain by the economic and political power of their creators. As Grewal points out, human rights are Eurocentric in origin and inspiration yet at the same time are some of the only tools available to struggle for rights of the disenfranchised.[86]

---

[85] Marc W. Steinberg, *supra* note 27.

[86] Inderpal Grewal, "On the New Global Feminism and the Family of Nations: Dilemmas of Transnational Feminist Practice" in Ella Shohat (ed.), *Talking Visions: Multicultural Feminism in a Transnational Age* (New Museum of Contemporary Art, New York and MIT Press, Cambridge, MA, 1998), p. 501 at 507.

This is the paradox of making human rights in the vernacular: in order to be accepted, they have to be tailored to the local context and resonant with the local cultural framework. However, in order to be part of the human rights system, they must emphasize individualism, autonomy, choice, bodily integrity, and equality, ideas embedded in the legal documents that constitute human rights law. Whether this is the most effective approach to diminishing violence against women is still an open question. It is certainly an important part of the expansion of a modernist view of the individual and society embedded in the global North, which promotes it along with democracy, the rule of law, capitalism and the free market. That translators vernacularize these transnational institutions and ideas and negotiate the differences reflects these global inequalities.

Chapter 11
Thinking About Indigenous Legal Orders

Val Napoleon*

> Indigenous law can be hard to see when we are used to seeing law as something the Canadian government or police make or do. Some people may even have been taught that Indigenous people did not have law before white people came here. This is a lie. Law can be found in how groups deal with safety, how they make decisions and solve problems together, and what we expect people "should" do in certain situations (their *obligations*).... They are often practiced and passed down through individuals, families, and ceremonies. This is why many still survive, after all the government's efforts to stop them and sneer at them. Because of the presence of Canadian law, and the lies and efforts to stop Indigenous law, some Indigenous laws are sleeping. It is time to awaken them.[1]

11.1 Introduction

One of my Indigenous students said to me, "Just because something has 'always been done that way' does not make it law." This is certainly a valid observation, but his actual concern was whether Cree law could be considered real law or whether it is merely habit. The student's skepticism is not uncommon, and he was simply

*This article has been revised from the original version, which was written for the National Centre for First Nations Governance and published in 2007 online at http://fngovernance.org. The ideas contained herein were reworked and substantially developed in Val Napoleon, *Ayook: Gitksan Legal Order, Law, and Legal Theory* (PhD Dissertation, University of Victoria, 2009) [unpublished]. This dissertation is available online at http://dspace.library.uvic.ca

[1] Hadley Louise Friedland, *The Wetiko (Windigo) Legal Principles: Responding to Harmful People in Cree, Anishinabek and Saulteaux Societies – Past, Present and Future Uses, with a Focus on Contemporary Violence and Child Victimization Concerns*. (LLM Thesis, University of Alberta, 2009) [unpublished] at 15–16 [Friedland] [footnotes omitted].

V. Napoleon (✉)
Faculty of Law, University of Victoria,
V8W 2Y2 Victoria, BC, Canada
e-mail: napoleon@uvic.ca

R. Provost and C. Sheppard (eds.), *Dialogues on Human Rights and Legal Pluralism*, Ius Gentium: Comparative Perspectives on Law and Justice 17,
DOI 10.1007/978-94-007-4710-4_11, © Springer Science+Business Media Dordrecht 2013

drawing from his recent reading of western legal theory. There, he had encountered widely held assumptions about Indigenous legal orders and law that too often remain unchallenged. To fully appreciate the implications of the student's statement for Indigenous peoples requires some careful analysis. This paper is about analysing and challenging this statement and other gross simplifications about Indigenous legal orders and law.

There are many ways to think about law. Basically, how we think about law is shaped by our experiences and history. As Indigenous peoples, much of our current understanding of law derives from our experiences with the western legal system in Canada. We know this system through its courts, legislation, and enforcement, and by its treatment of our peoples, lands, and resources. Given this, many Indigenous peoples have come to associate "law" with power, punishment, hierarchy, and bureaucracy. In the case of my student, "real" law was clearly associated with formal, centralized state processes of determining what law is and how to apply it.

There is a broader and more useful way to think about law, including Indigenous law, beyond what we have come to know as western law. In this paper, I will describe how we might think about law so that it is more helpful to Indigenous peoples' work generally. Such a discussion includes asking questions about the sources of Indigenous law[2] and what its functions are. Thinking about law also raises questions about its legitimacy and authority, and how law changes over time. Such rigorous critical thinking about law can support the building of non-colonial relationships among Indigenous peoples and between Indigenous peoples and Canada.

Indigenous peoples have many intellectual resources, legal and political, that are available to us from our own histories and societies and that are needed for reasoning through today's complex struggles. Indigenous law is a crucial resource for Indigenous peoples. It is integrally connected with how we imagine and manage ourselves both collectively and individually. In other words, law and all it entails is a fundamental aspect of being collectively and individually self-determining as peoples. Indigenous law is about building citizenship, responsibility and governance, challenging internal and external oppressions, safety and protection, lands and resources, and external political relations with other Indigenous peoples and the state.

I use the term Indigenous legal traditions when referring to Indigenous legal protocols and laws. Legal traditions are deeply rooted and comprise "historically conditioned attitudes about the nature of law, role of law in the society and the polity, about the proper organization and operation of the legal system, and about the ways law is or should be made, applied, studied, perfected, and taught".[3] Of course, it is usually preferable to use Indigenous peoples' own language when referring to law and legal concepts. For example, the Gitksan people's word for law is *ayook*, which means law, custom, or precedent.

---

[2] For a wonderful discussion on the sources of Indigenous law, see John Borrows, *Canada's Indigenous Constitution* (Toronto: University of Toronto Press, 2010) 23–58 [Borrows].

[3] J.H. Merryman, *The Civil Law Tradition: An Introduction to the Legal Systems of Western Europe and Latin America* (Stanford: Stanford University Press, 1985) 1.

I use the term "legal system" to describe state-centred legal systems in which law is managed by legal professionals in legal institutions that are separate from other social and political institutions. For example, Canada and other nation states have such central legal systems. In contrast, I use the term "legal order" to describe law that is embedded in non-state social, political, economic, and spiritual institutions.[4] For example, Gitksan, Cree, and Dunne za peoples have legal orders. Indigenous law is a part of and derives from an Indigenous legal order. By distinguishing between legal systems and legal orders, I hope to avoid imposing western legal ideas onto Indigenous societies.

11.2 Locating Myself

By way of establishing my own experience with these issues: My family is from Saulteau First Nation located in northeast British Columbia's *Treaty 8* area. I am of Cree and Dunne za heritage.[5] For over 25 years my work was mainly with Gitksan and Wet'suwet'en peoples in northwest BC and included community activism and support for the *Delgamuukw*[6] legal action. I am an adopted member of the Gitanyow (Gitksan) house of Luuxhon. When I became a grandmother, I went to law school, and I was called to the BC bar in 2002. In 2009, I completed a PhD with the Faculty of Law at the University of Victoria. Currently, I am an associate professor with the Faculty of Law at the University of Victoria. In the course of my research, I work with Aboriginal peoples locally and regionally. Both inside and outside my work at the university, I advocate for academic and political diversity among Aboriginal peoples, and for ongoing gender analysis of all aspects of the larger Indigenous political project.

11.3 Seeing Indigenous Law

This paper is not intended to be a prescription for all Indigenous peoples' legal traditions. Rather, it draws on my experience with non-state, decentralized societies such as the Gitksan, Wet'suwet'en, Tsimshian, Cree, Dunne za, and Carrier peoples.

---

[4] Harold J. Berman, *Law and Revolution* (Cambridge: Harvard University Press, 1983) at 49–50.

[5] Saulteau First Nation located in northeast British Columbia (BC). This region is covered by *Treaty 8*, one of the numbered treaties, which also covers northern Alberta and part of the Northwest Territories. Northeast BC is the homeland of the Dunnezah peoples. By 1911, a group of Saulteaux peoples had moved into Dunne za territories. In 1914, the Saulteaux were "admitted" into *Treaty 8* without the usual negotiated adhesion process. In 1918, the Saulteaux took up residence at the eastern end of Moberly Lake where a reserve was set out for them. This community prefers the spelling "Saulteau."

[6] *Delgamuukw v. The Queen* (March 8, 1991) Smithers 0843 (BCSC); *Delgamuukw v. British Columbia* (1993), 104 DLR (4th) 470 (B.C.C.A.); and *Delgamuukw v. British Columbia*, [1997] 3 SCR 1010.

It offers a way to think about law in a theoretical framework that can be shaped according to different cultures, experiences, and histories. It is intended to relate more specifically to Indigenous peoples in western Canada. It definitely is not intended to represent or describe all Indigenous legal traditions in Canada or beyond.

Indigenous peoples were and are reasonable and reasoning peoples,[7] and law is one of the ways we govern ourselves. It is law that enables large groups of people to collectively manage themselves "against a backdrop of deep-seated normative disagreement" and to fashion "collective positions out of the welter of disagreement".[8] Law is a not a thing; it is a process that people actually engage in. Indigenous peoples applied law to harvesting fish and game, access to and the distribution of berries, the management of rivers, and the management of all other aspects of political, economic, and social life. Since our legal orders and law are entirely created within our cultures, it can be difficult to see and understand law in other cultures. In other words, law is societally bound – it is only law within the society that created it. Gitksan law is not law to Cree peoples, and vice versa.

I am referring to culture in the broadest sense – that which forms our horizon in the world and which includes politics, law, economics, and social orders. We can learn how to see law across cultures and societies, and we can agree to recognize other people's law through our various international arrangements. To do this we must pay attention to our own cultural biases so that we recognize them in our expectations, responses, and judgments of other peoples.[9] We have to take the time to understand how law makes sense in that other society.[10]

Law is never static, but rather, lives in each new context. In fact, one of the most important things to understand about any law is how it changes. And it has to change in order to be an effective part of governance – it has to be appropriate to new contexts and circumstances or it simply will not work. It also has to be appropriate to the experiences of the people or it will have no meaning or legitimacy. Rules are only a part of law. It is the thinking and reasoning processes that make law. Law is the intellectual process of deliberating and reasoning to apply rules according to the context. This was part of what my student was missing when he was questioning the validity of Cree law.

[7] Friedland, *supra* note 1 at 45.

[8] Jeremy Webber, "Naturalism and Agency in the Living Law" in Marc Hertogh, ed, *Living Law: Reconsidering Eugen* Ehrlich, Oñati International Series in Law and Society (Portland, OR: Hart, 2009) 201 at 202 [Webber, "Naturalism"]. Webber defines a normative order as "a natural dimension of any human interaction, generated through the day-to-day business of human life, perhaps even definitional of the existence of society" (at 201).

[9] William Alford, "On the Limits of 'Grand Theory' in Comparative Law" (1986) 61 Wash L Rev 945.

[10] See generally, William Ewald, "Comparative Jurisprudence (I): What Was It Like to Try a Rat?" (1994–95) 143 U Pa L Rev at 1889–1905, 1912–16, 1924–25, 1936–43.

11.3.1 Sources of Law

It is helpful to think of different kinds of law as a spectrum. Where we place law on the spectrum is determined by where we think law comes from – the sources of law. It would look like this[11]:

Law from Central Processes of Enactment	Law from Social Interaction	Law from the Divine or from Outside Human Beings
Known as Positive Law (Legal Positivism)	Known as Customary Law	Known as Natural Law
Law comes from a central authority through a formal process. (E.g., Canadian Constitution, *Indian Act*, etc.)	Law comes from the interaction between human beings that enables people to generally predict behaviours in a group. (E.g., resource-management law of decentralized peoples)	Law comes from a divine authority or from basic human characteristics.[12] (E.g., Ecclesiastical law, etc.)

Another way to think about sources of law is provided by John Borrows who argues that Indigenous societies have at least five sources of law: sacred, deliberative, custom, positive, and natural.[13] Borrows cautions against treating these sources as separate or artificially watertight because, in actuality, "Indigenous legal traditions usually involve the interaction of two or more… sources".[14] Arguably, all sources of law require interpretive choices and deliberation; it is in the articulation of these processes that one can create the necessary intellectual space to critically examine norms, power, and assumptions – as a part of the healthy exercise of agency and citizenship.

Since law is a cultural institution, societies that are organized centrally will have centralized processes for enacting law. This is the case for Canada, which is centrally organized as a nation state with hierarchical levels of law-making authority and adjudication. However, decentralized societies do not have formal, centralized processes for enacting law. For example, the Gitksan are a decentralized society made up of kinship groups known as "Houses".[15] The House is the basic political

[11] This is an extremely brief outline. There are volumes written about each area of law.

[12] But see the extensive work of John Finnis, *Natural Law and Natural Rights*, Clarendon Law Series (Oxford: Clarendon Press, 1980).

[13] Borrows, *supra* note 2 at 23.

[14] *Ibid.* at 55.

[15] Each Gitksan person is born into his or her mother's House, a matrilineal kinship group of about 150 persons who share a common ancestry. It is the House (*wilp*) that is the territory- and fishing site-owning entity. The term House originates from the historic longhouses, although members of the same House did not actually live under the one roof. Rather, House members were and are widely scattered by marriage and occupation. House members have rights and responsibilities in other Houses by virtue of their roles as spouses and clan members. See Richard Daly and Val Napoleon, "A Dialogue on the Effects of Aboriginal Rights Litigation and Activism on Aboriginal Communities in Northwestern British Columbia" (2003) 47:3 Social Analysis, The International Journal of Cultural and Social Practice 108.

unit of Gitksan society, and each one is closely interrelated with other Houses through kinship, marriage, and other relationships. All the Houses are part of the four larger clans.[16] While each Gitksan person is born into the mother's House, there are many reciprocal obligations to the father's House, spouse's House, and so on. Territories are held in trust by the House chiefs on behalf of the House members. This is a decentralized system because there is no big boss of all the Houses.

If historically there was no centralized Gitksan society, there was no centralized or official Gitksan enactment of law. However, the Gitksan did and do have law, the *ayook*, decentralized law which derives from the long-term social, economic, and political interactions of the members, House groups, and clans, and their interactions with non-Gitksan peoples. Gitksan peoples had collective ways of formalizing the law that derived from such social interactions over time. These explicit legal teachings are part of how Gitksan peoples managed themselves historically, and arguably, they are still reflected in contemporary governance functions. The main point here is that how we structure law reflects how we structure our societies. Indigenous societies that were more centrally organized will likely have more centralized legal orders, and so on.

Turning to natural law and sacred law: Some Indigenous peoples equate their own laws with the laws of the natural world and so describe their law as "natural law".[17] Other Indigenous peoples believe that their laws come from the Creator, and therefore consider them to be sacred.[18] However, since laws have to be interpreted by human beings, and law is not just rules, the conception of law as being natural or sacred needs further consideration and discussion. What are the consequences of law being sacred or natural? Who gets to say whether the law has been broken? How can people disagree with sacred law or natural law? Can sacred laws change? Can natural laws change?

There is an important difference between, on the one hand, believing that the laws themselves are spiritual and sacred, and outside human control, and on the other hand, understanding that all law, including western law, is founded on a world view of one sort or another (i.e., how we see human beings, non-human life forms, and the spirits and the universe). It is hard to perceive this in western law because it is always described as "normal" and "rational". But all law, including western law, is based on a

---

[16] Each Gitksan House belongs to one of the four larger clans (*pteex*), which share a broader history: the *Ganeda* (Frog), *Gisgahast* (Fireweed), *Lax Gibuu* (Wolf), and *Lax Skiik* (Eagle).

[17] There are a number of theories about natural law, each with different perspectives on morality, authority of legal norms, and beliefs about human beings. For example, in one school of thought, the term "natural law" is about the laws of nature such as the law of gravity. Another school of thought holds that the organization of centralized states is a natural extension of natural individual rights. See generally, *Wikipedia, The Free Encyclopedia*, online: Wikipedia http://en.wikipedia.org/wiki/Natural_law; online: *Internet Encyclopedia of Philosophy* http://www.iep.utm.edu/n/natlaw.htm.

[18] See generally, Harold Cardinal & Walter Hildebrandt, *Treaty Elders of Saskatchewan: Our Dream is That Our Peoples Will One Day Be Clearly Recognized as Nations* (Calgary: University of Calgary Press, 2000).

formative societal understanding of humans (e.g., individual, competitive, communal, etc.) and of the larger world (i.e., how humans relate to non-human life forms).

So if we understand law as being founded on our world views, including our norms and morals, and our relationship with the spirit world, then human beings are responsible for the interpretation, reasoning, and application of law. However, if we believe laws are sacred, our understanding about the responsibility of human beings can become reduced to following rules. It should be noted that just as there is great diversity among Indigenous peoples, there is also diversity within Indigenous communities. In any given community, there is a range of beliefs and resultant behaviours. Furthermore, these norms, or understandings of right and wrong, are contested at every level on which human beings live with one another – as they should be.

For instance, this critical question relates to the trend of creating hierarchies and turning elders into priest-like beings that are also sacred. What are the consequences of treating elders as if they were priests? Does this allow elders to admit when they do not know something? How is this reconcilable with the high incidence of elder abuse in our communities? How is this reconcilable with elders who are abusive? Can we disagree with elders? Is it a form of fundamentalism? Is this good governance? These are serious questions that require fearless on-the-ground exploration and much, much more discussion.

11.3.2 Kinds of Law

Law may be described as "a language of interaction" that is necessary for people's social behaviour to be meaningful and predictable.[19] It is this language of interaction that makes possible social settings where people's behaviours generally fall within expected or known patterns.[20] Citizens can manage their lives within this interactive framework. They know what to expect from one another – at least generally.

Law still functions as law whether it is centralized or decentralized. So what is it that law does? The basic characteristic of law is that it lays down general rules or baselines that people figure out how to interpret and apply.[21] Decentralized Indigenous legal orders fulfill the basic functions of law and enable people to manage themselves.

As with any legal tradition, some Indigenous law is implicit, or unsaid.[22] In other words, many Indigenous peoples are not aware of the law they know – they just take it for granted and they act on their legal obligations without talking about it.

---

[19] Lon L. Fuller, "Human Interaction and the Law" (1969) 14 Am J Juris 1 at 1.

[20] *Ibid.* at 2.

[21] *Ibid.* at 23.

[22] See Gerald Postema, "Implicit Law" in Willem Witteveen & Wibren van der Burg, eds, *Rediscovering Fuller: Essays on Implicit Law and Institutional Design* (Amsterdam: Amsterdam University Press, 1999) 255.

Indigenous societies also have explicit law that is explained and talked about, recorded and recalled, and deliberated. However, sometimes Indigenous peoples think that their laws have to look like western laws and so they try to describe them in western terms. Other times, like my law student, they fail to see Indigenous law as real law. This is not to suggest that Indigenous societies do not also centrally enact law today in the fulfilment of governance responsibilities.

11.3.3 Legal Reasoning

So what is the reasoning process that enables people to collectively make rules into law? Why does this reasoning process matter? In the common law, which we follow in Canada (except in Quebec), legal reasoning is sometimes called "artificial reasoning". This is because its form and structure are designed for a public forum where the reasoning is open to challenge. The actual reasoning is the result of practical experience that people collectively reflect on through an agreed structure and process. This is different from the individual reasoning that we do every day.[23]

Take, for example, how a historic Gitksan crest dispute is resolved. This process contains all the legal reasoning elements of law.[24] The Gitksan chiefs consider Gitksan law, past cases, circumstances, and histories. The reasoning and interpreting process of the Chiefs is known to the participants because it is conducted through both formal and informal public gatherings. Numbers of people are involved: those with direct interests, those with related interests, and those who could be considered neutral. These Gitksan reasoning processes occur within the context of Gitksan culture, institutions, history, and experiences. In other words, appreciating the wisdom of Gitksan law "lies in recognition of the internal point of view of participants in the legal system".[25]

Other Indigenous peoples also have processes by which legal reasoning and deliberation takes place. The challenge is to learn to recognize these processes because they can be implicit, informal, and decentralized. And it is critical to consider these laws from within their cultural and historical perspective so that they make sense as part of governance. We can comprehend and explore these processes by looking at both historic and contemporary conflicts, agreements, and ongoing arrangements between people. It is also important to consider interactions and conflicts over time so that we can recognize overall patterns and roles.[26] For instance,

[23] Gerald J. Postema, "Classical Common Law Jurisprudence (Part II)" (2003) 3:1 OUCLJ 1 at 10. Postema contends that the reason common law is artificial is that "it is the disciplined practice of argument and disputation in a public forum – an art that had been called *ratio artificialis* long before Coke gave it currency in common law jurisprudence".

[24] Val Napoleon, "Living Together: Gitksan Legal Reasoning as a Foundation for Consent" in Jeremy Webber & Colin McLeod, eds, *Challenges of Consent: Consent as the Foundation of Political Community in Indigenous/Non-Indigenous Contexts* (Vancouver: UBC Press, 2009) 45 [Napoleon].

[25] Gerald J. Postema, "Classical Common Law Jurisprudence (Part I)" (2002) 2:2 OUCLJ 155 at 155.

[26] See generally, Roderick Macdonald, *Lessons for Everyday Law* (Montreal: McGill University Press, 2002).

there is a current dispute regarding the southern boundary of *Treaty 8* in British Columbia.[27] The community of Lheidli T'enneh negotiated a modern treaty under the British Columbia Treaty Commission, but its proposed boundary overlaps that of *Treaty 8*. One way to resolve this dispute would be to explore the historic relationships between the Lheidli T'enneh peoples and the *Treaty 8* peoples. What created the overlap and how did people manage the overlap area in the past? What were the trade and intermarriage arrangements? What were the land tenure laws that applied to the disputed lands? How might these former conflicts and arrangements inform today's dispute?

Indigenous law is not stuck in the past. Rather, despite the damage to our legal orders, Indigenous peoples continue to act on historic legal obligations in modern forms wherever they can. For example, it is arguable that the work that many people do at the community level with various Aboriginal justice initiatives is rooted in their historic legal obligations in their own legal orders.[28]

11.3.4 Legitimacy

All peoples have to believe that the legal order and law are legitimate before they will countenance them; if they do not, decisions will have no meaning. This does not mean that all parties involved in a decision will get what they want; rather, that even when they do not get their way, they will still abide by the decision. After all, as Jeremy Webber has pointed out, "all law – non-state law as well as state law – is inherently non-consensual, [and] is always to some extent peremptory and imposed, establishing a collective position against a backdrop of deep-seated normative disagreement".[29] What is important then, is to focus on the "means by which contestation is settled".[30]

This becomes another piece of the work involved with Indigenous legal orders and law. What makes the legal order and law legitimate? This question is complicated because in recent times, Indigenous laws have been broken without consequences (e.g., alienation of land and resources, violence, failed kinship obligations, etc.). When laws are broken with no recourse, the legal order begins to break down, and this has been the experience of Indigenous peoples. This is one of the reasons that western courts and lawmakers are so concerned with actions that might bring western law into "disrepute". If the law looks ridiculous, it fails as a governance function. It no longer enables groups of people to manage themselves.

This does not make working with Indigenous legal orders and law impossible. It is simply another factor in the work. It is a reality that our legal institutions have

[27] Val Napoleon, *Indigenous Legal Lodge Proposal for Treaty 8,* (2008) [unpublished, archived with author].

[28] Val Napoleon, Angela Cameron, Colette Arcand, & Dahti Scott, "Where Is the Law in Restorative Justice" in Yale Belanger, ed, *Aboriginal Self-Government* (Purich, 2008) 348.

[29] Webber, "Naturalism", *supra* note 8 at 202.

[30] Napoleon, *supra* note 24 generally.

been damaged, so we can consider the extent of the damage and start from there. And given that there is no pure, static law anyway, this is not a problem. We can learn from the present while drawing what is useful from the past.

For the Gitksan, the legitimization of the Gitksan legal order and law takes place horizontally among the members on a decentralized basis, and not vertically as when the government is centralized. Gitksan law was effectively approved and integrated into a body of law, and into people's daily lives. Also, approval of Gitksan law is evidenced in the ongoing management and resolution of disputes.[31] The nature of this consent, and therefore the authority of Gitksan law, is that Gitksan people agreed to live with how the disputes are handled and with the outcomes. The major agreements continue to be affirmed in the Feast hall through time and are witnessed in formal public processes.[32] That is, we know it exists because we can see it at work.

This becomes much more complicated when the various contemporary governing structures represent band and tribal organizations rather than kinship systems. The challenge is to effectively reconcile the modern and historic forms of governance and law-making authorities at the local level.

Many behaviours that create conflict today observe historical ethics regarding authority and legitimacy. For example, the Innu in Labrador practiced conflict avoidance. This worked well with small highly mobile groups of people that were able to travel across a large territory. However, since the establishment of settled communities, the cultural practice of conflict avoidance no longer works. In fact, when people are living close together, the practice of conflict avoidance actually makes the conflict worse.[33]

---

[31] *Ibid.* at 24.

[32] On this point, I agree with Jeremy Webber's scepticism as to the adequacy of the language of consent and whether consent can actually be deliberately and explicitly provided to form the political basis of societies. See Jeremy Webber, "Challenges of Consent" (Paper prepared for the Inaugural 2004 Conference of the Consortium on Democratic Constitutionalism: "Consent as the Foundation for Political Community"), online: University of Victoria http://www.law.uvic.ca/demcon/2004_program.htm at 2. According to Webber, dialogic theories of consent conceptualize "a community's legitimacy as a function of the quality of its interactions, rather than of an historic (and indeed generally mythical) act of adherence" (at 22).

[33] Hedda Schuurman suggests that the current conception of "community" does not derive from Innu language or culture, and the experience of living within a fixed settlement is entirely foreign. Historically, Innu lived in small, mobile social units with a dynamic pattern of social organization and coherent identities, but with shifting social and geographic boundaries. One of the consequences of 1960s settlements has been a social stratification of subgroups that were created by contact – external privileging according to the degree of acculturation or isolation of the subgroups. This hierarchy now determines status, social positions, and political leadership. For the Innu, settlement has meant individual households, a cash economy and dependence, changes to Innu economic and social practices, breakdown of social relationships, centralized schools, and increased conflict. According to Schuurman, settlement has resulted in an anti-community consciousness that raises particular difficulties for leadership and the implementation of self-government. See Hedda Schuurman, "The Concept of Community and the Challenge for Self-Government" in Colin Scott, ed, *Aboriginal Autonomy and Development in Northern Quebec and Labrador* (Vancouver: UBC Press, 2001) 379.

Among the Gitksan, this historical cultural ethic of decentralization still operates in the form of individual and collective resistance to hierarchy and centralization.[34] While these cultural ethics are powerful forces, for the most part they remain unexamined. This means that part of the work necessary for understanding Indigenous legal orders and laws is to identify underlying cultural ethics so that they can be discussed. People will have to explore the original purpose of the behaviour and decide how to change or reconcile cultural ethics in present-day circumstances. It may be that some of the behaviours are no longer appropriate, but first people have to "see" them and talk about them. Otherwise, the cultural ethics may be causing people to unknowingly react by sabotaging well-intentioned political efforts and organizations.

All peoples have conflict. Conflict in and of itself is not the problem. The challenge is not preventing conflict, but managing it effectively so that it does not paralyze people. This is one of the functions of law – including Indigenous law. Damage to Indigenous peoples' conflict management systems and law has resulted in increased conflict that is destructive. The result is that many people no longer know how to constructively deal with conflict.[35]

11.4 Where Is Indigenous Law Recorded?

> Some people say Indigenous laws can be found in stories, dreams, dances, art, in the world around us and in how we live our lives. Some people say they are "written on our hearts".[36]

How, then, do people in oral societies record their laws? The law of the Tlicho Nation is recorded in the place names.[37] The names are a record of the historic events that took place and are tied to the oral narratives. From listening to the name of a site, a Tlicho person is able to learn what happened at that place, who was involved, how it was resolved or dealt with, what was important in the event,

[34] Richard Daly, *Our Box Was Full: An Ethnography for the Delgamuukw Plaintiffs* (Vancouver: UBC Press, 2005) at 202.

[35] For example, Adrian Tanner explains that since settlement, the Innu have experienced an epidemic of general dysfunction and social breakdown. The former practice for dealing with disputes was primarily avoidance; when a dispute occurred, hunting groups split up. However, once people settled in villages, this conflict avoidance was not longer possible. According to Tanner, while self-government offers the Innu a way to address their problems, a new conception of community must be developed that is based on Innu values and that is acceptable to the larger Canadian society. See Adrian Tanner, "The Double Bind of Aboriginal Self-Government" in Colin Scott, ed, *Aboriginal Autonomy and Development in Northern Quebec and Labrador* (Vancouver: UBC Press, 2001) 397.

[36] Friedland, *supra* note 1 at 16.

[37] John B. Zoe, Chief Executive Officer of the Tlicho Nation, spoke at a public gathering in Edmonton at the University of Alberta on 20 March 2006.

and how this information applies to his or her own behaviour.[38] The place names also provide important information about the land itself, such as the type of vegetation, water and resources, and other conditions necessary to living and surviving on the land.

Indigenous peoples' law is also recorded in our traditions and practices.[39] Sometimes it takes more thinking to see the usefulness and practical application of these traditions – or, for that matter, their uselessness. And sometimes looking at traditions can be a little confusing. For example, I was told the following story: A dispute arose in a school regarding the keeping of sweet grass. Some of the community members were angry at what they saw as disrespectful treatment of sweet grass because it was left out on a desk. They argued that the sweet grass was supposed to be kept in a jar and put away in an enclosed place. An old person with a long memory was consulted. This person explained that it was because of the Church and the Indian agent's disapproval that it became "wrong" to have sweet grass out in the open. In response to this, people put the sweet grass in jars so that the priests and Indian agent could not smell it, and they hid it away so the priests and Indian agent could not see it. Now it is a different time and it is no longer necessary to hide the sweet grass. So in this case, it was important to recall the original purpose of hiding the sweet grass. Traditions have to have a useful purpose, and to figure out whether this is still the case, the practices have to be discussed. If the practice no longer has a useful purpose, then people need to think about changing it.[40]

Then what is the goal of a tradition? What is its effect? For example, what is the effect of celebrating the first saskatoon berry or the first spring salmon? What is the effect of making an offering of food to the spirits before eating at a feast? In part, this is about being grateful for the food, sharing the food, acknowledging the enormity of the universe and our place in it, and understanding our own place within the world. There is more, but this a start to drawing out some of the principles contained in the traditions that support Indigenous laws. We must be critical and rigorous about this. There is no room for romantic notions or idealism. Romanticism will not enable us to govern ourselves and relate to others on the power of our own ability to govern ourselves. We must apply the same critical thought to our Indigenous legal orders and laws as we do to western law.

Many Indigenous peoples recorded their laws in their oral histories and oral traditions. In the case of the Gitksan, it is the *adaawk* (owned, formal, collective

---

[38] See "The Habitat of Dogrib Traditional Territory: Place Names as Indicators of Bio-geographical Knowledge", online: West Kitikmeot Slave Study http://www.wkss.nt.ca/HTML/08_ProjectsReports/08_habitat/08_habDogribTT.htm

[39] See generally, H. Patrick Glenn, *Legal Traditions of the World, Sustainable Diversity in Law*, 2nd ed (Oxford: Oxford University Press, 2004).

[40] This incident was shared by Matthew Wildcat during a class discussion at the University of Alberta (spring term, 2006). It was related to Matthew by his father, Brian Wildcat. According to Matthew, the reason that this elderly person was so forthright was that he was not forced into a position of defending a cultural practice against imposed change. Rather, the issue was dealt with as a community education matter in which community members' experiences and ideas were valued.

oral histories) that preserves the identity and history of a House with its owned territories, crests, songs, names, major events, and relationships with other Houses. As Richard Overstall writes, this is a legal order of embedded law:

> The Gitxsan legal order has evolved as the result of people observing the consequences of their behaviour over time. When the behaviour is disrespectful of spirits, animals, and others, the consequences are dire and are often recorded in adaawk, especially if the behaviour alters a lineage's relationship with its territory. The adaawk thus have a role as legal precedents that inform later conduct.[41]

The Cheyenne,[42] Tlicho, Navajo, and many, many other Indigenous peoples recorded their law in their oral histories. Again, the work involves developing a careful perspective from inside the culture to identify and examine the legal precedents, principles, and content of the laws.

Finally, Indigenous law was often recorded inside peoples' relationships with one another. Turning again to the Gitksan: it is in the roles and relationships that peoples' legal obligations are found. Wherever one is within the Gitksan kinship network, there are definite roles and reciprocal obligations to others through that network. An individual's responsibility extends to the members in their mother's House and closely aligned Houses, father's House, grandparents' Houses on both sides, and spouse's House. Practically, this means that one is responsible for addressing injuries caused by others, education, providing access to land and resources, and so on. And since these are reciprocal obligations, there are obligations through these networks back to the individual.

The Cree also have reciprocal legal responsibilities and obligations that are contained within the kinship networks. Described as a Cree law, the doctrine of *wâhkôhtwowin* guides the conduct and behaviour that must be maintained in all types of relationships.[43] These relationships include mother and child, cousins and other relatives, and unrelated persons. All one has to know is where one fits, and the surrounding relationships determine what one has to do in order to fulfill their responsibilities in that society.[44] Similarly, the larger group, whether organized into matrilineal or into patrilineal kinship networks, will know their obligations to the individual. In considering social relationships and practices as a source of law, we must ask what people recognize and treat as law.[45]

---

[41] Richard Overstall, "Encountering the Spirit in the Land: 'Property' in a Kinship-Based Legal Order" in John McLaren, ed, *Despotic Dominion: Property Rights in British Settler Societies* (Vancouver: UBC Press, 2005) 22 at 40. Also see M. Jane Smith, *Placing Gitxsan Stories in Text: Returning the Feathers. Guuxs Mak'am Mik'Aax* (PhD Dissertation, UBC Faculty of Education, 2004) [unpublished, archived with the author].

[42] See generally, K.N. Llewellyn & E. Adamson Hoebel, *The Cheyenne Way* (Norman: University of Oklahoma Press, 1941).

[43] Cardinal & Hildebrandt, *supra* note 18 at 34.

[44] Conversation between the author and Wes Fineday, March 2005, Saskatoon, Sask.

[45] See Brian Z. Tamanaha, "A Non-Essentialist Version of Legal Pluralism" (2000) 27:2 JL & Soc'y 296 at 319. According to Tamanaha, "[L]egal pluralists currently tend to see law in far more places than general social practices would support"(at 320).

11.5 Territory – How Far Does the Legal Order Go?

External boundaries have always been sites of ongoing negotiations in accordance with each Indigenous group's laws and political structures. At the most basic level, each group's legal order extends over their territory, and at its farthest reaches, another group's territory begins.[46] Historically, each Indigenous group's territory was the area they could defend both physically and legally according to their Indigenous legal orders. International Indigenous laws and protocols enabled each group of people to maintain and protect their relationships with other peoples through time.

The discussion about resources and land raises three critical questions: Who is included in the Indigenous legal order? What territory does the legal order extend to? How does the law relate to other peoples' law at the farthest reaches of the territory? For the most part, these questions require Indigenous peoples to go beyond band structures in order to consider scale, the concepts of the public good and personal interests, accountability, and the full extent of the relationships and responsibilities within the society. The reserve boundaries created by the *Indian Act*,[47] which divided and grouped Indigenous peoples into bands, cut across the Indigenous legal orders. This division of Indigenous peoples and lands has undermined the management of the larger legal orders and the application of Indigenous laws. At the band level, the larger legal order becomes unworkable because it is disconnected, and some co-operative arrangements must be established to enable bands to draw upon broader-based relationships at a national level to more effectively implement their laws.

As an example, the Tsimshian people are divided into seven bands with a number of small reserves. Many Tsimshian people live off reserve. The Tsimshian legal order operates along kinship lines. In Tsimshian society, the legal obligations for dealing with a Tsimshian person's injuries are with his or her father's House. Members of the father's House can live anywhere, on or off reserve. If only the band membership is considered in the case of an injury to a Tsimshian band member, then all the other Tsimshian people, living either on other reserves or off reserve, that have obligations in the kinship system are excluded from fulfilling their responsibilities. The Tsimshian legal order extends throughout Tsimshian territory and cannot work if its orientation is only at the band level. So people should ask, who does the legal order apply to and how far does it extend? What happens at the edge of the territory with other peoples' laws?

---

[46] This is not to suggest that there could only be one system of law in a physical or geographic space. The reality is always much more complicated. Trade and other ways of establishing and maintaining international relationships meant that people were constantly negotiating different legal orders in the same space.

[47] *Indian Act*, RSC 1985, c. I-5.

11.6 Power and Gender

> I came to [Cree] *wetiko* law wanting help with a particular issue: How to respond to the violence and child victimization today in a principled and effective way? I have concluded that the *wetiko* can be seen as a legal concept, that the thinking and theorizing about *wetiko* dynamics is similar to the current thinking and theorizing about offenders and child victimization dynamics, and that there are several identifiable legal principles in the *wetiko* stories and accounts.[48]
>
> …
>
> …I think *wetiko* law is a meaningful and useful resource for facing the violence and victimization in some communities. We need something that teaches us how to protect those we love, from those we love.[49]

There are a couple of common arguments made against Indigenous law: First, that Indigenous law is incapable of dealing with complex present-day issues. Second, that Indigenous law will allow Indigenous peoples to violate human rights.

It is true that, historically, life was hard, but Indigenous peoples did not have to deal with the pervasiveness of violence, crime, and addictions found in some Indigenous communities today. (In fact, had these terrible conditions existed pre-contact, Canada would very likely have been truly *terra nullius*.) However, sorting out Indigenous legal traditions does not mean trying to return to the past. Rather, it is about drawing on the strengths and principles of Indigenous legal orders to deal with contemporary issues – including complex social dysfunctions as Hadley Friedland so effectively argues.[50] Such efforts should be developed in light of current problems as well as the western legal system. Again, if we understand law to be collaborative and to be a function of governance, then that could be a helpful basis for our responses to problematic social dysfunction.

Internal oppression and power imbalances present another reality that all Indigenous people – like anyone else – have to consciously guard against. Sexism is a reality. Homophobia is a reality. Ageism (despite the rhetoric) is a reality. Many of our communities are not safe places for our children and other vulnerable individuals.[51] Law is one way to deal with questions of oppression and the abuse of power. If we understand law as an intellectual process that all citizens engage in, then we can use that process to enable people to tackle the uncomfortable issues in our communities. In order to remain alive, Indigenous legal orders and law must be able to withstand internal challenges and change. It is this ongoing challenge to norms that keeps a culture alive and vital – and ensures continued relevance for younger people.[52]

---

[48] Friedland, *supra* note 1 at 123.

[49] *Ibid.* at 126.

[50] *Ibid.* generally.

[51] For the latest in the grim statistics on Aboriginal victims and offenders, see online: Statistics Canada www.statcan.ca/daily-quotedien/060606/dq060606b-eng.htm

[52] For a very interesting critique of how harmony is used to stifle internal conflict and challenges to the status quo, see Laura Nader, *Harmony Ideology: Justice and Control in a Zapotec Mountain Village* (Stanford, Cal.: Stanford University Press, 1990).

Otherwise, Indigenous law will fail to be useful in today's world, and if it is not useful, there is no point in teaching or practicing it. Our young people will continue to turn away in spite of our rhetoric.

On the subject of gender: One of the key issues is the inclusion of Indigenous women. If one examines the Aboriginal rights and title case law and discussion, it appears that Indigenous women have been erased from both the geographical and the legal landscape.[53] It is as if women did not have an important and active presence on the land. The literature and images of Indigenous peoples focus almost entirely on males and their activities – hunting, fishing, and trapping. In this colonial mythology, women's role is restricted to dealing with what the men bring home from the hunt.[54]

These issues are real and current, and it is our responsibility to deal with the tough stuff and ensure that our legal orders and law are up to the task. Since power dynamics are always a part of social relationships, we need to ask whose power is preserved through oppressive cultural, legal, or social norms. Whose voices are excluded? We have to be fearless in looking at our own cultural institutions too – not just those modelled on western governance. When an oppressive cultural practice is identified, determine what the goal of the practice is, then work out how to meet that goal without oppression.

11.7 Summing Up

I have proposed here that Indigenous legal orders and law should be understood as a necessary part of governance, including the safety and protection of those who are marginalized within Indigenous societies. It is not about trying to go back in time, but about drawing on the strengths and principles of the past to deal with modern-day problems and situations. A deeper and more critical understanding of Indigenous legal traditions can strengthen today's governance structures and functions.

The theory underlying this paper is that it is possible to develop a flexible, overall legal framework that Indigenous peoples might use to express and describe their legal orders and laws so that they can be applied to present-day problems. This framework must be able to (*i*) reflect the legal orders and laws of decentralized (i.e., non-state) Indigenous peoples, and (*ii*) allow for the diverse way that each society is reflected in their legal orders and law. In turn, this framework will allow each society to draw on a deeper understanding of how their own legal traditions might be used to resolve contemporary conflicts, complex social injustices, and human rights violations.

---

[53] Gerdine Van Woudenberg, "Placing Gender in the Mediation of Aboriginal Resource Claims and Conflicts" (2004) 34:3 Recherches Amérindiennes au Québec.

[54] Christine Miller & Patricia Chuchryk, eds, *Women of the First Nations* (Winnipeg: University of Manitoba, 1996).

The Canadian state is not going away and the past cannot be undone. This means that Indigenous peoples must figure out how to reconcile former decentralized legal orders and law with a centralized state and legal system. Any process of reconciliation must include political deliberation on the part of an informed and involved Indigenous citizenry. Rethinking Indigenous legal traditions is fundamentally about rebuilding citizenship. We have to answer the question, "Who are we beyond colonialism?"

Chapter 12
Wives' Tales on Research in Bountiful

Angela Campbell*

12.1 Introduction

Three years ago, while completing a research study on polygamy for Status of Women Canada (SWC),[1] I was contacted by several women from a community in British Columbia where plural marriage is a way of life. Known as "Bountiful," this community was founded 60 years ago by individuals who identify themselves as fundamentalist Mormons and adhere openly to polygamy as a central tenet of their faith. Some women from the community (or who had recently left it) who had

---

This chapter was first published as an article: (2008) 23: 1–2 Can J L & Soc 121. Since that time, the research project envisioned in this paper has been carried out, the results of which have been published elsewhere (see Angela Campbell, "Bountiful's Plural Marriages" (2010) 6:4 Int'l JL Context *343:* Angela Campbell "Bountiful Voices" (2009) 47 Osgoode Hall L J 183). Additionally, the reader should keep in mind that since the time of original publication, the constitutionality of Canada's criminal prohibition against polygamy has been tested and upheld in a reference conducted by the Supreme Court of British Columbia (*Reference re: Section 293 of the Criminal Code of Canada*, 2011 BCSC 1588). Prior to this reference judgment, two prosecutions were initiated on the basis of polygamy, although these were quashed on procedural grounds (*Blackmore v. British Columbia* (*Attorney General*), 2009 BCSC 1299). As of the date of this publication, no further criminal charges for polygamy have been laid in Canada.

*The author acknowledges support from the Social Sciences and Humanities Research Council of Canada and thanks: Kristin Ali, Sarah Berger Richardson, Robert Leckey, Desmond Manderson, Roderick Macdonald, Gillian Nycum, Krista Stout, Mariana Valverde and Shauna Van Praagh for insights and comments on earlier drafts of this paper and Maurice Onichino for encouragement while writing this text.

[1] Angela Campbell, "How Have Policy Approaches to Polygamy Responded to Women's Experiences and Rights? An International, Comparative Analysis" in Status of Women Canada, *Polygamy in Canada: Legal and Social Implications for Women and Children: A Collection of Policy Research Reports* (Ottawa: Status of Women Canada, 2005).

A. Campbell (✉)
Faculty of Law, Institute for Comparative Law,
McGill University, H3A 1W9, Montreal, QC, Canada
e-mail: angela.campbell@mcgill.ca

R. Provost and C. Sheppard (eds.), *Dialogues on Human Rights and Legal Pluralism*, Ius Gentium: Comparative Perspectives on Law and Justice 17,
DOI 10.1007/978-94-007-4710-4_12,

become aware of SWC's commissioned research on polygamy sought to initiate discussions about their polygamous life. They wished to be interviewed and consulted by researchers so that their experiences could form part of our knowledge bases. They asked: If the academic reports prepared for SWC were going to wield some impact on Canada's legal approach to polygamy, shouldn't the authors know what it is like to be a married to a polygamist, to live in a polygamous community and to raise children in this setting?[2]

While these points were compelling, logistical reasons precluded consultation with the women of Bountiful while preparing my report.[3] Since that time, however, my thoughts have been drawn to questions prompted by my conversations with these women. In particular, I have considered whether academics and policymakers can credibly assess and write about polygamy without hearing from those who abide by this practice, and if so how. Furthermore, because polygamy's most common manifestation is poly*gyny* (that is, where a man takes several concurrent wives), and very few societies globally espouse poly*andry* (the practice by women of having multiple husbands),[4] should we not focus specifically on accessing the experiences of *women* associated with this way of life? [5] Motivated by these questions, I now embark on a project that centres on consultation and dialogue with women in the plural marriage society of Bountiful, with a view to understanding the effectiveness of Canada's legal approaches to polygamy. My ambition is to gather insights from these women about what it means to be a "co-wife" in Bountiful, while simultaneously an "outlaw" in broader Canadian society.

This paper accomplishes the first step in this broader project by exploring research strategies designed to access and record the narratives of women within a plural marriage society, with a view to enhancing legal and popular knowledge about polygamy in Canada. It does so through reliance on scholarship that explores methods for conducting reflexive research from a feminist viewpoint. More specifically, as a professor of law interested in how normative frameworks affect – and are affected by – the ordinary experiences of individuals (in this case, polygamous wives), my focus here is on texts,

[2] Canadian law generally rejects polygamy. The *Criminal Code*, R.S.C. 1985, c. C-46, prohibits the practices of "bigamy" (s. 290(1)) and "polygamy" (s. 293(1)). Bigamy involves participating in the ceremony of marriage while already married, or with someone who is known to be married. Rather than the *act* of marriage, polygamy centres on the *status* of having more than one spouse, or being in a conjugal union with more than one person, simultaneously. See *ibid.* at 1. In this paper, "polygamy" refers to the simultaneous sharing of a husband by two or more women.

Canada's civil laws also resist the idea of plural marriage. See *Civil Marriage Act*, S.C. 2005, c.33, which limits the number of spouses who may marry to two.

[3] Two logistical reasons limited the ability to engage in empirical research that would have allowed for my SWC research to be based upon interviews with the women of Bountiful. The first of these was time, given that the SWC reports were prepared in just 3 months. A second obstacle was financial: because my budget from SWC did not plan for travel to Bountiful to conduct empirical research, I was unable to pursue this avenue of investigation.

[4] Campbell, *supra* note 1 at 9.

[5] For a discussion of the centrality of women's experiences to a feminist research inquiry focused on the interface between state law and religious law, and on the normative plurality within each of these frameworks, see Shauna Van Praagh, "The Chutzpah of Chasidism" (1996) 11 C.J.L.S. 193.

developed primarily by legal scholars, which debate methods for pursuing feminist research about genderized cultural practices.[6]

While this existing body of literature offers valuable research strategies for a project like mine on polygamy, it is limited by the fact that discussions are not grounded in any particular place, so as to apply and test the limits of the research techniques they develop. In this paper, I aim to do just this. That is, I examine two principal research strategies oriented toward promoting feminist and cultural pluralist objectives, and link these to the distinct setting of Bountiful, British Columbia. I rely on these strategies to develop a distinctly *juridical* analysis, that is, one which seeks to critique and test normative assertions about tradition, gender and community. More precisely, this analysis resists an uncritical acceptance of formal, state-based law as protector of women's interests, while at the same time rigorously assessing the legitimacy of bare claims about cultural norms and expectations. Thus, the application of this research framework to a study of polygamy in Bountiful should serve to expand our depth of knowledge about how women are affected by plural marriage, and by law's response to this practice, in this distinct setting.

12.2 Accessing and Giving Credence to Women's Varied Experiences

Current stories about plural marriage in Canada tell us little about how women experience quotidian life as polygamous wives. These stories, which emanate from: the media, government officials, popular non-fiction literature, and scholars who have relied primarily on secondary sources, often cast these women as exploited and damaged.[7] What fails to emerge, however, is knowledge about how apparently marginalized actors, like wives in Bountiful, might at once be both influenced by,

[6] Arguably, use of the term "cultural practices" is problematic; all practices can be traced to some idea of culture, and distinguishing between behaviours adopted for "cultural" versus other reasons (e.g., economic or social) is next to impossible. See discussion *infra* note 56 and accompanying text. However, in this paper, I refer to the terms "culture" and "cultural practices" as they appear in legal scholarship and in popular discussions in Canada pertaining to multiculturalism and approaches to accommodating diversity. At the same time, I recognize that this use leaves aside some of the most important complex questions inherent to the notion of culture, such as what exactly it embraces, and what ends can and should be effected by invoking this term.

[7] In terms of academic studies, see Rebecca J. Cook & Lisa M. Kelly, *Polygyny and Canada's Obligations Under International Human Rights Law* (Ottawa: Department of Justice Canada, 2006); Marla Peters, *Pearls Before Swine: Secrecy in a Mormon Polygynous Colony* (M.A. Thesis, University of Alberta, Department of Sociology, 1994) [unpublished]; Nicolas Bala *et al.*, "An International Review of Polygamy: Legal and Policy Implications for Canada" in Status of Women Canada, *Polygamy in Canada: Legal and Social Implications for Women and Children; A Collection of Policy Research Reports* (Ottawa: Status of Women Canada, 2005); and Alberta Civil Liberties Research Centre, "Separate and Unequal: The Women and Children of Polygamy" in Status of

and pivotal in shaping, the normative frameworks by which they live. This project seeks to garner such knowledge by moving beyond existing accounts of plural marriage, and by engaging in discussions with the women of Bountiful about how they interpret, manage and adhere to the rules of polygamy and the rules of the Canadian state. In this way, it seeks to leave aside assumptions about whether polygamy is inherently harmful and embedded in gender bias, and seeks to develop a more tangible sense of how women and the tenets of polygamy are affected by each other.[8]

While the value to my project of women's experiential knowledge is clear, the process of acquiring this knowledge is marred by practical and conceptual challenges. At a practical level, a researcher might face difficulty conferring with women in closed cultural groups who hesitate to speak with "outsiders" to their community. It might also be impossible to identify the constituents who would offer diverse and representative perspectives. At a more conceptual level, a researcher must contend with the argument that women in apparently oppressive patriarchal settings bear false consciousness. In this part, I consider these challenges and possible ways to address them.

12.2.1 The Value of Multiple Perspectives

Limits to understanding what a tradition means for various members of a cultural group arise when just the most powerful members of a community speak for the group and its traditions. Hearing just this elite tier further disenfranchises group

---

Women Canada, *Polygamy in Canada: Legal and Social Implications for Women and Children; A Collection of Policy Research Reports* (Ottawa: Status of Women Canada, 2005).

Similar insights are offered in popular accounts of polygamy: see Committee on Polygamous Issues, *Life in Bountiful – A report on the lifestyle of a polygamous community*, funded by the B.C. Ministry of Women's Equality (April 1993); Debbie Palmer & Dave Perrin, *Keep Sweet: Children of Polygamy* (Lister, B.C.: Dave's Press, 1994); Jon Krakauer, *Under the Banner of Heaven: A Story of Violent Faith* (New York: Anchor Books, 2004); Carolyn Jessop, *Escape* (New York: Broadway Books, 2007); and in media reports on the topic: see Richard C.C. Peck Q.C., *Report of the Special Prosecutor for Allegations of Misconduct Associated with Bountiful, BC: Summary of Conclusions*, online: <http://www.canada.com/vancouversun/news/extras/bountiful.pdf>; Stephanie Levitz, "Prosecutor tells BC: find out once and for all if anti-polygamy law stands" *Macleans* (1 August 2007), online: Macleans.ca <http://www.macleans.ca/education/wire/article.jsp?content=n0801135A>; and Daphne Bramham, "A Win for Those Who Want to Halt Abuses at Bountiful" *Vancouver Sun* (21 August 1997), online: Canada.com: <http://www.canada.com/vancouversun/features/polygamy/story.html?id=273ac6f3-9436-4ca6-8efe-1ab9072e8017&k=31961>.

[8] As Marie-Claire Belleau indicates in her work on mail-order brides, even apparently mundane questions – Does the bride drive, run errands, shop, and have money, a social network, and the ability to speak the language of the mainstream? – can allow us to access the narratives of women regarding the rationale underlying their adherence to practices that seem to undercut her liberty. Marie-Claire Belleau, "Mail-Order Brides in a Global World" (2003) 67 Alb. L. Rev. 595 at 602.

members without social or political influence. Women, especially those weakened by poverty, will often fall into this latter category.[9]

The challenge is to develop a framework that allows for a wider inclusion of perspectives, even of those who typically do not speak out within or for their communities. In this respect, Mari Matsuda's theory of "pragmatism", which sets out a methodology for learning about and garnering the experiences of women in postcolonial societies, is instructive. Pragmatism commands searching for and recording the experiences of the less privileged, so that their perspectives become part of legal knowledge.[10] Matsuda juxtaposes this emphasis on broad experiential knowledge against the traditional legal research method, which focuses intently on "the situated knowledge of the golden few."[11] Thus, for Matsuda, the promise of seeking out and listening to historically subordinated voices lies in the prospective of attaining "a truer account of social reality and human possibilities."[12] But this account is realized only when we first identify who is not present in discussions about community and culture, and when we examine why they do not participate. The researcher is thus called upon to seek out and attend to the viewpoints of those for whom presenting themselves, both physically and intellectually, in political contexts is not immediate or easy.

Hearing plural perspectives from within cultural groups requires the varied experiences of women to be uncovered and shared. Often relegated to the hidden, private sphere, women are clearly among those stakeholders whose voices must be heard and given effect before it is possible to know the meaning, impact and acceptance of practices said to be rooted in "culture".[13] Moreover, female perspectives are especially important to decisions within a multicultural state regarding the acceptance of cultural practices with gender implications, given that women tend to bear disproportionately any burden associated with policies of accommodation.[14] Delegation by the liberal state of power to cultural groups without attempting to unearth the multiplicity of perspectives within communities crystallizes the authority of acknowledged group leaders while their "hidden" constituents, often women, fade further into its background.[15]

---

[9] Maleiha Malik, "'The Branch on Which We Sit': Multiculturalism, Minority Women and Family Law" in Alison Diduck & Katherine O'Donovan, eds., *Feminist Perspectives on Family Law* (New York: Routledge, 2006) 211 at 217.

[10] Mari J. Matsuda, "Pragmatism Modified and the False Consciousness Problem" (1989–90) 63 S. Cal. L. Rev. 1763 at 1764.

[11] *Ibid.*

[12] *Ibid.* at 1768.

[13] Nancy Kim, "Toward a Feminist Theory of Human Rights: Straddling the Fence Between Western Imperialism and Uncritical Absolutism" (1993–1994) 25 Colum. H.R.L. Rev. 49 at 89–90.

[14] Some feminist scholars have noted that, it is not only women, but also children, who are typically the most vulnerable members of minority groups. See Shauna Van Praagh, "Faith, Belonging and the Protection of 'Our Children'" (1999) 17 Windsor Y.B. Access Just. 154; and Malik, *supra* note 9 at 215.

[15] Ayelet Shachar, "The Paradox of Multicultural Vulnerability: Individual Rights, Identity Groups, and the State" in Christian Joppke & Steven Lukes, eds., *Multicultural Questions* (New York: Oxford University Press, 1999) 87 at 94; Pascale Fournier, "The Erasure of Islamic Difference in Canadian and American Family Law Adjudication" (2001) 10 J.L. & Pol'y 51 at 71.

Efforts at seeking out more marginalized subgroups within cultural communities allow their members to speak for themselves, instead of having their interests determined by a set of assumptions or by dominant community figures who speak on their behalf.[16] A stark example of this is found in Abu-Lughod's ethnographic study of women in Bedouin Arab communities.[17] Her work demonstrates that the sexual segregation lived by these women was not experienced as seclusion or oppression. Instead, being separate and away from the "men's world" fostered independence, leadership, and sorority among women. These perspectives never could have emerged had the perspectives of male Bedouin community leaders been relied on solely as a frame of reference for their groups' cultural practices:

> The terms 'harem' and 'seclusion', so intertwined with popular and scholarly conceptions of Arab women, are in most respects grossly misleading. Conjuring up provocative images of groups of idle women imprisoned in sumptuous quarters awaiting the attentions of their master, or submissive veiled shadows scurrying down alleys, confined behind high walls, and excluded from the bustle of the public male world, these terms suggest the nadir of women's status and autonomy. [...] By shifting our gaze and assuming the perspective of those for whom this community of women is the primary arena of social life, we get a more accurate and nuanced view not only of its connection to the men's world, but of the nature of women's experiences and relationships within this community.[18]

Thinking about group dynamics and interactions from the perspective of women also reveals instances of their political power, mobility and activism. Looking only at what happens in public, explicitly "legal" spaces can leave us with a false impression about who in fact serves as the "Old Guards" of a given setting, shaping its normative structure.[19] This is especially true of patriarchal communities whose public face is most likely to be male. A closer look at the world of women inside the group might tell us more about their actual political engagement, and the extent to which they make law for themselves and for the group. In this way, research that strives to look out through the eyes of the women within cultural communities might tell a story that casts them as bearing more control and authority than would appear only by looking at the situation from the "outside".[20]

---

[16] See Annie Bunting, "Theorizing Women's Cultural Diversity in Feminist International Human Rights Strategies" (1993) 20 J.L. & Soc'y 6 at 18, who observes that "we should be wary of speaking for women whose culture is the object of scrutiny," and who would distinguish between recognizing alliance and solidarity among women as "keys to feminist politics" as opposed to an imposed politics.

[17] Lila Abu-Lughod, "A Community of Secrets: The Separate World of Bedouin Women" in Penny A. Weiss & Marilyn Friedman, eds., *Feminism & Community* (Philadelphia: Temple University Press, 1995) 21.

[18] *Ibid.* at 21.

[19] Roderick A. Macdonald, "Vieilles Gardes. Hypothèses sur l'émergence des normes, l'internormativité et le désordre à travers une typologie des institutions normatives" in J.G. Belley, éd., *Le Droit Soluble : contributions québécois à l'étude de l'internormativité* (Paris : Librairie générale de droit et de jurisprudence, 1996) 233 [Macdonald, "Vieilles Gardes"].

[20] See Kim, *supra* note 13 at 92, who notes that such internal reform prompted by female activists has frequently been ignored by human rights groups resistant to engaging with matters of "culture." Sunder also illustrates how women's activism in the Muslim world challenges the binary divide between law

This approach holds promise for a project on polygamy in Bountiful, British Columbia. Women in this community might appear to be subjugated to their husbands and the male leaders of the community: unlike the men, they are precluded from having plural spouses, and they do not wield public political leadership of the group. But, is it possible that a look at this community *from within* might deliver a different account of its power structures? That is, might we see polygamy as something other than "the nadir of women's status and autonomy"[21] if we try to see the practice and its meaning from the perspective of women? In particular, if we hear and record the voices and experiences of women, as Matsuda directs, could we learn more about the roles and responsibilities they carry out, for example, as parents, educators and midwives? In doing so, might we find that women exercise agency in shaping the way their marriages, families and the community look and operate? Moreover, would this approach reveal the polycentricity of relationships in Bountiful, exposing the way in which wives relate to one another directly, rather than just through the husband they share? Relationships and alliances forged between and among women could prove to be sites for developing agency and implicit power, bolstering their autonomy and influence in their families and community.[22]

By posing these questions, I do not mean to indicate that I assume anything about life for women in Bountiful; nor do I have any fixed opinion about whether this life is empowering or oppressive. Instead, I raise these questions with a view to thinking about the potential promise of seeing polygamous family and community life through the lens of women who live that life. More specifically, this research inquiry is developed so as to enrich the law's knowledge about polygamy which, until now, has been static, and based on monolithic sources and absolutist assumptions drawn without the benefit of experiential knowledge.

12.2.1.1 Practical Challenges to Finding Multiple Perspectives

While the discussion so far highlights the value of including the experiences of the marginalized in seeking to understand cultural practices and traditions, questions related to method or process have not been addressed. Answers to these questions

---

(typically viewed as a public space) on one hand, and religion and culture (usually seen as private zones) on the other. Such activism within cultural communities allows women opportunities to reclaim both spheres. Madhavi Sunder, "Piercing the Veil" (2003) 112 Yale L.J. 1399.

[21] Abu-Lughod, *supra* note 17 at 21.

[22] The way in which women's direct relationships with each other might shift power dynamics in a polygamous marriage and community is vividly illustrated by the marriage of Shelina Palmer and Lorraine Johnson, two celestial wives of the former Bishop of Bountiful, Winston Blackmore. Given that their marriages to Blackmore were not formally recognized, these women were free under Canadian law to marry one another. A televised interview with Blackmore suggested that he was not even aware of this formal union between women he considered as his own spouses, until the journalist covering the story broke the news to him. Thus while explicit religious and state-based

are not readily apparent in the literature that stresses the relevance of hearing different voices and perspectives. *How* then do we access those voices? More specifically, when a community is an insular one, perhaps sceptical of the world surrounding it, what are the risks of trying to penetrate it and speak to the women within it? Further, how do we know which women to contact, to communicate with, and to hear? If we are to resist essentialist assumptions that one woman, or one cluster of women, can speak for all within the group, what approach is needed to hear from a relevant cross-section of voices?

This challenge is an obvious one for my project, which seeks to consult with women in a closed religious community. That this community would be wary of outsiders is understandable: Bountiful has come under close scrutiny by the public and by law enforcement authorities. Because the community's way of life is explicitly prohibited by Canadian law, its members might perceive conversations with an outsider like me as risky. The state's interest in Bountiful is linked also to questions about immigration: a number of wives remain in Canada without permission after relocating here from the United States. Immigration Canada has thus investigated these women (many of them mothers to Canadian-born children), and threatened them with removal.[23]

Because women married to polygamists are cast as bandits or squatters under formal law, a researcher from the world that imposes these labels might bear little trustworthiness. Nevertheless, as indicated at the outset, the women of Bountiful seem willing to share their experiences with researchers interested in learning about polygamy. Furthermore, a number of them have interacted with the media and the public about what polygamy means to them and to their community.[24] These experiences indicate possible avenues for initiating conversations with the group.

Finding a meaningful cross-section of voices raises another practical difficulty. Since it is not feasible to hear from *all* members of a community like Bountiful, which individuals or "subgroups" should be approached and invited to share their perspectives?

normative structures operating in Bountiful might at first glance seem to disadvantage polygamous wives, this story illustrates how women might use these structures to their benefit as a possible route to enhanced liberation. Interview of Winston Blackmore by Hana Gartner (25 January 2006) "Bustup in Bountiful" on *The Fifth Estate*, online: CBC.ca <http://www.cbc.ca/fifth/bustupinbountiful/interview.html>.

[23] In May 2006, the CBC reported that Canada Immigration had ordered the deportation of three American women married to Winston Blackmore, The women, who among them have 16 Canadian children (all of whom are permitted to remain in Canada), saw their immigration claim on humanitarian and compassionate grounds denied. The women are ineligible to immigrate to Canada as spouses since their marriages are not legally recognized and they do not qualify as skilled workers or students. See "3 Bountiful wives ordered out" *CBC [British Columbia]* (12 May 2006), online: CBC.ca <http://www.cbc.ca/bc/story/bc_bountiful20060512.html>. Blackmore has stated that he has filed a complaint against Immigration Canada alleging that his wives were being discriminated against because of their polygamous marriages. See "Bountiful wives ready for immigration fight" *CBC [British Columbia]* (16 May 2006), online: CBC.ca <http://www.cbc.ca/bc/story/bc_bountifulwives20060516.html>.

[24] See *infra* note 44 and accompanying text.

The views of the most prominent women and those with experience in public discourse will surely be important to consider. But an obvious dilemma for feminist research is how to account for potential power hierarchies *among* the women in a group, which might operate to the particular benefit of "dominant" female community members. Consultation with just this top echelon of women ignores their disenfranchised and silent sisters whose experiences and stories might be most revealing to a research project like the one I contemplate here. At the same time, hearing and recording the stories of women who have not before spoken out about their way of marriage and family life, or who lack clout in their families or community will not necessarily be simple. There are risks and challenges to soliciting their opinions, such as determining who these women are, offending them by moving too abruptly and probing intrusively into their personal space, and provoking fear or distress if they feel that contact with an "outsider" researcher puts them at risk. A balance must be struck between the objective of including multiple experiences in a research project, while also respecting the space of women who opt not to share their insights. At the very least, the latter should be made aware of opportunities for participation and invited to do so.[25]

12.2.1.2 Conceptual Challenges to Finding Multiple Perspectives

Is it always possible to trust women's voices to be legitimate and authentic? What if women are so blinded by the control to which they are subject in patriarchal cultures that they fail to see the "truth", that is, their oppression within male-dominated social and legal orders? These questions and linked arguments about women's false consciousness complicate a research framework premised upon seeking out the narratives of women. More specifically, they seem to resist a *prima facie* acceptance of perspectives from women who do not acknowledge or resist their subjugation.[26]

[25] Careful deliberation about practical methodological skills and approaches is required before the actual initiation of fieldwork in a place like Bountiful. A reflection on the most appropriate and effective qualitative research techniques is beyond the ambit of this paper. Nevertheless, a body of writing on feminist methods for carrying out interviews and discussions within fieldwork will be invaluable to this later stage of my research. See *e.g.* Melanie Mauthner *et al.*, *Ethics in Qualitative Research* (Thousand Oaks, CA: Sage, 2002); Melanie Mauthner, "Snippets and Silences: Ethics and Reflexivity in Narratives of Sistering" (2000) 3 International Journal of Social Research Methodology 287; and I.E. Seidman, *Interviewing as Qualitative Research: a Guide for Researchers in Education and the Social Sciences* (New York: Teacher's College Press, Columbia University, 1991). Moreover, ethnographic studies that have investigated maligned cultural practices and groups, especially those that have focused on women, will be equally important sources. See *e.g.* Susan Friend Harding, *The Book of Jerry Falwell: Fundamentalist Language and Politics* (Princeton, NJ: Princeton University Press, 2000); Karen McCarthy Brown, *Mama Lola: A Vodou Priestess in Brooklyn,* (Berkeley: University of California Press, 2001).

[26] The radical feminist would say that such failure to perceive male dominance is linked to the overpowering influence of patriarchal ideology. See Catharine A. MacKinnon, *Toward a Feminist Theory of the State* (Cambridge, MA: Harvard University Press, 1989) at 115–17, 204; and Catharine A. MacKinnon, *Feminism Unmodified: Discourses on Life and Law* (Cambridge, MA: Harvard University Press, 1987) at 40–41.

If I were to accept the idea of false consciousness – a matter I explore here – I might be required to assume that a woman who claims to have made an autonomous and free choice about polygamous marriage has no sense of the truth. The hypothesis would assert that she has been "co-opted" by her culture.[27] If she articulates a desire to stay with her husband and share him with other women, should her claim be accepted as genuine, even though a Western feminist might see this woman as controlled (maybe even brainwashed) by her environment? Might this woman have a different sense of her family life and what she deserves within it if her consciousness were "raised" by greater contact with the world beyond her community?

While worth asking and investigating, these questions are problematic and largely unanswerable; as Kim points out, if false consciousness exists, then *all* women are subject to overriding patriarchal influences that prevent any of us from knowing or seeing "the truth."[28] Assumptions about false consciousness undermine the experiences and perspectives of women, especially those who decide (for whatever reason) to retain their cultural membership in settings that, at least from the outsider's perspective, fail to privilege gender equality. These women are cast as lacking in capacity and in need of protection, and in this way likened to children.

Furthermore, because the notion of false consciousness propagates a single "truth" about women's experiences, it is critiqued for unduly essentializing women and for failing to give appropriate weight to cultural difference and to women's experiences as a source of knowledge.[29] Thus, espousing the idea of false consciousness leaves women, especially those who offer their perspectives from within cultural minority groups, disempowered and "othered". Rather than bearing any agency, they continue to be spoken for in the discourse, only now it is by enlightened (Western) women who have somehow surmounted patriarchal brainwashing, rather than their male community leaders.[30]

These critiques are persuasive. Clearly research that emphasizes the relevance of experiential knowledge and multiple perspectives will be thwarted by an attempt to seek out only those voices that are untainted by false consciousness. My project's starting point thus resists presumptions about false consciousness and assumes the authenticity, "truth" and legitimacy of the stories women tell. These are the

---

[27] This language is used explicitly by Okin, who suggests that older women are especially vulnerable to subjugation that colours their ability to identify oppression in their community's cultural practices. Susan Moller Okin, "Is Multiculturalism Bad for Women?" in Joshua Cohen, Matthew Howard & Martha C. Nussbaum, eds., *Is Multiculturalism Bad for Women?* (Princeton, NJ: Princeton University Press, 1999) 8 at 24. See also Kim, *supra* note 13 at 94.

[28] Kim, *ibid.* at 99.

[29] Katharine T. Bartlett, "Feminist Legal Methods" (1990) 103 Harv. L. Rev. 829 at 875; Kim, *ibid.* at 99–100; and Colleen Sheppard, "Equality Rights and Institutional Change: Insights from Canada and the United States" (1998) 15 Ariz. J. Int'l & Comp. L. 143 at 167.

[30] See Karen Engle, "Female Subjects of Public International Law: Human Rights and the Exotic Other Female" (1992) 26 New Engl. L. Rev. 1509 at 1525. See also Karen Engle, "International Human Rights and Feminisms: When Discourses Keep Meeting" in Doris Buss & Ambreena S. Manji, eds., *International Law: Modern Feminist Approaches* (Portland, OR: Hart Publishing, 2005) 47 at 57*ff*; and Bunting, *supra* note 16 at 18.

stories that matter most to this research, and so I depend on them regardless of any influence exerted by "culture" on the narrators' accounts.[31] This approach makes room for the voices of women who "have different priorities and are in the process of articulating [the] issues" about which I seek to learn.[32]

However, in saying all this, I do not mean to imply that women's accounts should be accepted without critique or question. Clearly I cannot resolve debates about false consciousness in this paper. However, it is possible to formulate an inquiry that takes women's narratives about culture seriously, while at the same time rejecting strong cultural relativist passivity. This can be accomplished by applying a juridical analysis that seeks to evaluate rigorously claims advanced about law and normativity. In this connection, I find Macdonald's framework for testing claims for the recognition of cultural pluralism instructive. His analysis posits that the legitimacy of normative assertions grounded in cultural rules depends on three distinct features, namely: the **source** of the legitimacy or authority for these rules; the extent which the rules respect **due process**; and the **justifications** offered for the rules.[33] Applied to this project on Bountiful, Macdonald's framework gives rise to the following questions:

1. Source of authority underlying the normative order:
   - Who are the community leaders that propagate polygamy as morally essential?
   - How, if at all, is their authority over group members legitimized?
   - While community leaders might appear to "make law" for Bountiful, how are community members also sources of authority, committed to constructing, understanding, interpreting and implementing the norms of this place?
   - Might community "outsiders" operate as sources of authority for the normative orders operative in Bountiful? More specifically, do broad social perceptions in Canada about: whether polygamists are actually "married"; the palatability of this way of life; whether and how formal law should engage with the community; and why polygamy happens in Bountiful contribute to constituting and legitimating the rules governing this place? Or conversely, is it the case that broad social acknowledgement of plural marriage has no bearing on group members' perceptions of the legitimacy of this practice?
   - How do community members reckon with the plurality of normative commitments and authorities they perceive as binding?[34]

[31] In saying so, I am cognizant that it is always possible to argue that what we commonly call "culture" would impact the discourse of any narrator sharing her viewpoint as to the tolerability of the practices and habits that shape her everyday life.

[32] Bunting, *supra* note 16 at 18.

[33] Roderick A. Macdonald, "Pluralistic Human Rights; Universal Human Wrongs" (2007) [unpublished, on file with the author].

[34] A multiplicity of rules – often incompatible with one another – will operate simultaneously in any normative framework. Those subject to these rules become "legal actors" by attributing varying degrees of significance to these rules, and in constructing for themselves the particular normative

2. Due process in the formation and execution of community norms:

   - To what degree is there dialogue and consultation within the community about the propriety and desirability of plural marriage?
   - How, if at all, are group members informed about what polygamy entails within the contexts of faith-based and state-based legal orders? What alternatives (e.g., monogamous marriage, celibacy) are they offered, and in what way?
   - What factors drive a woman's entry into polygamous life? If she asserts a choice for this life, what factors motivate her decision?
   - How long does she know her husband before they marry?
   - Does she select (or have a role in selecting) her husband? If other community members are involved in "matching" spouses, what roles do they play? What determines these roles?
   - Must (or can) a woman consent to her spouse taking an additional wife?
   - What measures can a spouse take if dissatisfied with her marriage? Can she leave the marriage, or the community, if unhappy with either? If leaving is not possible, what strategies might she employ to manage her situation?
   - This last question is connected with the debate over the propriety of advancing a right of exit for women in ostensibly oppressive relationships and environments. A variety of factors – such as: emotional attachment, familial responsibilities and affections, economic dependence, limited education and skill, religious commitment – can make it impossible for a woman to "pick up and leave" her family or community, no matter how hard staying behind might be.[35] Thus, she cannot be understood as implicitly consenting to her lifestyle and the treatment she receives in a place only because she does not leave it.[36] At the same time, a woman who "remains behind" might still bear power and agency by mobilizing from within her community to seek reform of the group's most troubling practices or expectations.[37] Bearing voice within a community – that is, an ability to express sentiments that may influence the group's actions – thus might serve as a substitute for, or perhaps as a companion to, exit rights as a means to forging autonomy from within a cultural group.[38]

---

rubric that will shape their lives and relationships. See Roderick A. Macdonald & Thomas McMorrow, "Wedding a Critical Legal Pluralism to the Laws of Close Personal Adult Relationships" (2007) 1 European Journal of Legal Studies, online: European Journal of Legal Studies <http://www.ejls.eu/index.php?mode=present&displayissue=2007-04>; and Macdonald, "Vieilles Gardes", *supra* note 19.

[35] Malik, *supra* note 9 at 216; Shachar, *supra* note 15 at 100.

[36] This discussion of the form and substance of exit rights intersects with the historical juridical discourse surrounding domestic violence. Shachar thus critiques exit arguments by paralleling them to the historical claim that through the act of marriage, a woman communicated her implied consent to maltreatment of virtually any kind at her husband's hand. Shachar, *ibid.* See also the discussion of Wilson J. in *R. v. Lavallee*, [1990] 1 S.C.R. 852 at 887, which identifies how affective bonds and environmental factors can impair women's ability to leave violent relationships.

[37] Sunder, *supra* note 20 at 1442, 1457; and Malik, *supra* note 9 at 218.

[38] Dwight G. Newman, "Exit, Voice, and 'Exile': Rights to Exit and Rights to Reject" (2007) 57 U.T.L.J. 43 at 48–51.

3. Justifications for substantive rules:

- Which community members defend polygamy as a rule imperative to family life? Are there members who would reject the moral centrality of polygamy in Bountiful? What rationales are offered by proponents and dissenters?
- What factors (e.g., gender, wealth, education, political affluence within the group) drive the competing explanations that constituents might offer for the normative order within Bountiful?
- Who benefits from – and what good is achieved by – polygamous family structures in Bountiful?
- In articulations that explain plural marriage in Bountiful, what consideration is given to claims (which might be levied both within and outside the community) about the drawbacks, possibly even the harms, of this way of life?

In addition to these questions, a critical appreciation of women's narratives requires an analysis of the forces that shape their perspectives, and an inquiry into their level of reflection about life experiences and choices.[39] Some feminist scholars posit that opportunities for such reflection are created through shared "consciousness-raising" activities, that is, through "an interactive and collaborative process of articulating one's experiences and making meaning of them with others who also articulate their experiences."[40] Through consciousness-raising, subordinated voices become fortified and public, since the process typically develops collective self-knowledge through organized movements aimed at ending oppression.[41]

The notion that consciousness can be "refined" through collaboration and dialogue has a certain appeal. It illuminates the value of collective experiences and activism within populations that are otherwise politically and socially excluded. It also adds legitimacy to claims and ideas voiced by the disempowered because these are rooted in a shared – rather than individual – experience,[42] and because these claims and concepts were sparked by specific and concrete instantiations of them.

---

[39] Malik, *supra* note 9 at 226.

[40] Bartlett, *supra* note 29 at 863–64. Other descriptions of consciousness-raising are offered in the literature. For example, Schneider's perspective is influenced by her perception of a dialectical relationship between theory and practice or experience. She thus states that within consciousness-raising experiences, "learning starts with the individual and personal (the private), moves to the general and social (the public), and then reflects back on itself with heightened consciousness through this shared group process." Elizabeth M. Schneider, "The Dialectic of Rights and Politics: Perspectives from the Women's Movement" (1986) 61 N.Y.U.L. Rev. 589 at 602.

[41] Matsuda, *supra* note 10 at 1778–79.

[42] However, a search for the common experiences of women might be considered problematic, as representing an essentialist understanding of women's conditions in particular cultural settings. But as feminists have pointed out, essentialism – while problematic when imposed by a dominant group – can be instrumental when it is identified and used by subordinated groups to challenge dominant and oppressive ideologies. That is, relying on a basis of shared experiences and perspectives can be an important strategy for political mobilization and empowerment. See Bunting, *supra* note 16 at 12; and Malik, *supra* note 9 at 221.

There is some difficulty, though, in identifying what types of activities count as "consciousness-raising" or as rendering a woman's reflection of herself and her experiences more informed, critical or refined. What collective experiences suffice to elevate consciousness? Must they involve a mobilized, organized movement of solidarity to lift awareness, or can more private conversations among women ever be seen as having this effect? And what if these conversations allow for reflection of the self, but do not necessarily result in a perception of that self as oppressed or subjugated, but instead, in continued contentment with one's current state of being? If that occurs, can we still say that a woman's consciousness was raised?

It is suggested that consciousness-raising should allow for a challenge of "dominant versions of social reality".[43] But my own sense is that we should look for spaces in which storytellers have had occasion to engage collectively with their peers and counterparts to discuss their experiences and perhaps also, to pursue some action with a view to empowerment. The very occurrence of these conversations should be indicative of reflection and critical self-awareness, even if there are no immediate or obvious challenges to repression that follow.

In exploring polygamy in Bountiful, then, I am compelled to learn whether women affected by this practice have opportunities to share experiences and if so, what the fruits of such conversations might be. My investigation will be directed at trying to discern whether such occasions for exchange prompt introspection among wives about polygamous life, about their satisfaction with it, and about whether they perceive themselves as subjugated by their spouses, their religious leaders, the norms and expectations of their community, and by the social, legal and political frameworks imposed by the Canadian state. Finally, questions must probe whether women have used these exchanges as a springboard for activism – either within or outside of Bountiful – directed at challenging their current social and political circumstances.

In connection with all of this, a critical appraisal of women's voices and experiences in Bountiful also demands an inquiry into activities suggesting that women in this community bear considerable agency. Several women have moved into public and political spheres, broaching the media, politicians or the judiciary to make arguments (both supportive and critical) about plural marriage and its impact on women.[44]

---

[43] Bartlett, *supra* note 29 at 865. See also Matsuda, *supra* note 10 at 1779, who indicates that consciousness-raising involves the search for self-knowledge that occurs "in conjunction with organized movements to end existing conditions of domination."

[44] See "B.C. Mulling Charges Against Polygamist Sect" (10 May 2007), online: CBC News Online <http://www.cbc.ca/canada/story/2007/05/10/polygamy-community.html>; Mike D'Amour, "Sect Greets Abuse Probe." *The Calgary Sun* (27 July 2004), online: The Calgary Sun Online: <http://www.canoe.ca/NewsStand/CalgarySun/News/2004/07/27/558440.html>; Mike D'Amour, "Sect Wives Defend Lives: Women say Polygamy Choice is Theirs" *The Calgary Sun* (29 July 2004), online: The Calgary Sun Online: <http://www.canoe.ca/NewsStand/CalgarySun/News/2004/07/29/561063.html>; "B.C. Polygamists Want Age of Consent Raised" (19 February 2005), online: CTV News Online: <http://www.ctv.ca/servlet/ArticleNews/story/CTVNews/1108760102803_29/?hub=CTVNewsAt11>; and "Cdn. Polygamy Laws Need to be Reviewed: Activist" (26 January 2005), online: CTV News Online: <http://www.ctv.ca/servlet/ArticleNews/story/CTVNews/1106749304265_34?s_name=&no_ads>.

While these efforts indicate the presence of a collective discourse among women, a series of questions must be raised before assuming that they reflect consciousness-raising activities: How broadly do these public or political activities reflect the views of women in the community? Which women participate in this level of activism and which do not? What determines such participation? Do these activities foster a sense of solidarity and self-reflection among the women of the community? Is there dissent, and if so, on what basis and how is it expressed? Pursuing these questions in conversations with the women of Bountiful will illuminate the extent to which these activities truly lend themselves to enhanced self-reflection and critique.

12.3 Learning About Cultural Difference Through Self-Reflection

Malik suggests that while minority women's experiences and knowledge attribute to them "an authority that cannot be replicated by outsiders", there is a role of significance to be played by Western feminist "outsiders" who study these women and their cultural settings.[45] She asserts: "one of the most significant contributions that outsiders can make is to 'hold the line' by using key principles such as autonomy as the basis for a detailed and constructive critique of traditional communities and their family practices."[46] While this might be true, various factors complicate the contribution that Western feminists might actually make to forging rights for minority women.

First, given communities' fluid and dynamic boundaries, their "insiders" and "outsiders" are not always readily identified.[47] Second, as I explore in this part, the researcher who investigates traditions that differ from her own must also reckon with her ability to understand these traditions and assess them critically. For example, how might I – as a white, Canadian law teacher and researcher, but also as a mother of two sons, married to a male spouse pursuant to the rules of state law and the traditions of my faith – appreciate the experiences, for example, of an Islamic adolescent who wears the *hijab*, of the fundamentalist Mormon woman who marries a polygamist, or of the African mother who acquiesces in her daughter's genital cutting?[48]

[45] Malik, *supra* note 9 at 219.

[46] *Ibid.* at 218.

[47] Sally Engle Merry, *Human Rights & Gender Violence: Translating International Law into Local Justice* (Chicago: University of Chicago Press, 2006) at 17–18.

[48] Similar questions are raised by Gunning in relation to a Western feminist's ability to consider critically "culturally challenging practices". She asks:

> As I analyzed the practice [of female genital cutting] and my reactions, I was confronted with two major problems: (1) by what right did I, as a Western feminist, have to criticize as right or wrong the practices of an entirely different culture? and (2) should and can law, with its attribution of right and wrong, exoneration and punishment, be used to eradicate a cultural practice.

Isabelle R. Gunning, "Arrogant Perception, World-Travelling and Multicultural Feminism: The Case of Female Genital Surgeries" 23 Colum. H.R.L. Rev. 189.at 189.

Possibilities for understanding these practices "from the outside" are suggested by the research tactic just examined, that is, by learning and trying to appreciate the meaning of such practices through women's experiential narratives. A second strategy emergent in relevant feminist legal discussions is also valuable to this research project. This strategy prompts the researcher who studies a cultural practice as an "outsider" to initiate her inquiry by reflecting on the way in which her own perspectives, experiences and biases might influence her approaches and conclusions.[49]

This introspective process is crucial for revisiting ideas of difference and exoticism. Are the practices just named (the veil, plural marriage, genital cutting), commonly touted as oppressive to women, really so removed, foreign, or "other" to the life experiences of a Western, "modern" woman? A careful response that resists assumptions of difference requires a researcher to identify and critique the practices and norms of her own cultural setting that might in fact align with those she studies. "Turning the gaze back on itself"[50] thus invites the observer to identify parallels and intersections between the multiple experiences of women, and to reconsider the "otherness" of the practices and persons forming the subject of her inquiry.[51] It will also likely land the researcher at Matsuda's conclusion that "[w]e are not the same. But we are not so different that we are bereft of the chance of knowing anything at all about one another and thereby about ourselves."[52]

Reflecting on one's own normative assumptions is facilitated by "seeing oneself as the other sees you,"[53] that is, by imagining and accounting for the way that a woman from a cultural minority group might see the researcher and her culture. This is reflected in Slack's research on female genital cutting. She questions whether Western feminists are suited to judge this practice, given the tolerance within their own culture for activities that could easily be labelled oppressive to women:

> What would a Sudanese woman think if she were to hear about the women of America who have their ribs removed to appear thinner, their faces lifted to appear younger, and their noses made smaller and breasts made larger, all in the desire to become more attractive? How, in turn, would these American women feel if they were told that their actions were barbaric or immoral, or if they were prohibited by law to have such operations?[54]

Slack's analysis can be pushed further. Beyond plastic surgery, consider also Western acceptance of crude medical interventions aimed at purging disabled persons of their sexuality and reproductive capacity.[55] Such examples illuminate our

---

[49] Bunting, *supra* note 16 at 16.

[50] Brenda Cossman, "Turning the Gaze Back on Itself: Comparative Law, Feminist Legal Studies, and the Postcolonial Project" (1997) Utah L. Rev. 525.

[51] This approach is suggested also by Malik who considers the value of connecting practices cast as "different" to "a similar or analogous home practice." Malik, *supra* note 9 at 228–29.

[52] Matsuda, *supra* note 10 at 1777.

[53] Gunning, *supra* note 48 at 212.

[54] Alison T. Slack, "Female Circumcision: A Critical Appraisal" (1987–1988) 10 Hum. Rts. Q. 437 at 463.

[55] See Kristin Savell, "Sex and the Sacred: Sterilization and Bodily Integrity in English and Canadian Law" (2004) 49 McGill L.J. 1093. See also "Parents Defend Treatment to Keep Girl Child-Sized" (5 January 2007), online: CTV.ca <http://www.ctv.ca/servlet/ArticleNews/story/CTVNews/20070104/ashley_treatment_070104/20070105?hub=Health>.

own tolerance for practices that compromise bodily integrity, and the link between these practices and social perceptions of what is sexually desirable and proper, especially for women. We are thus warned against drawing pejorative assumptions about difference and reminded that culture is not only "out there" as some exotic concept, but everywhere, and that the observer/researcher is consistently subject to its influences.[56] And indeed, while the observer might find the Other's practices and beliefs intriguing, and possibly problematic, the opposite could also be true.[57]

Before considering the value of this strategy for investigating polygamy in Bountiful, I signal my awareness about the character of the scholarship relied on in this Part. Much of this scholarship is centred on gendered "foreign" or "immigrant" traditions. We thus might question its utility for addressing the experiences of women living in a Canadian community where the "problematic" cultural practice is indigenous to the West, given the heterogeneity that exists within the categories of "woman" and "minority woman".[58] But the sources relied on here should not be taken to suggest that it is possible to assimilate the experiences of women in minority cultural groups. Instead, they are considered useful to the extent that they offer a strategy premised on self-reflection as a way to acquire a fuller understanding of "othered" cultural practices. Thus, while the scholarship provides a broad methodological approach, it is only a point of departure for grasping the particularities of polygamy in Bountiful, which requires precise and contextual questions that account for the distinct features of this practice and community.

Applying this research approach to my own project would require me as the researcher to reckon with my own culture's current and historical understanding of marriage and family life and its outcomes, particularly for women.[59] It commands an acknowledgement that family law and policy – through its rules related to spousal and child support, divorce, and custody – has not always been friendly to women's interests.[60] The liberal state's governance of family life has commonly interacted

[56] Penelope Andrews, "Women's Human Rights and the Conversation Across Cultures" (2003) 67 Alb. L. Rev. 609 at 613. See also Engle Merry, *supra* note 47 at 10*ff*, 228–29, who posits that human rights – often pitted against culture – are best imagined as a cultural practice; and Richard Rorty, "Human Rights, Rationality and Sentimentality" in Richard Rorty, *Truth and Progress: Philosophical Papers*, vol. 3 (Cambridge: Cambridge University Press, 1998) 167, who adopts the language of a "human rights culture."

[57] Gunning thus writes: "[J]ust as a Westerner may view the [genital] surgeries as a cultural challenge, the street runs two ways: non-Westerners too can view Western practices as culturally challenging." Gunning, *supra* note 48 at 212.

[58] Malik, *supra* note 9 at 216.

[59] The importance of situating one's perceptions about culture in a *historical* context is emphasized by Gunning who demonstrates how this analysis reveals facts that could otherwise be neglected. In this connection, she critiques Western ideas about genital cutting in view of the acceptance and performance of this practice in the United States and England during the late nineteenth and early twentieth centuries. See Gunning, *supra* note 48 at 205*ff*.

[60] See Susan Boyd, "Legal Regulation of Families in Changing Societies" in Austin Sarat, ed., *The Blackwell Companion to Law and Society* (Oxford: Blackwell, 2004) 255; Margrit Eichler, *Family Shifts: Families, Policies, and Gender Equality* (Toronto: Oxford University Press, 1997); Colleen Sheppard, "Uncomfortable Victories and Unanswered Questions: Lessons from *Moge*" (1995) 12 Can. J. Fam. L. 283; Joan Williams, "Is Coverture Dead? Beyond a New Theory of Alimony"

with and embodied "social relations of power" drawn along lines of class, gender, race and sexual orientation.[61] Its success in protecting the social and economic interests of the vulnerable has thus been far from perfect, with women and children, especially those who are racialized or live within unorthodox family structures, sustaining disproportionately burdens imposed by poverty and restricted access to legal information and processes.[62] Thus, the superiority of formal regimes governing families over religious normative orders cannot be presumed without more rigorous analyses as to the substantive outcomes that each yields.[63]

With respect to polygamy, it must be acknowledged that while the practice has never been dominant in Canada, it has not been relegated exclusively to distinct cultural or religious settings. In the few cases where Canadian courts have decided prosecutions for polygamy or bigamy,[64] there is no indication that the accused were residents of Bountiful or other isolated religious sects.[65] Tolerance for this practice within the Canadian juridical ethos is apparent by the light penal consequences that have attached to convictions for this offence,[66] and by recognition of the effects of a polygamous marriage if celebrated in a jurisdiction permitting such a marital structure,[67] or if one of the parties was in good faith.[68] This partial acceptance of polygamy triggers questions about why law rejects and stigmatizes the practice so starkly when it materializes in a place like Bountiful.

(1994) 82 Geo. L.J. 2227 at 2246*ff*; Herma Hill Kay, "'Making Marriage and Divorce Safe for Women' Revisited" (2003) 32 Hofstra L. Rev. 71; and Dianne Post, "Why Marriage Should Be Abolished" (1997) 18 Women's Rights L. Rep. 283.

[61] Boyd, *ibid.* at 256.

[62] *Ibid.* at 258–59, 264.

[63] See Pascale Fournier, "In the (Canadian) Shadow of Islamic Law: Translating Mahr as a Bargaining Endowment" (2006) 44 Osgoode Hall L.J. 650.

[64] While just a few Canadian decisions have assessed criminal charges based on bigamy or polygamy (see *infra* notes 65–66), courts have considered the legality of polygamous marriages formed in foreign jurisdictions in a number of cases. See Amy J. Kaufman, "Polygamous Marriages in Canada" (2005) 21 Can. J. Fam. L. 315 at 318*ff*; and Campbell, *supra* note 1 at 31.

[65] See *R. v. Clarke* (1959), 124 C.C.C. 284 (Man. C.A.) [*Clarke*]; *R. v. Moore* (2001), WL 596386 (Ont. Ct. J.) [*Moore*]; *R v. Moustafa*, [1991] O.J. No. 835 (Ont. Ct. J. (Prov. Div.)) [*Moustafa*]; *R. v. Sauvé*, [1997] A.J. No. 525 (Alta. Prov. Ct.) [*Sauvé*]; *R. v. Young*, [1965] O.J. No. 498 (Ont. C.A.) [*Young*]. Although the accused in *Moustafa* was described as "of the Moslem religion", the judgment does not suggest that his decision to marry polygamously was propelled by faith. In other cases listed here, no reference is made to the accuseds' religious beliefs.

[66] See *ibid.*, where the sentences were of the following nature: imprisonment for 6 months (*Clarke*) and 2.5 years (*Young*); a conditional sentence of 3 months (*Moore*); time served (31 days) and 3 years' probation (*Moustafa*); and a $1,000 fine coupled with 12 months' probation (*Sauvé*).

[67] Provincial family law and successions legislation might extend the effects of marriage to polygamous spouses. See *e.g.* Ontario *Family Law Act*, R.S.O. 1990, c. F.3, s. 1(2), and Ontario *Succession Law Reform Act*, R.S.O. 1990, c. S.26, s.1(2), which include within the definition of "spouse" partners to a polygamous marriage if celebrated in a jurisdiction "whose system of law recognizes it as valid". See also *Yew v. British Columbia (Attorney-General)*, [1924] 1 D.L.R. 1166 (B.C.C.A.); and Kaufman, *supra* note 64 at 333.

[68] See *e.g. Civil Code of Québec*, art. 382, para. 1; and *G.P. v. B.M.* (2002), IIJCan 602 (QC C.S.).

Further and obviously, questions need to be raised about mainstream fidelity to the very idea of marital fidelity. Given Canada's legal and societal tolerance of adultery,[69] and even "swinging",[70] we must revisit what it is about plural marriage that makes it so juridically troubling.[71] And finally, there is critical notice to be taken about the subversion and limits on liberation that exist within my own cultural framework that cut across lines of gender and which result from difference linked to class, sexual orientation, age and disability. These markers of difference persist as bases for disparate social outcomes.

As a last point, it is imperative for a researcher's self-reflection to consider the way in which her own cultural and legal norms have contributed to any oppression observed in the setting she studies. For example, a superficial glimpse into the lives of women in Bountiful could possibly reveal economic and social hardship: some sources suggest that polygamous wives in this community experience severe financial depression,[72] and that their health and well-being is compromised by rivalry between co-wives, by strained (and possibly abusive) marital relationships, and by living in a community with a history of pervasive and systemic child abuse.[73] The reflective approaches to research developed in this article encourage the observer of such difficulties to refrain from linking them to the practice of polygamy *per se*, without probative investigation and analysis. As discussed, the perspectives of the women affected by these hardships are necessary to understanding whether these women perceive polygamy, or some other force, as the root source of such adversity. In addition, the researcher is prompted to think about the way in which her own cultural and legal order might contribute to any oppression that women in Bountiful experience. The following questions thus become central: In what way does fear of criminal prosecution deter women from seeking access to resources (related, for example, to health, social assistance, or education) that they, or their children, might need? Do Canada's immigration regulations, which curb the ability to sponsor foreign nationals when the sponsors and/or the prospective immigrants are married polygamously,[74] similarly limit women's access to social and economic resources?[75] Does the refusal to recognize polygamy as a valid form of marriage in Canadian family law curtail women's ability to exit their marriages and community

---

[69] There is no criminal sanction linked to adultery or infidelity despite its potential lack of moral approbation. However, until 1985 the *Criminal Code* did include a qualified offence related to adultery, which required the Crown to show that the action occurred in a child's home and compromised the child's moral well-being. *Criminal Code of Canada*, s. 172(1) [as rep. by R.S., 1985, c. 19 (3rd Supp.), s. 6].

[70] *R. v. Labaye*, 2005 SCC 80.

[71] For a discussion of how polygamy is broadly perceived in Canada as morally problematic, see Gillian Calder, "Penguins and Polyamory: Using Law and Film to Explore the Essence of Marriage in Canadian Family Law" (2009) 21(1) Canadian Journal of Women and the Law 55 at 78–81.

[72] Committee on Polygamous Issues, *supra* note 7.

[73] *Ibid.*; Palmer & Perrin, *supra* note 7; and Jessop, *supra* note 7.

[74] See Canada *Immigration and Refugee Protection Regulations*, S.O.R./2000-227, s.117(9)(c).

[75] See *supra* note 23.

when they or their children are unhappy, or experience harm?[76] And finally, how does Canada's decision to reject and prohibit polygamy from a legal perspective, in the face of broad public awareness of its occurrence in Bountiful, affect power structures in the community? In particular, in what ways might this approach undermine the interests of women and other vulnerable group members?[77] These reflections are crucial to assessing law's current impact on women in Bountiful, and to rethinking Canadian legal and policy approaches to this topic with a view to preserving women's needs and interests.

12.4 Conclusion

This paper explores some of the challenges and tactical decisions inherent to an empirical research project about how women are affected by polygamous life, and by the way in which law imagines and treats this way of life. It also bears a broader objective, which is to develop an inquiry that might be applied to investigate and test normative assertions about any genderized practice claimed or perceived to be grounded in culture. In pursuing these aims, this paper reflects on two key research strategies developed within feminist legal scholarship. This first of these stresses the vitality of women's experiences to understanding tradition and culture, and is considered crucial for ensuring that research gives voice and meaning to multiple claims about culture and cultural identity. That said, the idealism inherent in "giving voice" to women is tempered by realities associated with penetrating closed communities, and by questions about false consciousness. I argue that these complicating dynamics can be addressed while still privileging narrative accounts delivered by women.

[76] Because polygamous marriages are generally unrecognized under the federal *Divorce Act*, R.S. 1985, c.3 (2nd Supp.) and provincial family law legislation, the wives of a polygamist (except the first he formally married) generally cannot claim spousal support. Financial dependence on a husband could thus be an important deterrent to leaving a marriage.

It is worth noting that some legislation might allow polygamous wives to make simultaneous claims against a shared husband as dependants. Consider s.85.1 of British Columbia's *Estate Administration Act*, R.S.B.C. 1996, c. 122, which recognizes that two or more persons might be recognized in law as "spouses" entitled to share in the spousal portion of an intestate's estate. This provision envisages the situation of a person who, before his death, set up a common law relationship with a partner without having formally terminated a prior marriage. But this structure for spousal entitlement might also extend to polygamous circumstances where a man was legally married to one woman, but "celestially" married to one or more other wives with whom he cohabited.

[77] Law's decision to remain outside of a family or community can bear an impact on women by reinforcing gendered power dynamics within it. Boyd, *supra* note 60 at 256. The legal community's decision to accept the status quo in Bountiful is thus problematic, not necessarily because prosecutions for polygamy should be pursued, but because the state's neglect of the community risks solidifying its hierarchies at women's expense. For a discussion of law's privatization of religion and the potentially nefarious effects of this for women, see Sunder, *supra* note 20 at 1424.

A second strategy seeks to prompt an abandonment of judgment of the Other through the researcher's preliminary self-reflection and an examination of her own cultural framework and normative assumptions. This approach emphasizes a relinquishing of existing presumptions by looking openly at difference, without measuring it against any set benchmark or standard. It also commands contemplation of the way in which the dominant cultural order and formal legal rules might undermine women's interests.

I rely on these strategies as tools for developing a juridical inquiry that rejects the presumed preference of state over cultural "law", while at the same testing rigorously claims about gender and tradition arising within cultural normative orders. These strategies also prompt research that looks beyond formal and explicit norms and rules set out by the state or by community leaders to uncover more unobvious sites of power and authority within specific settings and relationships. So whereas research premised on assumptions about women and culture, and preoccupied with formal rules and institutions alone might cast women as vulnerable and controlled, they can in fact emerge as bearing considerable agency through the methods advanced here.

An approach that listens critically to women's narratives, and that examines rigorously one's own cultural and normative starting points, thus enables us to spot the ways in which women might shape the rules and expectations by which they, and their families and communities, live. This approach also allows us to unpack common expectations about the universality of culture by unearthing the multiplicity of visions and views within normative orders perceived from the outside as static and monolithic. Finally, this approach forces the researcher to question presumptions about the moral superiority of the dominant legal culture and formal rules, particularly insofar as securing gender equality and protecting vulnerable or disadvantaged group members is concerned. While each of these attributes suggests the potential of feminist legal research for learning about how polygamy unfolds and is understood in Bountiful, they also reveal the overarching utility of such research for investigating traditions, relationships and practices that operate as sites for competing normative claims about gender and culture.

Selected Bibliography on Human Rights and Legal Pluralism

Alston, Philip, Academy of European Law, and New York University. 2009. *Non-state actors and human rights*. Oxford/New York: Oxford University Press.

Andrews, Penelope. 2003. Women's human rights and the conversation across cultures. *Albany Law Review* 67(2): 609.

Arthurs, H.W. 1985. *"Without the law": Administrative justice and legal pluralism in Nineteenth-Century England*. Toronto: University of Toronto Press.

Bakht, Natasha. 2004. Family arbitration using sharia law: Examining Ontario's arbitration act and its impact on women. *Muslim World Journal of Human Rights* 1(1). doi:10.2202/1554-4419.1022. http://www.bepress.com/mwjhr/vol1/iss1/art7

Barzilai, Gad. 2008. Beyond relativism: Where is political power in legal pluralism?. *Theoretical Inquiries in Law* 9(2). doi:10.2202/1565-3404.1191. http://www.bepress.com/til/default/vol9/iss2/art4

Bauer, Joanne. 1999. *The East Asian challenge for human rights*. Cambridge/New York: Cambridge University Press.

Baxi, Upendra. 2007. *Human rights in a posthuman world: Critical essays*. New Delhi/New York: Oxford University Press.

Bell, Gary. 2011. Indonesia – The challenge of legal diversity and law reform. In *Law and legal institutions of Asia: Traditions, adaptations and innovations*, ed. Ann Black and Gary Bell, 262–298. Cambridge: Cambridge University Press.

Belley, Jean-Guy. 1986. L'État et la régulation juridique des sociétés globalesdeuxpointsPour une problématique du pluralisme juridique. *Sociologie et Societes* 18(1): 11–32.

Belley, Jean-Guy. 1997. Law as terra incognita: Constructing legal pluralism. *Canadian Journal of Law and Society* 12: 17.

Bello, Emmanuel G. 1985. The African charter on human and peoples' rights: A legal analysis. *Recueil des Cours* 194: 9–268.

Benda-Beckmann, Franz. 2005. *Mobile people, mobile law: Expanding legal relations in a contracting world*. Aldershot Hants/Burlington: Ashgate.

Berman, Paul Schiff. 2006. Global legal pluralism. *Southern California Law Review* 80: 1155.

Berman, Paul Schiff. 2009. The new legal pluralism. *Annual Review of Law and Social Science* 5: 225–242.

Blackett, Adelle, and Colleen Sheppard. 2003. Collective bargaining and equality: Making connections. *International Labour Review* 142(4): 419–457. doi:10.1111/j.1564-913X.2003.tb00539.x.

Borrows, John. 2010. *Canada's indigenous constitution*. Toronto: University of Toronto Press.

Bunn-Livingstone, Sandra. 2002. *Juricultural pluralism vis-à-vis treaty law: State practice and attitudes*. The Hague/Boston: Martinus Nijhoff Publishers.

R. Provost and C. Sheppard (eds.), *Dialogues on Human Rights and Legal Pluralism*, Ius Gentium: Comparative Perspectives on Law and Justice 17,
DOI 10.1007/978-94-007-4710-4, © Springer Science+Business Media Dordrecht 2013

Bunting, Annie. 1993. Theorizing women's cultural diversity in feminist international human rights strategies. *Journal of Law and Society* 20(1): 6.

Campbell, Angela. 2008. Wives' tales: Reflecting on research in bountiful. *Canadian Journal of Law and Society* 23(1–2): 121–141.

Campbell, Angela. 2009. Bountiful voices. *Osgoode Hall Law Journal* 47: 183.

Campbell, Angela. 2010. Bountiful's plural marriages. *International Journal of Law in Context* 6(4): 343–361. doi:10.1017/S1744552310000297.

Campbell, Angela, and Alberta Civil Liberties Research Centre.;Canada. 2005. *Polygamy in Canada: Legal and social implications for women and children: A collection of policy research reports*. Ottawa: Status of Women Canada.

Charney, Jonathan I. 1998. Is international law threatened by multiple international tribunals? *Recueil des cours – Académie de Droit International de La Haye* 271: 101–382.

Clapham, Andrew, and Academy of European Law. 2006. *Human rights obligations of non-state actors*. Oxford/New York: Oxford University Press.

Cook, Rebecca. 1994. *Human rights of women: National and international perspectives*. Philadelphia: University of Pennsylvania Press.

Coutu, Michel. 2007. Legal pluralism, labour law and the Sovereign state. *Canadian Labour and Employment Law Journal* 13: 169–185.

Cover, Robert M. 1983. The Supreme Court, 1982 term. *Harvard Law Review* 97(1): 1–68. doi:10.2307/1340787.

Cowan, Jane. 2001. *Culture and rights: Anthropological perspectives*. Cambridge/New York: Cambridge University Press.

D'Sa, R.M. 1981. The African charter on human and peoples' rights: Problems and prospects for regional action. *Australian Yearbook of International Law* 10: 101.

Daly, Richard. 2003. A dialogue on the effects of aboriginal rights litigation and activism on aboriginal communities in Northwestern British Columbia. *Social Analysis* 47(3): 108.

Delmas-Marty, Mireille. 2004. *Les forces imaginantes du droit*. Paris: Éditions du Seuil.

Delmas-Marty, Mireille. 2006. *Le pluralisme ordonné: Les forces imaginantes du droit (II)*. Paris: Éditions du Seuil.

Delmas-Marty, Mireille, and Marie-Laure Izorche. 2000. Marge nationale D'Appreciation et internationalisation du Droit: Rééflexions sur la validité formelle d'un commun pluraliste. *McGill Law Journal* 46: 923.

Desrosiers, Julie. 2005. *Isolement et mesures disciplinaires dans les centres de réadaptation pour jeunes*. Montréal: Wilson et Lafleur.

Engle, Karen. 2001. From skepticism to embrace: Human rights and the American anthropological association from 1947–1999. *Human Rights Quarterly* 23(3): 536–559.

Fischer-Lescano, Andreas, and Gunther Teubner. 2003. Regime-collisions: The vain search for legal unity in the fragmentation of global law. *Michigan Journal of International Law* 25: 999.

Fuentes, Carlos Iván. 2008. Normative plurality in international law: The role of soft law in the jurisprudence of the Inter-American court of human rights. *SSRN eLibrary* (October 13). http://papers.ssrn.com/sol3/papers.cfm?abstract_id=1134101

Fuller, Lon. 1969. *The morality of law*. Rev. ed. New Haven/London: Yale University Press.

Gagnon, Alain, and Institute for Research on Public Policy. 2003. *The conditions of diversity in multinational democracies*. Montreal: Institute for Research on Public Policy (IRPP).

Gaudreault-DesBiens, Jean-François. 2009. *Le droit, la religion et le raisonnable: Le fait religieux entre monisme étatique et pluralisme juridique*. Montréal: Éditions Thémis.

Glenn, Jane Matthews. 2008. Informal formality: Tenantries, ejidos and family land. *International Journal of Law in Context* 4(02): 135–148. doi:10.1017/S1744552308002036.

Glenn, Patrick H. 2010. *Legal traditions of the world: Sustainable diversity in law*, 4th ed. Oxford/New York: Oxford University Press.

Grenfell, Laura. 2006. Legal pluralism and the rule of law in Timor Leste. *Leiden Journal of International Law* 19(02): 305–337. doi:10.1017/S0922156506003323.

Griffin, James. 2008. *On human rights*. Oxford/New York: Oxford University Press.

Griffiths, John. 1986. What is legal pluralism. *Journal of Legal Pluralism and Unofficial Law* 24: 1.

Hart, H.L.A. 1994. *The concept of law*, 2nd ed. Oxford/New York: Clarendon Press/Oxford University Press.

Hertogh, M., and Oñati International Institute for the Sociology of Law. 2009. *Living law: Reconsidering Eugen Ehrlich*. Oxford: Hart publishing.

International Council on Human Rights Policy. 2009. *When legal worlds overlap: Human rights, state and non-state law*. International Council on Human Rights Policy. http://www.ichrp.org/files/reports/50/135_report_en.pdf

International Law Commission, and Martti Koskenniemi. 682. Report of the study group – Fragmentation of international law: Difficulties arising from the diversification and expansion of international law.

Jensen, Erik. 2003. *Beyond common knowledge: Empirical approaches to the rule of law*. Stanford: Stanford University Press.

Jouannet, Emmanuelle. 2007. Universalism and imperialism: The true-false paradox of international law? *European Journal of International Law* 18(3): 379–407. doi:10.1093/ejil/chm029.

Kasirer, Nicholas. 2003. Legal education as metissage. *Tulane Law Review* 78: 481.

Kennedy, David. 2007. One, two, three, many legal orders: Legal pluralism and the Cosmopolitan Dream. *N.Y.U. Review of Law and Social Change* 31: 641–659.

Kleinhans, Martha-Marie, and Roderick A. Macdonald. 1997. What is a critical legal pluralism. *Canadian Journal of Law and Society* 12: 25–46.

Koch, Ida Elisabeth. 2005. Dichotomies, trichotomies or waves of duties? *Human Rights Law Review* 5: 81–103. doi:10.1093/hrlrev/ngi004.

Koskenniemi, Martti. 2006. International law: Between fragmentation and constitutionalism. In Camberra: Australian National University, November 27. http://cigj.anu.edu.au/cigj/link_documents/KoskenniemiPaper.pdf

Legrand, Pierre. 1997. The impossibility of legal transplants. *Maastricht Journal of European and Comparative Law* 4: 111–124.

M'Baye, Keba. 1992. *Les droits de l'homme en Afrique*. Paris: Éditions A. Pedone.

MacDonald, Roderick A. 1996. Les Vieilles Gardes. Hypothèses sur l'émergence des normes, l'internormativité et le désordre à travers une typologie des institutions normatives. In *Le droit soluble: Contributions québécoises à l'étude l'internormativité*, ed. Jean-Guy Belley. Paris: Librairie générale de droit et de jurisprudence.

MacDonald, Roderick A. 1998a. Metaphors of multiplicity: Civil society, regimes and legal pluralism. *Arizona Journal of International and Comparative Law* 15: 69.

MacDonald, Roderick A. 1998b. Critical legal pluralism as a construction of normativity and the emergence of law. In *Théories et émergence du droit: Pluralisme, surdétermination, effectivité*, ed. Andrée Lajoie, 12. Montréal: Éditions Thémis.

MacDonald, Roderick A. 2003. The legal mediation of social diversity. In *The conditions of diversity in multinational democracies*, ed. Alain Gagnon, François Rocher, and Maria Montserrat Guibernau, 85–114. Montreal: Institute for Research on Public Policy (IRPP).

MacDonald, Roderick A. 2008. Three metaphors of norm migration in international context. *Brooklyn Journal of International Law* 34: 603.

MacDonald, Roderick A., and Thomas McMorrow. 2009. Myths of miscegenation. In *The law/politics distinction in contemporary public law adjudication*, ed. B. Iancu, 89. Utrecht: Eleven International Publishing.

MacDonald, Roderick, and Queen's University (Kingston, Ont.).;Law Commission of Canada. 2002. *Lessons of everyday law*. Montreal: Published for the Law Commission of Canada and the School of Policy Studies Queen's University by McGill-Queen's University Press.

Malik, Charles, and Centre for Lebanese Studies (Great Britain);Charles Malik Foundation. 2000. *The challenge of human rights: Charles Malik and the universal declaration*. Oxford: Charles Malik Foundation/Centre for Lebanese Studies.

Mautner, Menachem. 2008. From 'honor' to 'dignity': How should a liberal state treat non-liberal cultural groups?. *Theoretical Inquiries in Law* 9(2). doi:10.2202/1565-3404.1199. http://www.bepress.com/til/default/vol9/iss2/art12

Mayer, Ann. 1999. *Islam and human rights: Tradition and politics*, 3rd ed. Boulder: Westview Press.

McCorquodale, Robert. 2002. Overlegalizing silences: Human rights and nonstate actors. *Proceedings of the Annual Meeting (American Society of International Law)* 96: 384–388.
Mégret, Frédéric. 2005. In defense of hybridity: Towards a representational theory of international criminal justice. *Cornell International Law Journal* 38: 725.
Mégret, Frédéric. 2008. The disabilities convention: Human rights of persons with disabilities or disability rights? *Human Rights Quarterly* 30(2): 494–516.
Melissaris, Emmanuel. 2004. The more the merrier? A new take on legal pluralism. *Social and Legal Studies* 13(1): 57–79. doi:10.1177/0964663904040192.
Melissaris, Emmanuel. 2006. Perspective, critique, and pluralism in legal theory. *Northern Ireland Legal Quarterly* 57: 597.
Melissaris, Emmanuel. 2009. *Ubiquitous law: Legal theory and the space for legal pluralism*. Farnham Surrey/Burlington: Ashgate Publishing.
Merry, Sally. 1988. Legal pluralism. *Law and Society Review* 22(5): 869–896.
Merry, Sally Engle. 2003a. Rights talk and the experience of law: Implementing women's human rights to protection from violence. *Human Rights Quarterly* 25: 343.
Merry, Sally Engle. 2003b. Human rights law and the demonization of culture (and anthropology along the way). *PoLAR: Political and Legal Anthropology Review* 26(1): 55–76. doi:10.1525/pol.2003.26.1.55.
Merry, Sally. 2005. Anthropological currents – The female inheritance movement in Hong Kong: Theorizing the local global interface with CA comment. *Current Anthropology* 46(3): 387.
Merry, Sally. 2006a. *Human rights and gender violence: Translating international law into local justice*. Chicago: University of Chicago Press.
Merry, Sally Engle. 2006b. Human rights and transnational culture: Regulating gender violence through global law. *Osgoode Hall Law Journal* 44: 53.
Merry, Sally Engle. 2008. International law and sociolegal scholarship: Toward a spatial global legal pluralism. *Studies in Law, Politics and Society* 41: 149–168.
Michaels, Ralf. 2005. The re-state-ment of non-state law: The state, choice of law, and the challenge from global legal pluralism. *Wayne Law Review* 51: 1209.
Michaels, Ralf. 2009. Global legal pluralism. *Annual Review of Law and Social Science* 5: 243–262.
Mickelson, Karin. 1998. How universal is the universal declaration. *University of New Brunswick Law Journal* 47: 19.
Miller, Jonathan M. 2003. A typology of legal transplants: Using sociology, legal history and argentine examples to explain the transplant proces. *The American Journal of Comparative Law* 51(4): 839–885. doi:10.2307/3649131.
Moore, Sally Falk. 1978. *Law as process: An anthropological approach*. London: Routledge and K. Paul.
Motoc, Iulia. 2008. Conception of pluralism and international law. In *Select proceedings of the European society of International Law*. Oxford: Hart Publishing.
Na'īm, 'Abd. 1992. *Human rights in cross-cultural perspectives: A quest for consensus*. Philadelphia: University of Pennsylvania Press.
Na'īm, 'Abd. 2002. *Cultural transformation and human rights in Africa*. London/New York: Zed Books; Distributed in the USA by Palgrave.
Nader, Laura, and Wenner-Gren Foundation for Anthropological Research. 1969. *Law in culture and society*. Chicago: Aldine Publishing Company.
Napoleon, Val. 2010. Living together: Gitksan legal reasoning as a foundation for consent. In *Between consenting peoples: Political community and the meaning of consent*, ed. Jeremy Webber and Richard Daly, 45. Vancouver: UBC Press.
Napoleon, Val, Angela Cameron, Colette Arcand, and Dahti Scott. 2008. Where is the law in restorative justice. In *Aboriginal self-government in Canada: Current trends and issues*, 3rd ed, ed. Yale Belanger, 348. Saskatoon: Purich Publishing.
Ouguergouz, Fatsah. 2003. *The African charter of human and people's rights: A comprehensive agenda for human dignity and sustainable democracy in Africa*. Hague/New York: Kluwer Law International.

Parker, Christine. 2008. The pluralization of regulation. *Theoretical Inquiries in Law* 9(2). doi:10.2202/1565-3404.1189. http://www.bepress.com/til/default/vol9/iss2/art2

Perez, Oren. 2003. Normative creativity and global legal pluralism: Reflections on the democratic critique of transnational law. *Indiana Journal of Global Legal Studies* 10(2): 25–64.

Petersen, Hanne, and Henrik Zahle, eds. 1995. *Legal polycentricity: Consequences of pluralism in law*. Brookfield: Dartmouth Publishing company.

Posner, Eric. 2009. *The perils of global legalism*. Chicago: University of Chicago Press.

Provost, René. 2002. *International human rights and humanitarian law*. Cambridge: Cambridge University Press.

Provost, René. 2007. The international committee of the red widget – The diversity debate and international humanitarian law. *Israel Law Review* 40: 614.

Provost, René. 2008. Judging in splendid isolation. *American Journal of Comparative Law* 56: 125.

Raz, Joseph. 2009. *The authority of law: Essays on law and morality*, 2nd ed. Oxford/New York: Oxford University Press.

Riles, Annelise. 1998. Infinity within the brackets. *American Ethnologist* 25(3): 378–398.

Riles, Annelise. 2006. Anthropology, human rights, and legal knowledge: Culture in the iron cage. *American Anthropologist* 108(1): 52–65. doi:10.1525/aa.2006.108.1.52.

Rocher, Guy. 2006. *Sociologie et société québécoise présences de Guy Rocher*. Montréal: Presses de l'Université de Montréal.

Rorty, Richard. 1998. *Truth and progress: Philosophical papers*, vol. 3. Cambridge: Cambridge University Press.

Rüsen, Jörn. 1993. Human rights from the perspective of a universal history. In *Human rights and cultural diversity*, ed. Wolfgang Schmale. Goldblach: Keip Publishing.

Sen, Amartya. 2004. Elements of a theory of human rights. *Philosophy and Public Affairs* 32(4)): 315–356.

Sezgin, Yüksel, ed. 2010. Special issue on human rights and legal pluralism. *Journal of Legal Pluralism and Unofficial Law* 60.

Shachar, Ayelet. 2001. *Multicultural jurisdictions: Cultural differences and women's rights*. Cambridge/New York: Cambridge University Press.

Shachar, Ayelet. 2008. Privatizing diversity: A cautionary tale from religious arbitration in family law. *Theoretical Inquiries in Law* 9(2). doi:10.2202/1565-3404.1198. http://www.bepress.com/til/default/vol9/iss2/art11

Sheppard, Colleen. 1998. Equality rights and institutional change: Insights from Canada and the United States. *Arizona Journal of International and Comparative Law* 15: 143.

Sheppard, Colleen. 2010. *Inclusive equality: The relational dimensions of systemic discrimination in Canada*. Montreal: McGill-Queen's University Press.

Stone, Katherine. 1992. The legacy of industrial pluralism: The tension between individual employment rights and the new deal collective bargaining system. *The University of Chicago Law Review* 59(2): 575.

Tamanaha, Brian. 2000. A non-essentialist version of legal pluralism. *Journal of Law and Society* 27(2): 296.

Tamanaha, Brian. 2001. *A general jurisprudence of law and society*. Oxford/New York: Oxford University Press.

Tasioulas, John. 2007. The moral reality of human rights. In *Freedom from poverty as a human right: Who owes what to the very poor?* ed. Thomas Pogge, 75–102. New York: Oxford University Press.

Teubner, Gunther. 1983. Substantive and reflexive elements in modern law. *Law and Society Review* 17(2): 239.

Teubner, Gunther. 1996. Global Bukowina: Legal pluralism in the world-society. In *Global law without a state*, ed. Gunther Teubner. Aldershot: Dartmouth.

Twining, William. 2009a. Normative and legal pluralism: A global perspective. *Duke Journal of Comparative & International Law* 20: 473–517.

Twining, William. 2009b. *General jurisprudence: Understanding law from a global perspective*. Cambridge/New York: Cambridge University Press.

Vallée, Guylaine. 2006. Le droit du travail comme lieu de pluralisme juridique: aspects historiques et enjeux actuels. In *Sociologie et société québécoise. Presences de Guy Rocher*, ed. C. Saint-Pierre and J.P. Warren, 241–265. Montréal: Presses de l'Université de Montréal.

Vallée, Guylaine, Michel Coutu, and Marie-Christine Hebert. 2001. Implementing equality rights in the workplace: An empirical study. *Canadian Labour and Employment Law Journal* 8: 71.

Van Praagh, Shauna. 1996. The chutzpah of chasidism. *Canadian Journal of Law and Society* 11(2): 193–216.

Van Praagh, Shauna. 1999. Faith, belonging, and the protection of 'our' children. *Windsor Yearbook of Access to Justice* 17: 154.

Webber, Jeremy. 2006. Legal pluralism and human agency. *Osgoode Hall Law Journal* 44: 167.

Weeramantry, Christopher, and Nathaniel Berman. 1998. The Grotus lecture series. *American University of International Law Review* 14: 1515.

Index

A

Abu-Lughod, Lila
- Bedouin Arab communities, 252
- cultural practices, 214–215
- harem, 252
- patriarchal communities, 253

Accommodation
- burqa, 33
- religious observance, 33

Actors
- non-state (*see* Co-legislators)
- state, 4, 62–63, 65, 66

Act Respecting Industrial Accidents and Occupational Diseases, 152

Act Respecting Labour Standards, 152, 158–159

Act Respecting Occupational Health and Safety, 152

Adolescents. *See* Youth protection; *Youth rehabilitation centres*

Adverse effects, 7, 131, 132

African Charter on Human and Peoples' Rights
- colonialism, 143
- legal philosophy, 50
- M'baye, Kéba, 43, 49–50
- Organization of African Unity, 49
- responsibilities, 50
- rights of peoples, 43, 50
- specificity, 50

Agency
- human, 20, 23, 30, 36
- legal actors, 4, 5
- women (*see* Matsuda, Mari; Researcher)

Alvarez, Alejandro, 46

American International Law
- Alvarez, Alejandro, 46

Anaya, James
- self-determination, 135

Appadurai, Arjun
- globalization from below, 139

Asad, Talal, 215

Asia. *See also* China; Domestic violence; Hong Kong; India; Women
- non-governmental organisations, 10, 65, 191

B

Batshaw Committee, 183–184

Battered women. *See also* Hawai'i; Merry, Sally Engle; Vernacularization
- Hong Kong, 213–214
- intermediaries (*see* Translators)
- local legal institutions, 214

Berman, Paul Schiff
- global legal pluralism, 3, 70, 99, 130, 133, 135, 138, 139

Best interest of the child
- *Baker v. Canada (Minister of Citizenship and Immigration)*, 140
- Convention on the Rights of the Child, 140

Bohannan, Paul. *See also* Gluckman-Bohannan debate
- folk categories, 210
- Tiv, 210

Borrows, John
- sources of law in Indigenous societies, 230

Bountiful. *See also* Researcher
- children, 265–266
- closed religious community, 254
- collective discourse, 261

R. Provost and C. Sheppard (eds.), *Dialogues on Human Rights and Legal Pluralism*, Ius Gentium: Comparative Perspectives on Law and Justice 17,
DOI 10.1007/978-94-007-4710-4,

Bountiful (*cont.*)
community norms
bindingness, 87–94
competing normative claims, 267
co-wife, 148
Criminal Code, 247, 248, 265
cultural membership, 256
experiential knowledge, 250, 251, 253, 256
fundamentalist mormons, 247, 261
gender equality, 256, 263, 267
genderized practice, 248–249, 266
hierarchies among women, 252, 253, 260, 261
immigration, 254, 265
narratives of women, 248, 250, 255
plural marriage, 247–250, 257–260, 262, 265
polycentricity of relationships, 253
polygamy, 247–250, 253, 254, 257–260, 263–267
recognition of cultural pluralism, 257
right of exit, 258
storyteller, 260
Brierly, James, 63
British Columbia. *See also* Gitksan
bountiful, 247, 249, 253
Treaty 8, 231, 236–237

C
Canadian Charter of Rights and Freedoms
governing instrument, 22
Cassin, René
author, 40–41
Universal Declaration on Human Rights, 40–41, 45
CEDAW. *See* Convention on the Elimination of All Forms of Discrimination Against Women (CEDAW)
Charter of Human Rights and Freedoms, Québec, 103, 126, 152, 153, 191
Children, 7, 25, 31, 32, 51, 58, 80, 86, 104, 140, 165, 187, 219, 243, 248, 254, 256, 264–266
Children's rights. *See also* Youth; Youth protection
right to childhood, 21
China, 220, 221. *See also* Hong Kong
cultural nationalism, 218
Churchill, Winston
International Committee of Movements for European Unity, 44
Church of Latter Day Saints. *See* Polygamy
Citizenship. *See also* Indigenous citizenry; Industrial citizenship
economic citizenship
cosmopolitan self, 115
Civil Code of Québec, 112, 152, 158–160, 166, 183, 197, 264
Codes of Conduct
community, 3
corporate, 85–86, 89
informal, 3, 6, 129, 139
institutional
human rights violation, 7–8, 180
informal, 6, 129, 139, 180
workplace, 3
youth rehabilitation centres
Québec, 169
Cold War, 39, 41
Co-legislators, 8, 164
Colonial. *See also* Colonialism; Colonization
laws, 75–77
legal systems
local law, 75
nations, 2
powers, 101
principles of civilization, 75
repugnancy clause, 75, 76
Colonialism, 38, 49, 75–77, 222, 245
Colonization. *See also* Decolonization
formal laws, 2
nations, 2
Colonizing nations, 2
Communities
aboriginal, 10, 136, 233
community-based customs/practices, 138
discrete (*see also* Insular)
Church of Latter Day Saints, 9
marginalization, 9–11, 252
sub-groups, 9, 252
indigenous (*see* Gitksan)
linguistic
anglophones, 137
educational policy, 137–138
empowerment, 138
equality rights, 21, 137
francophones, 137
locus, 2
minority, 130, 132, 135, 137–138, 140, 142
object of study, 2
political autonomy, 135
practice, 9–11, 135, 138, 142, 238, 252, 263
religious community (*see* Bountiful)
semi-autonomous communities (*see* Moore, Sally Falk)

structure, 2, 10, 11, 266
values, 11, 32
women
domestic violence, 9
wives, 10
Conciliator, 11
Convention
coexistence, 47
regional, 47, 48, 80, 139
universal, 47
Convention on the Elimination of All Forms of Discrimination Against Women (CEDAW), 51, 83, 141, 188, 209
Convention on the Rights of migrant workers, 80
Convention on the Rights of Persons with Disabilities, 80, 130
Convention on the Rights of the Child, 51, 83, 140, 165, 183, 188
Cosmopolitan law
plurality, 29, 32, 71
Cover, Robert
jurisgenesis, 5
narrative, 5, 52, 61
nomos, 5, 61
Criminal Tribunals
ad hoc, 55–56
hybrid, 55–56
Critical legal pluralism
modes of law
plurality, 23
multiple legal orders, 26–27
sites of law
plurality, 23
Cross-cultural. *See* Trans-cultural values
Cultural
exceptionalism, 5
local frameworks, 139, 228
practices, 31, 33, 67, 238, 240, 244, 248–249, 251–253, 255, 256, 261–263
reservations, 5
specificity, 5, 28, 33
Cultural defence, 25, 26, 31–34
Cultural translator. *See also* Vernacular
hybridization, 9, 222–226
replication, 9, 218–222
Culture
technological culture, 106
Custom. *See also* Customary law(s)
laws, 135, 230, 233
norms, 2, 129, 130, 133
Customary law(s)
indigenous customary law, 2
indigenous legal orders, 233
Customary norm(s)
implicit canonical norms, 27

D

Declaration on the Rights of Indigenous Peoples, 136–137
Decolonization, 101, 108
Delocalization
human being, 110
human dignity
infringements, 110
international legal standards, 5
legal personality, 109, 110
monist doctrine, 108–109
national centralization of law, 109
state-centric
positive law, 109
Diplomatic immunity
law of, 54
Disaggregation of rights
discrete rights, 8
Discrimination. *See also* Adverse effects; Disparate impact; Sturm, Susan
adverse effects discrimination, 7, 131, 132
anti-discrimination
as facilitative law, 134
participatory forms of governance, 134
socio-legal backlash, 134
indirect discrimination, 7, 131
structural discrimination
workplace processes
and decision-making, 133, 134
systemic discrimination, 131, 132, 135
Disparate impact, 7
Domestic violence, 2, 9, 58, 219–224, 226
Dupuy, Pierre-Marie, 64

E

Economic and social rights. *See also* Housing; Labour law; Right to housing
access to justice, 8
adjudicative space, 203–204
disaggregation, 8
discrete rights, 8, 203
enforceability (*see also* Housing)
complaints procedure, 191–192
shadow reports, 191
intersecting forms of normativity, 203
justiciability, 8, 188, 191, 194, 203

Economic and social rights (*cont.*)
legal effect
implementation of rights, 188
recognition of rights, 188, 191
public interest standing, 163
state obligations
fulfill, 89, 124
protect, 192, 193
respect, 107, 192, 193
Economic globalization. *See also* Second modernity
corporate economy, 107
corporate liberalism
efficiency of the economic system, 112
global village, 112
multinational organizations, 107
openness of borders, 112
transnational organizations, 107, 125
Elder(s)
aboriginal communities, 10
female, 10
South Africa
interpretation of traditional customs, 139
leadership, 139
Emergence of legal persons, 65
Equal
protection, 122, 126
Equality. *See also* Equality rights; Non-discrimination
in everyday life, 1, 6, 129, 132–134
gender, 21, 22, 33, 139, 219, 223, 225, 256, 263, 267
legal regulation
affirmative action, 132
proactive measures, 132
prism of legal pluralism, 7, 129–143
Equality rights
educational policy
critical strategy, 137
minority linguistic communities, 137–138
equitable representation, 142
global human rights
informal practice, 131
group-based equality, 138, 139, 142
informal law
social institutions, 142
institutional codes of conduct, 129
legal instruments, 129
lens
community, 130, 253
institutional, 129–135
transnational, 130
mobilization strategies, 143
municipal human rights documents, 129
protection of vulnerable individuals, 142
European Commission of Human Rights. *See also* European Court on Human Rights
Beer and Regan, 53
extinct, 53
Richard Waite and Terry Kennedy, 53
European Convention on Human Rights. *See also* Margin of appreciation
European Union, 44, 45
European Court on Human Rights, 53
European Social Charter, 188–189, 191

F

Family. *See also* Bountiful
adultery, 265
governance by state, 263–264
as mini-legal order, 86
Female genital cutting
bodily integrity, 262–263
clitorectomy, 21
plastic surgery, 262
Fiduciary duties
aboriginal peoples, 202
breach, 202, 203
First Nations. *See also* Indigenous
colonialism, 22, 26–29, 38, 49, 75–77
colonization, 2, 76, 136
Formal law(s). *See also* Colonization
domestic law, 3, 54, 60, 62, 75, 76, 103, 130, 140
instruments, 4
international law, 3–5, 32, 37–68, 73–76, 84, 103, 112, 136, 139, 141, 218, 224
regional law, 3

G

Gitksan. *See also* First Nations; Indigenous; Indigenous legal orders
British Columbia, 231
legitimation of Gitksan legal order, 238
Global legal pluralism. *See also* Berman, Paul Schiff
colonial societies, 71
counter-hegemonic globalization, 94
post-colonial societies, 71
third generation, 71
Gluckman-Bohannan debate
difficulties of translation, 210

Gluckman, Max. *See also* Gluckman-Bohannan debate
  Barotse, 220
  reasonable man, 10
Goffman, Erving
  house rules, 177
  total institutions
    absence of privacy, 174–176
    admissions, 169–172
    identity, 172–174
    minute regulation of daily life, 177–180
Governance. *See also* Family
  autonomy, 130, 135, 138, 142
    social relations of power, 263–264
  Gitksan, 234
  group-based equality, 130, 135–136, 138, 142
  indigenous, 136, 230, 232, 234, 236–238, 243, 244
  indigenous legal orders, 136, 230, 232, 234, 236–238, 243, 244
  kinship systems, 238 (*see also* Local; Locality)
  market-based approach, 188
  neoliberal approach, 188
  self-governance
    group-based equality, 130, 135–136, 138, 142
Griffiths, John
  legal pluralism
    strong, 72, 81
    weak, 72, 74, 94

H
Hawai'i
  domestic violence program, 222
  Hawaiian sovereignty movement, 222
  oppression by colonialism, 222
  symbolic indigenization, 222
Hong Kong. *See also* Ling, Chan Ko
  cultural nationalism, 218
  domestic violence program, 219
Honour killings, 21
Housing. *See also* Economic and social rights; Right to housing
  justiciability, 8, 188, 191, 192, 194, 203
Human dignity
  central marker of democratic constitutionalism, 103
  equal dignity, 103–105
Humanism
  individualist, 108
  legal personality, 108
  philosophical, 105, 106
Humanitarian intervention, 75, 87
Humanitarian organizations
  field rules, 88
  standards of conduct, 88
Human rights
  action
    sub-state entities, 82–84
  actor-oriented, 94
  alternative dispute resolution mechanisms, 91
  circulation, 227
  community, 2, 3, 5, 10, 11, 18, 37, 62, 80, 130, 208, 227
  cosmopolitan, 6, 32, 69, 71, 125, 207
  cultural pluralization, 80–81
  culture, 30, 31, 38, 67, 73, 85, 87, 93, 252
  discourse
    essentialism, 4
  Drittwirkung, 2
  emergence of, 4, 5, 38–52, 58, 60–61, 63, 78, 126
  enlightenment view of
    ancient régime, 70
    corps intermédiaire, 70
  idea
    aspiration, 18, 35–36
    rights claims, 18
  individual, 1–3, 6, 25, 29–31, 66
  law
    fragmentation, 5, 52–60, 66
  legal phenomenon, 35
  local settings, 209
  natural rights, 73
  nomadic character, 6
  normative fragmentation, 5
  normative project, 69
  norms, 1–11, 26, 28, 31, 51–52, 58–61, 67, 69, 75, 79, 83, 89, 90, 93, 95, 130, 139, 140, 211
  pluralist agenda, 88, 93
  pluralization, 80–81
  privileged sites, 4, 6
  standards, 1, 2, 4–6, 9–11, 51, 56, 61, 163, 209
  violence against women, 2, 10, 207, 209, 212, 218–219, 223, 224, 228
Human Rights Code, Ontario, 156
Human Rights Codes
  discrimination, 34
Human rights discourse, 4, 6, 10, 18, 21, 25, 34, 71, 84, 88, 93–95, 210

Humphrey, John
author, 39, 40
UDHR, 39–41, 43

I

ICESCR. *See* International Covenant on Economic, Social and Cultural Rights (ICESCR)
Identity
individual, 108, 167, 172, 177
markers, 5, 34
states, 5
Inclusion. *See* Discrimination; Equality
India. *See also* Vernacularization
dalits, 223, 224
domestic violence, 223, 224
empowerment program, 223
Gujarat, 223, 224, 226
mahila panch, 225
nari adalats
authority, 224, 225
levels of translation, 225–226
panchayat, 225
sahyoginis, 224–226
sangha, 223–225
shakti, 226
Uttar Pradesh, 223, 224
women's collectives, 223, 224
Indigenization
framing
collective action frames, 212
resonance, 212–213
symbolic dimension, 212
Indigenous. *See also* Colonization; Colonizing nations; First Nations; Indigenous legal orders
citizenry, 245
customary law(s), 2
global indigenous rights, 80, 222
local practice, 33
Indigenous citizenry, 245
Indigenous legal orders. *See also* Borrows, John; Governance
carrier, 231
Cree
reciprocal legal responsibilities, 241
cultural institution, 233
Dunneza, 231
elders, 235
explicit law, 236
Gitksan
ayook, 230, 234
cultural ethic, 239
decentralized society, 233
Feast hall, 238
kinship network, 241
legitimation of legal order, 238
matrilineal, 233, 241
oral traditions recording law, 240
reasoning process, 236
reciprocal obligations, 241
implicit law, 235
inclusion of indigenous women (*see also* Elder(s))
colonial mythology, 244
Indian Act, 242
Innu
conflict avoidance, 238, 239
oral tradition, 40
practices, 240
reserve boundaries, 242
as societally bound, 232
spirit world, 235
sweet grass, 240
tradition, 240, 243, 244
Tsimshian
kinship system, 242
on/off reserve, 242
Wet'suwet'en, 231
Industrial citizenship, 149
Informal law(s). *See* Customary law(s)
Institution(s)
formal institutions, 5–6, 91–92, 224
instruments, 5–6, 168
jurisdiction, 6
private, 6
public, 6, 7, 61
Institutional
level
human rights entities, 59
multiplication, 38, 60
regionalism, 60
Institutional norms, 3, 6, 7, 79, 129–130, 134
Institutional practices
community codes of conduct, 3
workplace, 3
Insular, 11, 254
Insular communities. *See* Bountiful
Integrity
physical, 6, 103
psychological, 6
Inter-American Conference on Problems of War and Peace, 46
Inter-American Convention on the Protection of Human Rights
Roman Catholic identity, 48

Inter-American Court of Human Rights
  Velasques-Rodriguez case, 64
International
  human rights law
    cultural profiling, 61
    dislocation, 58, 93
    hegemonic model, 61, 62
    universality, 51, 52, 58
  human rights regime
    paradox, 11, 139
International Committee of Movements for European Unity
  Churchill, Winston, 44
  Teitgen, Pierre-Henri, 44, 45
International Court of Justice
  African Charter of Human and Peoples' Rights
    interpretation, 56
International Covenant on Civil and Political Rights, 48, 140, 191
International Covenant on Civil and Political Rights, Optional Protocol
  Lovelace v. Canada
    discrimination against indigenous women, 140
    indian status, 140
    legislative reform, 140
International Covenant on Economic, Social and Cultural Rights (ICESCR), 188, 191, 192, 203
International Criminal Tribunal for the former Yugoslavia
  prohibition on torture
    as peremptory norm, 55
International human rights
  actors (*see* Non-state)
  dynamic
    centralization, 72
    decentralization, 72
  net cost, 93
  normative system, 69–71
  pluralization
    functional, 80–81
    indigenous, 80
    personal, 80
  regional instruments, 58
International law. *See also* International Law Commission (ILC)
  fragmentation
    horizontal, 68
    phenomenon, 52
  plural, 60
  public
    matrix, 74
  soft law
    institutional codes of conduct, 6
International Law Commission (ILC). *See also Jus cogens;* Koskenniemi, Martti
  Report of the Study Group–Fragmentation in International Law: Difficulties arising from the Diversification and Expansion of International Law
    hierarchization, 54
    proliferation of institutions, 54
    regionalism, 54
    self-contained regimes, 54
International Monetary Fund, 187
  Internormative. *See also* Internormativity
  challenge, 31
  trajectories
    plurality, 27
Internormativity
  phenomenon, 19
  trajectories, 27
Islamic Law. *See* Shari'a law

J

Jus cogens
  definition
    international law commission, 59

K

Koskenniemi, Martti
  International Law Commission, Report of the Study Group-Fragmentation in International Law: Difficulties arising from the Diversification and Expansion of International Law, 54

L

Labour law. *See also* Economic and social rights; Rocher, Guy
  arbitrator
    adjudicator, 146, 149, 155
    as interpreter, 149, 164
  autonomous sources of law, 146
  collective agreements
    as privileged site of norms, 149
  collective bargaining law
    new era, 150
  collective negotiation, 149, 151, 152, 157, 159, 161
  compatibility with state law
    method employed, 159–160

Labour law (*cont.*)
contractual freedom, 147, 151
duty to accommodate, 160
emergency of statutory norms, 158, 164
employment contract
certification, 150
between employer and employee, 150, 160
individual contract of employment, 150
working conditions, 147, 150
enterprise
democratic project, 148, 151, 163
grievance arbitration
analysis of decisions, 153, 154, 157
binding decisions, 153
contractual autonomy of the parties, 153
external law, 155–156
institutional coherence, 156
internal law, 155
jurisdiction, 154, 156, 157, 161, 162
specialized tribunal, 153
hierarchy of sources of law, 162
industrial citizenship, 149
industrialization, 146–147
industrial pluralism doctrine
fundamental values, 156
normative impact, 151, 163
project of democratization, 163
residual rights, 151
widening scope, 157
jurisdictional issue, 161–162
liberal individualism, 146–147
rights in the workplace
collective, 152–153
individual, 148, 152
social relationships, 146–147
union representation
as legitimate source of opposition, 149
unions
as co-legislators, 164
Labour Relations Act, 156, 157
Law
pluralisation, 4, 5, 62
social control, 21, 29
Law and society
legal regulation, 21–23, 108–109, 115
multiple legal orders, 6–9, 26
plural legal orders, 3
political project, 34
relationship
factual, 100
legal, 100
as resource for an implementation of group-based equality, 142
socio-legal discourse, 70
soft version, 78–79
third generation (*see* Global legal pluralism)
truth claim, 4, 35
understanding of, 62
Westphalian compromise, 74
Legal agents. *See also* Agency
cultural plurality, 5
plurality, 5, 27
Legal centrism, 71
Legal culture
first modernity
decolonization, 108
delocalization, 108–109
liberal democracy, 108–111
monist doctrine, 108–109
second modernity
best practices, 118
corporate liberalism, 111–123
cybernetic regulation of action, 115
de-individualization, 113, 114
de-territorialization, 115
evolution, 112–116, 118, 121
harmonization of rights, 118
ideal self, 116
legal personality, 114, 119–123
organizational pluralism, 117
organizational society, 123
paradox, 112
postmodern person, 118–119
reversal of paradigmatic status, 120
right to social benefits, 113
science of organizational systems, 115
state as stakeholder, 116–117
state relationships, 117, 119
technocratic governance, 113
welfare state, 111, 113
third modernity
contemporary legal pluralism, 124
cosmopolitan humanism, 125
hegemony of organizations, 125
human dignity, 123–125, 128
new dimensions of the right to life, 127
primacy of human principle, 125
Legal narrative. *See also* Cover, Robert
alternative, 62
formal, 62
Legal normativity, 1, 11, 24, 25, 27, 60, 62
notion, 60
Legal orders
indigenous, 9–10, 136, 229–245

Legal personality
general theory, 120
human beings, 110, 119, 120, 123
impersonal entities (*see* Emergence of legal persons)
pluralist ascription of, 121
Legal pluralism
challenge
state centrism, 71
communities of commitment, 74–75
constitutive dimension, 146
epistemological status
autonomous status, 101
scientific construct, 101–102
social ideology, 101, 102, 105–106
explanatory dimension, 146
fundamental dimensions, 4
global (*see* Global legal pluralism)
historical development, 100
internal, 72, 74
labour law, 8, 104, 145–164
Legal plurality
social diversity, 15
Legal regulation
effects
instrumental, 21–23
symbolic, 21–23
Legal subject, 24, 35, 36
Legal tradition, 11, 79, 230, 232, 233, 235, 243–245
Lex specialis derogate legi generali, 58
Ling, Chan Ko. *See also* Merry, Sally Engle
Chinese conceptions of masculinity, 221
domestic violence, 220, 221
Hong Kong, 219
as translator, 221
Yi, 220–221
Local. *See also* Locality; Vernacular
law(s), 3, 29, 31–33, 75, 76, 130–131, 142
norm(s)
entrepreneur, 32
Locality
decentralization, 9
legal orders
indigenous, 9–10
reconciliation, 9
translation, 9

M

Macdonald, Roderick A. *See* Critical Legal Pluralism
Margin of appreciation
elaboration, 11
elasticity of, 80
Matsuda, Mari
plural perspectives, 251
theory of pragmatism, 251
M'baye, Kéba
African Charter on Human and Peoples' Rights, 43, 49–50
author, 43
drafter, 43, 50
Merry, Sally Engle
transnational consensus building, 87–88
Moore, Sally Falk
intermediary bodies, 84–86
semi autonomous social fields, 84, 130
Municipal law, 61, 196, 198

N

Nadeau, Denis, 153–155, 162
Nari adalats, 223–226
Narrative. *See also* Vernacular
dominant, 10
internal, 10
Non-discrimination, 6, 190
Non-State. *See also* Co-legislators
actors
legal personality, 65, 66
emergence of new legal persons, 65
Norm(s). *See also* Customary law(s); Human Rights
emergence of
supranational, 72
hierarchy, 54, 59–60
institutional governance, 6, 7
production
bindingness, 87–94
universal, 3
Normative
fragmentation, 5
Métissage, 66
orders
competing, 26, 267
Normativity
canonical forms
modes of law, 23, 27
global, 31
implicit, 23
inferential, 23, 27
intersecting forms (*see* Economic and social rights)
legal, 11, 24, 25, 27, 60, 62
overlapping, 8, 11, 70, 129

O

Organization of African Unity
  African Charter on Human and Peoples' Rights, 48, 49
  M'baye, Kéba, 49

P

Policy
  decisions, 8, 138, 195, 203
Polygamy. *See also* Bountiful; Researcher
  children, 6, 7, 25, 31, 32, 51, 80, 86, 104, 140, 141, 165, 168, 187, 219, 243, 247–251, 254, 256, 264–266
  criminal prosecution, 265
  state recognition, 121
Positivism, 23, 24, 28, 36, 62, 233
Post-World War II
  international law, 4
  legal reform
    equality rights, 131
  universal human rights, 1, 4
Power
  bureaucratic corporate, 7
  technocratic, 7
Prescriptive law, 30
Principle(s). *See* Norm(s)
Privacy
  corporate codes of conduct, 85, 89
  right (*see also* Goffman, Erving)
    absence from African Charter on Human and Peoples' Rights, 49, 50
    absence from youth rehabilitation centres in Québec, 174–176
Private law, 3, 17, 32, 109, 112–114, 118, 126, 136, 194–197, 200, 203
Professional ethics
  American Anthropological Association, 86, 90
  Hippocratic oath, 90
Project on international courts and tribunals
  institutional density, 55
  permanent institutions
    judicial, 55
    quasi-judicial, 55
  synoptic chart, 55
Protection
  groups, 6
  vulnerable individuals, 6
Public Law, 3, 33, 65, 103, 109, 112–114, 116, 134, 195–198, 201, 203
Public resources, 8, 203

R

Regional
  mechanisms, 39
Religious tribunals
  religious private law, 3, 32
  secular civil law, 32
Researcher
  collective discourse, 261
  conceptual challenge, 255–261
  consciousness
    refined, 259, 260
  empowerment, 138, 214, 223, 225, 259, 260
  experiential knowledge
    challenges, 251
  false consciousness, 250, 251, 255–257, 266
  introspective process, 262
  marginalized subgroups, 252
  minority women's experiences and knowledge, 261
  outsider
    otherness, 262
    risk, 255
  plural perspectives, 251
  reflexive research
    feminist viewpoint, 248–249
    self-reflection, 260–266
  research strategies
    juridical analysis, 249, 257
  storytellers, 260
  theory of pragmatism (*see* Matsuda, Mari)
  traditions, 250–251, 261, 263, 266
  women's narratives, 248, 250, 255, 257, 259, 267
  women's voices, 255, 260–261
Right to housing. *See also* Economic and social rights
  adequacy of housing
    private sector, 196
  assistance
    financial, 200–203
    social, 187, 192, 200–203
  enforcement, 188, 190–193
  European Social Charter, 188, 191
  explicit recognition, 188
  homeless, 193–194, 196, 199
  implicit recognition, 189
  International Covenant on Economic, Social and Cultural Rights (ICESCR), 188, 191, 192, 203
  land use policies, 196, 198
  legal regimes
    intersection, 190, 193

mortgage, 188, 190, 193, 194, 196–197, 201
municipal law
duty of care, 194
reading in, 190
soft-law documents, 188, 189
state spending power, 199
tenants' rights, 197, 198, 204
Rocher, Guy
sociology of law, 145, 146
Roosevelt, Eleanor
author, 11
UDHR, 11, 41
Rottenburg, Richard
chains of translation, 216–217
Rule of Law
capital punishment, 19
foreign rendition, 19
Guantanamo, 19
Rwanda
Gacaca system, 93

S
SARS outbreak. *See* Severe acute respiratory syndrome (SARS) outbreak
Second modernity, 100, 103, 106–108, 111–123
Security of the person, 6, 126, 165, 193, 202
Self-determination. *See also* Anaya, James
indigenous peoples, 135–136
Self-regulation
private, 89
Severe acute respiratory syndrome (SARS) outbreak
duty of care, 195
Shari'a law
alternative to human rights, 218
Nigeria, 11, 208, 218
Social solidarity
practices, 17
symbols, 17
Soft law
alternatives, 7
Statehood, 63, 85, 223
State legal order
centralism, 23, 24, 71
chirographism, 24, 28
monism
liberal individualism, 107
official
explicit canonical references, 27
explicit inferential norms, 27
implicit canonical references, 27
implicit inferential norms, 23, 27
positivism, 23, 24, 28, 36
prescriptivism, 24, 28
States
actors, 2, 62, 65, 81–87, 94, 95, 117, 134, 146, 151
human rights norms, 2–3, 5, 6, 28, 83
legal positivism (*see* State legal order)
nomopoly, 24
norm entrepreneurs, 5, 17, 32
norms, 161, 162
vision of law, 19, 60, 62, 131, 142
Status of Women Canada (SWC)
research study on polygamy, 247
Stolen Sisters campaign, Amnesty International
awareness of violence against Indigenous women, 141–142
global solidarity, 141
human rights abuse, 141
Sturm, Susan
structural discrimination, 133
Suttee, 21

T
Teitgen, Pierre-Henri
International Committee of Movements for European Unity, 44, 45
Teubner, Gunther, 115, 133
Theory of justice, 73
Tolstoy, Leo
Anna Karenina, 16
Epigram, 16, 19
Torture
prohibition, 55, 59
Trans-cultural values, 60
Translators. *See also* Nari adalats; Rottenburg, Richard
authority, 9
cultural translators, 9
double consciousness, 214
human rights translators, 9, 211, 215, 217, 221
intermediaries, 214, 226
power, 215, 226–228
process
hybridity, 226, 227
replication, 9, 221, 226, 227
systems
global, 211–212
local, 211
top-down process, 227
vulnerability, 9, 215, 226–228

Transnational
corporations
effective regulation, 107
institutions, 228
multinational
effective regulation, 107
Transnationalism, 211
Treaty
ratification
dualist tradition, 83
Westphalia, 106

U
UDHR. *See* Universal Declaration of Human Rights (UDHR)
Universal
human rights
contemporary critiques, 17, 23, 25, 28
ethnocentric, 20
justiciability, 8, 188, 191, 192
methodology, 10, 22, 26, 29–31
local, 29–31, 33, 34, 76, 113, 130, 141, 209, 211–212, 217
norms
interplay, 34
truths, 15
values, 6–9, 38, 39, 60–61
Universal Declaration of Human Rights (UDHR)
ambiguities, 41, 86
binding norm
fear, 42
normative unity, 38
political compromise, 40
relativism, 35, 40, 73
Trojan horse, 39
Universalism of rights
tension
application, 79
rights, 79, 142
Universality
chimera, 17
pluralistic understanding, 38
Universe
legal agents, 4, 27, 35
normative
choice, 4
physical, 4

V
Vernacular. *See also* Merry, Sally Engle; Translators; Vernacularized
global, 6, 10, 211–212, 217–218, 222, 226
law, 32, 218–219, 224, 225, 228
local
norms, 9, 32, 139, 211
paradox, 139, 228
regional, 79
Vernacularization
process
hybridity, 217, 222–227
replication, 217–222
symbolic dimension
indigenization, 211–212
Vernacularized, 211, 227
Vulnerability
economic and social rights, 8, 188, 189
translators, 9, 215, 226–228
women, 9, 169–170, 226, 228

W
War crimes, 2
War on terror
American Bar Association, 90–91
American Psychological Association, 90
Webber, Jeremy
Naturalism, 232, 237
Wives, 10, 219, 220, 247–267
Women. *See also* Elder(s); Wives
human rights
localization, 80, 211
marginalization, 10, 11, 249–250
narrative, 10–11, 248, 250, 255, 257, 259, 262, 266, 267
prisons, 169–170
rights, 86, 138, 208, 224, 225, 264
Workplace, 3, 8, 85, 91, 129, 132–135, 145, 146, 148–158, 160, 163, 164
World Bank, 118, 187, 188

Y
Youth. *See also* Youth protection
decision-making power, 7
interpersonal relationships, 175, 176
voice, 7, 169, 177, 178, 182
Youth protection
institutional rules, 7, 166
Québec
Youth Protection Act, 165, 166, 183, 184
regulations, 177–180
transformation of
institutional cultures, 183–185
professional cultures, 167, 185

Youth rehabilitation centres
  absence of privacy, 174–176
  admissions, 167, 169–172
  disciplinary measures, 166–167, 169, 174, 181, 182, 184, 185
  educators (*see also* Goffman, Erving)
    recurring institutional paradox, 167, 168
    total institutions, 167–170, 172, 174–177
  identity
    deprivation, 172
    image, 172
    re-engineering, 169, 172–174
  institutional framework
    codes of conduct, 167–183
    house rules, 177
    privileges, 168, 177, 180
    rigidity, 166
    sanctions, 168, 174, 179–180
  juvenile marginality, 173
  minute regulation of daily life, 177–180
  normative universe, 167, 183, 184
  processes of socialization, 174
  right to an education, 183
  schedule, 177–179
  secure rehabilitation units, 168, 169, 180
  sexual decency, 173

Printed by Printforce, the Netherlands